Living Standards and the Wealth of Nations

Living Standards and the Wealth of Nations
Successes and Failures in Real Convergence

edited by Leszek Balcerowicz and Stanley Fischer

The MIT Press
Cambridge, Massachusetts
London, England

MIT Press books may be purchased at special quantity discounts for business or sales promotional use. For information, please email special_sales@mitpress.mit .edu or write to Special Sales Department, The MIT Press, 55 Hayward Street, Cambridge, MA 02142.

This book was set in Sabon on 3B2 by Asco Typesetters, Hong Kong and was printed and bound in the United States of America.

Library of Congress Cataloging-in-Publication Data

Living standards and the wealth of nations : successes and failures in real convergence / edited by Leszek Balcerowicz and Stanley Fischer.
    p.   cm.
Includes bibliographical references and index.
ISBN 0-262-02595-7 (alk. paper)
1. Economic development. 2. Convergence (Economics). 3. Cost and standard of living. 4. Wealth. I. Balcerowicz, Leszek. II. Fischer, Stanley.

HD75.L59   2006
339.4′2—dc22   2005054008

10   9   8   7   6   5   4   3   2   1

Contents

Contributors

Anders Åslund, Carnegie Endowment for International Peace

Leszek Balcerowicz, President, National Bank of Poland

Manuel Balmaseda, Research Department, Banco Bilbao Vizcaya Argentaria

Iain Begg, European Institute at the London School of Economics and Political Science

John Bradley, Economic and Social Research Institute

Vittorio Corbo L., Central Bank of Chile

Stanley Fischer, Vice Chairman, Citigroup Inc.

Leonardo Hernández T., Central Bank of Chile

Philip Keefer, World Bank

Olle Krantz, University of Umeå

Abel Moreira Mateus, Bank of Portugal, New University of Lisbon

Thomas O'Connell, Central Bank of Ireland

Stephen L. Parente, University of Illinois at Urbana-Champaign

Edward C. Prescott, Federal Reserve Bank of Minneapolis, Arizona State University

Jacek Rostowski, Central European University in Budapest

Isaac D. Sabethai, Bank of Greece

Miguel Sebastián, Universidad Complutense de Madrid

Diarmaid Smyth, Financial Services Authority of Ireland

Athanasios Vamvakidis, International Monetary Fund

José Maria Viñals, Bank of Spain

Wing Thye Woo, University of California at Davis

Nikolai Zoubanov, University of Birmingham

I

Some General Remarks on the Process of Catching Up

Introduction and Summary

Leszek Balcerowicz and Stanley Fischer*

This volume contains revised versions of papers presented at the Conference on Successes and Failures in Real Convergence, which was held at the National Bank of Poland in Warsaw in October 2003. The conference took place fifteen years after the Polish and east European transition processes began and less than a year before ten countries, including Poland, were scheduled to join the fifteen existing members of the European Union (EU).

Given the time and the place of the conference, it is natural that several of the chapters in this volume discuss the convergence processes of countries—Spain, Portugal, Ireland, and Greece—that had recently joined the EU. But the focus of the conference was wider than the impact of EU membership on the convergence of income levels in member countries toward or even above the EU average.

The question of convergence in economics is part of the economic-growth literature. The general issue of what determines the wealth of nations—and the related specific question of whether poor countries can catch up to rich countries economically—has been at the center of economics for centuries. And it is the most important and all-encompassing question in economics.

The professional debate on convergence begins from the implication of the closed-economy Solow growth model that per-capita income in a given country converges to its steady-state level as capital is accumulated and that steady-state income grows at the rate of technical progress. If economies are open, capital would flow from the capital-rich to the

* The authors are grateful to Adam Burchat and Marek Radzikowski for their assistance in preparing this volume.

capital-poor countries to take advantage of the higher rates of return implied by the relative scarcity of capital in poorer countries, and per-capita income (gross domestic product, GDP) levels in the poorer countries should converge toward those in the richer countries.

Yet this theoretical prediction is not taking place in practice, certainly not with the uniformity that is implied by the analytic models. Because convergence should be possible, has happened for many countries, and appears to be taking place now in China, India, and many other countries, the question of under what circumstances income levels in poorer countries will converge toward those of the rich countries is critical for understanding economic growth and development.

The pervasive issue at the conference and in this volume is *what factors make for successful convergence.* The general conclusion is that *reliance on market forces within an open economy in a stable macroeconomic environment, with assured property rights, are the keys to rapid economic growth.* The chapters are divided into five sections.

Part I   Growth and Convergence

Chapter 1 by Stephen L. Parente and Edward C. Prescott provides a broad perspective on growth and convergence. Parente and Prescott present a model of an economy with two sectors—traditional and modern. Countries differ in the efficiencies of the two sectors. The key to development and rapid growth is to switch to the modern technology. But that happens only when modern technologies become more efficient than traditional technologies. In the Parente-Prescott model, relatively small differences in efficiency in the modern sector can produce very long lags in convergence, for rapid catch-up begins only when the modern sector in the converging country becomes sufficiently large.

Parente and Prescott attribute increases in efficiency to policy changes. They predict that a country will catch up to the leading industrial countries only if it eliminates constraints on the use of technology—but, they emphasize, removal of these constraints is bound to be contentious since the constraints are typically imposed to protect particular interest groups.

They conclude by recommending membership in a free-trade club as a method for eliminating the constraints that hinder the adoption of efficient technologies. The importance of opening up trade is a persistent theme of the other chapters in the volume. One of the most important examples is provided by China's inspired use of its membership negotiations for the World Trade Organization (WTO) as a means of imposing an externally oriented pro-market policy framework on itself.

The second chapter in part I is by Philip Keefer, whose starting point is the difficulty of establishing an empirical link between democracy and growth. The argument that there should be a positive correlation is that growth cannot take place without secure property rights and that property rights are best secured in democracies. However, many hold the opposite view, arguing on the basis of examples such as Pinochet's Chile and modern-day China that authoritarian governments are better for growth. These are good examples, but there are far more examples of authoritarian governments that failed to produce growth than of those that succeeded in doing so.

Keefer's chapter is empirical. The evidence supports the view that nondemocratic forms of government hinder growth. But the evidence also supports the view that what matters most for growth is not elections *per se* but rather the presence of political checks and balances. The checks and balances help protect property rights. It is good to know that the data support such a sensible proposition.

Part II Non-European Union Case Studies

Olle Krantz presents an interesting chapter (chapter 3) on similarities and differences in the long-term development paths of the Nordic countries. The data on Nordic per-capita income relative to that in the United States start in 1870 and are summarized in figure 3.1. They show considerable convergence toward the income level in the United States and among the Nordic states—with some shifts in relative position among them—over the period.

Krantz focuses particularly on Finland's catch-up to the level of Sweden during the 1950 to 1990 period. He attributes the catch-up to the increasing rigidity of the Swedish business system over that period relative to that in Finland. He concludes that if "political measures and institutions ... are constructed in a way that makes the economy flexible and adaptable to changes, they can promote growth and counteract stiffness [rigidity] of the economic structure."

No conference that focuses on growth and convergence can ignore China's extraordinary growth performance over the past twenty-five years. Some of the major controversies about what permitted China to grow at near double-digit annual rates over that period are revisited and analyzed in chapter 4 by Wing Thye Woo.

The main controversy Woo discusses is that between the experimentalist and convergence schools. The former attributes China's success to its constant experimentation with reforms, which allowed the country to find out what worked and implement those changes on a larger scale. The convergence school attributes China's success to its more or less steady movement toward implementing a market-based private ownership economy. Woo is an adherent of the convergence school and deploys his considerable forensic skills to make that case.

He emphasizes that the experimentalist-convergence debate is not about the speed of reform. On that issue, he notes that some reforms can be done rapidly (for example, agricultural reform) in China, whereas others (for example, privatization) cannot. If anything, he argues that the evidence favors more rapid reform, quoting, for instance, the evidence from Vietnam and Laos. On a related topic, Woo deals decisively with the role of the dual-track pricing system (DTPS), which some see as the source of China's ability to move without major social unrest toward a market system. Woo argues that, on the contrary, because the DTPS creates massive opportunities for corruption, it produced major societal strains, including within the Chinese political leadership—and that that is why it was abolished.

Woo concludes that China's decision to bind its future policies through its WTO admission is decisive evidence that the convergence school is now dominant in China. Of course, the experimentalist and convergence schools are not mutually exclusive, since experimentation could have resulted in the emergence of the market-based system. Woo makes almost that point at the end of his chapter, arguing that the experimentalist and convergence schools are themselves converging in the light of China's entry into the WTO.

In chapter 5, Vittorio Corbo L. (president of the Central Bank of Chile) and Leonardo Hernandez T. examine Chile's economic performance over the past thirty years. Chile has grown rapidly over that period. It has also strengthened both institutions and policies to the point that it has become the most stable economy in Latin America and one of the most stable emerging-market economies in the world.

Corbo and Hernandez look for lessons in Chile's recent history about what worked and also about what policies failed so that others can benefit from Chile's successes and failures. They start from 1973, when the Chilean economy was in deep crisis. The military government rapidly strengthened fiscal policy and began to put in place institutional reforms that moved the economy away from socialism and toward a market system.

However, among the negative lessons of the Chilean experience, in 1979 Chile instituted a pegged exchange rate to reduce inflation. As a result of a largely private-sector spending boom, the external deficit ballooned, and a classic debt crisis ensued in 1982. GDP fell by a cumulative 16 percent in 1982 to 1983. At the same time, the financial system had been severely weakened during the precrisis boom, and the government ended up taking over a large part of the financial system, as well as important nonfinancial corporations.

In the face of this massive crisis, the government focused thereafter on privatization again and on strengthening the economy's institutional framework, including that for monetary policy. This allowed the economy to reach record growth rates during the period 1985 to 1997 and to withstand the impact of the Asian crisis—albeit with a short recession and with a subsequent reduction in the growth rate. Of special note is the fact that all this happened as the country transited from an authoritarian to a democratic regime.

One of the most provocative essays in the volume (chapter 6) is by Anders Åslund, who examines the changing relative growth performances of the group of central and east European (CEE) transition economies versus those of the Commonwealth of Independent States (CIS)—the twelve non-Baltic states of the former Soviet Union.

Åslund's stylized fact is that the CEE economies grew more rapidly than those of the CIS up to 1999 and that the CIS economies grew much more rapidly than the CEE economies thereafter. Painting with a broad and interesting brush, Åslund attributes this change to the adoption of elements of the East Asian model in the CIS countries—particularly low taxes, limited social transfers, reasonably free labor markets, and limited environmental regulation. The CEE countries, by contrast, were generally moving toward membership in the European Union, implementing a set of measures that would likely result in a larger role for the state.

Among the questions raised in the conference discussion of the Åslund paper was whether the more rapid growth in the CIS was due to the growing role of oil and gas in the major CIS economies. While this was a positive factor for those economies, the management of an oil economy is difficult, implying that it took careful management by the authorities in these economies not to dissipate the potential gains from their natural resource booms. Further, the raw-material argument does not apply in the case of Ukraine, where growth has also increased rapidly. The Åslund hypothesis thus remains on the table for further consideration and research.

The four chapters on growth and convergence in non-EU countries, including China, thus point toward the same conclusion as the introductory chapters—namely, that increasing reliance on market forces within an open economy in a stable macroeconomic environment, with increasing assurance of property rights, enhances economic growth.

Part III   Case Studies on Accession to the European Union

Seven chapters examine the impact of accession to the European Union on the economies of Spain, Portugal, Greece, and Ireland—with two papers for each country except Portugal.

The first chapter on Spain in the EU is by José Viñals of the Banco de España (chapter 7), and the second is by Manuel Balmaseda and Miguel Sebastián (chapter 8). Sebastián is now the chair of the Economic Bureau of the President in Spain and, as such, is chief economic adviser to the prime minister.

The authors of these chapters reach similar conclusions. Both chapters emphasize that EU membership, achieved in 1986, gave a formidable impulse to the opening of Spain's economy, with the share of foreign trade in GDP (imports plus exports) rising from 27 percent in 1985 to 63 percent in 2002. The financial opening of the economy was far more dramatic, with the volume of payments linked to international transactions rising as a share of GDP more than eightyfold over the same period.

This financial opening, along with the constraints on macroeconomic policy implied by EU membership, led reasonably rapidly to nominal convergence of the economy with that of the EU. This can be seen clearly in the figures and tables presented at the end of chapter 7 by Viñals. However, both chapters emphasize the difficulties faced by Spain in the run-up to membership in 1986 and in the years following, with Spain being hard hit in the exchange-rate mechanism (ERM) crisis of 1992 to 1993.

Up to 1986, economic expansion was propelled in part by a very expansionary fiscal policy, reflected both in a rising government budget deficit and in a rapid increase in general government spending as a share of GDP. Government spending continued to rise after Spain's EU entry, peaking as a share of GDP in 1993 to 1994 at 45 percent and gradually declining subsequently. The budget deficit rose sharply during the ERM crisis to over 6 percent of GDP but has been reduced to the point where the budget is now in balance and the debt-to-GDP ratio declining. Viñals thus emphasizes the differences in macroeconomic policy following the ERM crisis as a key factor in Spain's macroeconomic convergence in the last decade.

The path of unemployment in Spain looks remarkably similar (with a rescaling of the axes) to the path of the debt-to-GDP ratio. At the time of Spanish entry to the EU, the unemployment rate was near 20 percent; it then declined for a few years and rose sharply following the ERM crisis, peaking at nearly 25 percent. Viñals emphasizes the differential rates of progress in different sectors after 1986: progress was rapid in the goods and financial markets, which were open to international competition; it was much slower in the markets for services and labor, which required politically difficult policy actions by the Spanish authorities.

Overall, Spain made considerable progress after joining the EU. Its per-capita income was 73 percent of the EU average in 1986 and 84 percent in 2002. This is impressive, but it still leaves a considerable gap between Spain and the rest of the EU. Balmaseda and Sebastián emphasize the need to close that gap—to achieve real as well as nominal convergence—and argue that doing so requires making goods and services and labor markets more flexible, particularly in light of the challenges posed by the enlargement of the EU.

The Spanish story is not only interesting and important but also instructive. The goods and financial market opening of the economy as a result of EU membership helped Spain grow fast, but incomplete liberalization, especially in the labor and services markets, prevented real convergence from taking place. Thus although Spain has made significant progress in many respects, including in fiscal policy, important reform challenges remain before it can expect to achieve real convergence. And as Balmaseda and Sebastián argue, that convergence should be to the income levels of the most advanced countries of the EU.

Abel Mateus presents the Portuguese case in chapter 9. He argues that Portugal's experience provides lessons both about what should be done to grow and converge and what should not be done. This experience is especially useful for the former transition economies, since Portugal started far behind the EU average and had also to deal with the heritage of a large state-owned sector of the economy.

From 1960 to 2002, per-capita GDP in Portugal rose from 43 percent of the average of the EU15 to 72 percent. This relative convergence was achieved essentially in two spurts, from 1960 to 1974 and then from 1986 to 1997, with a period of socialism with nationalization between those periods, following the transition to democracy. Unlike in the case of Spain, Portugal's growth was achieved while unemployment stayed well below double digits.

During this period, the Portuguese economy opened up significantly. Mateus attributes much of the first growth spurt to the opening of the economy associated with Portugal's joining the European Free Trade Association (EFTA). This was accompanied by a removal of barriers to competition and a rapid increase in the investment ratio.

Portugal entered the EU in 1986, together with Spain. Mateus identifies four progrowth factors resulting from EU accession: increased trade, increased investment, fiscal transfers that financed infrastructure, and a strengthening of Portugal's institutional framework. Over the period 1985 to 1997, these helped produce a sharp productivity-growth increase. At the same time, Portugal achieved nominal convergence that allowed it to become a founding member of the European Monetary Union (EMU).

But progress since 1998 has been slow. Mateus attributes this to an unwillingness to tackle politically difficult structural reforms, an excessive debt buildup as nominal interest rates declined in the process of nominal convergence, and the undertaking of wasteful investment projects financed in part by EU funds. Mateus notes, in particular, that Portugal has the lowest level of human capital in the EU15, well below the levels of the leading CEE 2004 entrants. He suggests that EU structural funds should be available for investment in human as well as physical capital.

There are two chapters each on Greece and Ireland, two countries whose contrasting performances provide valuable lessons on the potential impact of EU accession. Greece joined the EU in 1981 with per capita GDP at 59 percent of the EU15 average. By the mid-1990s, its relative income had *fallen* to 48 percent; by 2002, the ratio had risen to 56 percent. Thus Greece's first fifteen years in the EU provide an example of nonconvergence; that of the last decade, an example of convergence.

Isaac D. Sabethai (chapter 10) and Athanasios Vamvakidis (chapter 11), in their respective chapters, seek to explain why Greece first diverged from and then began to converge to the average European performance. Vamvakidis attributes the period of divergence to deterioration in macroeconomic policies and serious structural impediments to growth —and the subsequent period of convergence to macroeconomic adjustment and progress in structural reforms. He notes also that Greece's labor-market performance since EU accession has been disappointing and that major labor-market inflexibilities remain even now.

The question arises of what made it possible to strengthen policies in the mid-1990s. Vamvakidis's answer is that the conditions for entering the EMU made the reforms politically feasible. Nonetheless, a substantial reform agenda remains: fiscal consolidation (particularly since Greece's debt ratio is very high), pension reform, further progress on inflation reduction, privatization and product-market liberalization, and labor-market reform. Absent significant progress in these areas, the authors fear that Greek convergence may not continue.

The lesson to be drawn from this thoroughly mixed performance is stated succinctly by Vamvakidis: "EU participation alone does not lead to convergence; good policies do."

Ireland's stellar performance in the EU is addressed by Thomas O'Connell and Diarmaid Smyth (chapter 12) and John Bradley (chapter

13). Ireland joined the EU in 1973 with a relative GDP just above 60 percent. It took until 1989 for relative income to reach the 70 percent level. Less than fifteen years later, Irish per-capita income exceeded 120 percent of the EU15 average.

Why the slow growth for the first sixteen years in the EU and the spectacular performance subsequently? Fiscal policy in the period up to 1985 was extremely loose (see the data in table 12.2 in O'Connell and Smyth's chapter). The general government fiscal deficit exceeded 10 percent of GDP in 1985, with total government spending exceeding 50 percent of GDP and the national debt at nearly 100 percent of GDP.

By the mid-1980s, it was generally accepted that policy needed to be changed radically. The main changes, instituted in 1987, were to cut public spending; to reach a tripartite agreement on wage and tax behavior among unions, employers, and government; and to devalue by 8 percent within the EMU. By 1990, the budget deficit was just over 2 percent of GDP, total government spending was below 40 percent of GDP, and the debt-to-GDP ratio at 88 percent was declining as a share of GDP—a decline that took the ratio down to 36 percent in 2000. This macroeconomic stabilization was an essential step toward the recovery of growth in the early 1990s.

In addition, a structural reform process was put in place, inspired in part by the deregulation process in the United Kingdom. It included a tax reform, a labor-market reform that reduced disincentives to work, and a generally light regulatory touch. Corporate taxes were set low to encourage foreign direct investment. Foreign direct investment increased substantially, while structural funds from the EU contributed to increasing infrastructure investment.

The last fifteen years have seen a remarkable growth boom in Ireland. Productivity growth during the boom period was not exceptional. Rather, there was a sizable increase in employment, most of it accounted for by the services and construction sectors.

Both chapters emphasize the importance of Ireland's strong commitment to free trade and its flexible and well-educated labor force. These, together with the strong macroeconomic framework and a lightly regulated competitive environment, are seen by O'Connell and Smyth as key prerequisites for rapid economic growth.

Taken together, the case studies on the consequences of accession to the EU present a consistent picture. Entry into the EU opens up the potential for more rapid growth by enforcing a commitment to free trade within a large market. But convergence is not guaranteed by membership alone; it requires also good policies, with regard to both the macroeconomic and structural frameworks, in which the size of government and the impact of the tax system on incentives are key factors. Foreign direct investment (FDI) has played an important role in increasing growth in several of the accession countries studied. The importance of the quality of the labor force and of human-capital investment is a consistent theme in the chapters in this section—one that may not have received as much attention as it should have in the policy discussions on growth within the EU. Some of the authors also express reservations about the role of the structural funds.

Part IV   European Monetary Union Entry and Economic Growth

The two chapters in this section, by Jacek Rostowski and Nikolai Zoubanov (chapter 14) and by Iain Begg (chapter 15), both focus on real convergence. In the Rostowski-Zoubanov paper, the question is whether the CEE countries that joined the EU in 2004 should be required to demonstrate real convergence of their economies with those of the rest of the EU before they are allowed to join the Economic and Monetary Union (EMU) or whether nominal convergence will suffice. "Nominal convergence" means meeting the Maastricht criteria and presumably the requirements of the Stability and Growth Pact however it will be revised. Real convergence would require in addition a sufficient degree of convergence of key structural features of the economy, including, for instance, the financial and labor markets and the ownership of enterprises.

Rostowski and Zoubanov argue firmly that nominal convergence should be sufficient for entry to the EMU. They analyze at some length one argument against that view—namely, that the Balassa-Samuelson effect will require higher inflation in the new entrants because their more rapid rate of productivity growth will cause the prices of nontraded goods, particularly services, to rise more rapidly than other prices. There will thus be an inflationary bias in the poorer countries, implying that their inclusion in the EMU would raise the overall inflation rate.

The authors argue that Eurozone enlargement would be good for both the existing members and the potential new members and should take place once the Maastricht criteria are satisfied. However, they warn that it is critical for the slower-growing members of the EU to have labor markets flexible enough to align the real wage with real labor productivity.

Begg addresses the closely related question of whether full participation in the EMU favors or slows real convergence. EMU participation could slow real convergence because the absence of an independent monetary policy, and the associated fiscal policy constraints embodied in the Stability and Growth Pact take away some of the policy flexibility that countries need to keep growing as fast as possible. Begg argues that although this possibility exists, the longer-term benefits of early EMU membership outweigh the risks. But he notes that governments cannot relax following EMU membership because further policy adjustments are inevitably needed to deal with the evolving situations that every entrant will face. This warning echoes that of Rostowski and Zoubanov that labor-market flexibility is essential for real convergence.

In this section, too, the message is simple. Governments cannot relax: there are many benefits to entry into the EU and later into the EMU, but these can be dissipated unless governments maintain and strengthen the policy framework. Another way of stating the message is to say that while the prospect of entry into the EU and the EMU is good for growth—because it forces countries to strengthen policies to meet the entry criteria—the benefits of entry can be disappointing if governments do not stay on the path of macroeconomic stability and ongoing promarket structural reforms.

Part V   Concluding Remarks[i]

In the final chapter, Leszek Balcerowicz, president of the National Bank of Poland, the conference host, presents his concluding reflections. Bal-

[i] This section was written by Fischer.

cerowicz was a student and started his professional career as an economist in pretransition Poland. To understand the economy in which he lived and how to change it, he had to teach himself modern economics.

He was able to put that knowledge into effect a few years later as finance minister in the first posttransition Polish government. Balcerowicz is generally credited with designing and implementing the highly successful Polish reform program. Doing that required an understanding of the economics of transition and a keen grasp of political economy.

Balcerowicz summarizes the conclusions of both his own unique experience and the chapters in this volume in three strong propositions: (1) no poor country has lastingly converged under any variation of a statist institutional system; (2) all successful cases of sustained convergence have happened under more or less free-market systems or during and after the transition to such systems; and (3) not all market-oriented reforms have led to lasting convergence.

He expands on the meaning of these propositions and explains how they relate to a number of countries—for instance, China—that the reader might be tempted to cite as counterexamples. In particular, he emphasizes that convergence may begin well before a free-market economy is in place, provided that the transition to such a system is under way.

In sum, the chapters in this volume, produced by different authors and covering a wide range of countries, provide a remarkably consistent picture of the requirements for growth and convergence: *reliance on market forces within an open economy in a stable macroeconomic environment, with assured property rights, are the keys to rapid economic growth.*

1

What a Country Must Do to Catch Up to the Industrial Leaders

Stephen L. Parente and Edward C. Prescott

Introduction

Today, differences in international incomes are huge. Even after adjusting for differences in relative prices and factoring in household production, the typical person living in a rich country, such as the United States, is twenty to thirty times richer than the typical person living in a poor country, such as Haiti. This is in stark contrast to the differences that existed prior to 1700. In 1700 and before, the living standard of the richest country was less than three times the living standard of the poorest country. Moreover, in the pre-1700 period, living standards showed no significant increases over time.

After 1700, this all changed as some countries started experiencing sustained increases in their living standards. England was the first country to develop—that is, to realize sustained increases in per-capita income. Western European countries and countries that were ethnic offshoots of England began to develop shortly thereafter. At first, the increases in income experienced by these early developers were irregular and modest in size. However, since the start of the twentieth century, these increases have been larger and relatively regular, with income doubling every thirty-five years in these countries—a phenomenon Kuznets (1966) labels *modern economic growth.*

Over time, more and more countries started experiencing sustained increases in living standards, and today virtually all have accomplished this feat. Even sub-Saharan Africa has started to experience sustained increases in living standards, although it has yet to start the process of modern economic growth. On account of these later starts, the gap in

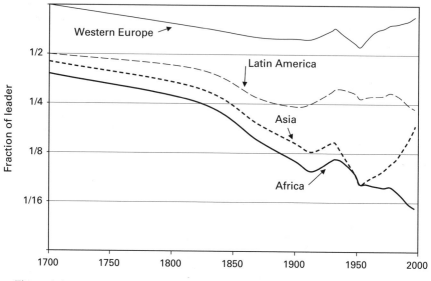

Figure 1.1
Evolution of international incomes, 1700 to 1990 (fraction of leader)

incomes between early and late developers widened over time, and huge differences in international incomes emerged. The implication of this evolution of international incomes since 1700 is shown in figure 1.1 for the four major regions of the world.

The United Kingdom was the first country to start the transition to modern economic growth and was the industrial leader until about 1900 when the United States assumed the role. The western European countries, which started the transition to modern economic growth later, lost ground relative to the leader prior to 1900. Once this region entered into modern economic growth, it ceased to lose ground and in the last half of the twentieth century has nearly caught up in terms of productivity.

What, if anything, can a late starter do to catch up to the leaders? This chapter provides an answer to this question. It begins by setting out a theory that accounts for the evolution of international income levels and by examining the policy implications of that theory. The theory represents a unification of two theories: the Hansen and Prescott (2002) theory of economic development and growth and the Parente and Prescott (2000) theory of relative efficiencies. The essence of this unified theory is that a country starts to experience sustained increases in its living standard when the efficiency at which it can use resources in modern technologies reaches a critical level. Countries reach this critical level of efficiency at different dates not because they have access to different stocks of knowledge but rather because they differ in the amount of constraints placed on the technology choices of their citizenry. These constraints, which are the result of explicit policies, exist in many instances to protect the interests of groups vested in current production processes. If these constraints are removed, the theory predicts that a late starter will catch up to the leaders.

The chapter follows this review with an examination of the record of catch-up in the world and the reason for catch-up. As constraints typically are put in place to protect the interests of industry groups associated with current production processes, their removal is most likely to be contentions. For this reason, we examine the record on catch-up in greater depth for the purpose of determining the circumstances under which barriers to the efficient use of technology were reduced in some countries and catching up with the efficiency leaders occurred. We conclude from this examination that membership in a free-trade club is an important way by which a country can eliminate these constraints. This reason for this is that when a country belongs to a free-trade club, it is no longer in the interest of industry groups to prevent the efficient use of resources.

The chapter is organized as follows. The next section presents the model economy and describes the equilibrium properties of the model, and the following section then examines the record of catch-up in the world economy and the reasons for this catch-up. A conclusion discusses the prospects for catch-up for some individual countries that are not currently members of a free-trade club.

A Theory of the Evolution of International Incomes

The Model Economy
The theory is embedded in a dynamic general-equilibrium model. In the model, infinitely lived households determine how much of their incomes to consume and how much to invest each period. The representative

household's income in each period consists of three components: wage income, land rental income, and capital rental income. There is a single composite commodity in the economy that can be produced by means of two technologies: a traditional technology and a modern technology. The key difference between the two technologies is that the traditional one uses a fixed factor in the form of land. In each period, firms decide which technology to use and how much capital, land, and labor to hire.

The number of households in an economy varies over time. In the era prior to 1700, when incomes stagnated, the theory has an economy's population vary to maintain a given level of households' consumption. We do not see this relation resulting from the fertility decisions of individual households. Our modeling strategy reflects the fact that societies have devised social institutions and policies that give them their desired population size. In the pre-1700 era, when land was an important input, countries set up social institutions that controlled population to maintain the highest possible living standard consistent with the ability to defend itself from outside expropriators. After 1700, when land became less important, societies did not need such a large population and set up social institutions that limited their population size. In modern China, for example, a law effectively limits many households to one child. In other periods and in other countries, social norms that led to later marriage had the consequence of reducing fertility.

For reasons of space, we omit formal descriptions of the household side of the economy and of the model's demographics. We refer the reader to Parente and Prescott (2005) for a detailed description of these features of the model. For the points we wish to establish here, it is sufficient to limit our description to the technology side of the model economy.

The Traditional Technology   The traditional technology is given by a Cobb-Douglas technology,

$$Y_{Mt} = A_{Mt} K_{Mt}^{\phi} N_{Mt}^{\mu} L_{Mt}^{1-\phi-\mu}. \tag{1.1}$$

In equation (1.1), Y_{Mt} is output, K_{Mt} is capital, N_{Mt} is labor, and L_{Mt} is land in period t. A_{Mt} is a total factor productivity (TFP) parameter,

ϕ is the capital-share parameter, and μ is the labor-share parameter. TFP is assumed to grow exogenously at a constant rate γ_M; that is, $A_{Mt} = (1 + \gamma_M)^t$ to reflect the fact that technology was not stagnant after 2000 B.C. (Mokyr 1990).

The Modern Technology   The modern technology is also given by a Cobb-Douglas production function. In contrast to the traditional technology, the modern technology includes no fixed factor of production. The modern technology is

$$Y_{St} = EA_{St}K_{St}^{\theta}N_{St}^{1-\theta}. \tag{1.2}$$

In equation (1.2), output is Y_{St}, capital is K_{St}, and labor is N_{St}. Capital's share is given by the parameter θ, and a country's TFP corresponds to EA_{St}.

TFP in the modern technology is decomposed into the product of two components. The first component is an efficiency component, denoted by E. The second component is a pure knowledge or technology component, denoted by A_{St}. The technology component of TFP is common across countries. It is the same across countries because the stock of productive knowledge that is available for a country to use does not differ across countries.[1] It is assumed to increase exogenously through time. The efficiency component E is not common across countries. It differs across countries on account of economic policies and institutions. The efficiency component is a number in the $(0, 1]$ interval. An efficiency level less than one implies that a country operates inside the production possibilities frontier, whereas an efficiency level equal to one implies that a country operates on the production possibility frontier. Differences in efficiency therefore imply differences in TFP.[2]

Relative Efficiency   To see how a country's policies and institutions determine its relative efficiency, consider a type of policy that effectively constrains firms in how a given plant technology is operated. An example of this type of policy is a work rule, which dictates the minimum number of workers or machines that must be used when operating a plant technology. In particular, suppose constraints are such that a given plant technology could be operated with K units of capital and N units of labor but that a law requires a firm to use $\phi_K K$ units of capital and $\phi_N N$ units of labor where ϕ_K and ϕ_N each exceed one. This rule implies that a particular technology, if operated, must be operated with excessive capital and labor. With these constraints, the aggregate modern technology is

$$Y_{St} = EA_{St}K_{St}^{\theta}N_{St}^{1-\theta}, \tag{1.3}$$

where $E \equiv \phi_K^{-\theta}\phi_N^{\theta-1}$. If the nature of the constraints were to double the capital and labor requirements, then the efficiency measure would be one-half. If the nature of constraints were to quadruple both the capital and labor requirements, then the efficiency measure would be one-fourth.

This is just one type of policy that affects a country's efficiency. There are a numerous other types of policy that affect a country's efficiency. For example, Parente and Prescott (1994) show how constrains on the choice of the plant technology that can be operated also affects a country's relative efficiency.[3] Any policy that increases the amount of resources the production unit must spend to adopt a better technology is a constraint of this nature. Such policies and practices take the form of regulation, bribes, and even severance packages to factor suppliers whose services are eliminated or reduced when a switch to a more productive technology is made. In some instances, the policy is in the form of a law that specifically prohibits the use of a particular technology.[4] For another example, Schmitz (2001) suggests a mapping from government subsidies of state-owned enterprises to aggregate efficiency.

The evidence strongly suggests that production units in poor countries are severely constrained in their choices, and the costs associated with these constraints are large. This prompts a question: why does a society impose these constraints? A large number of studies, several of which are surveyed in Parente and Prescott (2000), suggest that constraints are imposed on firms to protect the interests of factor suppliers to the current production process. These groups stand to lose in the form of reduced earnings if new technology is introduced. These losses occur either because the input the group supplies is specialized with respect to the current production process or because they were granted a monopoly over the supply of a factor input to the current production.[5]

Equilibrium Properties of the Model

The equilibrium properties of the model are quantitatively consistent with the process of economic development and growth and the evolution of international incomes over the last two thousand years.

Economic Development and Growth With respect to the process of economic development and growth, the model predicts a stagnant living standard in all countries up until some date. This stagnant era corresponds to the period of time where the economy uses only traditional technology. As long as an economy specializes in traditional technology, any increases in TFP in traditional technology translate entirely into increases in population. Total output increases, but these increases are offset by population growth because land is a fixed factor and society must have a sufficiently large population to protect this fixed factor.

An economy specializes in the traditional technology as long as TFP associated with the modern technology is below some critical level. More specifically, an economy will specialize in the traditional technology if

$$EA_{St} < \left(\frac{r_M}{\theta}\right)^{\theta} \left(\frac{w_M}{1-\theta}\right)^{1-\theta}, \tag{1.4}$$

where r_M and w_M are the rental prices of capital and labor when the economy specializes in the traditional technology. Equation (1.4) is the condition required for the profits of a firm using modern technology to be negative. The condition follows from profit maximization and the fact that capital and labor are not specific to any technology.

When TFP associated with modern technology reaches the critical value given by the above inequality, modern technology begins to be used. This marks the beginning of a country's industrial revolution— namely, the long transition from a stagnating traditional economy to a modern industrial economy. At some date, inequality (1.4) must be violated, so eventually every economy will start using the modern technology no matter how small is its E. This is because as long as an economy specializes in the traditional technology, the rental prices of capital and labor are essentially constant. Consequently, the right-hand side of (1.4) is a constant. The left-hand side, however, is unbounded since TFP in modern technology is assumed to grow forever at a rate bounded uniformly away from zero. This result is independent of the size differences in the growth rates of TFP associated with traditional and modern production functions.

Once an economy starts using modern technology, it begins to realize increases in per-capita output. Traditional technology will continue to be used, as only traditional technology uses land as an input and the supply of land is inelastic. However, over time, its share of economic activity continually declines. In the limit, the equilibrium path of the economy converges to the constant growth-path equilibrium of a model economy where only modern technology is used. Asymptotically, per-capita output, consumption, real wages, investment, and the capital stock all grow at the same rate. This rate is independent of a country's population growth rate and its relative efficiency. Along this equilibrium path, capital's share of income and the real interest rate are constant. These are just the well-known modern growth facts.

Hansen and Prescott (2002) find that the model is quantitatively consistent with the development and growth process experienced by today's leading industrialized countries. They calibrate the parameters of traditional technology to match pre-1700 observations and the parameters of modern technology to match post-1900 observations for the United Kingdom and United States. The model predicts that an economy that begins the transition in 1700 will be approximately twenty-eight times richer in 1990 than it was in 1700. This is consistent with the historical record, as shown in figure 1.2, which plots period t per-capita output relative to 1700 per-capita output for the model economy and the industrial leader as reported by Maddison (1995, tables 1.1 and C.12). The model predicts a long transition period. Roughly 150 years elapse before 95 percent of the economy's output is produced using the modern technology. The growth rate of per-capita output rises slowly over the transition period. This is shown in figure 1.3. The growth rate of per capita output only reaches the one percent level one hundred years after the start of the transition, and reaches the modern growth era level of two percent after two hundred years have elapsed.

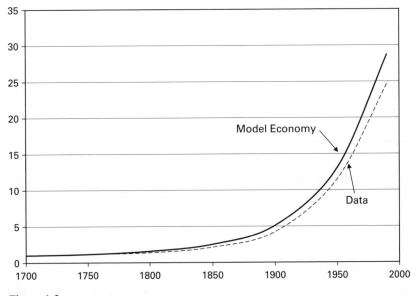

Figure 1.2
Per-capita output relative to 1700

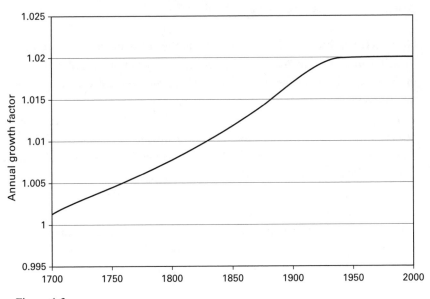

Figure 1.3
Growth rate of per-capita output

Evolution of International Income Levels   Parente and Prescott (2005) show that the theory accounts well for the evolution of international income levels once differences in relative efficiencies across countries and differences in relative efficiencies across time within a given country are introduced into the model. The theory predicts that all countries will eventually switch to modern technology but that the exact date will vary depending on the relative efficiencies of countries in modern technology. As inequality (1.4) suggests, countries with lower levels of relative efficiencies switch to modern technology at much later dates. Thus, the theory attributes a delay in a country's start toward economic development to its having a lower efficiency in modern technology relative to other countries.

Parente and Prescott (2005) compute the relative efficiency of a late starter required to delay the start of its transition by a given length of time. They find that the required size of the required efficiency difference between the leader and the laggard to generate delays observed in the data are not implausibly large. In particular, they find that a factor difference in relative efficiencies of less than 5 is sufficient to give rise to a 250-year delay in the start of economic development.[6]

No Catch-Up after the Transition   A number of countries, particularly those located in Latin America, started to experience sustained increases in living standards in the nineteenth century and yet failed to eliminate their income gap with the leader over the twentieth century. Is this observation consistent with the predictions of the theory? Parente and Prescott (2005) analyze what happens to a country's income relative to the leader after it switches to modern technology, assuming that the country's efficiency level does not change subsequently. They show that there is no subsequent elimination of the income gap with the leader if the country's relative efficiency does not change.

Figure 1.4 plots the path of per-capita GDP predicted by the model for late starters relative to the leader over the 1700 to 2050 period. Asymptotically, the relative income of a late starter is just the constant growth-path level associated with the neoclassical growth model, and so asymptotically the factor income difference between two countries is just $(E_s^i/E_s^j)^{1/(1-\theta)}$. The theory does not predict any catch-up for late starters.

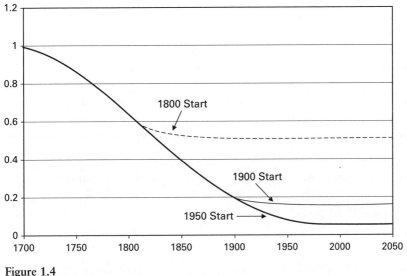

Figure 1.4
Late start (output relative to the leader)

In fact, the income gap with the leader continues to increase for a while even after the country starts using the modern technology. There are two reasons for this. First, the disparity continues to increase because the traditional production function is still widely used at the start of the transition and the growth rate of TFP associated with the traditional production function is lower than the growth rate of TFP associated with the modern production function. Second, the population growth in these countries tends to be higher compared to the leader over the comparable period.[7]

The increase in an economy's income gap with the leader once it starts using modern technology is small relative to the increase in the gap with the leader while the country specializes in traditional technology. The disparity with the leader stops increasing only after the modern production function starts being used on a large scale. For the country that starts the transition to modern economic growth in 1800, its income gap with the leader continues to increase until 1850. This is effectively the case of Latin American countries. Since 1900, they have remained at about 25 percent of the leaders. For the 1900 starter, the gap effectively continues to widen until 1950, and for the 1950 starter, the disparity with the leader continues to widen until 2000. This is effectively the case of sub-Saharan Africa. Most countries there started to experience sustained increases in per-capita income only after 1950, and their gap with the leader has widened over the 1950 to 2000 period.

Catch-Up and Growth Miracles   A key feature of the evolution of international income levels is that many countries have been able to narrow the gap with the leader in the twentieth century, with some realizing large increases in output relative to the leader in a relatively short period of time. Botswana, China, Japan, South Korea, and Taiwan doubled their living standards in less than a decade at some point in time over the post-1950 period. These growth miracles are a relatively recent phenomenon and are limited to countries that were relatively poor prior to undergoing their miracle. No country at the top of the income distribution has increased its per-capita income by a factor of four in twenty-five years, and the leader has always taken at least eighty years to quadruple its income.

Does the theory account for the experience of these countries and the record of catch-up in general? To account for catch-up, including growth miracles, the theory requires an increase in the efficiency of a country relative to the leader.[8] In light of the Parente and Prescott (2000) theory, these changes in relative efficiency are easy to understand—namely, they reflect policy changes. Following an improvement in policy that leads to a significant and persistent increase in efficiency, the theory predicts that the income of a late starter will go from its currently low level relative to the leader to a much higher level. As it does, its growth rate will exceed the rate of modern growth experienced by the leader countries, and the gap in incomes will be narrowed.

Parente and Prescott (2005) consider a change in relative efficiency in the model economy and find that the model is quantitatively consistent with the growth miracle experiences of countries such as Japan. The theory is consistent with the fact that growth miracles are a relatively recent phenomenon and are limited to initially poor countries. Growth miracles are a relatively recent phenomenon because differences in relative incomes between a low-efficiency country and a high-efficiency country widen over time before leveling off. This widening is due to growth in the stock of pure knowledge associated with the modern production function, which the high-efficiency country uses from a very early date. Thus, as one goes back in time, the gap that a low-efficiency country could close by becoming a high-efficiency country becomes smaller and smaller. If the gap is less than 50 percent, the low-efficiency country cannot double its income in less than a decade. For the same reason, the unified theory is consistent with the fact that late starters have been able to double their incomes in far shorter times compared to early starters. Growth miracles are limited to the set of initially poor countries because a growth miracle in the theory requires a large increase in a country's relative efficiency. A large increase in efficiency can occur only in a poor country with a currently low-efficiency parameter. This rules out a rich country, which by definition uses its resources efficiently.

Catching Up

The implication of the theory is that countries will be rich if they constrain the choice of technologies and work practices of its citizenry. Currently poor countries will catch up to the industrial leaders in terms of production efficiency if existing barriers to efficient production are eliminated and an arrangement is set up to ensure that barriers will not be re-erected in the future. The removal of such constraints is a necessary condition for catching up. As discussed above, strong evidence suggests that these constraints exist to protect the interests of industry groups vested in the current production process. As such, their removal is likely to be contentious. For this reason, it is instructive to examine the record on catch-up in greater depth for the purpose of determining the circumstances under which barriers to efficient use of technology were reduced and catching up occurred with the efficiency leader.

Catch-Up Facts

Catching up is not uniform across regions, as can be seen in figure 1.1. Latin American countries began modern economic growth in the late nineteenth century, and this set has not subsequently closed the living-standards gap with the industrial leader; the per-capita income of this set remained at roughly 25 percent of the industrial leader throughout the twentieth century. In comparison, Asian countries, with the exception of Japan, began modern economic growth later. This set of countries, however, experienced significant catching up in the last half of the twentieth century.

The large Western European countries—namely, Germany, Italy, and France—caught up to the industrial leader in the post–World War II period after trailing the leader for one hundred years. Modern economic growth in these countries began about 1840. At that time, their living standard was about 60 percent of the industrial leader, which at that time was the United Kingdom. For nearly one hundred years, these countries maintained an income level that was about 60 percent that of the industrial leader. In the post–World War II period, output per hour worked in these countries (which is a good measure of living standards because it recognizes the value of nonmarket time) increased from 38 percent of the U.S. level in 1950 to 73 percent in 1973 and to 94 percent in 1992. Per-capita output in Western Europe is still lower compared to the U.S. level, but this difference is accounted for by differences in the fraction of time that people work in the market and not in the efficiency with which resources are used.

Another important example of catching up is the U.S. development experience in the 1865 to 1929 period. In 1870, U.K. per-capita GDP was nearly a third higher than that of the United States. By 1929, the United Kingdom's per-capita GDP was a third lower than that of the United States. The dramatic growth performance of the United States in this period is an important fact that needs to be explained.

Reasons for Catching Up or Not Catching Up

The United States   We begin with the question of why the United States caught up with and surged past the United Kingdom in the 1865 to 1929 period. Our answer to this question is that the United Sates was and continues to be a free-trade club, while the United Kingdom was not a member of a free-trade club in this earlier period. Our definition of a *free-trade club* is a set of states that cannot impose tariffs and other restrictions on the import of goods and services from other member states and that must have a considerable degree of economic sovereignty from the collective entity. Just as no single state is able to block the movement of goods between states, the collective entity cannot block the adoption of a superior technology in one of its member states. Thus, a free-trade club in our definition is far more than a set of countries with a free-trade agreement.

The United States certainly satisfies these two conditions and thus is a free-trade club. The individual state governments have a considerable degree of sovereign power over the federal government. Additionally, the Interstate Commerce Cause of the U.S. Constitution gives the federal government the right to regulate interstate commerce and prevent individual states from imposing tariffs and other restrictions on the import of goods and services. With the formation of the North American Free Trade Association (NAFTA) and the recent approval of free-trade agreements with Chile and Singapore, the set of states constituting the free-trade club to which the United States belongs may be getting larger.[9]

A free-trade club—which prohibits individual states from discriminating against the goods produced in other member states and against producers from other member states operating within their borders—has the advantage that industry insiders in the various member states face elastic demand for what they supply. As a consequence, they are not hurt by the adoption of more efficient production methods as the increase in output leads to an increase in employment of the factor they supply in that industry. If demand were inelastic, an increase in efficiency would lead to a fall in employment, something that industry insiders do not like and would strongly oppose.[10] Thus, a free-trade club provides less incentive for groups of factor suppliers to form insider groups and block the adoption of more efficient technologies.

A free-trade club need not be comprised of individual democratic states, as is the case with the United States. However, in a free-trade club made up of democratic states with legislatures representing districts, vested interests in one district will be far more limited in their ability to block the adoption of technology in some other district if the citizens of the other district want that technology adopted. In the United States, for example, Toyota was able to locate an automobile plant with its just-in-time production in Kentucky in 1985. Those with vested interests in the less efficient technology in Michigan and other states with a large automotive industry were not able to prevent this from happening. The people in Kentucky wanted the large construction project in their state and the high-paying jobs in the automobile factory. In 1995, political pressure mounted to block the import of luxury automobiles from Japan. Toyota responded by building plants in other states, including Indiana and West Virginia in 1998 and Alabama and Texas in 2003. These location decisions were as much politically motivated as economically motivated, and now Toyota is the third-largest automobile producer in the United States.

Western Europe   The reason that Western Europe caught up with the United States in terms of labor productivity in the 1957 to 1993 period is the same. With the creation of the European Union, Western Europe has become an equally important free-trade club. Its states enjoy even greater sovereignty than do U.S. member states. The German state cannot block the Toyota introduction of just-in-time production in Wales even though German politicians would if they could in response to domestic political pressures. If Toyota starts gaining market share, it will not be long before the auto industry throughout Europe adopts the superior technology and productivity in the automobile industry increases. This is competition at work.

The historical statistics lend strong empirical support to the theory that a trading-club arrangement results in greater efficiency of production. Table 1.1 reports labor productivity defined as output per work hour for the original members of what became the European Union and the labor productivity of members that joined in the 1970s and 1980s. Productivities are reported for an extended period before the EU was formed as well as for the period subsequent to its creation. The Treaty of Rome was signed in 1957 by Belgium, France, Italy, Netherlands, Luxembourg, and West Germany to form the union. In 1973, Denmark, Ireland, and the United Kingdom joined, and in 1981, Greece joined, followed by Portugal and Spain in 1986. The most recent additions are Austria, Finland, and Sweden in 1995.

One striking fact is that prior to forming the European Union, the original members had labor productivity that was only half that of the United States. This state of affairs persisted for over sixty years with no

Table 1.1
Labor Productivities of European Union members as a percentage of U.S. productivity

Year	Original Members	Members Joining in 1973
1870	62	
1913	53	
1929	52	
1938	57	
1957	53	57
1973	78	66
1983	94	76
1993	102	83
2002	101	85

Note: The prewar numbers are population-weighted labor-productivity numbers from Maddison (1995). The postwar numbers are also population weighted and were obtained from Maddison's Web page, ⟨http://www.eco.rug.nl/GGDC/index-series.html#top⟩.

catching up. However, in the thirty-six years after forming what became the EU, the Treaty of Rome signers caught up with the United States in terms of labor productivity. The factor leading to this catch-up is an increase in the efficiency with which resources are used in production. Changes in capital-to-output ratios are of little significance in accounting for the change in labor productivity (Prescott 2002).

Also reported in table 1.1 is the productivity of the EU countries that joined the union in 1973. These countries experienced significant productivity catch-up subsequent to joining the union. It will be interesting to see if Greece and Portugal, the two EU countries that have significantly lower productivity than the other EU members, continue to improve their relative productivity performance.

Another interesting comparison is between the productivity performance of the set of original EU members and the set of Western European countries that either joined in 1995 or still have not joined the EU. This latter set consists of Switzerland, Austria, Finland, and Sweden ("the others").[11] Table 1.2 reports labor productivities of the others to the original EU countries.

Table 1.2
Labor productivity of other Western European countries as a percentage of original EU members

Year	Others/Original
1900	103
1913	99
1938	103
1957	106
1973	96
1983	85
1993	81

Note: The prewar figures are from Maddison (1995). For this period, GDP per capita is used as a proxy for productivity. The postwar numbers are also population weighted and were obtain from Maddison's Web page, ⟨http://www.eco.rug.nl/GGDC/index-series.html#top⟩.

The important finding is that the original EU countries and the others are equally productive in the pre–World War II period. In the thirty-six years from 1957 to 1993, the others fell from 1.06 times as productive as the original EU countries to only 0.81 as productive in 1993. This constitutes strong empirical evidence that membership in the EU fosters higher productivity.

Latin America   Latin America failed to catch up because it has failed to develop into a free-trade club. For this reason, Latin America per-capita income has remained at the same level relative to the leader for the last century. There was no free movement of goods and people between the set's relatively sovereign states. A consequence of this is that industry insiders in the sovereign states often faced inelastic demand for their products or services, and this led them to block the adoption of more efficient production practices. If Latin American countries were to decentralize and restrict the authority of their central governments to be like the United States in the 1865 to 1929 period, then they too would quickly become as rich as (or maybe richer than) Western Europe and the United States.

Southeast Asia   The reasons for catch-up in Asia are slightly more involved. Countries such as South Korea, Taiwan, and Japan were forced to adopt policies that did not block efficient production as a condition for support from the United States. Further, the need to finance national defense made protecting those with vested interests in inefficient production too expensive for South Korea and Taiwan. The success of these countries along with the Hong Kong and Singapore growth miracles made it clear to the people of other states in the region such as Thailand and Malaysia that the policy their leaders followed mattered for their living standard. The leaders of these countries had no choice but to cut back on the protection they afforded to industry insiders with vested interests in inefficient production or risk losing power. Perhaps as the political systems of these states become more democratic, these pressures will increases and protection will be further reduced, which will allow these countries to continue their catch-up with the leaders. Additionally, these countries should benefit from the closer economic ties they have recently forged with the advanced economies.

The recent catching up done by China is primarily a result of its becoming a free-trade club. The rapid development of China began in 1978 when the Chinese government became more decentralized, with much of the centralized-planning system dismantled. Although the central government gave more power to regional governments, it did not give the regional governments the right to restrict the flow of goods across regions. In fact, when individual regions attempted to erect trade barriers in the late 1980s and early 1990s, the central government immediately took steps to restore the free flow of goods and services (Young 2000). The resulting competition between businesses in different provinces led to rapid growth in living standards.

While China's performance since its transition to capitalism has been spectacular, the same cannot be said for Russia's performance since its transition to capitalism: China has closed some of its income gap with the leader, but Russia has fallen further behind the leader. Between 1985 and 1998, Russia's per capita GDP fell from 30 percent to 22 percent of the U.S. level. Why has Russia failed to catch up to the leader following its switch to capitalism?

Russia, in contrast to China, does not belong to a free-trade club and remains economically isolated from Western Europe. It is large enough both in terms of population and land for its regions to make up a free-trade club, but this is not the case. Local and regional governments in Russia have the power to discriminate against producers from other member states operating within their borders and to restrict the flow of goods and people into and out of their region. For example, in response to the financial crisis of August 1988, regional governments prohibited exports of food goods from their regions and put in place price ceilings for many of those items. Regional governments further have the discretion to use federal funds for purposes they see fit. Often, these funds are used to keep inefficient industries afloat. Local governments also have control over the use and privatization of land. There are essentially no land and real estate markets. In general, the purchase of land and the conversion of nonindustrial structures for new commercial activity are not possible. During the privatization phase, local governments refused to lease any property that had not been used commercially.[12]

Concluding Remarks

Will the whole world be rich by the end of the twenty-first century? The implication of the theory reviewed in this chapter is that a country will catch up to the leading industrial countries only if it eliminates the constraints relating to the use of technology. But removing the constraints to the efficient use of resources is bound to be contentious because such constraints typically exist to protect specialized groups of factor suppliers and corporate interests.

The historical record of catch-up suggests that joining a free-trade club is an important way by which a society can eliminate barriers that were erected to protect specialized groups of factor suppliers and corporate interests and reduce the likelihood that such groups will seek similar protection in the future. The European Union has and continues to be an important free-trade club. The European Union was scheduled to expand from fifteen to twenty-five members in May 2004. The new countries include the Czech Republic, Hungary, Poland, and the Slovak Republic, which are all former Communist states located in Central Europe. If history is any guide, these countries will narrow the productivity gap with the original European Union members and the United States.

Three of the ten scheduled joiners—Cyprus, Malta, and Slovenia—already have relatively high GDP per capita and have little catching up to do. They are all small countries that are highly economically integrated with Western European states and have been de facto members of the Western European trading club for a number of years. Countries that are economically integrated with other sovereign states can be rich. Australia and New Zealand are additional examples of rich countries that are not members of a formal free-trading club. These countries, of course, are members of the British Commonwealth, which was a trading club before the United Kingdom joined the European Union in 1973. Poor countries in the world would be wise to heed the lessons of these countries.

Notes

Edward C. Prescott thanks the National Science Foundation and the University of Minnesota Foundation for research support. The views expressed herein are those of the authors and not necessarily those of the Federal Reserve Bank of Minneapolis or the Federal Reserve System.

1. Much of the stock of productive knowledge is public information, and even proprietary information can be accessed by a country through licensing agreements or foreign direct investment.

2. The efficiency parameter E can change as the result of a change in a country's policies, but for now we treat it as constant over time and index it by country only and not by time.

3. In this theory, the corresponding concept of capital also includes intangible capital.

4. See Parente and Prescott (2000) for a survey of this evidence.

5. Parente and Prescott (1999) show in a model with no capital how a monopoly right granted to factor suppliers can significantly lower a country's efficiency. Herrendorf and Teixeira (2003) extend this model to include physical capital and show that these monopoly rights have even larger effects on a country's efficiency.

6. The size of these required differences is shown to decrease as the size of the capital-share parameter in modern technology increases.

7. Ngai (2004) also uses the Hansen and Prescott (2002) model of economic development to account for the evolution of international incomes. Unlike Parente and Prescott (2005), Ngai examines the effect of policy on the starting date within Hansen and Prescott's overlapping-generations model. On account of this, she

finds that some part of the income gap will be eliminated once poor countries start their transitions.

8. Additionally, an increase in efficiency can hasten the start of the transition to modern growth for countries that have not already begun this phase of development.

9. The United States was probably more of a free-trade club in the 1865 to 1929 period than in the post-1929 period. This is because the Interstate Commerce Clause was interpreted in the earlier period to mean that states could not interfere with interstate commerce. After 1929, the interpretation changed when the meaning of the clause was broadened to allow the federal government to regulate interstate commerce.

10. Dowrick and Spencer (1994) review empirical literature that finds union resistance to the adoption of labor-saving innovations occurs within an industry when employment and wages will fall as the result of the adoption of the innovation. They go on to establish conditions under which this will and will not occur.

11. Norway is not included in this set of countries because of the large size of its oil industry.

12. Parente and Ríos-Rull (2001) document the greater prevalence of specialized groups of factor suppliers in Russia compared to China and the successful efforts by local governments in Russia to prevent the adoption of better technologies.

References

Dowrick, S., and B. J. Spencer. (1994). "Union Attitudes to Labour-Saving Innovation: When Are Unions Luddites?" *Journal of Labor Economics* 12: 316–344.

Hansen, G. D., and E. C. Prescott. (2002). "Malthus to Solow." *American Economic Review* 92: 1205–1217.

Herrendorf, B., and A. Teixeira. (2003). "Monopoly Rights Can Reduce Income Big Time." University of Carlos III Working Paper, July.

Kuznets, S. (1966). *Modern Economic Growth*. New Haven, CT: Yale University Press.

Maddison, A. (1995). *Monitoring the World Economy: 1820–1992*. Paris: Organisation for Economic Co-operation and Development.

Mokyr, J. (1990). *The Lever of Riches: Technological Creativity and Economic Progress*. New York: Oxford University Press.

Ngai, L. R. (2004). "Barriers and the Transition to Modern Economic Growth." *Journal of Monetary Economics* 51: 1353–1383.

Parente, S. L., and E. C. Prescott. (1994). "Barriers to Technology Adoption and Development." *Journal of Political Economy* 102: 298–321.

Parente, S. L., and E. C. Prescott. (1999). "Monopoly Rights: A Barrier to Riches." *American Economic Review* 89: 1216–1233.

Parente, S. L., and E. C. Prescott. (2000). *Barriers to Riches*. Cambridge: MIT Press.

Parente, S. L., and E. C. Prescott. (2005). "A Unified Theory of the Evolution of International Incomes." In P. Aghione and S. Durlauf, eds., *The Handbook of Economic Growth*. Amsterdam: Elsevier Press.

Parente, S. L., and J.-V. Ríos-Rull. (2001). "The Success and Failure of Economic Reforms in Transition Economies." Manuscript, University of Illinois.

Prescott, E. C. (2002). "Prosperity and Depression." *American Economic Review* 92(2): 1–15.

Schmitz, J. A., Jr. (2001). "Government Production of Investment Goods and Aggregate Labor-Productivity." *Journal of Monetary Economics* 47: 163–187.

Young, A. (2000). "The Razor's Edge: Distortions and Incremental Reform in the People's Republic of China." *Quarterly Journal of Economics* 115: 1091–1135.

2

Elections, Political Checks and Balances, and Growth

Philip Keefer

Many authors argue that universal suffrage, competitive elections, and restraints on the executive branch are necessary for secure property rights, which in turn are important for economic growth (e.g., Acemoglu, Robinson, and Johnson 2002). There is also strong evidence that insecure property and contract rights slow growth (Acemoglu et al. 2002; Knack and Keefer 1995). Nevertheless, despite substantial effort, scholars have found little robust evidence that democracies grow more rapidly than nondemocracies. This has become a puzzle of increasing concern, since the number of countries holding competitive elections has doubled from 53 to 101 between 1985 and 2000, and the number exhibiting some checks and balances has risen from 62 to 112.[1]

This chapter revisits the issue of democracy and growth using multiple measures of democracy to isolate the different dimensions of democracy. The evidence supports the claim that nondemocratic forms of governance are a significant hindrance to growth. However, it turns out that it is not elections that matter most for growth but rather the presence of political checks and balances. Previous difficulties assessing the democracy-growth relationship seem to be due to the use of data that overly emphasizes the former at the expense of the latter. However, in addressing the theme of convergence of the poor countries with the developed economies, less support is found for the hypothesis that democracy is a significant determinant of convergence and catch-up. Almost surely because of data limitations, the evidence does not support the claim that the ability of poorer countries to catch up to richer countries is conditioned on their political regime.

Growth and Measures of Democracy

Clear statements of how democracy might accelerate growth come from North and Weingast (1989) and Acemoglu, Robinson, and Johnson (2002), who argue that political checks and balances restrain expropriatory tendencies of government, enhancing investor confidence and thereby spurring growth. Acemoglu, Robinson, and Johnson (2002) also suggest that voting and the full enfranchisement of citizens help to check expropriatory tendencies of government. Counterarguments have been advanced that democracies give rise to the potential for expropriation of the investments of the rich by the poor (Przeworski and Limongi 1993, review these arguments). Such competing hypotheses do not explain why the poor are more apt to expropriate than a dictator (who could be rich or poor). Possibly because democracy has offsetting positive and negative effects on growth, researchers have not uncovered robust causal relationships between democracy and growth (e.g., de Haan 1996).

Some scholars have rejected the democracy-growth link because it is not robust to the inclusion of different control variables. Barro (1994) shows that democracy has a significant effect on growth only when the rule of law and education variables are not controlled for. However, substantial theory suggests that democracy influences these variables, so it is reasonable to exclude them from the list of control variables. Similarly, Rivera-Batiz (2002) argues that democracy operates through the Hall and Jones (1999) index of social infrastructure, which rises the more secure property rights are and the more free trade is.

Scholars' approach to endogeneity issues—especially the joint determination by omitted variables of both democracy and growth—is another source of variation in results. Tavares and Wacziarg (2001) adopt an elaborate econometric strategy for evaluating the channels through which democracy might affect growth, though they do not include the security of property rights among these. They use a large number of instrumental variables that "determine" democracy but are uncorrelated with the error terms in the various "channel" equations, ranging from ethnolinguistic fractionalization to whether a country was ever a colony to dummy variables capturing the predominant religion in a country. They find that the net effects of democracy are negative, primarily because democracy suppresses investment. This result is puzzling, since the effect of secure property rights—the channel through which others argue democracy exerts the strongest positive influence on growth—has been found to have a large effect on investment (Knack & Keefer 1995). Using the same Freedom House variable to measure democracy but using only religious dummies and the gap between female and male school attainment as instruments, Svensson (1999) finds that democracy is weakly but positively associated with growth.

Finally, though, it is possible that the relevant aspects of democracy are not well captured in the data. This is the concern of the analysis in this chapter. The most common measure of democracy is the Freedom House indicators of political freedoms and civil liberties, used in one form or another by most authors in the literature of this subject. Another commonly used measure is taken from the Polity Database, the most recent version of which is Polity IV. All countries are scored in this database on both their autocratic and democratic characteristics.

These measures apparently take into account the multidimensionality of democracy. How precisely they weight democracy's different attributes is not clear, however. For example, the fact of election may have a greater impact on democracy scores than the extent of restraints on the executive. Przeworski, Alvarez, Cheibub, and Limongi (2000) employ an objective measure of democracy that puts almost all weight on whether elections occur in a country and whether elections lead to a change of government. Using this clear, objective, and unidimensional measure of democracy, they find no difference in growth rates between democracies and dictatorships. This raises the question of whether more general measures of democracy have little effect on growth because they underweight other characteristics along which democracies vary, such as political checks and balances.

To get at this possibility, the influence of four different measures of democracy is evaluated. The Freedom House indicators of civil and political liberties reflect whether countries embrace a wide range of "democratic" norms, ranging from freedom of assembly and speech to the existence of competitive elections and human rights more generally. Freedom House scores are based on expert evaluations of country conditions. As is typical, the estimates use the sum of the political freedom and civil liberties indicators.

The Polity indicators are subjective assessments of a narrower range of phenomena, including whether elections are competitive and whether there are restraints on the executive. Both indicators reflect *outcomes* of the political process rather than the formal rules of political decision making: countries could exhibit both elections and checks and balances on paper, but these may in practice not operate to restrain arbitrary government behavior. Similarly, countries could fail to exhibit formal checks and balances, but informal restraints on the executive branch would raise country scores on the Polity democracy indicators. The Polity scores permit countries to have both democratic and autocratic characteristics. Again as is common practice, therefore, the variable used is the democratic score less the autocratic score.

Two other *objective* indicators of democratic characteristics are further considered. These are the two criteria that are most prominent in the construction of the Polity IV democracy indicator. The *checks* indicator from the *Database of Political Institutions* (Beck, Clarke, Groff, Keefer, & Walsh 2001) measures how many political actors can veto proposed legislation. Beginning from a value of one (meaning that there is only one veto player and no checks and balances), this variable increments by one if countries have potentially competitive elections of the executive; by one in presidential systems if the legislature and presidency are controlled by different parties; in parliamentary systems, by the number of parties in the government coalition whose departure would cause the government to lose a majority; and in all systems by one for each party supporting the government in the legislature whose ideological stance strongly differs from that of the executive's party (see the *Database of Political Institutions* codebook for more details). The key to this variable is that it captures the two essential ingredients identified by Acemoglu, Robinson, and Johnson (2002) for secure property rights: elections and checks on the executive branch.

The *DPI* also contains variables assessing the competitiveness of elections. The Executive Index of Electoral Competitiveness (EIEC) is used for this purpose. It reaches its highest score (7) when multiple parties can and do compete for executive election and no party gets more than 75 percent of the vote. A 6 means that one party receives more than 75 percent of the vote; a 5 that only one party ran for office though others could have; and so on until 1, indicating that no elections were held. Since most scholars would agree that only the most competitive category of EIEC is a reasonable approximation to elections, a dummy variable is used in the regressions, equaling 1 when EIEC is 7 and 0 otherwise.

Specification

This chapter compares the effects of different democracy indicators on growth. To focus the comparison sharply, a parsimonious empirical specification is used:

$$Growth\ in\ income\ per\ capita_i = \beta_1 + \beta_2\ ln(initial\ income/capita)_i$$
$$+ \beta_3\ (democracy\ indicators)_i + \varepsilon_i.$$

This parsimonious specification has several advantages. First, there is little disagreement that institutions have a strong influence on a range of determinants of growth that often enter independently in growth regressions (evidence below shows this explicitly to be the case for education enrollment, for example). This specification allows the institutional variables to reflect these effects. Second, Hall and Jones (1999) employ such a specification when looking at the determinants of per-capita income, arguing both that income is an equilibrium or long-run outcome and that social infrastructure is the fundamental determinant of income. Finally, arguments below are robust to including other more exogenous variables, ethnolinguistic polarization, land area, and total population.

Several of the democracy indicators are available from only 1975 to 2000. This is the period over which growth is evaluated; the regressions are all cross-section. To minimize simple problems of reverse causation, the determinants of growth are limited to the 1975 values of the democracy variables and the 1986 values of the security of property rights (the earliest available).

Of course, the determinants of democracy may include omitted variables that themselves influence growth. Countries that are inherently more prosperous may also be inherently more democratic. Instrumental variables are a typical solution to this problem, particularly in the literature of the subject. Scholars first estimate

$$Democracy_i = \gamma_1 + Y'_i\gamma_2 + \eta_i$$

and substitute the predicted value of democracy from this equation into the main growth equation above. The choice of instrumental variables in this chapter differs from that in the literature. Rather than use lagged values of democracy to instrument for current values, as in Helliwell (1994) and de Haan (1996), the argument here takes advantage of the instruments that have been employed in assessing the relationship between the security of property rights and growth.

The literature evaluating the importance of secure property rights for growth typically justifies the use of instruments for the security of property rights by reference to their connection to the underlying institutions that give rise to secure property rights. This is the case with urban population in 1700 in Acemoglu, Robinson, and Johnson (2002) and latitude and language in Hall and Jones (1999), for example. The implicit argument is the following: fundamental country characteristics (such as distance from the equator) influence unobserved institutions, which themselves guarantee the security of property rights. However, this argument provides an even stronger justification for using such instruments in democracy-growth regressions. The broad instrument set used here consists of distance from the equator (Hall and Jones 1999, use this to instrument for their index of social infrastructure) and colonial heritage and years since the creation or independence of a country (used frequently to instrument for the institutional choices of countries, as in Persson, Tabellini, and Trebbi 2001). All of the instrument variables estimates below use three sets of these instruments: first, all of them; second, only time since independence and distance from the equator; and third, the dummy variables indicating a country's colonial heritage, if any.

Democracy and Growth

The effects of these democracy variables on growth, using the different instrument sets, are summarized in table 2.1. Significant results are in

Table 2.1
The effect of democracy on growth: parsimonious specification, 1975 to 2000

| | | Instrumental Variables Estimates | | |
	OLS	All Instruments	Only Latitude and Years since Independence	Only Colonial Heritage Dummies
Polity IV	.0008	.0008	.0017	.001
	(.02)	(.27)	(.34)	(.16)
Freedom House	.0014	.0028	.012	.0037
	(.04)	(.14)	(.27)	(.11)
EIEC	.0065	.019	.035	.014
	(.135)	(.235)	(.16)	(.50)
Checks	.0035	.0078	.01	.0087
	(.003)	(.01)	(.26)	(.008)

Note: All specifications include the log of initial income per capita and a constant, not reported. Robust standard errors are used to calculate p-statistics. p-statistics are in parentheses.

bold. Only the democracy coefficient is reported. There are a number of interesting conclusions to be drawn here. First, although Polity IV and Freedom House indicators are highly significant in ordinary least squares (OLS) regressions, they are not robust to different instrument sets used to control for endogeneity. This is consistent with results in the literature.

The estimated coefficients, though much less significant, are actually higher in the IV estimates than in the OLS. This is likely because the Polity IV and Freedom House indicators inaccurately assess the true institutional (democratic) environment in countries and, moreover, the errors are negatively correlated with measured institutions. As a consequence, the estimated OLS democracy coefficient is biased downward in growth regressions. Such mismeasurement can occur for several reasons. The most important is that some aspects of democracy promote growth while others may not. To the extent that the construction of the Polity IV and Freedom House indicators puts excessive weight on the former and insufficient weight on the latter, their association with growth is attenuated.

In particular, as the third row of table 2.1 demonstrates, if one isolates the effect of elections, there is no significant effect at all on subsequent growth. Elections in one year might be expected to have little effect on growth ten or fifteen years later, as is assumed in the estimation. However, the same claim can be made of the other democracy indicators, all of which are measured in 1975. Furthermore, average EIEC scores over the period 1975 to 2000 are only slightly more significant as determinants of growth over the same period.[2] Elections, however, are the cornerstone of most characterizations of democracy. To the extent that they receive significant weight in the subjective Freedom House and Polity IV indicators, these indicators are not robust indicators of growth.[3]

Although elections themselves seem to be unimportant for growth, the last row of table 2.1 supports that political checks and balances are important. Checks—consistent with arguments by North and Weingast (1989), Keefer and Knack (1997, 2002), and Acemoglu, Robinson, and Johnson (2002)—are strongly associated with growth. However, checks are robust only to IV estimations that use colonial heritage as instruments, not the specification that uses only latitude and years since independence. This pattern of results is revealing about the democracy-growth relationship. Colonial heritage says something about the formal institutional endowment of a country, and checks and balances are determined in large part by the institutions of government: whether there are elections or whether there is a presidential or parliamentary system. On the other hand, underlying country characteristics (such as those described by latitude) and the opportunity for political competitors to form reputations (as might be captured by years since independence) are important regardless of the formal institutions and therefore need have no *a priori* relationship to colonial heritage.

Table 2.2 presents results that control, additionally, for average ethno-linguistic polarization over the period, average population, and land area.[4] These variables are relatively exogenous to government policy (though less so in the case of population), they affect market size and the potential for growth, and at the same time they are likely to mediate the influence of the institutional indicators. Democracy under conditions of social polarization, for example, might have different effects than when voters are not polarized.

Table 2.2
The effect of democracy on growth with more controls, 1975 to 2000

	Instrumental Variables Estimates		
	All Instruments	Only Latitude and Years since Independence	Only Colonial Heritage Dummies
Polity IV	.0008	.0002	.001
	(.27)	(.90)	(.16)
Freedom House	.003	.0005	.0036
	(.06)	(.95)	(.04)
EIEC	.005	−.002	.004
	(.07)	(.76)	(.14)
Checks	.0077	−.0004	.0067
	(.02)	(.96)	(.04)

Note: All specifications as in table 2.1, adding total population, land area, and ethnic polarization. Robust standard errors are used to calculate *p*-statistics. *p*-statistics are in parentheses.

Most of these variables are not significant in any growth regression. Their inclusion does improve the precision of two of the Freedom House and one of the EIEC regressions. However, of the nine Polity IV, Freedom House, and EIEC regressions, in six the institutional coefficients remain insignificant. Table 2.2 is therefore supportive of the discussion surrounding table 2.1, which argues that political checks and balances, rather than elections alone, are a key characteristic of democracy that drives growth.

Three IV estimations of the effects of EIEC and Freedom House are significant in table 2.2, where none were significant in table 2.1. This is also consistent with the arguments presented in this chapter. In the first-stage regressions (not reported), population is a significant predictor of EIEC, and average polarization is a significant—but positive—predictor of the Freedom House variable. To the extent that these instruments condition the functioning of democratic institutions, this is precisely the result that one would expect. The positive effect of polarization on Freedom House variables is most likely an indication that Freedom House evaluations take into account the difficulties presented by social polarization. The evaluations therefore appear to give more polarized countries the benefit of the doubt. In fact, Freedom House scores and polarization are correlated at 0.58. Removing this source of noise in the evaluations improves the precision of the Freedom House evaluations.

The Effects of Democratic Institutions on Catch-Up

These arguments have implications for convergence and "catch-up" effects. Keefer and Knack (1997) demonstrate that poverty confers a catch-up advantage conditional on poor countries offering secure property rights to economic actors. As in the literature more generally, that analysis considers only briefly the institutional origins of secure property rights and not at all in the context of convergence. The evidence is clear that secure property rights accelerate growth and convergence, and the preceding sections suggest that competitive elections and political checks and balances, two essential attributes of democracy that are believed to enhance the security of property rights, also accelerate growth. The evidence in this section suggests, however, that these same democratic institutions may do little to hasten convergence.

To see this, an interaction term is added to the empirical specifications in table 2.1, the product of initial income per capita and the different institutional variables. Evidence for convergence exists when the coefficient on initial per-capita income is negative: poorer countries grow faster. A negative coefficient on the interaction term indicates that in the presence of "better" institutions, the convergence effect is greater. The significance of the linear terms in table 2.3 is conditional on the value of the other linear terms. Hence, only the significant interaction terms are highlighted in bold.

Consistent with each of the foregoing sections, elections and the two traditional subjective measures of democracy from Freedom House and Polity IV exhibit no significant impact on convergence. However, inconsistent with the previous results, convergence appears to be little affected by checks and balances. There are two possible explanations. First, the interactive specification (in which institutional variables enter twice—once linearly and once nonlinearly) places excessive demands on inexact instruments. That is, to the extent that instruments introduce noise into the estimation, there is less to distinguish the linear and interactive terms and multicollinearity drives down significance levels. Second, there is

Table 2.3
The effect of democracy on convergence, 1975 to 2000

	OLS	All Instruments	Only Latitude and Years since Independence	Only Colonial Heritage Dummies
		Instrumental Variables Estimates		
Polity IV:				
Initial polity	.002	.0028	.004	.003
	(.414)	(.21)	(.25)	(.211)
Initial GDP	−.0001	.0006	−.005	−.002
per capita	(.97)	(.90)	(.54)	(.64)
Polity * GDP	−.0001	−.0003	−.0003	−.0002
	(.64)	(.37)	(.44)	(.52)
Freedom House:				
Initial FH	.004	.0063	.022	.0045
	(.49)	(.102)	(.013)	(.25)
Initial GDP	.002	.0008	**−.029**	−.005
per capita	(.77)	(.93)	**(.063)**	(.62)
FH * GDP	−.0003	−.0005	−.0009	−.0001
	(.67)	(.39)	(.14)	(.86)
EIEC:				
Initial EIEC	.007	.005	−.0009	−.001
	(.22)	(.44)	(.93)	(.89)
Initial GDP	.0035	−.002	.008	−.008
per capita	(.487)	(.72)	(.52)	(.32)
EIEC * GDP	−.0007	−.00006	−.0002	.0009
	(.40)	(.95)	(.88)	(.46)
Checks:				
Initial checks	.008	.0227	.024	.011
	(.36)	(.089)	(.16)	(.42)
Initial GDP	.002	.0014	−.003	−.003
per capita	(.63)	(.76)	(.70)	(.54)
Checks * GDP	−.0006	−.002	−.0016	−.0003
	(.59)	(.24)	(.35)	(.85)

Note: All specifications include the log of initial income per capita and a constant, not reported. Robust standard errors are used to calculate p-statistics. The p-statistic for the linear terms is valid only at the point where the other linear term is zero. Only significant interaction coefficients are highlighted in bold. p-statistics are in parentheses.

simply much less variation in the checks indicator at low income levels (where the standard deviation is approximately one) and higher incomes (where the standard deviation is approximately 1.6). The seventeen poorest countries exhibit no checks and balances at all (checks equal to one for each of them). This inevitably attenuates estimates of the effect of checks and balances on the ability of low-income countries to catch up with richer countries.

Conclusion

The analysis in this chapter addresses two questions raised by the literature on property rights, democracy, and growth. First, can we distinguish the effects of different democratic attributes on growth? Second, are democratic institutions helpful in accelerating the convergence process? The findings here on the first question are clear: the usual subjective measures of democracy have little influence on growth, neither directly nor indirectly. One explanation for this is that these indicators may be simply too noisy to capture a true underlying relationship. However, an objective indicator of elections from the DPI shows no systematic relationship to growth, either, just as earlier work by Przeworski and colleagues (2000) using a similar variable. Instead, it appears that key democratic attributes that mediate the democracy-growth relationship go beyond elections to include political checks and balances that constrain government decision making. Unlike elections alone, elections with political checks and balances appear to have a strong direct effect on growth, robust to and even strengthened by controls for endogeneity.

Although striking, the results are preliminary in several senses. First, the results do not extend to a democracy-based explanation of why some poor countries can catch up and others do not. Second, other instruments are common in the literature of the subject and need to be taken into account. Third, the proper role of other policy and exogenous variables should continue to be examined. For example, do ethnic polarization, land, and population belong in the growth equation, or are they properly considered instruments themselves?

Finally, more qualitatively, stories are needed that connect these statistical findings to actual experiences of successful and unsuccessful countries. For example, the lack of statistical robustness in the democracy and growth literature seemed consistent with real-world experiences in which non- or weak democracies managed to grow rapidly over decades. The analysis here at least provides evidence that the simple fact of elections should not be expected to distinguish the growth record of countries. The analysis does not directly explain the growth of nondemocracies. It does, however, provide hints. Like democracies, nondemocracies are not created equal. Specifically, some, particularly those with entrenched and deeply organized single parties, seem to instill checks and balances despite the absence of competitive elections. In such countries, the removal of sharp policy distortions (e.g., on land use in China) can trigger much greater responses from economic actors than in nondemocracies in which autocratic rule is unconstrained. Hypotheses such as these require further exploration.

Notes

1. Based on World Development Indicators purchasing-power parity (PPP) adjusted income per capita, and using the Database on Political Institutions variables Executive Index of Electoral Competition (EIEC) and Legislative Index of Electoral Competition (LIEC), and Tenure of System (tensys), which are explained in more detail below. Democracies are defined as those countries with competitive elections for both the legislative and executive branches, $EIEC = LIEC = 7$.

2. The OLS coefficient is nearly significant; the others are not.

3. In fact, a one standard deviation increase in the EIEC dummy in 1975 is associated with a one-third standard deviation increase in the Polity and Freedom House 1975 values, even controlling for checks.

4. Ethnolinguistic polarization is a transformation of ethnolinguistic fractionalization that is discussed in Keefer and Knack (2002). Fractionalization is the probability that any two random people do not belong to the same ethnic or linguistic group. Polarization assigns the highest values to countries where this value is closest to one-half and the lowest values where this value is close to one or to zero.

References

Acemoglu, D., J. A. Robinson, and S. Johnson. (2002). Reversal of fortune: Geography and institutions in the making of the modern world. *Quarterly Journal of Economics, 117*: 1231–1294.

Barro, R. (1994). Democracy and growth. NBER Working Paper 4909 (October).

Beck, T., G. Clarke, A. Groff, P. Keefer, and P. Walsh. (2001). New tools in comparative political economy: The database of political institutions. *World Bank Economic Review, 15*(1): 165–176.

de Haan, J. (1996). New evidence on the relationship between democracy and economic growth. *Public Choice, 86:* 175–198.

Hall, R. E., and C. I. Jones. (1999). "Why do some countries produce so much more output per worker than others?" *Quarterly Journal of Economics, 114*(1): 83–116.

Helliwell, J. F. (1994). Empirical linkages between democracy and economic growth. *British Journal of Political Science, 24:* 225–248.

Keefer, P. (2000). "DPI2000, Database of political institutions: Changes and variable definitions." ⟨http://econ.worldbank.org/staff/pkeefer⟩.

Keefer, P., and S. Knack. (1997). Why don't poor countries catch up? A cross-national test of an institutional explanation. *Economic Inquiry, 35*(3): 590–602.

Keefer, P., and S. Knack. (2002). Polarization, property rights and the links between inequality and growth. *Public Choice, 111*(1–2): 127–154.

Knack, S., and P. Keefer. (1995). Institutions and economic performance: Cross-country tests using alternative institutional measures. *Economics and Politics, 7*(3): 207–228.

North, D. C., and B. R. Weingast. (1989). Constitutions and commitment: The evolution of institutions governing public choice in seventeenth-century England. *Journal of Economic History, 49*(4): 803–832.

Persson, T., and G. Tabellini. (2000). *Political economics: Explaining public policy.* Cambridge, MA: MIT Press.

Persson, T., G. Tabellini, and F. Trebbi. (2001). Electoral rules and corruption. National Bureau of Economic Research Working Paper 8154 (March).

Przeworski, A., M. E. Alvarez, J. A. Cheibub, and F. Limongi. (2000). *Democracy and development: Political institutions and well-being in the world, 1950–1990.* New York: Cambridge University Press.

Przeworski, A., and F. Limongi. (1993). Political regimes and economic growth. *Journal of Economic Perspectives, 7*(3): 51–69.

Rivera-Batiz, F. (2002). Democracy, governance and economic growth: Theory and evidence. *Review of Development Economics, 6*(2): 225–247.

Svensson, J. (1999). Aid, growth and democracy. *Economics and Politics, 11*(3): 275–297.

Tavares, J., and R. Wacziarg. (2001). How democracy affects growth. *European Economic Review, 45:* 1341–1378.

II

Case Studies of Successes and Failures in Catching Up

3

The Nordic Countries in the Nineteenth and Twentieth Centuries: Economic Growth in a Comparative Perspective

Olle Krantz

The Nordic countries are sometimes also called the Scandinavian countries, a designation that is not wholly adequate, especially from a geographical point of view. In this chapter, the countries involved—Denmark, Finland, Iceland, Norway, and Sweden—are compared with other countries, including the United States. First, some characteristics of the countries are described where country size takes a prominent place; second, a quantitative overview of the countries' growth is given; and third, some institutional features are discussed with special reference to Finland and Sweden.

Some Characteristics of the Nordic Countries

The Scandinavian countries have certain characteristics in common, but they are different in many respects. Finland and Sweden formed one state up to 1809, when Finland was ceded to the Russian empire. Then Finland formed a grand duchy with great autonomy up to 1917, when it became a sovereign state. Today, Finland and Sweden are in many respects similar: both are industrial countries, big in surface, and sparsely populated. They are dissimilar in other important respects, particularly geopolitical position and income levels up to the late twentieth century. Denmark and Norway formed one state for many centuries up to 1814, when Norway was ceded to Sweden. Sweden and Norway then formed a union up to 1905, when they got the shape that they have today. Norway, at the edge of the Atlantic, has been formed by the fishing and shipping industries and in recent decades by the offshore oil industry. Denmark, in contrast to Finland, Norway, and Sweden, is a small country[1] and has been formed by its exceptionally good agricultural conditions and its closeness to the developed countries on the European continent. Iceland is a special case with a small number of inhabitants and a position at an island in the north Atlantic. Its economy has always been dominated by fishing.

One important characteristic is the size of the countries. Around the year 2000, Denmark had 5.3 million, Finland 5.1 million, Iceland 0.28 million, Norway 4.5 million, and Sweden 8.8 million inhabitants. Thus, they are all small in population, a characteristic that makes the Scandinavian countries a special group—small, Western European, highly developed states.

One special property of small countries is that their foreign trade is big relative to total output: they have high trade ratios—exports or exports plus imports expressed as a percentage of gross domestic product (GDP). This has given rise to what may be called the *economic small-state theory* (Kuznets 1960; Krantz 2003). In small countries, exports are more likely to be concentrated in a few commodities than in larger nations (and this is especially true for less developed countries or countries in the early phases of development where these commodities are often raw materials). On the other hand, imports are more diversified because many commodities cannot be produced in an economically satisfactory way within the countries. Imports and particularly exports are also likely to be concentrated with respect to country of destination or origin. A large proportion of total exports is destined for one large country, and a large proportion of imports comes from that country. This means that a small country is heavily dependent on the surrounding world for its economic performance but, due to its limited size, has to take this world as given; it has no or very limited possibilities to influence the international economic situation.

Small countries are said to suffer *diseconomies of scale*. According to standard economic theory, production requires a certain size to be efficient. When the market is seen as synonymous with the domestic market, a small country is said to have too tiny a market for its production to be efficient. Consequently, the growth possibilities are more problematic than for a large country, which has a big home market that facilitates

Table 3.1
Export as a percentage of GDP (the export share) in some countries, 1970 and 2001

	Export Share, 1970	Export Share, 2001
Denmark	28	44
Finland	25	43
Norway	36	47
Sweden	23	46
France	15	29
United Kingdom	22	28
United States	6	11

Source: Own calculation based on OECD data. Current prices.

economic growth. To overcome these shortcomings, the small country has to seek larger markets via exports.

Based on this theory, the international environment and foreign trade have to play a major role, directly or indirectly, in the economic growth of the Nordic countries. They are small countries and therefore have a significantly higher foreign trade ratio than large ones. This is clearly shown in table 3.1.

However, foreign trade is not the only factor that matters. In the beginning of the era of modern economic growth in the nineteenth century, for instance, it was of utmost importance that the Nordic countries' trade could grow in relation to GDP and thus have link effects to the rest of their economies. However, at the same time, had there not been a certain degree of development and an adaptation ability in the rest of the economy regarding institutional setting, entrepreneurship, education, technological knowledge, and so on, enclave economies could have been the outcome and no modern economic growth would have occurred. Thus expansion of foreign trade was substantial and its contribution to the growth process was great, but domestic economic issues mattered as well.

When foreign trade grew in relation to GDP from the 1970s onward, however, it was not accompanied by an acceleration GDP per-capita growth, which was slower than in preceding decades when the foreign trade ratio had been lower. Thus, in the late twentieth century, the institutional and economic setting had a different impact on economic growth than it did in the liberal era in the late nineteenth century when trade was expanding relatively. Hence, free foreign trade is important but certainly not the only thing that matters for high rates of growth.

The Nordic countries can be considered as belonging to a group of states with success stories of economic growth in the nineteenth and twentieth centuries. Their long-run economic development has been rapid since the start of the era of modern economic growth, even since the beginning of industrialization. In this long-term perspective, there has been a convergence toward the richest countries in the world, and today they themselves belong to this group of countries. However, their growth experiences are complex and far from identical.

Quantitative Evidence

Economic growth was high in the Nordic countries for most of the nineteenth and twentieth centuries compared to the United States, as is demonstrated in table 3.2.

Table 3.2
Growth rates between five-year averages, 1872 to 2000

	Denmark	Finland	Iceland	Norway	Sweden	USA
1872–1890	1.1	0.8	1.0	0.9	1.0	1.8
1890–1910	2.0	1.8	2.0	1.3	2.3	1.8
1910–1930	1.6	1.6	1.7	2.2	2.2	1.0
1930–1950	1.2	2.5	3.8	2.4	2.7	2.3
1950–1970	3.5	4.0	2.9	3.2	3.2	2.0
1970–1990	2.1	2.8	3.1	3.1	1.6	1.7
1970–2000	2.1	2.5	2.6	3.0	1.6	2.9
1872–1970	1.9	2.2	2.3	2.0	2.3	1.8
1872–2000	1.9	2.2	2.4	2.2	2.2	1.8

Source: Hansen (1974), Hjerppe (1989), Jonsson (1999), Krantz (2001b), Maddison (2001), NOS XII (1965), and complements from the statistical offices of the respective countries.
Note: GDP per capita, constant prices.

Except for the first and the last subperiods, the United States, the economically leading country in the world (Maddison 2001), experienced a slower growth than the Nordic countries. Thus, this table shows a convergence toward the American economic level, and this process went on for most of the twentieth century. However, there are differences during the period, as is more clearly shown in figure 3.1, where the income levels[2] are compared for certain years during the period under study. The average levels for the five-year period 1998 to 2002 form the points of departure. The original data for these levels were calculated by Eurostat and are comparable for currency, which is made possible by using PPS (purchasing power standards). Here the five-year averages have been linked to the series for GDP per capita for the countries under review so that the ratios between the income levels of the countries for all years of the period could be computed. Needless to say, this method of

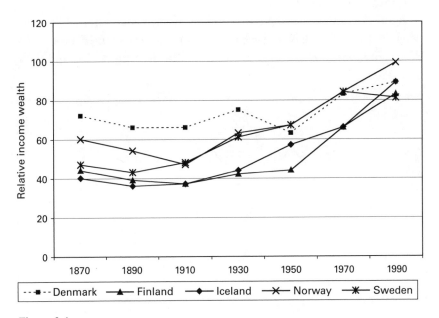

Figure 3.1
Income levels of the Nordic countries in relation to the United States, selected years 1870 to 2000
Source: OECD and Eurostat.
Note: Constant prices, EU15 = 100.

measurement involves margins of error, but they probably are not wide enough to distort the result. With these data, the time perspective is much longer than it is in most recent studies on convergence.

Until 1910, there were minuscule changes in the relations between the countries. Then they successively approached the United States, taking slightly differing paths. In general, the catching-up was slower before 1950 than after. Between 1930 and 1950, it seems that Denmark and Finland were slower growers than the other countries, and this has to do with their different experiences in wartime. In the second half of the century, the catching-up was very clear for all but for Sweden after 1970.

Changes also occurred in the ranking of the five Nordic countries, and thus convergence and divergence are also found within this group of countries. These changes are summarized in figure 3.2, which shows the coefficient of variation for these countries. This is a common way to illustrate processes of this kind.

Figure 3.2 shows that there was no long-term change from 1870 up to roughly 1910. World War I meant a short but very marked process of divergence, which changed to the opposite in the early 1920s and con-

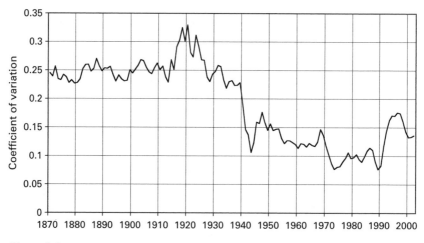

Figure 3.2
Dispersion of income per capita among the Nordic countries (coefficient of variation), 1870 to 2000
Source: OECD and Eurostat.
Note: Constant prices.

tinued a downward tendency until the 1960s or early 1970s. World War II meant a deep but short disturbance in the long-term process of change. The period from the late 1960s or the early 1970s was marked by greater fluctuations than before, and it is possible that the 1990s meant the commencement of a growing divergence. Anyhow, a very clear and long-run tendency of convergence within this group of countries is not visible in the same way as it is against the United States.

Thus, the quantitative data show convergence in the period from 1870 up to 2000, and this is summarized in table 3.3. There is a tendency toward higher growth figures for countries with lower rank in the beginning of the period.

Economy and Institutions: Rigidity and Flexibility

This section emphasizes a comparison between two countries, Finland and Sweden, which are of interest since the difference between them regarding income levels was great up to 1950, but around the year 2000 they were equal (see figure 3.1).[3]

From the 1890s to the late 1940s was Sweden's most successful period of growth. The country saw an industrial breakthrough in the decades around the turn of the nineteenth century, which resulted in a favorable industrial structure. Furthermore, Sweden was a nonbelligerent in the two world wars, which was positive for growth. Finland had as good a

Table 3.3
Relation between the income levels of the countries in 1870 and their average annual growth rate in years 1872 to 2000

	Relation, 1870	Growth, 1872 to 2000
United States	100	1.8
Denmark	72	1.9
Norway	60	2.2
Sweden	47	2.2
Finland	44	2.2
Iceland	40	2.4

Source: OECD and Eurostat.

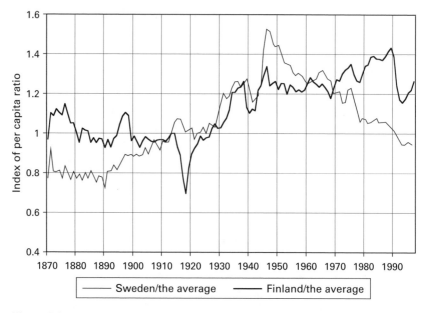

Figure 3.3
Finland's and Sweden's GDP per capita in relation to the average of sixteen industrial countries, 1870 to 1998
Source: Maddison (2001), Hjerppe (1989), Krantz (2001b). Index 1913 = 1.
Note: The countries involved are Australia, Austria, Belgium, Canada, Denmark, Finland, France, Germany, Italy, Japan, Netherlands, Norway, Sweden, Switzerland, United Kingdom, and United States.

performance as Sweden in the 1920s and 1930s, decades that saw a definitive industrial breakthrough in Finland (Krantz 2001a). Before that, with the exception of certain short periods, especially the late 1910s with the civil war, Finnish growth was average. From the late 1940s, there were great differences between growth in the two countries, which is clear when seen in an international perspective as in figure 3.3. In the 1950s and 1960s and more so from the 1970s onward, Sweden experienced a lower growth than the average for the sixteen countries involved. Finland, on the other hand, followed the international average in the 1950s and 1960s and then had a conspicuous growth spurt. The early 1990s saw a great depression, which was more severe in Finland than in Sweden, but after some years the economy recovered. The problem to be discussed here is why the Finnish performance differ so much from the Swedish in the second half of the twentieth century.

Catching-up in a technological sense could be an explanation. However, if by catching-up is meant that Finland experienced and exploited technological backwardness in relation to Sweden to reach a high growth rate, it is doubtful whether such backwardness did exist. The same international technology was available to both countries, and the main difference between them was that the Finnish manufacturing industry in the 1950s simply constituted a smaller share of total output than the Swedish one and that this share grew in the decades to come (Lindmark and Vikström 2003). Thus, explanations for the differences in growth rates between the Nordic countries have to be sought elsewhere.

An obvious option is to explore the countries' economic structures as well as their institutional and political regimes. These could be more or less appropriate for rapid economic growth, and moreover, they could change over time. The institutional and political aspects were pertinent in the second half of the twentieth century when the governmental sector grew in importance in all countries, but at different rates, which is shown in table 3.4. There Sweden stands out with its large share of government final expenditure even if Denmark is not far below. If government total expenditure had been used (that is, expenditure including transfers), the differences would have been wider. In 1996, the share of general government expenditure of GDP was 64 percent in Sweden and 49 percent in Norway. The average for fourteen highly industrialized countries was 45 percent (Tanzi and Schuknecht 1997, table I:1).[4]

Another feature of great importance was the so-called democratic corporatism that culminated in the 1960s and 1970s. This refers to the close collaboration between the labor unions, particularly the blue-collar workers' union (LO), the employers' organizations (SAF), and the government. The structure of industry was essential in this setting, especially the size distribution of firms. In these respects, there were clear differences between the countries.

In Sweden, there was a conspicuous consensus between the organizations mentioned above in the first decades after World War II. This consensus was colored by the fact that in Sweden there was a clear

Table 3.4

Government final expenditure in a number of countries expressed as percentage of GDP (expenditure approach), 1970 to 2000

Year	Denmark	Finland	Iceland	Norway	Sweden	Average of 23 Indus- trialized Countries
1970	21%	15%	13%	16%	23%	16%
1975	25	18	17	19	26	19
1980	27	19	17	19	31	20
1985	26	20	18	18	29	20
1990	26	22	20	21	29	20
1995	26	23	22	22	27	20
2000	25	21	24	19	27	19

Source: OECD.
Note: Current prices.

dominance of big firms,[5] which put its mark on the industrial associations. Furthermore, these companies were old and well established. As shown in table 3.5, many of them emanated from the industrial breakthrough in the decades around the turn of the nineteenth century. Very few were founded in the last fifty years of the period.

Probably the consensus among the organizations mentioned contributed to political measures getting a special shape. Profit taxation, for instance, was designed in a way to lock in the profits in the companies, which meant high reinvestment. Furthermore, the so-called investment funds allowed companies to save profits in tax-free accounts in the central bank and use them in troughs. These arrangements were favorable to existing companies and contributed to creating a rigid structure that was not suitable for new ventures.

In the 1960s, Swedish industry went through an intensive rationalization, which in the short run meant great increases in productivity and output. One-sidedness of investments toward old lines of production was, however, typical, and in the long run this led to overcapacity and profitability problems. What could be expected in such a situation is a restructuring or closedown of production units, but this did not happen. Instead, in the second half of the 1970s and the early 1980s, vast govern-

Table 3.5
Founding year for Sweden's 50 largest companies

Year	Number of Companies
Before 1870	6
1871–1890	10
1891–1913	15
1914–1945	11
1946–1969	8
1970–2000	0

Source: NUTEK-ALMI (2001).

ment subsidies were introduced to support firms and industries that were close to discontinuance or, in other words, on the negative side of the development. The shipbuilding industry provides a good example. It should be added that this kind of policy, which hampered economic renewal, was pursued irrespective of the color of the government.

However, there were conspicuous exceptions from the corporate consensus in Swedish economic policy. A first sign of this was the question of general supplementary pensions for all employees, which was a highly debated issue in the 1950s. After a lively debate, these pensions were made compulsory. Furthermore, they were publicly administered, which was also the case with the vast capital funds that were built up. They grew bigger and exerted more and more influence on economic performance. It is very likely that these funds and their administration had an impact on capital formation in the country in the sense that the flexibility of capital provision in general was negatively affected (Vikström 2002, pp. 146 ff.).

As time went by, the exceptions from the corporate consensus tended to become more and more of a rule, especially from the 1970s onward. They also made industry more and more hostile to the Social Democrats and their governments, and such a situation was not growth promoting. Several of the political measures not agreed on by industry concerned the labor market. Laws making it difficult to change the composition of the labor force or to reduce it—such as the law on security of employment (LAS)—are one example. Another example is trade union representation on corporate boards of directors and codetermination in all questions at all places of work (MBL). In practice, however, this did not mean real codetermination but obligatory information only. It took a long time and a lot of resources for firms to adjust to these measures.

LAS and MBL as well as other measures of a similar kind raised suspicions between the industrial employers, on the one hand, and on the other LO (the blue-collar trade union) and the Social Democrats. The so-called wage earners' funds were even more controversial. In the first half of the 1970s, a proposal came from LO that a fraction of the firms' profits should be paid to central funds, which thereby should be owners of an increasing number of shares of the firms. These funds eventually would be majority owners of the companies. Furthermore, the funds would be managed by the trade unions. The industry owners did not like this proposal, and the debate was intensive and disruptive. In the early 1980s, a social democratic government carried through a diluted variant of wage-earners' funds, but when the bourgeois parties eventually came into office, the funds were abolished. This question brought distrust for a long time between the former constituent parties of the democratic corporatism. Furthermore, in all probability, the propensity to invest as well as the incentives to launch new entrepreneurial ventures were negatively affected, and this was not advantageous to economic growth.

Two more policy areas will be mentioned. One has to do with unemployment policy. Sweden began early conducting an economic policy directed toward full employment, and measures were taken to keep unemployment low from the 1950s. Support for people moving geographically is one example, and another one is retraining of workers. This active employment policy as well as other welfare measures led to high taxes and probably to inflationary tendencies that could have had a negative impact on economic growth. The other policy area was the so-called solidaristic wage policy. Originally this meant equal pay for equal work, but later the meaning changed to equal pay for all work. The solidaristic wage policy was launched early in the postwar period and together with a highly progressive tax system had the effect of making income differences successively smaller. This became more and more pronounced until the late 1980s, and the economy and its growth were probably influenced in a negative way through the preference structure.

All these policy measures and a number of others made the Swedish governance system less adaptable to the ongoing internationalization and globalization and to economic growth. In the 1950s and 1960s, corporatism was, as mentioned, characteristic where the employers' organization was one of the cooperating parties. Then, however, measures were taken that were more and more out of line with industrial interests. In other words, the balance within the corporative system changed. As the blue-collar workers' organization in alliance with the government got more and more power, governmental policy was designed in such a way as in practice to create rigidities. Structural changes and economic adaptations were hampered and resulted in slow economic growth.

When the Swedish governance and institutional regime is compared to that of Finland, important differences are found. The Swedish system has been described as state interventionism in the economy, and the Finnish system has been described as the economy's intervention in the government. Finnish interest groups, particularly industry and the big companies, were stronger than in Sweden and could influence politics more (Pekkarinen and Vartiainen 2001, pp. 260 ff.). Finland's Social Democratic Party and labor union, on the other hand, were relatively weaker than their Swedish counterparts due to historical reasons. In other words, the balance between the parties in the corporate alliance differed between the two countries and made their political measures differ.

Unemployment, for instance, was treated quite differently in Finland and Sweden. Furthermore, there was no Finnish counterpart to Sweden's solidaristic wage policy and to the investment funds (Lindmark and Vikström 2003, p. 35). It could be added here that the supplementary pension systems differed between the countries. In Sweden, as mentioned above, publicly governed with huge funds built up. In Finland, pension administration became a function of private insurance companies. Private employers supported this system since the proportion of the contributions that is not paid out as pensions is loaned back to business at favorable terms. It is likely that Finland's system favored flexibility in the capital market to a much higher extent than Sweden's system.

Thus, the Finnish system was flexible, and its policy measures did not contribute to a stiff economic structure in the same way as Sweden's did. All in all, this provided a more adaptable economic setting and thus allowed the forces favorable to economic growth to play a more active role.

Conclusion

Over the last one and a half centuries, the Nordic countries have joined the ranks of countries with the world's highest standards of living. There have been similarities as well as differences in their development paths. The growth and convergence process has not been smooth over this period. The differences are due to factor endowments, geographical conditions, and political and institutional factors. Some of the similarities and differences have been touched on in this chapter, and the overall impression is that there has been a convergence of incomes per capita.

The convergence in the second half of the twentieth century was addressed in a comparison of Finland and Sweden. It can be concluded that political and institutional factors played an important role in hampering economic growth in Sweden in the second half of the twentieth century, in contrast to the first half of the century, when the country had had the most rapid progress of the industrialized countries. In other words, the Swedish business system became less and less adaptable to changing growth incentives. This is in contrast to Finland, where the political and institutional factors had another shape and stimulated growth; the business climate was different. The contrast between the two countries was especially clear from roughly 1970, when Finland's economy grew very fast while Sweden lagged behind.[6]

If there is a lesson to be learned from the comparison between Finland and Sweden it is that political measures and institutions are of great importance for the functioning of the economy. If they are constructed in a way that makes the economy flexible and adaptable to changes, they can promote growth and counteract stiffness of the economic structure. Hence, they can exert a great impact on processes of convergence and divergence in the international economy.

Notes

1. Here, Denmark proper is treated and not "Denmark overseas" (Greenland and other islands).

2. The terms *income level* and *economic level* are used here synonymously with *GDP per-capita level.*

3. Another reason for concentrating on Finland and Sweden is that this case has been studied more than the other countries (see, e.g., Andersson and Krantz 2003, and Lindmark and Vikström 2003).

4. Unfortunately, the other Nordic countries were not included in this table.

5. The number of the largest firms (more than five hundred employees) as a share of all firms in 1988 to 1991 was on average for eleven industrialized European countries 2.2 percent. Sweden had the largest share of all, 3.8; Finland had 3.1; Norway, 2.1; and Denmark, 1.6 percent. See Henrekson and Johansson (1999, p. 145).

6. It could be added that Norway in this period was a special case since its offshore oil deposits made the economy grow very fast. Denmark became a member of the European Union and took special political measures to adapt to this situation. Iceland, too, was a special case with its fishing economy and its strategic position, which made the United States actively interested in it. Thus, we find that these countries, often considered as very similar, in reality differed a lot.

References

Andersson, Lars Fredrik, and Olle Krantz. (2003). "Finland och Sverige. En jämförelse av den ekonomiska utvecklingen under 1800- och 1900-talen" (Finland and Sweden: A Comparison of the Economic Performance in the nineteenth and twentieth Centuries). In Juhana Aunesluoma and Susanna Fellman (Eds.), *Finland i Sverige, Sverige i Finland (Finland in Sweden, Sweden in Finland)*. Helsinki: Svenska Litteratursällskapet i Finland.

Hansen, Svend-Aage. (1974). *Økonomisk vækst i Danmark* (Economic Growth in Denmark). Book 2: 1914–1970. Copenhagen: Institute for Økonomisk historie ved Københavns universität.

Henrekson, Magnus, and Dan Johansson. (1999). "Sysselsättnings- och företagsstrukturen: Endast Sverige snapsglas har eller?" (The Employment and Firm Structure: Sweden Is Special Or?). *Ekonomisk debatt, 3:* 139–149.

Hjerppe, Riitta. (1989). *The Finnish Economy 1860–1985: Growth and Structural Change.* Helsinki: Bank of Finland.

Jonsson, Gudmundur. (1999). *Hagvöxtur og iðnvæðing: Þróun landsframleiðslu á Islandi 1870–1945* (Economic Growth and Industrialisation: Iceland's GDP, 1870–1945). Sérrit 3. Reykjavik: National Economic Institute.

Kettunen, Pauli. (2001). "The Nordic Welfare State in Finland." *Scandinavian Journal of History, 3:* 225–247.

Krantz, Olle. (2001a). "Industrialisation in Three Nordic Countries: A Long-Term Quantitative View." In Hans Kryger Larsen (Ed.), *Convergence? Industrialisation of Denmark, Finland and Sweden 1870–1940.* Helsinki: Suomen Tiedeseura.

Krantz, Olle. (2001b). Swedish Historical National Accounts 1800–1990: Aggregated Output Series. Mimeo, Umeå.

Krantz, Olle. (2003). "Small European Countries in International Organisations: A Perspective on the Small-State Question." In Timo Myllyntaus (Ed.), *Small European Economies and International Organisations*. Manchester, UK: Manchester Unversity Press.

Kuznets, Simon. (1960). "Economic Growth of Small Nations." In E. A. G. Robinson (Ed.), *Economic Consequences of the Size of Nations: Proceedings of a Conference held by the International Economic Association*. London: Macmillan.

Lindmark, Magnus, and Peter Vikström. (2003). "Growth and Structural Change in Sweden and Finland, 1870–1990: A Story of Convergence." *Scandinavian Economic History Review, 1:* 46–74.

Maddison, Angus. (2001). *The World Economy: A Millennial Perspective*. Paris: OECD.

NOS XII. (1965). *Nasjonalregnskap 1865–1960*. Oslo: Statistisk Sentralbyrå.

NUTEK-ALMI. (2001). *Tre näringspolitiska utmaningar—Allianser för hållbar tillväxt* (Three Industry Political Challenges: Alliances for Sustainable Growth). Stockholm: NUTEK: ALMI företagspartner.

Pekkarinen, Jukka, and Juhana Vartiainen. (2001). *Finlands ekonomiska politik. Den Långa linjen 1918–2000* (Finland's Economic Policy: The Long Line 1918–2000). Stockholm: Stiftelsen Fackföreningsrörelsens institut för ekonomisk forskning.

Vikström, Peter. (2002). *The Big Picture: A Historical National Accounts Approach to Growth, Structural Change, and Income Distribution in Sweden 1870–1990*, Umeå Studies in Economic History No. 26. Umeå: Department of Economic History, Umeå University.

Tanzi, Vito, and Ludger Schuknecht. (1997). "Reforming Government: An Overview of Recent Experience." *European Journal of Political Economy, 3:* 395–417.

4

The Experimentalist-Convergence Debate on Interpreting China's Economic Growth: A Cross-Country Perspective

Wing Thye Woo

Two Approaches to Understanding China's Growth

The literature on China's impressive growth in the post-1978 period is littered with terms like *miracle, institutional innovations, virtuous cycle, bottom-up reform versus top-down reform*, and *evolutionary*. These terms reflect the many creative attempts to understand the large differences in growth rates between post-1978 China and post-1990 Eastern Europe. Why is a country that espouses socialist practices among the fastest-growing countries in the world, when virtually all other socialist economies have collapsed? Is China's gradual pace of reform the source of success, and if so, what are the mechanisms behind this outcome? Are the nonmarket aspects of China's economy, such as the large state ownership that persists today, a potential source of destabilization in the years ahead?

Broadly speaking, two schools of thought have emerged to interpret the Chinese experience. One school of thought gives great credit to the *evolutionary, experimental*, and *incremental* nature of China's reforms. In this view, China has been groping, with considerable success, toward a unique Chinese economic model with new viable noncapitalist institutions that produce economic outcomes as efficient as those produced by (best-practice) capitalist economic institutions. Most notably, there is no need to privatize farmland because long-term leases (say, of fifteen-year duration) would generate the same outcome; there is no need to have privately owned small and medium enterprises (SMEs) because SMEs owned collectively by the local communities would also generate the same outcome; and competition among state-owned enterprises (SOEs) is more important than privatization of SOEs in improving performance in the enterprise sector. A faster approach to reforms, according to the experimentalist school, would have led to more social conflict, instability, and poorer economic policies (because of less experimentation). Barry Naughton (1995, pp. 5–13) is a clear proponent of the experimentalist view:

Reforms have been gradual and evolutionary.... Reforming without a blueprint, neither the process nor the ultimate objective was clearly envisaged beforehand.... It can be seen, ex post, that there is substantial coherence to these different elements. Reduction of the state's monopoly led to rapid entry of new firms. Entry of new firms, combined with adoption of market prices on the margin, led to enhanced competition, and began to get state-sector managers accustomed to responding to the marketplace. Gradual price decontrol was essential. Competition eroded initially high profit margins for state firms, and induced the government, as owner of the firms, to become more concerned with profitability. The government experimented with better incentive and monitoring devices, and this improved state-sector performance.[1]

The other school of thought denies that the Chinese approach has produced new viable noncapitalist economics and claims instead that the essence of the Chinese approach is really to allow its socialist economic institutions to converge gradually and surreptitiously with capitalist economic institutions (especially the particular forms of these institutions in East Asia) under a terminological haze of socialist rhetoric. We therefore use the term *convergence school* to characterize this point of view. This convergence, it is argued, is occurring despite official pronouncements to the contrary (including the stated intention to build a socialist market economy), as well as despite inconsistencies of many reforms in the short term. In this view, the faster the convergence, the better will be the outcomes. Gradualism-cum-experimentation, in this view, has not been a strategy so much as a result of continuing political conflict and other difficulties inherent in setting a policy course in a country of some 1.2 billion people. According to the convergence school of thought, China has achieved the greatest success in precisely the areas (agriculture and coastal provinces) where market reforms have gone the furthest.[2] Table 4.1 sums up the key differences between how the two schools interpret China's achievements.

Table 4.1
Experimentalism versus convergence

	Experimentalism School	Convergence School
Speed of reform	Sequential trial and error	Rapid and comprehensive liberalization of agriculture and of international trade in coastal provinces; slow deregulation of SOEs and of international trade in interior provinces
Reasons for gradualism (increm$_{Price}$)	Economic experimentation	Political compromise; ideological commitment to state ownership
Sources of rapid growth	Unintended virtuous cycle and few dislocations from large shifts in policies	Existence of surplus agriculture labor; East Asia pattern of labor-intensive export-led growth
Outcomes in the SOEs	Substantial improvements in production efficiency	Little technical progress; overcompensation of SOE personnel and overinvestment that weaken the fiscal situation
Interpretation of the TVEs	Adaptations to China's economic conditions of still developing markets	Continuing legal restrictions on private ownership
Future directions and pace of reform	Policies that change to reflect evolution in material conditions and lessons from continuing experiments	Policies that push China toward a normal private market economy with characteristics similar to other East Asian economies

In an early appraisal of economic transition, the *World Development Report 1996* (1996, pp. 20–21) concluded that

Despite the industrialization efforts of the 1950s and 1960s, China was very poor and largely rural at the start of its reforms. Agriculture employed 71 percent of the work force and was heavily taxed to support industry. Social safety nets extended only to the state sector—about 20 percent of the population. Poor infrastructure and an emphasis on local self-sufficiency led to low regional specialization and large numbers of small and medium-sized firms. The economy was far less centrally planned and administered than the Soviet economy. Local governments had greater power and developed considerable management capacity, preparing them for a more decentralized economy. Chinese industry also received subsidies, but cross-subsidization was less pervasive [than in the Soviet Union].

Because the agricultural sector had been so heavily repressed, freeing it up had immediate payoffs. Between 1981 and 1984 agriculture grew on average by 10 percent a year, largely because the shift to family farming improved incentives. This allowed for the reallocation of surplus agricultural labor to new rural industries, which generated 100 million new jobs between 1978 and 1994 and encouraged further reform. China thus started transition largely as a peasant agrarian economy and with far greater scope for reallocating labor than Russia.

However, the above conclusions were rejected just three years later by Joseph Stiglitz (1999a, 1999b), then vice president and chief economist at the World Bank. He claimed that the economic reform programs in central and eastern Europe and the former Soviet Union (CEEFSU) were wrong and had caused unnecessary suffering. In particular, Stiglitz (1999a, p. 3) rejected the conclusion of the *World Development Report 1996* that "countries that liberalise rapidly and extensively turn around more quickly [than those who do not]."

Stiglitz is not alone in his complaints. A number of recent papers have also claimed that the transformational recession was unnecessary (for example, Lau, Qian, and Roland 2000) and that gradual experimentation with the forms of economic institutions was superior to rapid wholesale adoption of the economic institutions of the market economies (for example, Rawski 1999). The implication of these recent papers is that CEEFSU should have imitated the Chinese reform strategy, which has not produced a transformational recession. More relevantly, the experimentalist school would recommend that North Korea and Cuba trust the "induced innovations" mechanism to spawn country-specific virtuous cycles that would cumulate into the type of economic system that best suits each country's circumstances.

Clearing the Terminological Thicket

Before discussing the relative merits of these two schools, it is first necessary to comment on the obfuscating terminology that the debate over transition strategies has generated. A wealth of oxymorons has appeared because protagonists have sought to attach undeserved positive connotations to their viewpoints. A number of authors have labeled rapid, comprehensive reforms (big-bang reforms) as top-down reforms, and slow, partial reforms (incremental reforms) as bottom-up reforms. Big-bang reforms were hence associated with a reform style that is reminiscent of central-planning coercion, and incremental reforms with a democratic trial-and-error market-learning process. These two associations are largely false and self-contradictory as suggested by the following two considerations.

First, the reliance on markets to allocate resources represents decentralized economic management achieved by empowering individual initiatives. Markets are naturally occurring phenomena because they render both buyers and sellers better off. The only time when markets are absent is when they are suppressed by the central plan of the state. Marketization means allowing the bottom-up process to run its natural course. Second, reform of a centrally planned economy means the marketization of economic transactions and the deep entrenchment of market-supporting institutions such as the criminal justice system to maintain law and order, commercial courts to enforce contracts, bankruptcy courts to encourage prudent lending and enable fresh starts for entrepreneurs, and social safety nets to lower the costs of resource reallocation. By its nature, marketization can be accomplished fairly quickly if desired, but the firm entrenchment of market-supporting institutions cannot be achieved quickly even if desired.

In short, big-bang reforms (quick marketization) means the unleashing of the bottom-up process of individual initiatives on a grand scale, while incremental reforms (slow marketization) means incremental legalization of the bottom-up process. The amazing semantic sleight of hand that has happened is that the advocates of gradual reform have identified themselves as advocates of the bottom-up approach to economic management. It is time to drop misleading terms such as *top-down reform* and *bottom-up reform* from the transition strategy debate.

The terms *evolutionary* and *path-dependent* are often encountered in the transition literature, and while they are always accurate, they are not always useful. In the strictest sense, rational policy making is evolutionary and path-dependent by necessity. Policy making has to be evolutionary because new exogenous shocks are always appearing, and it is nearly always path-dependent because reversals can be expensive, if not impossible. For example, China's tariff policy is contingent on whether China is already a World Trade Organization (WTO) member or not.

There is one important sense in which the term *evolutionary* is analytically useful. Take the case of bankruptcy procedures. They were not needed during the planning period, and so they were nonexistent prior to 1990. With the transition to a market economy, the state faces two policy choices. The first policy is to adopt the bankruptcy procedures of another country after modifying them to accommodate relevant differences in national circumstances and then to continue to modify them in light of experience. The second policy is to rely on the bottom-up process in the most fundamental sense by encouraging its citizens to come up with private contractual arrangements that would cover the contingency of financial difficulties that the borrowers might encounter. Comparing these two policies, we see that the first promotes institutional evolution in the local sense, and the second choice promotes institutional evolution in the global sense.

In practice, institutional evolution in the local sense entails a proactive state in the sphere of institution building where the usual operational principle is to adopt a foreign prototype and then modify it through practice.[3] Institutional evolution in the global sense, on the other hand, requires a state that is agnostic and passive about institution building because of its unbridled faith that the demand for institutions will inevitably induce the appropriate institutional innovations. This first approach is the convergence school of institution building, and the second approach is the experimentalist school of institution building.

The misunderstanding over these two approaches to institution building has caused the biggest obfuscation in the debate over transition strategies. The truth is that there is a fundamental difference between the nature of the transition strategies debate within China and the nature of the transition strategies debate within CEEFSU. The transition debate *within China* has primarily been a debate over the origins of institutions and the desired direction for institutional evolution and only very secondarily been a debate over the speed of implementing the reform program, even though the debate did focus on speed in the beginning. The real question in the transition debate within China still remains whether a third way exists between socialist planning and capitalist markets.

In sharp contrast, the fundamental academic issue in the postmortem debate on transition strategies within CEEFSU is the desired speed for institutional changes because leading CEEFSU economists (such as Kornai 1992) take it for granted that there is no third way. There is clearly no simple answer to the speed issue because "the transition from socialism to capitalism ... is a curious amalgam of revolution and evolution" (Kornai 2000, p. 25). Some reforms, such as macroeconomic stabilization, have to be done very quickly, and some reforms, such as privatization, have to be done much slower. In all cases, the decision on speed has to take into account the administrative capacity of the state and the political situation in the country.

It is clear that most of the countries of CEEFSU have embraced the convergence school of institution building (albeit with different speeds in implementation), but would it be accurate to say that China has followed the experimentalist school of institution building, since many of the critics of quick marketization have explained the gradual pace of Chinese reform as being due to the time-consuming process of experimentation to discover policies and institutions that are optimal for China's economic situation? The remainder of this chapter shows that the critics of quick marketization are wrong in their reading of the Chinese reform experience.

We want to point out that if the experimentalist interpretation of China's phenomenal growth is correct, then China's recent WTO membership is a negative development and that if the convergence explanation is true, then China's WTO membership would allow China to reap large benefits. This is because WTO, being an organization for private-market economies, defines the broad institutional features of a prototype market economy and requires its members to possess these institutional features. In short, China's WTO membership would drastically constrain China's scope for experimentation. This means that if the experimentalist interpretation is correct, then China's WTO membership would have deleterious effects on China's economic performance in the future. On the other hand, if the convergence school is correct, then WTO membership is a positive development that will lock China on to the path of deepening economic reform and openness.

Reform without Losers? A Comparative Perspective

Lau, Qian, and Roland (2000) have attributed the absence of a transformational recession in China to the dual-track pricing system (DTPS) that was implemented in the 1984 to 1990 period. They interpret the DTPS as a Pareto-improving way of introducing price flexibility that encourages growth without arousing political opposition from entrenched interest groups. We find their claim of gain without pain to be either factually wrong or politically implausible. We will make our case against the Lau, Qian, and Roland interpretation by

• Examining the analytics of the DTPS in both the partial equilibrium context and the general equilibrium context;

• Comparing the predictions of the model against the data;

• Explaining why the political economy of the DTPS made its demise in China inevitable;

• Pointing out the failure of the DTPS in the Soviet Union; and

• Pointing out the impressive sustained growth in Laos and Vietnam beginning in 1989 despite the absence of the DTPS.

The Partial-Equilibrium Analysis (PEA) of Dual-Track Pricing

The analytics can be summarized by the following example when there is a light industrial good and a heavy industrial good, with the following supply-and-demand relationships in a free-market setting.

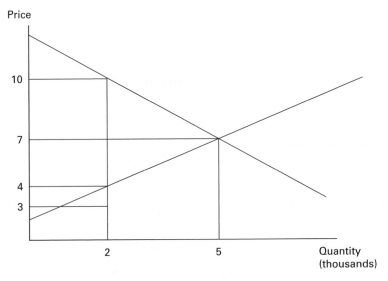

Figure 4.1
Light-industrial good

- For the light industrial good, we assume

  Supply curve (marginal cost curve): $P = 2 + Q$

  Demand curve: $P = 12 - Q$, where Q is in units of millions

- For the heavy industrial good, we assume

  Supply curve (marginal cost curve): $P = 3 + 2Q$

  Demand curve: $P = 12 - Q$, where Q is in units of millions

- Under the free market (see figures 4.1 and 4.2), we assume

  In the light industrial good market: $P = 7$ and $Q = 5$

  and

  In the heavy-industrial-goods market: $P = 9$ and $Q = 3$

  For the central-plan situation, assume the modus operandi to be where the planner picks the output level in each industry and sets the plan price to equate revenue with production costs of the output quota. Furthermore, assume that the planner creates the typical Stalinist outcome where the light industrial good is underproduced compared with the free-market

Price

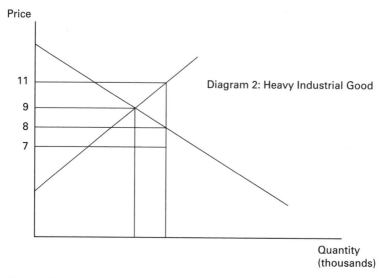

Diagram 2: Heavy Industrial Good

Quantity
(thousands)

Figure 4.2
Heavy-industrial good

situation and the heavy industrial good is overproduced compared with the free-market situation.[4]

Say, for light industrial goods, the planner picks $Q = 2$ and hence sets $P = 3$. The result is a black-market price of 10 with the marginal cost being 4. And, say, for heavy industrial goods, the planner picks $Q = 4$ and hence sets $P = 7$. The result is a black market price of 8 with the marginal cost of 11.

The dual-track pricing system is the situation where the producer is allowed to sell his above-quota output at a freely determined price. Then for the light industrial good, we have

Market price $= 7$
Market quantity $= 3$
Plan price $= 3$
Plan quantity $= 2$

The total quantity of 5 represents an increase in the output of the light industrial good, with no decrease in quantities sold at the lower plan price to the privileged buyers. This is a Pareto-improving situation.

For the heavy industrial good, we have

Market price   = 8

Market quantity = 0 (because the marginal cost exceeds the market price)

Plan price   = 7

Plan quantity   = 4

The total quantity produced remains at 4 with no losers and no winners. So the overall situation from the DTPS is a Pareto-improving situation.

Complete price liberalization (big-bang reform), as is clear from figures 4.1 and 4.2, is not Pareto-improving. The privileged buyers of both goods under rationing will now have to pay higher prices, and there will be laid-off workers in the heavy-industrial-goods sector. A big bang will cause a collapse in the production of heavy industrial goods, and the resulting disorganization (Blanchard and Kremer 1997) could cause a temporary drop in the production of light industrial goods as well—a situation that is reminiscent of Poland and Russia on the marketization of their economies in January 1990 and January 1992, respectively.

The key lesson from the partial-equilibrium analysis is that partial price flexibility is superior to total price flexibility.

The General-Equilibrium Analysis (GEA) of Dual-Track Pricing

The inadequacy of PEA is obvious if these two goods comprise the entire production structure and if there were full-employment and maximum production efficiency under the original central-planning situation. In this context, the introduction of dual-track pricing cannot cause an increase in the output of the light industrial good unless there is a decrease in the output of the heavy industrial good—and how could the occurrence of the latter still make the DTPS Pareto-improving?

Lau, Qian, and Roland (2000) answered this question by claiming that the light-industrial-good supplier will execute the following sequence of actions:

1. Go into the market for the heavy-industrial good, and buy (at the free-market price) the rights to some of the planned output that was

allocated to privileged consumers (at the free-market price). Say that he bought the rights to X units of the heavy-industrial good.

2. Tell the heavy-industrial-good producer to reduce his production by X units, and send the released workers to work in the light-industrial-good sector.

3. Hire the newly released workers from the heavy-industrial sector, and expand the production of the light-industrial good by Y units.

The heavy-industrial-good producer is happy to cooperate because he now makes a positive profit from having his costs decrease more than his revenue. One of the possible outcomes is that $X = 1$ and $Y = 3$, which makes the dual-tracking outcome the same as the free-market outcome. The important prediction is that the DTPS, in a general-equilibrium setting, will cause one sector to expand and the other sector to shrink as in complete price liberalization, and this DTPS-induced adjustment is contractual and mutually beneficial in nature.

For policy purposes, both PEA and GEA offer the same advice: limited price deregulation is better than complete price deregulation. Complete price deregulation might produce the same input allocation and output composition as the DTPS, but the former definitely generates resentment against the government while the latter does not.

Critique of the Preceding Two Analyses of the Dual-Track Pricing System

It is ironic that the supposedly flawed PEA is factually more correct than the theoretically coherent GEA. Table 4.2 shows that the output of both the light- and heavy-industrial sectors went up every year following the introduction of the DTPS in 1985.[5] Light-industrial output increased 64 percent in the 1984 to 1987 period, and heavy-industrial output increased 55 percent. The Lau, Qian, and Roland's prediction of a (voluntary) contraction in heavy-industrial output on marketization of the economy is contradicted by the data, suggesting that their elaborate general-equilibrium analysis could be an exercise in false precision. Clearly, we need an explanation other than the DTPS to explain why China grew so fast after marketization.

Table 4.2 shows two interesting facts that suggest an alternative explanation for what really happened in China. First, output from industrial

SOEs increased every year in the reform era, but the state sector's share of total industrial output declined secularly from 78 percent in 1978 to 28 percent in 1998. This means that the bulk of the increase in industrial output came from the nonstate sector. Hence, fast growth of industrial output should not be attributed entirely to the incentive effect of dual-track pricing. Most of the credit, in our judgment, should be given to the legalization of the dual-track ownership system in the industrial sector in 1984. The legalization of nonstate firms allowed nonstate industrial enterprises to be established in the rural areas—the famous township and village enterprises (TVEs).

Second, the nonstate sector did not grow by obtaining their labor from the state sector through contractual agreements, the key mechanism behind Lau, Qian, and Roland's (2000) assertion of "gain without pain." State employment was 17.9 percent of the labor force in 1984 (the eve of the introduction of the DTPS to the industrial sector), and it rose to 18.3 percent in 1989 (the eve of the replacement of the DTPS with almost complete price decontrol). The state sector in 1989 employed 14.7 million workers more than in 1984 and 26.6 million more than in 1978. In employment terms, China was certainly not growing out of the plan either in absolute or in relative terms.[6]

The labor that fueled the fast expansion of the nonstate industrial sector came out from agriculture, a sector that was not identified by Lau, Qian, and Roland (2000) as an important contributor to China's high growth rates after 1984. Part A of table 4.3 shows that employment in the primary sector declined from 71 percent in 1978 to 50 percent in 1998.[7] Therein, we have the *deus ex machina* of China's growth. The marketization and internationalization of economic activities generated substantial productivity increases—not only by enlivening the agricultural sector in the 1979 to 1984 period and by creating a dynamic nonstate sector from 1984 onward but also by moving low-productivity agricultural workers into higher-productivity jobs in the secondary and tertiary sectors. Chow (1993) found the marginal value product of labor in China in 1978, measured in 1952 prices, to be 63 yuan in agriculture, 1,027 yuan in industry, 452 yuan in construction, 739 yuan in transportation and 1,809 yuan in commerce; and Woo (1998) estimated that the reallocation of Chinese agricultural labor into industries and services

Table 4.2
Production of light- and heavy-industrial goods and state-sector employment, 1978 to 1998

	Index of Gross Industrial Output (1978 = 100)		Composition of Gross Industrial Output (in 1995 prices, percentage)		Proportion of Labor Force in State-Owned Units (percentage)	Proportion of Gross Industrial Production by State-Owned Units (current prices, percentage)
	Light Industry	Heavy Industry	Light Industry	Heavy Industry		
1978	100.0	100.0	38.9	61.1	18.6	77.6
1979	110.0	108.0	39.3	60.7	18.8	78.5
1980	130.8	110.1	43.1	56.9	18.9	76.0
1981	149.5	105.1	47.5	52.5	19.1	74.8
1982	158.2	115.5	46.6	53.4	19.1	74.4
1983	172.9	130.6	45.7	54.3	18.9	73.4
1984	200.7	152.2	45.6	54.4	17.9	69.1
1985	246.3	182.9	46.1	53.9	18.0	64.9
1986	278.5	201.6	46.8	53.2	18.2	62.3
1987	330.3	235.3	47.2	52.8	18.3	59.7
1988	403.3	280.9	47.7	52.3	18.4	56.8
1989	436.4	305.9	47.6	52.4	18.3	56.1
1990	476.6	324.9	48.3	51.7	16.2	54.6
1991	548.0	372.0	48.4	51.6	16.5	56.2
1992	657.7	479.8	46.6	53.4	16.6	51.5
1993	835.2	611.8	46.5	53.5	16.5	57.3
1994	1,032.3	762.3	46.3	53.7	16.2	37.3

1995	1,268.7	899.5	47.3	52.7	16.1	34.0
1996	1,573.2	1,013.7	49.7	50.3	15.9	36.3
1997	1,801.3	1,132.4	50.3	49.7	15.5	31.6
1998	2,013.9	1,242.2	50.8	49.2	12.6	28.2

Note: Data calculated from State Statistical Bureau of China (1999).

Table 4.3
Production in employment structure in China, the Soviet Union, and the United States

Part A: China: Change in Production and Employment, 1978 to 1998

	Composition of GDP (1995 prices, percentage)			Composition of Employment (percentage)		
	Primary	Secondary	Tertiary	Primary	Secondary	Tertiary
1978	41.2	34.0	24.7	70.5	17.3	12.2
1979	40.9	34.2	24.9	69.8	17.6	12.6
1980	38.0	37.0	24.9	68.7	18.2	13.1
1981	38.4	35.6	26.0	68.1	18.3	13.6
1982	39.0	34.2	26.7	68.1	18.4	13.4
1983	38.1	34.2	27.8	67.1	18.7	14.2
1984	37.3	33.9	28.8	64.0	19.9	16.1
1985	33.8	35.9	30.3	62.4	20.8	16.8
1986	32.2	36.5	31.3	60.9	21.9	17.2
1987	30.3	37.5	32.2	60.0	22.2	17.8
1988	28.2	38.8	33.0	59.4	22.4	18.3
1989	28.0	38.4	33.6	60.0	21.6	18.3
1990	28.9	38.0	33.0	60.1	21.4	18.5
1991	27.2	39.7	33.0	59.7	21.4	18.9
1992	25.1	42.3	32.6	58.5	21.7	19.8
1993	23.2	44.8	31.9	56.4	22.4	21.2
1994	21.5	47.3	31.2	54.3	22.7	23.0
1995	20.5	48.8	30.7	52.2	23.0	24.8
1996	19.7	50.0	30.3	50.5	23.5	26.0
1997	18.8	50.7	30.5	49.9	23.7	26.4
1998	18.1	51.5	30.4	49.8	23.5	26.7

Part B: Cross-Country Comparison of Production and Employment Structure

	Composition of GDP (1995 prices, percentage)			Composition of Employment (percentage)		
	United States 1986	Soviet Union 1988	China 1978	United States 1986	Soviet Union 1988	China 1978
Agriculture	1.9	9.3	41.2	2.7	19.3	70.5
Industry	23.5	48.9	28.9	17.6	28.9	17.3*
Contruction	6.1	10.7	5.1	4.6	11.5	**
Services	68.5	31.1	24.7	75.1	40.3	12.2

Note: China data from State Statistical Bureau of China (1999). Statistics for United States and Soviet Union are from Lipton and Sachs (1992).

* = Data include construction.

** = Data included in industry category.

added 1.3 percentage points annually to the GDP growth rate over the 1985 to 1993 period. In short, China's marketization and international-ization policies initiated the non-zero-sum process of economic develop-ment, moving China away from a subsistence peasant economy and causing agriculture to drop from 41 percent of GDP in 1978 to 18 per-cent in 1998. This is the true source of the Pareto-improving outcome in China's economic reform, not the dual-pricing system.

The Political Economy of the DTPS in China

One of the biggest claims of virtue for the DTPS is that by avoiding the creation of losers, it does not generate political opposition to economic reform (except, of course, from central-planning ideologues). We find such a claim to be dubious because dual-track pricing creates opportuni-ties for corruption, and serious corruption can undermine the political legitimacy of the government and even the political stability of the coun-try. In our understanding of the history of Chinese reforms, the DTPS was an unsustainable economic mechanism from the management view-point of extreme difficulties in administration and also from the political viewpoint of maintaining the cohesion of the ruling coalition.

To see this point, it is important to first note that the DTPS was only one component of the serious attempt (beginning in 1984) to improve the rationality of the state-owned enterprise (SOE) system; the other component was the devolution of decision-making power to the SOEs. The political cost of the DTPS came from its interaction with the opera-tional autonomy of the SOEs in an unexpected way.

The plan track for inputs conferred instant profits on the favored pur-chaser on reselling quota inputs in the free market. Many children of top leaders were able to make purchases of inputs at plan prices and resell them at large profits. The general public was not happy with this widespread corrupt practice. The devolution of operational autonomy to SOEs in a soft budget situation caused demand for investment credit to soar, and the accommodation by the state banks of this demand en-abled inflation in 1985 to 1989 to reach levels not seen since 1949 (see Fan and Woo 1996). It was therefore natural that the general public linked the large illegal profits of the dual-pricing system with high inflation and perceived the inflation to be the result of price gouging by corrupt officials. This general perception brought public unhappiness with the corruption to new heights, which led to demonstrations against corruption and inflation in quite a number of large cities at the end of 1985 and 1986.

To address this social unrest, Hu Yaobang, then head of the Chinese Communist Party (CCP), started arresting corrupt officials, and the sons of several top conservative leaders were apprehended. This crackdown was interpreted by some conservative leaders as an excuse by the liberal faction to depose them, and this intensified the opposition to the continued leadership of Hu Yaobang on the grounds of administrative incompetence (look at the high inflation) and ideological revisionism (look at his introduction of material incentives). By aggravating the infighting inside the ruling coalition, the plan track contributed to the dismissal of Hu Yaobang as general secretary of the CCP in January 1987.

It is worthwhile to quote two accounts of this matter at length. According to Richard Baum (1994, pp. 176–177):

[In 1986,] Hu Yaobang raised the ire of Hu Qiaomu [Politburo member] by proposing to formally charge the latter's son, Hu Shiying, with criminal corruption.... [The] incident provoked an immediate reaction among powerful party elders.... A campaign to oust Hu Yaobang quickly took shape. At the same time, Hu Qiaomu reportedly threw himself at Deng Xiaoping's mercy, tearfully imploring the paramount leader to show mercy toward his errant offspring.

The highest level *gaogan zidi* [offspring of a high-ranking cadre] to be judicially punished was the daughter of General Ye Fei, the former commander of the Chinese Navy.... In 1982 the general ... had sharply criticized Hu Yaobang for failing to halt the spread of bourgeois liberalization.

Other *gaogan zidi* who came under criminal investigation in this period included the prodigal offspring of conservative party elders Peng Zhen and Wang Zhen [both Politburo members]. Like Ye Fei and Hu Qiaomu, Peng and Wang had been vocal critics of bourgeois liberalization, and the raising of allegations of corruption against their children thus carried a strong hint of political retaliation.

According to Joseph Fewsmith (1994, p. 177):

In January 1986, Hu Yaobang presided over a huge rally of 8,000 cadres ... called to address the issue of corruption.... A special committee headed by Hu Yaobang's associate Qiao Shi was established within the Central Committee to root out corruption. In February,... three sons of high-level cadres were executed. There were soon reports that the children of a number of conservative party leaders, including Peng Zhen, Hu Qiaomu, and Ye Fei, were under investigation, suggesting that Hu Yaobang was targeting his critics. Moreover, the decision to set up a special committee within the Central Committee to tackle this issue appeared to be a challenge to the CDIC [Central Discipline Inspection Commission], headed by Chen Yun [leader of the conservative faction], as the agency of discipline within the party.

Deng Xiaoping's solution to the growing unrest within society and within the ruling coalition was not to arrest the profiteers but to end the dual-track pricing system that fostered such conflicts within the ruling coalition as a by-product. This is why, in the middle of unprecedented (since 1949) inflation, in May 1988 Deng Xiaoping publicly urged that comprehensive price reform be finished within three to five years. The memorable slogan for this campaign was *zhuang jiage guan* (crash through the price obstacle).

The reality was that the working of the dual-track pricing system generated great social pressures to punish the profiteers but such acts threatened the viability of the ruling coalition. The choice facing the CCP elite was to either maintain the political coalition or maintain the dual-track pricing system. For the Chinese politicians, the choice was a no-brainer. This is why price liberalization was brought to virtual completion in the 1990 to 1991 period even though this was the time that the proplan conservative faction had the upper hand in policymaking (in the aftermath of the June 1989 Tiananmen incident). Political reality is the reason why the plan track was reduced steadily even though this act was not Pareto-improving and even though this contradicted the ideological position of the conservative faction.

The Soviet Experience with Dual-Track Reform

Market reforms in Russia did not start in 1992 with the Boris Yeltsin government. The gross inefficiency of the Soviet economy and its slide into technological stagnation during the *nomenklatura* communism of Leonid Brezhnez in the 1970s had fermented much reformist thinking among Soviet economists. By the time Mikhail Gorbachev assumed political power in May 1985, there were already many established influential economists urging market-oriented reforms. Boris Kurashvili, for example, argued for Hungarian-style market socialism, and Oleg Bogomolov for Chinese-style incremental liberalization.[8]

Gorbachev was not a quick convert to market reforms, however. The first two years of his rule were spent trying to propel the economy out of its doldrums by accelerating the technological level of Soviet industries through large investments in the machine-tool industry. The acceleration strategy failed, leading Gorbachev to seek "radical reforms" of the economy. The influence of China's reform strategy is clearly seen in Gorbachev's arguments in August 1987 "in favor of family contract, family teams and ... leasehold" (Åslund 1991, p. 103) to be introduced in Soviet agriculture. Gorbachev's radical reform program was unveiled in June 1987 at the Soviet economic plenum, which passed the Law on State Enterprises and Basic Provisions for Fundamental Perestroika of Economic Management to devolve decision-making power from the ministries to the SOEs. Just as in China, Soviet SOEs were given more freedom in choosing outputs, entering into long-term contractual agreements for purchases and sales, and retaining part of their profits to use at their discretion (for example, for technological upgrading and as incentive bonuses). In return, the SOEs were required to do "full economic accounting," a euphemism for holding SOEs responsible for their losses. As in China, deliveries to the state would still be required (state orders), for which subsidized inputs would be made available to the SOEs, but state orders would be reduced over time to cover only 40 to 60 percent of all production.[9]

The explosive growth China's nonstate industrial sector had made a deep impression on the Russian reformers and inspired them to push for a double track on ownership as well. Academician Leonid Abalkin, a prominent leader in reform thinking, predicted in 1986 that the radical reforms of Gorbachev would, within a decade, enable cooperatives to account for 10 percent of GDP and private enterprises for 4 percent of GDP (Åslund 1991, p. 168). Various decrees had been issued earlier to stimulate the cooperative sector, and they were greatly expanded with the adoption of the Law on Cooperatives in May 1988.

The Law on Cooperatives was categorical in making the formation of cooperatives an easy task: "A cooperative is organized at the desire of citizens, exclusively on a voluntary basis. The creation of a cooperative is not conditional upon any special permission whatsoever by Soviet, economic or other bodies" (quoted in Åslund 1991, p. 169). There was no ceiling set on the number of members, and there was no limit on the number of nonmembers that could be hired on contract. Furthermore, cooperatives could set their prices according to market conditions. In the words of Yevgenii Yasin, a senior member of the State Commission on Economic Reform (Ellman and Kontorovich 1998, p. 169):

The 1987 reform was in many ways an attempt to implement the Chinese model in Russia. It envisioned enterprises, and joint ventures would constitute the free sector, existing alongside the state sector, with its mandatory state orders, fixed prices, and centralized allocation of inputs.

The outcome of these market-oriented reforms of the dual-track variety was the disintegration of the Soviet economy from 1989 onward.[10]

Part B of table 4.3 explains why Russia's GDP fell after marketization of its economy. The Russian industrial sector, especially the heavy-industrial component, was much bigger than what a market economy would require. Lipton and Sachs (1992) made this point very well when they showed the production of the following metals expressed in thousands of metric tons per U.S. billion dollars of GDP for various countries in 1988 (table 4.4).

Industrial output accounted for 49 percent of Russia's GDP in 1988 compared to 24 percent of U.S. GDP in 1986. Given the relatively small proportion of labor in Russian agriculture compared to China, 19 percent versus 71 percent, a substantial amount of the labor needed for the growth of new light industries and new service activities had to come

Table 4.4
Steel, copper, and aluminum, various countries, 1988

	Soviet Union	United States	West Germany	Japan
Crude steel	280.0	18.49	34.35	36.47
Refined copper	1.71	0.38	0.36	0.33
Primary aluminum	4.28	0.80	0.62	0.01

Source: Lipton and Sachs (1992).
Note: Metric tons per U.S. billion dollars of GDP.

from the heavy industrial sector. The collapse of Russia's heavy industries was necessary to release the labor put there by the central plan.[11] The salient point is that the marketization of the overindustrialized Russian economy triggered the almost zero-sum (certainly so, in the short run) process of economic restructuring. The existing heavy industrial sector had to shrink because its value added at market prices was negative.[12]

No Transformational Recessions in Laos and Vietnam Despite Absence of DTPS

Under prodding by Gorbachev, Vietnam and Laos implemented partial reforms, inspired by an Oskar Lange–type of market socialism, near the end of 1986. There was, however, not a marked improvement in Vietnam's growth rates to these partial decentralization reforms (see table 4.5). The average annual GDP growth rate was 4.5 percent in the 1984 to 1985 period versus 4.8 percent in the 1987 to 1988 period. The really big response to the partial reform was in Vietnam's inflation rate. The decentralized reforms of SOEs unleashed an investment hunger that caused inflation to explode. The average annual rise in the consumer price index went from 178 percent in 1984 to 1985 to 373 percent in 1987 to 1988.

The growth performance of Laos actually worsened after the introduction of the partial reforms. The GDP growth rate was 6.5 percent in 1985, 9.5 percent in 1986, −5.2 percent in 1987, and 0.9 percent in 1988.

It was with this background of lackluster reform performance that Laos and Vietnam launched big-bang reforms in March 1989, a development that was much against the expectations of most external observers. This new round of reforms consisted of

• Drastic macrostabilization achieved by immediate slashing of budget deficits and bank credits to SOEs,

• Overnight comprehensive price liberalization,

• Discrete devaluation of currency to black-market level, and

• Relaxation of control on private ownership and acceleration of agricultural decollectivization.

Table 4.5
Output and price performance in Vietnam and Laos

	Output Growth				Inflation	
	GDP	Agri-culture	Industry	Services	GDP Deflator	Retail Price
Part A: Vietnam						
1984	3.3	4.2	12.0	NA	NA	164.9
1985	5.7	4.5	12.0	−1.0	102.315	191.6
1986	3.4	1.9	4.1	6.3	506.9	487.3
1987	3.7	−0.6	8.8	5.5	362.2	371.6
1988	5.9	3.9	5.3	9.2	407.3	374.2
1989	8.0	6.9	−2.6	18.3	68.7	95.8
1990	5.1	4.6	−2.4	10.8	42.1	36.4
1991	6.0	2.2	9.0	8.3	72.5	82.7
1992	8.6	7.1	14.0	7.0	32.6	37.7
1993	8.1	3.8	13.1	9.2	14.3	8.4
1994	8.8	3.9	14.0	10.2	14.5	9.3
1995	9.5	4.7	13.9	10.9	19.5	16.8
1996	9.3	4.8	15.6	8.9	6.1	5.6
Part B: Lao						
1985	6.5	NA	NA	NA	NA	
1986	9.5	9.4	6.6	11.6	44.6	
1987	−5.2	−8.5	−16.4	9.4	31.0	
1988	0.9	2.1	5.6	−3.6	33.7	
1989	14.5	10.8	35.0	14.5	59.0	
1990	7.3	8.7	16.2	−0.5	34.6	
1991	3.4	−1.7	19.9	6.5	13.3	
1992	7.0	8.3	13.0	9.1	9.3	
1993	5.2	2.7	10.3	7.7	6.4	
1994	8.0	8.3	10.6	5.6	7.7	
1995	6.7	3.1	13.1	10.2	19.7	
1996	6.7	2.2	17.3	8.7	13.9	
1997	7.6	7.5	8.1	7.3	17.7	

Source: Vietnam 1984 data refers to (Soviet definition) national income. Laos 1985 GDP growth based on 1988 prices, the rest on 1990 prices.

The output response to the big-bang reforms was stunning in both countries. GDP growth in Vietnam jumped from 5.9 percent in 1988 to 8.0 percent in 1989, and GDP growth in Laos jumped from −0.9 percent in 1988 to 14.5 percent in 1989. These two cases clearly refute the notion that big-bang reforms necessarily cause output to fall. In fact, when the experiences of China, Laos, and Vietnam are considered together, all the three East Asian Communist countries could be said to have experienced growth regardless of the speed of reform and regardless of the existence of dual-track reform. These three countries grew because they were largely agricultural economies with vast amounts of underemployed peasants. Once agricultural prices were raised and land tenure made more secure, their agricultural sectors boomed. Furthermore, in coastal China, and coastal Vietnam, export-oriented industries blossomed once trade and investment restrictions were relaxed.

To summarize, the 1985 to 1991 Soviet reform experience showed that dual-track reform did not guarantee reform without losers. The 1985 to 1996 reform experiences of Vietnam and Laos show that the absence of dual-track reform did not guarantee transformational recessions either. The key determinant behind the outcome of reform without losers was the existence of surplus agricultural labor and not the existence of a dual-track reform approach.

The Debate on State Enterprise Reform in China

The debate on state enterprise reform in China is markedly surreal. The experimentalist school sees China, unlike anywhere else in the world, as having succeeded in reforming its SOE sector, even though Chinese officialdom is not aware of it. This paradoxical stance of the experimentalist school is seen in the following thesis, antithesis, and suggested synthesis:

• *Thesis*: "This review leads to the conclusion that reform has pushed China's state-owned enterprises in the direction of 'intensive' growth based on higher productivity rather than expanded resource consumption.... We observe a consistent picture of improved results—higher output, growing exports, rising total factor productivity, and increased innovative effort—against a background of gains in static and dynamic efficiency that reflect the growing impact of market forces." (Jefferson and Rawski 1994, p. 58)

• *Antithesis*:   "The current problems of SOEs are excessive investments in fixed assets with very low return rates, resulting in the sinking of large amounts of capital, and a low sales-to-production ratio, giving rise to mounting inventories. The end result is that the state has to inject an increasing amount of working capital through the banking sector into the state enterprises."[13]

• *Suggested synthesis*:   "Focusing on profitability, [state bureaucrats] see the erosion in state sector profits as a profound crisis of the state sector. Without good measures of total factor productivity, they conclude that state sector performance is deteriorating. Foreign observers, hearing the cries of alarm from the state planners, shake their heads knowingly as they perceive still further evidence that state ownership is intrinsically inefficient. Neither party sees that the difficulties are the result of an ultimately beneficial transition to a different type of economy and are entirely compatible with gradually improving efficiency." (Naughton 1995, p. 314)

We find Naughton's synthesis implausible because it sees top Chinese officials as ignorant of elementary economic theory ("competition from new non-SOEs erodes SOE profits") and ignorant of the technically sophisticated literature on total factor productivity (TFP) estimations. In any case, the government had by 1993 decided to clarify the property rights of SOEs to salvage its SOE reform program. The CPC publicly committed itself in July 1997 to convert most of the SOEs to publicly traded shareholding corporations. This convergence to a form of industrial organization that originated in capitalist economies was possibly motivated more by a concern over the soaring loss of the SOE sector than by its continued inefficiency. The losses at the beginning of the 1990s were so severe that it was common for even government officials to say that "one-third of the country's state enterprises were in the red, and another one-third were in a latent loss-making state."[14] This financial situation has worsened over time. A national audit of 100 SOEs in 1999 found that eighty-one falsified their books and sixty-nine reported profits that did not exist, and an audit of the Industrial and Commercial

Bank of China and the China Construction Bank found that accounting abuses involving RMB 400 billion, of which RMB 200 billion was over-statement of assets.[15]

The difference between the experimentalist and convergence interpretations of the sharp collapse in SOE profit rates lies in the different weights that they put on each of the three factors that the literature has identified: increased competition from the nonstate enterprises, failure of the SOEs to improve their efficiency, and overcompensation of SOE personnel. The experimentalist school tended to emphasize only the first and second factors and to downplay the empirical validity of the second factor on the basis of the empirical work done by its members. The problem with the competition explanation is that the profit rates of SOEs in the sectors of industry that experienced little entry by non-SOEs showed the same dramatic drop as the profit rates of SOEs in sectors with heavy penetration by non-SOEs (see Fan and Woo 1996). Profits in SOEs fell regardless of whether they faced competition from non-SOEs.

The convergence school has emphasized continued inefficiency and *de facto* asset stripping and embezzlement of firm profits by managers and workers as the primary causes for the general decline in SOE profits, with the latter being the more important. The devolution of financial decision-making power to the SOEs, and the steady reduction in discrimination against the private sector have made it increasingly easy for the managers to transfer state assets to themselves.[16] The Chinese leadership recognizes clearly the increasingly serious economic and political problems created by the agency problem innate in the decentralizing reforms of market socialism. This is why the debate between the conservative reformers and the liberal reformers has progressed from whether privatization is necessary to the question of the optimal form and amount of privatization.

Even then the state's decision in 1997 to accelerate diversification of the ownership structure of the SOEs has to be recognized as a bold move because the experiences with mass privatization in central and eastern Europe and the former Soviet Union (CEEFSU) show that the task is extremely difficult and that the outcomes have consistently fallen below initial expectations. For example, in Russia, the "loans-for-shares" privatization transferred the country's enormous mineral wealth to a group of oligarchs, and the weak administrative and legal structures allowed many managers to take effective control of the privatized firms and loot them instead of improving their operations. Furthermore, the CEEFSU experiences warn that *mass* privatization is an exceedingly dangerous business politically, no matter how it is done—whether by outsider privatization or insider privatization. This is because the mass privatization of SOEs generates so much rent that massive corruption has not been avoided, and the resulting corruption inevitably delegitimizes the government (consider Vaclav Klaus in the Czech Republic and Boris Yeltsin in Russia).

Despite the mediocre to poor privatization outcomes in CEEFSU, privatization still seems to be inevitable and desirable for China for two main reasons. The first reason comes from John Nellis (1999), who points out that "governments that botch privatization are equally likely to botch the management of state-owned firms." The answer is not to avoid privatizations but to implement more careful privatizations— privatizations that involve much less corruption and that assume forms that are politically more acceptable to society. Governments in transition economies should "push ahead, more slowly, with case-by-case and tender privatizations, in cooperation with the international assistance community, in hopes of producing some success stories that will lead by example." The second reason is that the delay of privatization can be costly to China's government politically. Stealing by managers does occur during privatization and creates a social backlash against the government, but the maintenance of the status quo has become increasingly difficult because SOE managers in China know from the CEEFSU experience that they are in an endgame situation. The widespread spontaneous privatization by SOE managers could create grave social instability.

To be accurate, we believe that the solution to the SOE problem in China is not privatization but a transparent, legal privatization process that society at large can accept, at the minimum, as tolerably equitable. Because an adequate privatization program must compensate the retired and layoff workers, permit takeover by core investors, and respect the rights of minority shareholders, it is important that legal reforms be carried out simultaneously. Only with a transparent, equitable privatization process that is overseen by an adequate legal framework, would China be likely to avoid a state-created Russian-style *kleptoklatura* that would fuel social dissatisfaction.

Recently, there has been some questioning of whether the case for privatization has been overstated (e.g., Nolan and Wang 1999). When Zhu Rongji was designated the new premier in 1997, he announced that he would solve the SOE problem in three years. In 2000, he declared victory on the SOE front when the profits of the industrial SOEs leaped from 53 billion yuan in 1998 to 241 billion in 2000. This is indeed favorable news but should be put in context. This improvement in SOE profitability was actually part of a general phenomenon; the profits of the industrial non-SOEs increased from 93 billion in 1998 to 199 billion in 2000 for a variety of macroeconomic reasons.[17] While the rise in profits surely gives some breathing space, the capacity of SOEs to "dissipate rents" through high payments to managers and workers, if not illegal transfer of assets, should remain clearly in the policy makers' minds. Thus, any gains could well be squandered, if not reversed, in a relatively short period of time.

Table 4.6 summarizes a study by Zhou and Wang (2002), who quantified the sources of the financial turnaround. They found that

• The lower interest rate in 2000 increased profits by 52 billion yuan (28 percent of the increase in SOE profits);

• The higher oil prices boosted overall SOE profits by 79 billion yuan because almost all oil companies are state-owned (42 percent of the increase);[18] and

• The conversion of the bank loans of SOEs into equities held by state asset-management companies raised profits by 10 billion yuan (5 percent of the increase).

About 75 percent of the increase in the profits of industrial SOEs in the 1998 to 2000 period was not due to actions taken within these enterprises but to external factors. When Zhou and Wang (2002) calculated the profit rate after deducting the profits from the more favorable external environment, they found that it had increased from 0.7 percent in 1998 to 1.2 percent in 2000 for the SOE sector and from 2.8 percent to 4.8 percent for the non-SOE sector. Despite the recent good news on

Table 4.6
Analyzing sources of profit growth in SOEs and non-SOEs, 1998 to 2000

	SOE				Non-SOE			
	1998	2000	Change	Exp	1998	2000	Change	Exp
Total profit	525	2,408	1,883	(100%)	933	1,985	1,052	(100%)
From								
Interest-rate reduction			523	(27.8%)			300	(28.5%)
Higher oil price			791	(42.0%)			−341	(−32.4%)
Loan-equity swap			101	(5.4%)				
Residual = own effort			468	(24.8%)			1,093	(103.9%)
Real return rate	0.7%	1.2%	0.5%		2.8%	4.8%	2.0%	

Source: Zhou and Wang (2002). Units: 100 million yuan. Some terms used here differ from the source.
Note: Data in parentheses under "Exp" are share of contribution by different factors to total profit changes. "Real return rate" for 2000 is calculated as the ratio of total profit, excluding profits that resulted from the three external factors, to total assets. The estimate on the effect of higher oil prices has taken into account the additional production cost of the non-oil SOEs.

SOE profitability, the fact remains that the SOE sector still lags considerably behind the non-SOE sector in efficiency.

Is Localized Socialism the Viable Form of Socialism?

The single largest contributor to China's economic growth in the 1985 to 1993 period was the collectively owned sector, which consisted mostly of rural industrial enterprises that were registered as owned by villages, townships, or counties collectively and hence were known as *township and village enterprises* (TVEs). According to the experimentalist school, TVEs represent localized socialism just as SOEs represent centralized socialism—that is, ownership by the local community instead of ownership by the national community:

China's "collectively" owned enterprises are not cooperatives.... All members of the local community are *de jure* owners of "collectively" owned enterprises. (Nolan 1993, p. 297)

The surprising thing about TVE's is not that they function without clearly specified property rights, but rather the fact that *local government ownership* turns out to be a fairly robust ownership form. (Naughton 1994, p. 268, emphasis added)

An elaborate vocabulary of denial obscures the uncomfortable reality that these firms, widely described as collectives, TVEs, non-state, quasi-private or even private enterprises, *are typically owned and controlled by local governments*. (Rawski 1995, p. 1172, emphasis added)

The experimentalist school has argued that collective ownership is an effective way to raise capital funds for rural enterprises and to reduce the principal-agent problem by shortening the distance of supervision. For example, Naughton (1994, p. 269) has interpreted the TVE ownership structure as a good adaptation to market failures caused by China's underdeveloped markets for factors of production:

Banks are ill-equipped in the early stages of transition to process small-scale lending applications and assess risks. Local government ownership in China played a crucial role in financial intermediation. Local governments could better assess the risks of start-up businesses under their control ... and serve as guarantors of loans to individual TVEs.

In contrast, the convergence school holds that the TVE label serves mainly the useful political function of sheltering from view the occurrence of economic convergence in rural industries. It sees three main types of TVEs: genuine collectively owned enterprises, partnerships between local officials and private entrepreneurs, and privately financed and privately operated enterprises seeking political shelter and avoiding legal discrimination.[19] It predicts that over time and if political circumstances permit, the genuine collectively owned enterprises would evolve toward the other two types of ownership structure.[20] The convergence school is skeptical of the experimentalist school's functionalist explanation of the TVE ownership form, especially its emphasis on the state's superiority in financial intermediation. Taiwan's small and medium-size private enterprises exhibited dynamic growth in the 1960 to 1985 period even though they were heavily discriminated against by Taiwan's wholly state-owned banking system. They thrived because informal financial markets (curb markets) emerged to cater to their needs. When tolerated by the local authorities, the power of market forces to induce financial institutional innovations was also seen in Wenzhou city when economic liberalization began in 1979. Yia-Ling Liu (1992) reported that "Ninety-five per cent of the total capital needed by the local private sector has been supplied by 'underground' private financial organizations, such as money clubs, specialized financial households, and money shops."

In our opinion, the TVE ownership structure is the product of political and not economic circumstances. First, private ownership was heavily discriminated against in many areas until recently, and thus collective ownership of rural industry arose as the primary response to the profitable niches created by central planning. Many private enterprises evaded discrimination by registering themselves as collectively owned, a charade that Chinese observers have called "wearing the red cap." Second, the collective ownership of TVEs is rendered more manageable by the low labor mobility in the countryside, which, in turn, is the result of the system of political control known as the household registration system (*hukou*) that tied the peasants to the land. Community ownership was hence workable because the community members expected to remain in the same place indefinitely and there was also no complicating factor of inward migration.

To us, the most salient point about the TVE ownership structure is that it is highly unusual by international standards. In most East Asian countries with rural industry, such as Indonesia and Thailand, ownership of small enterprises is private, often within a family. By contrast, TVE ownership is collective, at least officially. Some scholars have argued that collective ownership reflects deep Chinese cultural patterns (Weitzman and Xu 1994). However, this "cooperative-culture" hypothesis would appear to be called into question by the dominance of small private enterprises in rural Taiwan, as well as by the prevalence of small, Chinese-owned private firms throughout East Asia. If there is any cultural affinity regarding small business, it would seem to be for private, family-owned businesses rather than collectively owned businesses. Since the cross-country experiences suggest that the reason for collective ownership in China is neither economic nor cultural in origin, our identification of political ideology as the reason seems very plausible.

It is hence not surprising that with the steady reduction in discrimination against private ownership since early 1992 (partly in response to the change in ideological climate after Deng's *nanxun* and partly to ameliorate rural unemployment), many TVEs have been taking off their "red hats"—albeit with difficulties in many cases:

As China heads toward a market economy, an increasing number of private companies are no longer feeling the need as register as "red cap," or collectively-owned ventures ... [because the] difference in preferential treatment between private and public units has been narrowed.... But there is a problem. The collective units are now arguing that private firms could not have developed without their help. As the so-called "owners" of the companies,... [they] usually ask for high compensation for the "divorce" or ask the companies to merge with them.[21]

By December 1997, the privatization of TVEs had gathered enough momentum that the state came out supporting it. Wan Baorui, vice-minister for agriculture, "called for carrying out ownership reforms on rural collective enterprises.... All organizational forms, such as joint-stock partnerships, joint-stock cooperatives, enterprise groups, leasing, and mergers, should be utilized boldly."[22]

An important reason that the central leadership started supporting the earnest privatization of TVEs was that the corruption of local officials was fomenting rural unrest. The depiction of rural industrialization as local corporatism by the experimentalist school is just too harmonious an image to be true. According to Jieh-Min Wu (1998, pp. 356–357), since a large part of rural industrialization has been undertaken under cadre leadership, the

Chinese village seems to have stratified into two groups: the coalition of cadre-entrepreneurs and powerful clans, and the powerless villagers deprived in the process of industrialization.... [The informal approach of privatization has sowed the seeds of distributional conflict in the village, creating the possibility that a] massive peasant protest movement may erupt at a time of weakened authoritarian control.

The fact is that TVEs are not optimal adaptations to China's economic circumstances; they are adaptations only to China's political circumstances. With the increasing recognition within China's leadership that it is to China's benefit to move quickly to a normal market economy, the great decline in state and collective forms of ownership was inevitable and desirable. As pointed to earlier in the discussion of SOE privatization, the maintenance of social stability requires that the privatization of collectively owned enterprises be a transparent, equitable process undertaken within an adequate legal framework.

Final Remarks

Gradualism in China is less the result of a particular theory of reform and more the result of (1) political deadlock and compromises within the Chinese Communist Party (CCP) between the conservative reformers and the liberal reformers and (2) a general lack of consensus in the society at large. The conservative reformers enunciated what Chen Yun has labeled the doctrine of a "bird-cage economy": the central plan is the cage, and the bird is the economy. The premise is that without central planning, production would be in chaos: without the cage, the bird will fly away. The amount of market activity that is to be tolerated to keep the economy working is analogous to the amount that the cage needs to be swung to create the illusion of greater space that is required to keep the bird happy.

The liberal reformers, on the other hand, reject the bird-cage ideal as a bird-brain idea because they recognize that the capitalist market economies have been more successful than the socialist planned economies. The East Asian developmental experience convinced the liberal reformers that only a market economy that is open to the outside world could promote long-term economic development.

With these basic differences in economic strategy, it is not surprising that partial reform was the compromise solution. Both conservative reformers and liberal reformers were able to implement part of their programs. All the special economic zones were located in southern China, for example, far away from the important political centers. This repeated factional struggle and compromise is the primary reason that the CCP has continually altered its stated goals for economic reform, which has progressed from the 1999 ideal of "a planned economy supplemented by market regulations" to the 1992 ideal of "a socialist market economy with Chinese characteristics."

The experimentalist-convergence debate has unfortunately been often miscast as a slow-fast debate. The key question in the debate about China's economic growth is whether the growth was generated by the appearance of new, noncapitalist economic institutions or by the convergence to a private market economy. The slow-fast characterization of the debate has to be seen in this context. For example, the relevant question in the present policy debate in Vietnam over the strategy of rural industrialization is "collectively owned enterprises versus private enterprises" and not "slow development of collectively owned enterprises versus fast development of collectively owned enterprises." The important issue is not speed but the direction of reform.

The slow-fast depiction of transition strategy also misses the fact that *instant* convergence to *all* the institutions of a private market economy is not technically achievable. It is possible to implement big-bang macrostabilization, and big-bang price and trade liberalization in a grossly policy-distorted economy, but it is technically impossible to conjure up instantly a legal infrastructure that could ensure a transparent, equitable privatization process.[23] An *immediate commitment to mass privatization* at the start of reforms is desirable, but immediate privatization that results in *nomenklatura* privatization is not. This is the primary difference between the Polish and Russian privatization programs, and this difference explains a large part of their different economic performances.

China's accession to WTO constitutes a watershed in the debate between the convergence school and the experimentalist school. To appreciate this point fully, the WTO membership must be viewed in the context of the comprehensive transformation of China's economy and society that began with the Twelfth Party Congress in 1992 and accelerated after the Seventeenth Party Congress in 1997. Most of the small and medium SOEs in the rich coastal provinces have been privatized, and the government is now exploring ways to sell the state shares of the large SOEs that are listed on the domestic stock markets. The constitution has been amended to accord legal protection to private property, and the latest ideological breakthrough, the Three Represents, allows the admission of capitalists into the Party. The rural landscape has also changed greatly by the ongoing privatization (since 1993) of the collectively owned TVEs. The extension of land leases from fifteen years to thirty years will be recognized as a landmark on the way to private land ownership in the countryside. WTO membership is hence only one of the many policy actions led by the state to promote the continued convergence of China's economy to the norms of its East Asian neighbors and integration with the world's major economies so that economic growth would be sustained. More important, China's leaders know that explicit embrace of capitalist institutions under WTO auspices would be welcome by the general Chinese public as a step forward in the reform process rather than as surrender of China's sovereignty in economic experimentation.[24]

Notes

1. Naughton (1995, p. 320) thus concluded that: "Big bang transitions thus sacrifice most aspects of the virtuous cycle that characterized the Chinese reforms." Other distinguished members of the experimentalist school include Thomas Rawski (1994), Peter Nolan and Robert Ash (1995), Qian (2000), and Justin Lin, Fang Cai, and Zhou Li (1996).

2. Members of the convergence school include Michael Bruno (1994), Gang Fan (1990), Sachs, Woo, and Yang (2000), and Geng Xiao (1997).

3. The earliest country in the industrial age to implement this operational principle successfully and hence attain first world status is Japan.

4. As is documented later, in 1988, the Soviet Union produced fifteen times more crude steel per dollar of GDP than the United States and eight times more than West Germany and Japan. The Soviet Union also produced five times more refined copper per dollar of GDP than the United States, West Germany, and Japan.

5. The rise of the light industrial component of the industrial sector from 39 percent of total industrial output in 1978 to 48 percent in 1988 and 51 percent in 1998 reflected, in part, its suppression under central planning.

6. State employment was 109.5 million in 1996 compared with 74.5 million in 1978.

7. This decline in agricultural employment is likely to be understated because it does not take illegal migration into account.

8. See Ellman and Kontorovich (1998) for more discussion of the range of alternatives.

9. Ellman and Kontorovich (1998, p. 103); but Åslund (1991, p. 127) reported the intended range to be 50 to 70 percent.

10. For contemporary accounts, see Central Intelligence Agency and Defense Intelligence Agency (1989, 1990). Malia (1994) gives an excellent analysis of the politics of the period.

11. Sachs and Woo (1994) pointed out that there had to be a big cut in welfare subsidies provide by the government through the state enterprises before workers could be induced to seek employment in the new nonsubsidized private sector.

12. Berg, Borensztein, Sahay, and Zettelmeyer's (1999) thorough econometric investigation of CEEFSU economies support this value-subtracting view of the Soviet-type industrial sector.

13. Vice-Premier Zhu Rongji: "Guo you qiye sheng hua gaige ke burong huan" (No time shall be lost in further reforming state-owned enterprises), speech at the Fourth Meeting of the Eighth People's Congress, *People's Daily, Overseas Edition*, March 11, 1996.

14. Lin, Cai, and Li (1996, p. 215).

15. "China: Finance Ministry Reveals Widespread Accounting Fraud," *Financial Times*, December 24, 1999. In January 2000, auditors in Hebei caught sixty-seven SOEs covering up losses of RMB 600 million ("Beijing Moving to Improve Quality of Statistics," *South China Morning Post*, February 29, 2000).

16. "State Asset Drain Must End," *China Daily*, December 13, 1995.

17. The non-SOE data exclude small non-SOEs with sales at or below 5 million yuan. Data in this paragraph are from Zhou and Wang (2002).

18. This estimate has taken into account the additional production cost of the nonoil SOEs.

19. In "Private Firms Jump to Take 'Red Caps' Off," the *China Daily*, November 4, 1994, reported that "hundreds of thousands of private companies have registered as branches of publicly owned units on the condition that they pay money to their so-called owners ... [because private companies face] complicated registration procedures, heavy levies, and less preferential treatment than State firms [in fund raising and fund use. For example, one] private company had to

write 46 receipts of 10,000 yuan each for goods worth 460,000 yuan because nonstate firms were only allowed to issue bills under 10,000 yuan."

This third type of TVE is not rare; its number may be greater than the number of registered private enterprises in many places. This is certainly true for Wenzhou: "In the 1980s, almost all private business people ... described their enterprises as *collective*, which indicated that they *belong* to local governments, or to a State enterprise." *China Daily*, October 31, 1996. A 1993 survey found that in one county in Hebei province where there were "at least 1,000 private businesses, the official number was eight." "Enterprises Shake Protection Cover," *China Daily*, March 31, 1995.

20. In fieldwork in southern Jiangsu, Wenzhou, Pearl River delta, and Zhengzhou, Jieh-Min Wu (1998, p. 355) found "that most of the rural enterprises were private in disguise."

21. "Private Firms Jump to Take 'Red Caps' Off," *China Daily*, November 4, 1994.

22. "Rural Ownership Reforms to Move Forward," *China Daily*, December 4, 1997.

23. The debate is therefore trivialized when big-bang advocates are unfairly depicted as proposing something that is technically infeasible.

24. For a quantification of the positive economic impact of China's WTO membership on China and of the net economic impact on the rest of the world, see McKibbin and Woo (2003) who use a dynamic, multisectoral, multicountry, macroeconomic model to conduct the analysis.

References

Åslund, Anders. (1991). *Gorbachev's Struggle for Economic Reform.* 2nd ed. London: Pinter.

Baum, Richard. (1994). *Burying Mao: Chinese Politics in the Age of Deng Xiaoping.* Princeton: Princeton University Press.

Berg, Andrew, Eduardo Borensztein, Ratna Sahay, and Jeromin Zettelmeyer. (1999). "The Evolution of Output in Transition Economies: Explaining the Differences." International Monetary Fund, WP/99/73.

Blanchard, Oliver, and Michael Kremer. (1997). "Disorganization." *Quarterly Journal of Economics,* 112(4): 1091–1126.

Bruno, Michael. (1994). "Our Assistance Includes Ideas as Well as Money." *Transition* (World Bank), 5(1): 1–4.

Central Intelligence Agency and the Defense Intelligence Agency. (1989). *The Soviet Economy in 1988: Gorbachev Changes Course.* Report to the Subcommittee on National Security Economics, Joint Economic Committee, Congress of the United States.

Central Intelligence Agency and the Defense Intelligence Agency. (1990). *The Soviet Economy Stumbles Badly in 1989.* Report to the Technology and National Security Subcommittee, Joint Economic Committee, Congress of the United States.

Chow, Gregory. (1993). "Capital Formation and Economic Growth in China." *Quarterly Journal of Economics, 108*(3): 809–842.

Ellman, Michael, and Vlaclimor Kontorovich. (1998). *The Destruction of the Soviet Economic System: An Insiders' History.* Armonk, NY: Sharpe.

Fan, Gang. (1990). *Macroeconomic Analysis of Public Ownership* (in Chinese). Shanghai: Shanghai United Press.

Fan, Gang, and Wing Thye Woo. (1996). "State Enterprise Reform as a Source of Macroeconomic Instability." *Asian Economic Journal, 10*(3): 207–224.

Fewsmith, Joseph. (1994). *Dilemmas of Reform in China: Political Conflict and Economic Debate.* Armonk, NY: Sharpe.

Jefferson, Gary, and Thomas Rawski. (1994). "Enterprise Reform in Chinese Industry." *Journal of Economic Perspectives, 8*(2): 47–70.

Kornai, Janos. (1992). *The Socialist System: The Political Economy of Communism.* Princeton: Princeton University Press.

Kornai, Janos. (2000). "Ten Years after 'The Road to a Free Economy': The Author's Self-Evaluation." Paper presented at the World Bank, Annual Bank Conference on Development Economics, April.

Lau, Lawrence J., Yingyi Qian, and Gerard Roland. (2000). "Reform without Losers: An Interpretation of China's Dual-Track Approach to Transition." *Journal of Political Economy, 108*(1): 120–143.

Lin, Justine Yifu, Fang Cai, and Zhou Li. (1996). *The China Miracle: Development Strategy and Economic Reform.* Hong Kong: Chinese University Press.

Lipton, David, and Jeffrey D. Sachs. (1992). "Prospects for Russia's Economic Reforms." *Brookings Papers on Economic Activity, 2*: 213–265.

Liu, Yia-Ling. (1992). "Reform From Below: The Private Economy and Local Politics in the Rural Industrialization of Wenzhou." *China Quarterly, 130*: 293–316.

Malia, Martin. (1994). *The Soviet Tragedy: A History of Socialism in Russia, 1917–1991.* New York: Free Press.

McKibbin, Warwick J., and Wing Thye Woo. (2003). "The Consequences of China's WTO Accession on Its Neighbours." *Asian Economic Papers, 2*(2): 1–38 (translated into Polish: "Konsekwencje Przystapienia Chin Do WTO Dla Krajow Sasiednich," Zeszyty Bre Bank-CASE 69, BRE Bank SA and Centrum Analiz Spoleczno-Ekonomicznych, Warszawa, 2003).

Naughton, Barry. (1994). "Chinese Institutional Innovation and Privatization from Below." *American Economic Review, 84*(2): 266–270.

Naughton, Barry. (1995). *Growing Out of the Plan: Chinese Economic Reform, 1978–1993.* Cambridge, UK: Cambridge University Press.

Nellis, John. (1999). "Time to Rethink Privatisation in Transition Economies?" International Finance Corporation Discussion Paper No. 38, World Bank.

Nolan, Peter. (1993). *State and Market in the Chinese Economy: Essays on Controversial Issues*. London: MacMillan.

Nolan, Peter, and Robert Ash. (1995). "China's Economy on the Eve of Reform." *China Quarterly, 144:* 980–998.

Nolan, Peter, and Wang Xiaoqiang. (1999). "Beyond Privatization: Institutional Innovation and Growth in China's Large State-Owned Enterprises." *World Development, 27*(1): 169–200.

Qian, Yingyi. (2000). "The Institutional Foundations of China's Market Transition." In Boris Pleskovic and Joseph Stiglitz (Eds.), *Annual World Bank Conference on Development Economics 1999* (pp. 377–398). Washington, D.C.: World Bank.

Rawski, Thomas. (1994). "Progress without Privatization: The Reform of China's State Industries." In Vedat Milor (Ed.), *The Political Economy of Privatization and Public Enterprise in Post-Communist and Reforming-Communist States* (pp. 27–52). Boulder, CO: Lynne Rienner.

Rawski, Thomas. (1995). "Implications of China's Reform Experience." *China Quarterly, 144:* 1150–1173.

Rawski, Thomas. (1999). "Reforming China's Economy: What Have We Learned?" *China Journal, 41:* 139–158.

Sachs, Jeffrey D. Sachs, and Wing Thye Woo. (1994). "Structural Factors in the Economic Reforms of China, Eastern Europe, and the Former Soviet Union." *Economic Policy, 18:* 101–145.

Sachs, Jeffrey D., Wing Thye Woo, and Xiaokai Yang (with Jeffrey D. Sachs). (2000). "Economic Reforms and Constitutional Transition." *Annals of Economics and Finance, 1*(2): 435–491.

State Statistical Bureau of China. (1999). *Comprehensive Statistical Data and Materials on Fifty Years of New China*. Beijing: China Statistical Press.

Stiglitz, J. E. (1999a). "Quis Custodiet Ipsos Custodes? Corporate Governance Failures in the Transition." Paper presented to the World Bank Annual Bank Conference on Development Economics, Paris, June 21–23. Accessed 16 August 2001. Available online at ⟨http://www.worldbank.org/research/abcde/eu/stiglitz.pdf⟩.

Stiglitz, J. E. (1999b). "Whither Reform? Ten years of the Transition." Paper presented at the World Bank Annual Bank Conference on Development Economics, Washington, DC, June 28–30. Accessed August 16, 2001. Available online at ⟨http://www.worldbank.org/research/abcde⟩.

Weitzman, Martin, and Chenggang Xu. (1994). "Chinese Township Village Enterprises as Vaguely Defined Cooperatives." *Journal of Comparative Economics, 18:* 121–145.

Woo, Wing Thye. (1998). "Chinese Economic Growth: Sources and Prospects." In Michel Fouquin and Francoise Lemoine (Eds.), *The Chinese Economy*. London: Economica (translated into Chinese: "Zhongguo Quan Yaosu Shengchan Lu: Laizi Nongye Bumen Laodongli Zai Pei Zhi de Shouyao Zuoyong," in *Jingji Yanjiu*, 3 (1998)).

World Development Report 1996. (1996). Washington, D.C.

Wu, Jieh-Min. (1998). "Local Property Rights Regime in Socialist Reforms: A Case Study of China's Informal Privatization." Ph.D. dissertation, Columbia University.

Xiao, Geng. (1997). *Property Rights and Economic Reform in China* (in Chinese). Beijing: China Social Science Press.

Zhou, Fangsheng, and Xiaolu Wang. (2002). "The Way of State-Owned Enterprise Reform in China." Beijing: National Economic Research Institute.

5

Successes and Failures in Real Convergence: The Case of Chile

Vittorio Corbo L. and Leonardo Hernández T.

The literature on economic growth has been trying for decades to provide an explanation for the enormous differences in growth that are observed between richer and poorer countries.[1] To do this, economic growth has been decomposed into factor accumulation and productivity gains (Solow's decomposition). In this regard, empirical evidence shows that improvements in total factor productivity (TFP) are as or more important as factor accumulation as a source of economic growth. However, in recent years the profession seems to have reached a near consensus: the ultimate cause of economic growth is neither capital accumulation nor factor productivity but the institutional setting that makes such accumulation or productivity gains possible. According to this view, adequate institutions and good policies—rule of law, good governance, protection of property rights, a market-oriented economy—promote rapid innovation and technological progress, leading to faster capital accumulation, increased employment, and growing factor productivity. Conversely, weak institutional settings and poor policies—lax protection of property rights, widespread corruption, low fiscal capacity, weak supervision, and lenient regulation of financial institutions—deter investment, innovation, employment, and capital accumulation, ultimately slowing economic growth. Empirical evidence strongly supports this view (figures 5.1, 5.2, 5.3, and 5.4).[2]

The conclusion above is supported also by the Chilean experience over the past thirty years. During this period, the country's authorities implemented major reforms in the economy—moving from a high-inflation, centralized, and protected economy to a low-inflation, market-oriented economy highly integrated with the rest of the world. But that was not

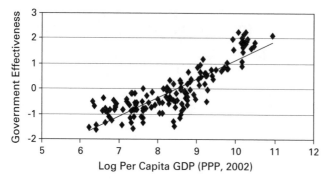

Figure 5.1
Government-effectiveness index and per-capita GDP
Source: Government-effectiveness index from Kaufmann, Kraay, and Mastruzzi (2003); per-capita GDP from the World Bank.
Note: 150 countries.

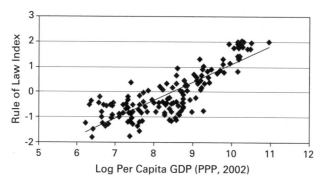

Figure 5.2
Rule-of-law index and per-capita GDP
Source: Rule-of-law index from Kaufmann, Kraay, and Mastruzzi (2003); per-capita GDP from the World Bank.
Note: 150 countries.

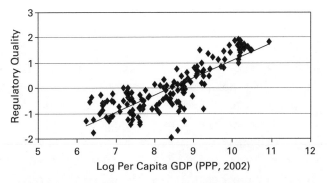

Figure 5.3
Regulatory-quality index and per-capita GDP
Source: Regulatory-quality index from Kaufmann, Kraay, and Mastruzzi (2003);
per-capita GDP from the World Bank.
Note: 150 countries.

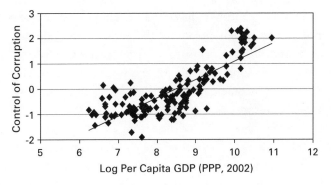

Figure 5.4
Control-of-corruption index and per-capita GDP
Source: Control-of-corruption index from Kaufmann, Kraay, and Mastruzzi
(2003); per-capita GDP from the World Bank.

all. Important institutional changes were introduced, such as granting full independence to the Central Bank and upgrading banks' regulatory and supervisory framework to match international standards. In addition, the authorities privatized most of the state-owned enterprises (SOEs), adopted an individual-capitalization (as opposed to the prevailing pay-as-you go) pension system, privatized the management of pension funds, and introduced competition in telecommunications. Further, they helped to rebuild the country's infrastructure through an innovative build-operate-and-transfer (BOT) framework and targeted social spending toward the poor, among other changes that are discussed in greater detail below. As a result, after the debt crisis and until the Asian crisis, the country grew by an annual average of about 7.3 percent—the longest period of rapid and sustained growth ever—and became one of the fastest-growing countries among emerging-market economies (figure 5.5). During this period Chile's social indicators improved substantially, the incidence of poverty was sharply reduced, and the per-capita income gap with developed countries fell markedly. In parallel, the country completed a successful transition to democracy. In contrast, in the region at large, poverty fell only marginally, while for every other Latin American country the per-capita income gap with developed countries either broadened or remained constant.

This chapter reviews the Chilean experience from 1973, the last pre-reform year, until 2002 to 2003. The rest of the chapter is divided into five sections discussing policies and reforms in the period leading to the debt crisis; reforms following the debt crisis years and until the Asian crisis; reforms implemented in the aftermath of the Asian crisis; the empirical evidence for the Chilean case and an explanation for Chile's performance compared with other Latin American countries; and finally, a few policy conclusions.

Stabilization and First-Generation Reforms: Moving toward a Market-Oriented Economy, 1973 to 1981

After World War II, the Chilean economy was in complete disarray as the government intervened increasingly in virtually every area of produc-

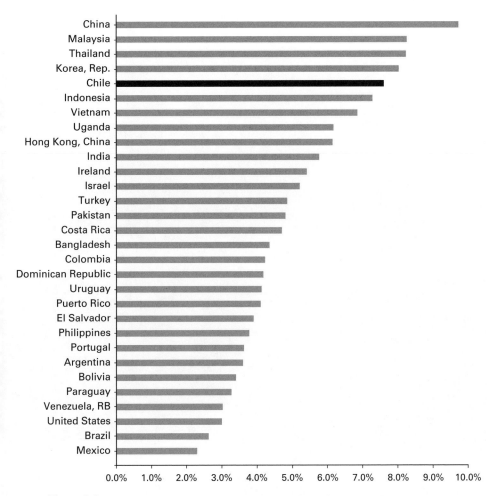

Figure 5.5
Real GDP: Average growth, selected countries, 1985 to 1997
Source: World Development Indicators 2002.

Table 5.1
Chile: Main macroeconomic indicators, 1973 to 2002

	Inflation (Dec.–Dec., percent)	Real GDP Growth (percent)	Fiscal Balance* (percent GDP)	Current Account Deficit (percent GDP)	Unemploy- ment Rate (percent)	Gross Fixed Capital Formation (percent GDP)	Gross National Savings (percent GDP)	Real Exchange Rate** (1977 = 100)
1973	508.1%	-5.6%	-30.5%					
1974	369.2	1.0	-5.4	0.5%		17.0%		
1975	343.3	-13.3	-2.0	6.4	14.9%	15.0	9.5%	
1976	197.9	3.2	4.0	-1.4	12.7	12.4	16.9	
1977	84.2	8.3	0.4	3.9	11.8	13.7	13.8	100.0
1978	37.2	7.8	1.6	6.8	14.2	14.9	15.3	83.8
1979	38.9	7.1	4.8	5.6	13.6	15.9	16.7	81.3
1980	31.2	7.7	6.1	7.1	10.4	18.8	19.3	93.9
1981	9.5	6.7	0.8	14.5	11.3	20.9	14.2	107.9
1982	20.7	-13.4	-3.4	9.0	19.6	14.2	4.9	96.8
1983	23.1	-3.5	-3.0	5.5	14.6	12.3	6.9	80.6
1984	23.0	6.1	-4.3	10.8	13.9	14.7	6.5	77.2
1985	26.4	3.5	-2.6	8.6	12.0	15.9	7.8	62.8
1986	17.4	5.6	-2.1	6.7	10.4	15.4	11.5	57.1
1987	21.5	6.6	1.9	3.6	9.6	17.4	17.3	54.7
1988	12.7	7.3	1.0	1.0	8.0	18.5	22.3	51.3
1989	21.4	10.6	1.4	2.5	7.1	21.6	23.3	52.6
1990	27.3	3.7	0.8	1.6	7.4	21.4	23.2	50.7

1991	18.7	8.0	1.5	0.3	7.1	19.8	22.3	53.7
1992	12.7	12.3	2.2	2.1	6.2	21.7	21.5	58.5
1993	12.2	7.0	1.8	5.4	6.4	23.8	20.9	58.9
1994	8.9	5.7	1.6	2.9	7.8	23.8	21.1	60.6
1995	8.2	10.6	2.4	1.9	6.6	26.1	23.8	64.2
1996	6.6	7.4	2.1	4.1	5.4	26.4	21.4	67.4
1997	6.0	6.6	1.8	4.4	5.3	27.4	21.6	73.0
1998	4.7	3.2	0.4	4.9	7.2	27.0	21.2	73.2
1999	2.3	-0.8	-1.4	-0.1	8.9	22.2	21.0	69.4
2000	4.5	4.2	0.1	1.0	8.3	23.0	20.6	66.4
2001	2.6	3.1	-0.3	1.7	7.9	22.9	20.0	59.5
2002	2.8	2.1	-0.8	0.8	7.8	22.7	21.0	58.5

Source: Central Bank of Chile.
* Central government.
** An increase indicates an appreciation.

tion and interfered in many economic decisions. Furthermore, fiscal deficits were rampant, and the economy was isolated from the rest of the world through a complex battery of trade restrictions. In a nutshell, by 1973 inflation was running at above 500 percent per year, the fiscal deficit was about 30 percent of GDP (table 5.1), and the peso was artificially overvalued. There were many capital and current-account restrictions aimed at containing the external imbalance (including a multiple exchange-rate system, for example). In addition, the average tariff was about 105 percent, though effective protection varied across economic sectors due to a wide range of restrictions (including nontariff barriers), and many prices were set (artificially low) by the government, creating a shortage of goods and services in many markets. Further, the state owned about 600 enterprises, accounting for about 40 percent of GDP, and financial repression in the form of controlled (negative) real interest rates and restrictions on credit allocation was widespread.

The military government that took power in late 1973 inherited an economy in complete disarray. Consequently, in the early years of the military government, exchange rates were unified, prices were liberalized for most goods and services, and several enterprises, farms, and banks that had been intervened and controlled by Salvador Allende's administration were returned to their previous owners. In addition, a major fiscal package comprising drastic cuts in public investment and subsidies, and a freeze in public wages, brought the fiscal deficit down to only 5 percent of GDP in 1974. The fiscal adjustment continued, bringing— helped by the economic recovery that followed—a 4 percent surplus only two years later.

But reforms went far beyond achieving stabilization and correcting macroeconomic imbalances. In 1975, for example, the sales tax was replaced by the value-added tax (VAT) at a flat rate of 20 percent, thus improving the efficiency of resource allocation. Over time, the VAT became the most important source of government revenue, amounting to about 50 percent of total taxes (table 5.2). Also, nontariff trade barriers were lifted, while both the dispersion and the level of tariffs were unilaterally reduced for most goods. This process continued into 1979, when a flat tariff of 10 percent was set for most goods (only a few exceptions remained, like cars and luxury items such as fur and jewelry).

Table 5.2
Fiscal revenues composition, 1987 to 2002

	1987	1989	1996	1999	2002
Income tax	14.5%	18.2%	23.6%	22.6%	27.7%
Value-added tax	45.1	45.9	47.9	48.4	48.4
Specific taxes (alcohol, tobacco, gas, etc.)	15.5	11.8	11.0	14.1	13.7
Legal acts tax	7.0	8.2	3.8	4.2	4.4
Trade taxes	14.5	14.8	11.9	9.2	5.7
Others	3.4	1.0	1.8	1.4	0.2
Total	100%	100%	100%	100%	100%

Source: Budget office, Chile.
Note: Percentages.

Major reforms were also introduced in the financial sector, where interest rates were liberalized, banks privatized, mandatory credit allocation abolished, entry restrictions lifted, and the scope of permitted activities broadened. But the end of financial repression was not preceded or accompanied by an upgrade—or even better, an overhaul—of the supervisory and regulatory framework, thus exacerbating moral hazard and adverse-selection problems. Furthermore, early on in the process one commercial bank went bankrupt and the government provided full protection to depositors, thus intensifying moral-hazard problems. Unsurprisingly, after the financial liberalization process began, connected lending grew unchecked, partly motivated by the simultaneous privatization of banks and enterprises that had led to a high concentration of wealth. Along with overborrowing, banks incurred in highly concentrated portfolios and underprovisioning of nonperforming loans—the latter due to both low provisioning requirements and lax rules that allowed nonperforming loans to be rolled over. Also, bank borrowers incurred in huge currency mismatches in their balance sheets, a risk that was overlooked by both banks and supervisory agencies (that is, banks' exchange-rate risk exposure became a credit risk). In addition, a de facto deposit insurance system precluded depositors from exerting any kind of market discipline, further aggravating moral-hazard problems. This financial fragility made the overall system prone to crisis and proved to be costly when the economy suffered severe shocks in the early 1980s.

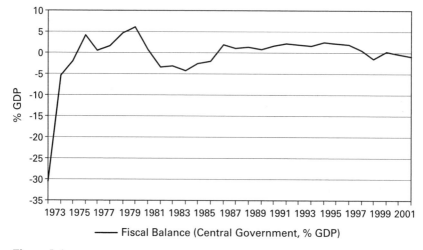

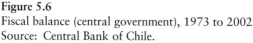

Figure 5.6
Fiscal balance (central government), 1973 to 2002
Source: Central Bank of Chile.

The outcome of all the above combined reforms was a quick economic recovery and a sharp reduction in both the fiscal deficit and the inflation rate (figures 5.6, 5.7, and 5.8; see table 5.1). Indeed, after a sharp recession in 1975 that resulted from the fiscal stabilization program, the first oil shock, and the fall in the price of copper on the world market, GDP grew on average by about 6.8 percent per year during 1976 to 1981 (7.5 percent in 1977 to 1981). Similarly, inflation reached the two-digit level just a few years into the stabilization program, although it remained around 30 percent until 1980 and was slightly below 10 percent only in 1981, while the fiscal balance was in surplus through the entire 1976 to 1981 period.

But three major imbalances arose during this period. First, the real exchange rate appreciated significantly, especially after the nominal exchange rate was pegged to the dollar in mid-1979 in an attempt to accelerate the reduction of inflation[3] (figure 5.9; see table 5.1). Second, because of a private-sector spending boom, the current-account deficit went steadily from a small surplus of 1.4 percent of GDP in 1976 to a large deficit of 14.5 percent of GDP in 1981 (figure 5.10; see table 5.1). And third, the financial sector weakened as major risks and vulnerabil-

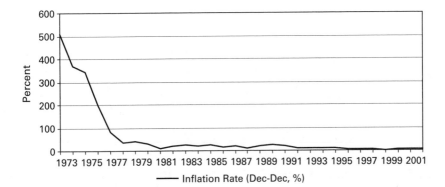

Figure 5.7
Inflation rate (December to December), 1973 to 2002
Source: Central Bank of Chile.

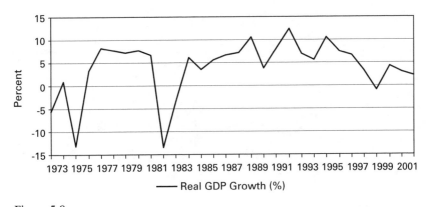

Figure 5.8
Real GDP growth, 1973 to 2002
Source: Central Bank of Chile.

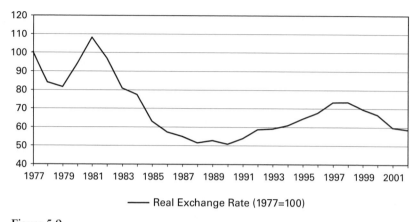

Figure 5.9
Real exchange rate
Source: Central Bank of Chile.
Note: An increase is an appreciation. 1977 = 100.

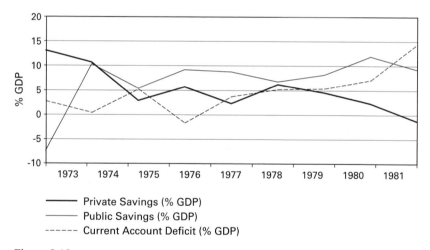

Figure 5.10
Private savings, public savings, and current-account deficit, 1973 to 1981
Source: Central Bank of Chile.

ities grew unchecked (unmatched currency liabilities of banks' debtors, weak asset-classification system, underprovisioning, and the like), leading to weak portfolios and undercapitalized banks, many of which accumulated potential losses several times their capital base.

All in all, the second oil shock in 1979, the appreciation of the U.S. dollar (to which the peso was pegged) compared to other major currencies in the early 1980s, along with the sharp rise in international interest rates that followed Paul Volcker's appointment to the U.S. Federal Reserve Board, and the fall in commodity prices caused by the global slowdown created an external situation that was difficult to sustain. As the country had become increasingly dependent on foreign capital, especially debt, the whole situation ended in a balance-of-payments crisis when private capital inflows came to a halt in 1982. The external crisis forced the abandonment of the nominal exchange-rate peg just two months before Mexico stopped servicing its foreign debt in August 1982. The real depreciation that ensued further aggravated the financial situation of corporations and banks because of their large balance-sheet currency mismatches, leading to a deep financial crisis and economic recession (see figure 5.8; tables 5.1 and 5.3).

The Golden Period and Second-Generation Reforms, 1984 to 1997

The economic and financial crisis of the early 1980s, with a cumulative fall in real GDP during 1982 to 1983 of about 16.4 percent, caused a setback on some of the policies and achievements of previous years. Indeed, the government had to intervene and take over nineteen financial institutions, whereby it ended up controlling about half of total bank credit (the intervened institutions were later on privatized, merged, or shut down). Along with this, the government took over several enterprises and nonbank financial intermediaries (such as insurance companies, mutual funds, and the like) that belonged to the conglomerates whose flagship banks were near collapse and had required intervention.[4] In addition, the government was forced to provide guarantees on most of the foreign debt incurred by the private sector, de facto socializing the country's foreign debt, while import tariffs were raised—albeit temporarily—to help the fiscal adjustment. All of this represented a major setback to

Table 5.3
Past-due loans over total loans, banks and financial companies

Year	Percentage
1979	1.6%
1980	1.1
1981	2.3
1982	4.1
1983	8.4
1984	8.9
1985	3.5

Source: Held (1989).

the market-oriented economic model implemented since 1974 and forced the government to incur in a fiscal deficit and allow higher inflation rates (in addition to tariffs) to finance it.

But important lessons were learnt that led to a reshaping of the institutional framework in the aftermath of the debt crisis, thus improving the capacity of the economy to absorb shocks and better aligning incentives. However, before proceeding with the discussion of all the changes made during this period, it is important to single out two reforms that were implemented just before the debt crisis and that played a major role in the subsequent period: the new constitution of 1980 and the pension system reform of 1981.

The new constitution of 1980 is important because it set the timetable for the return to a democratic regime in Chile and also because it granted the power to allocate government spending exclusively to the executive branch, thus closely linking expenditures with revenues. Prior to this legal change, the legislative branch shared the power to allocate public money but was not required to provide the necessary funding, thus exacerbating the bias toward having a large fiscal deficit because of political interests. Thus, today the Chilean Congress can either pass or reject the budget law presented to it by the government but cannot amend such law. This has proven to be an important factor for maintaining fiscal discipline. In addition, in the new constitution the Central Bank was prohibited from buying securities issued by the government, thus precluding the monetization of the fiscal deficit. It was also given the explicit man-

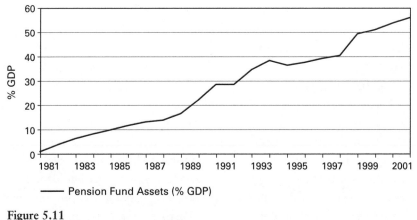

Figure 5.11
Pension-fund assets, 1981 to 2002
Source: AFPs Superintendency.

date to pursue the stability of prices (or of the currency), the stability of external payments, and the stability of the domestic payment system. Finally, it was granted full independence by the way its authorities would be designated.[5] (Although legislated earlier, these changes came into effect de facto in 1989 with the country's return to democracy.)

The pension-system reform of 1981 consisted of the phasing out of the bankrupt pay-as-you-go system and the creation of a fully funded capitalization system run by private, competing entities. In the new system, workers make mandatory monthly contributions into personal savings accounts that are managed by specialized private entities, and those balances cannot be withdrawn before retirement. This reform led to an increase in total savings and, at the same time, contributed to the development and deepening of the domestic capital markets, thus indirectly helping to raise total factor productivity (Corbo and Schmidt-Hebbel 2003). In fact, as the private entities managing these funds have become large lenders to both banks and corporations, over the years they have induced an improvement in corporate governance (figure 5.11).

Thus, in the aftermath of the debt crisis, the government focused its policies on two areas: redoing some of the work of previous years (privatizing banks and enterprises taken over during the crisis, continue reducing the budget deficit and inflation) and overhauling the institutional framework to correct the problems and regulatory shortcomings that had been diagnosed during (and were partly responsible for) the crisis. The most important institutional changes and policies are discussed below in chronological order.

A new tax law was enacted in 1984, which provided special incentives for saving and investment. For instance, profits became nontaxable if reinvested (taxes accrued only when profits were distributed in the form of dividends) and the corporate tax rate was reduced. At the same time, double taxation on dividends was abolished by giving shareholders a tax credit to be used in their personal income tax, equal to the proportional corporate tax paid by the company. This way the tax-induced bias in favor of corporate borrowing to finance investment was eliminated (Modigliani and Miller 1963). In addition, special incentives were provided for the issuance of equity. Buyers of new shares received a tax credit that was equal to a fraction of the new investment, which would last for as long as they held on to the new shares (Hernández and Walker 1993).

Also, new banking and bankruptcy laws were enacted in 1986. The new banking law granted more powers to the supervisory and regulatory agencies, while updating specific regulations to keep up with international standards and best practices. For instance, stringent restrictions were imposed on loans granted to related parties and on the reporting of nonperforming loans, thus significantly reducing the scope for connected lending and bad-loan rollover. Furthermore, new rules governing asset rating and provisioning by banks were put in place, closely following international standards. With respect to bankruptcy procedures, the new law set forth clear steps for the liquidation and closure of banks. Also, clear seniorities were established for the payment of debts to creditors, while bankruptcy procedures were expedited.

Other important institutional changes included the privatization of SOEs, comprising not only banks and other firms taken over during the debt crisis but also utilities formerly owned and operated by the state, such as electricity generation and distribution, long-distance and local telephone companies, and the setting of a framework for controlling and monitoring monopolistic practices. The privatizations undertaken during this period, as opposed to those implemented during 1974 to 1981, were designed to spread ownership among a larger group of investors, so that the high concentration of wealth that had resulted before could be avoided. For this purpose, tax and other incentives, such as low-cost loans, were provided to individuals for them to buy the shares of the privatized companies. The new privatization program brought the share of SOEs in GDP down from 24 percent in 1983 to only 13 percent in 1989. In addition, an antitrust law was passed, and specific rules were approved for the setting of prices in natural monopolies, such as electric companies, and in other industries such as public transportation.

In 1989, a new Central Bank law was enacted whereby the Central Bank's sole objectives are the stability of prices, the stability of the domestic payment system, and the stability of Chile's external payments. This new charter led the Central Bank, now autonomous, to adopt in 1991 a monetary-policy scheme based on inflation targeting and a widening exchange-rate band. The exchange-rate band was abolished in 1999, leading to a free-floating regime in which the Central Bank intervenes only when the exchange-rate market becomes dysfunctional and the exchange rate is clearly misaligned. As a result of all these changes, the inflation rate in Chile today has converged to the Central Bank's steady-state target, a range of 2 to 4 percent per year, a level that nobody thought feasible just a decade ago[6] (see figure 5.7; tables 5.1 and 5.4).

Also, new legislation allowing the participation of the private sector in infrastructure development was passed in 1991. According to it, roads, airports, seaports, and other infrastructure projects may be developed by the private sector under build, operate, and transfer (BOT) arrangements. As of 1998, twenty-one projects for a combined total of about $3.6 billion had been developed under this arrangement. And in 1994, a new law was passed permitting free entry to the until then monopolistic long-distance telecommunications market, the so-called multicarrier system. This change has shaped a highly competitive market and caused a drastic fall in long-distance telephone rates. And amendments to the banking law in 1997 allowed banks to undertake new businesses (including lending internationally) and upgraded some regulations (e.g., the Basel capital accord was adopted).

Table 5.4
Actual inflation and inflation target

Year	Inflation Target (percentage)	Effective Inflation (percentage)
1991	15–20%	18.7%
1992	13–16	12.7
1993	10–12	12.2
1994	9–11	8.9
1995	9	8.2
1996	6.5	6.6
1997	5.5	6
1998	4.5	4.7
1999	4.3	2.3
2000	3.5	4.5
2001	2–4	2.6
2002	2–4	2.8

Source: Central Bank of Chile.

Finally, it is important to mention that during this period the country successfully transited from an authoritarian to a democratic regime. Despite all the uncertainties surrounding this transition, the change was smooth in part because the new administration confirmed most of the market-economy elements already in place, while concentrating on a social agenda. This way the institutions created in previous years were validated and in many cases strengthened, so that uncertainty vanished. For instance, early on in 1990 the new democratic government deepened the opening up process by reducing the maximum import tariff from 15 to 11 percent. In fact, all three governments that have been in power since 1990 have strengthened the market economy model, accelerated the opening up process, consolidated the fiscal position, and improved regulations, while, at the same time, they have emphasized social policies and implemented new programs to alleviate poverty. However, in labor-market flexibility there has been some backtracking.

All the reforms listed above resulted in the highest growth rates ever in the country's history and for the longest period. During 1985 to 1997, the country's real GDP grew on average by 7.3 percent annually, while,

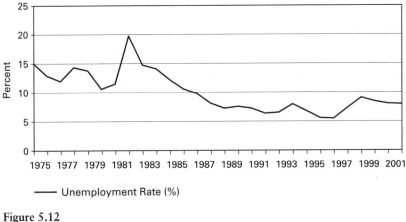

Figure 5.12
Unemployment rate, 1975 to 2002
Source: Central Bank of Chile.

at the same time, inflation fell steadily from about 27 percent into the low one-digit range. In addition, the current-account deficit was reduced from about 9 percent to the 3 to 5 percent range, while international reserves increased from about 10 percent of GDP in 1985 to about 22 percent of GDP in 1997. Meanwhile, the government balance was quickly turned into a surplus and stayed like that for more than a decade. Also during this period the savings and investment rates reached the highest levels seen in a long time (19.6 and 21.5 percent of GDP, respectively), and unemployment fell to a record low for the last thirty years (5.3 percent; see table 5.1; figures 5.6, 5.7, 5.8, 5.12, 5.13, and 5.14). The country risk rate decreased steadily and today is one of the lowest among emerging-market economies. As a consequence of rapid economic growth, the country's poverty rate fell sharply—from 33 percent in the early 1990s to 17 percent in 2000—and the existing gap in per capita GDP with industrial countries was reduced significantly, albeit less than in some Asian countries (figure 5.15). In contrast, poverty reduction in the region at large was modest (from 41 to 36 percent in the same period), while the gap in per capita GDP with industrial countries either increased or remained the same for all other Latin American countries.

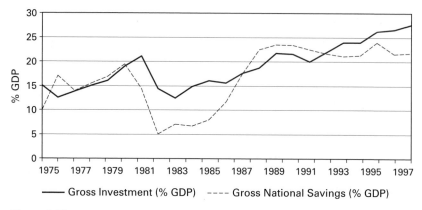

Figure 5.13
Gross fixed capital formation and gross national savings, 1975 to 2002
Source: Central Bank of Chile.

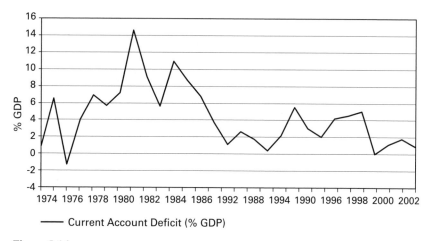

Figure 5.14
Current-account deficit, 1973 to 2002
Source: Central Bank of Chile.

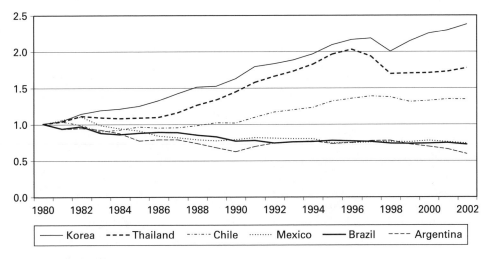

Figure 5.15
Relative gross domestic product (country's *j* per-capita GDP over U.S. per-capita GDP)
Source: Authors' estimations.
Note: 1980 = 1.

Reforms in the Aftermath of the Asian Crisis, 1998 to 2003

The Asian crisis hit the country through a sharp drop in the terms of trade and through contagion in financial markets. But because of the sound fundamentals—especially a strong and highly capitalized banking system—permanent effects were limited. In other words, as opposed to other emerging-market economies, the Asian and Russian crises of 1997 and 1998, respectively, had neither systemic nor permanent effects in Chile.

However, at the height of the turmoil, in the first and third quarters of 1998, the market pressure on the exchange rate was contained by sharply raising domestic interest rates. This policy response was motivated mainly by two reasons—first, the need to restrain aggregate spending (a necessary adjustment that was not properly supported by a restrained fiscal policy) and, second, a concern with the potential inflationary impact and balance-sheet effects of a large depreciation of the currency—or worse, an overshooting. This response, along with the

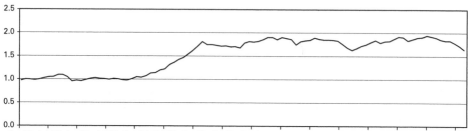

—— Non Performing Loans to Total Loans Ratio

Figure 5.16
Nonperforming loans to total loans ratio, 1996 to 2003
Source: Central Bank of Chile.

global slowdown and the drop in terms of trade, led to a short-lived recession in 1999. But the recession had a minor impact in banks' portfolios—nonperforming loans remained below 2 percent (figure 5.16) —although the sharp increase in interest rates in 1998 caused some distress in small and medium-sized enterprises whose effects have taken a while to fade away. All in all, the economy quickly recovered and resumed growth in 2000, though the average growth rate in the past three years has been much lower than during 1985 to 1997 (about 3 percent) (see table 5.1 and figure 5.8), mainly attributable to the global slowdown.

But during this latter period, the government has continued introducing policies and institutional changes to further consolidate the market-oriented economic model and to improve the resilience of the Chilean economy to shocks. Thus, in 1998 a law was passed unilaterally reducing the import tariff by one percentage point every year, stopping at 6 percent in January 2003. Furthermore, in 2002 Chile signed a free-trade agreement with the European Union, in 2003 with the United States, and in 2004 with South Korea, thus consolidating the process of integration with the world economy. Also, in 2001 the government committed to achieve and maintain a 1 percent structural fiscal surplus. Under this commitment, government expenditures are set to be 1 percent of GDP less than the government's *structural revenues*, which are defined as the revenues that would occur in steady state. In other words, expenditures are 1 percent less than the revenues that would occur if the economy were on its long-term path (after eliminating cyclical variations in taxes and other key variables such as the price of copper and the level of international interest rates). This rule is intended to guarantee that the government will remain solvent in the long run. And in the same year, all remaining capital controls were abolished, ending with more than half a century of a partly closed capital account. Also during this period, regulatory and tax changes were introduced to increase the efficiency of capital markets and provide incentives to save. The tax on capital gains in the stock market was abolished, voluntary (tax-free) contributions into the personal retirement savings accounts were allowed, the tax on interests paid to foreign investors in peso-denominated bonds was reduced from 35 to 4 percent, and some regulations affecting mutual funds and insurance companies were lifted.[7] And as already mentioned, during this period the exchange-rate band was abandoned, consolidating both the inflation targeting and the free-floating regimes. Finally, in 2003, three new laws were passed that (1) established a clearer career path for public servants, based on merits, by significantly reducing the scope for the government to appoint political allies in senior positions; (2) provided public funding for political parties; and (3) regulated private donations to political parties and candidates. These three laws should increase transparency, reduce the scope for corruption, and allow the public sector to attract more qualified personnel. The benefits derived from all the reforms above are expected to materialize in the future in the form of a higher and more sustainable economic growth when the world economy recovers from the current slowdown.

Growth and Institutions: Empirical Evidence on Chile

In the past three decades, the Chilean economy went from suffering a high degree of government intervention, being isolated from world markets, and running large macro imbalances to becoming a stable market-oriented economy where the private sector plays the main role in deciding what and how to produce. In this setting, market prices are the main device used for resource allocation decisions. In addition, self-correcting mechanisms have been put in place, and market discipline has been strengthened so that large imbalances are less likely to occur and the economy has become increasingly more resilient to shocks. Among these mechanisms are a floating exchange rate, limited deposit insurance, more stringent disclosure standards for banks, mandatory risk-rating of securities by specialized agencies,[8] a structural fiscal balance rule, and an inflation-targeting regime administered by an independent Central Bank. This economic transformation has led to a much more dynamic and fast-growing economy than in the past, supported by solid institutions as well as adequate economic policies.

As mentioned in the introduction, empirical studies show that large jumps in the rate of growth are driven mainly by changes in total factor productivity as opposed to greater usage of resources or factor accumulation, which, in turn, are determined by institutional factors.[9] It can be argued that Chile, after stabilizing its economy in the early 1970s, focused on strengthening and improving the quality of its institutions, although some mistakes were made and corrected along the way, particularly after the debt-crisis years. This whole process is still ongoing, but the country has already benefited from it.

Indeed, empirical analyses of the Chilean experience show that of the average annual growth of 7.3 percent during 1985 to 1997, more than one-third can be explained by gains in total factor productivity (figure 5.17). Furthermore, the gains in total factor productivity that appear when comparing the 1990s to previous decades can be explained mainly by the institutional changes and structural reforms of the 1970s that were deepened and improved during the 1980s (see tables 5.5 and 5.6).[10] For instance, Gallego and Loayza (2002) conclude that structural macro policies and the institutional buildup explain the bulk of the total difference in annual growth between 1970 to 1985 and 1986 to 1998 (table 5.6).

At this point, it is worth trying to figure out what explains the contrasting experience of Chile compared with the rest of the region, where despite a significant reform effort that began in the mid-1980s or early 1990s, countries have not yet seen the same kind of growth benefits. At least two explanations arise in this regard—(1) the time elapsed since Chile began its economic transformation and (2) the all-encompassing characteristic of the Chilean reform process including the pension system

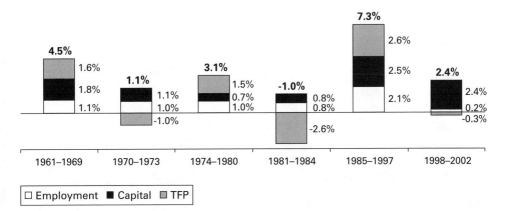

Figure 5.17
Solow's decomposition of Chile's economic growth
Source: Authors' estimations.

Table 5.5
Determinants of the jump in TFP growth during 1990 to 1998, compared to previous decades

	Compared to:		
	1961–1969	1970–1979	1980–1989
Total to be explained	2.5	4.6	4.5
Structural reforms	2.5	1.7	0.6
Fall in inflation	0.7	4.5	0.4
External conditions	−0.1	−3.2	0.9
Political rights	−0.7	1.6	2.3
Others	0.2	0	0.3

Source: Jadresic and Zahler (2000).

Table 5.6
Contribution to the change in growth, 1986 to 1998 and 1970 to 1985

Contribution	Percentage
Total difference in growth to be explained	4.74%
Unexplained	1.11
Explained	3.63
Initials conditions	0.14
Human capital	1.45
External conditions	−1.44
Structural macro policies	0.99
Institutions	1.23
Policy complementarities	1.26

Source: Gallego and Loayza (2002).

reform of the early 1980s, which provides a large savings base and has contributed to the development of the domestic capital markets and the adoption of better practices in corporate governance. With respect to the first argument, it should be acknowledged that Chile started its reforms in the mid-1970s, about a decade earlier than Mexico, the second country to reform. And the same logic applies to the second argument: Chile's reforms included macro, financial, and micro (overall set of incentives) areas. But more important, the reform process in Chile has continued (despite a few short-lived setbacks in the 1980s) over time and has been of much greater scope and depth, including the reshaping and strengthening of many of the country's institutions. In contrast, many Latin American countries have not even completed the so-called first-generation reforms. A clear example is Argentina, where the adoption of a Currency Board in the early 1990s did not put an end to the prevalent fiscal problems that have their origin in the provinces. Similarly, while as of 2002 Chile appeared to be the best-ranked emerging market economy in terms of the quality of its institutions,[11] in several countries in the region corruption and bureaucracy have not been reduced and property rights remain uncertain, while in a few others political instability has exacerbated recently.

In sum, Chile's outstanding performance can be attributed to its reform process, which has been more comprehensive (it has included not only economic policies but also institutions and has gone far beyond attaining macroeconomic stability), internally consistent, and persistent in time. The latter two points are worth emphasizing. Deciding on the adoption of a particular monetary or exchange-rate regime is not as important as ensuring the consistency of the policy framework. A currency board may work fine, as it does in Hong Kong, if other conditions are met—namely, fiscal discipline and price (wage) flexibility. Finally, the reform process must be continuous. Institutions and policies must be revised and upgraded constantly as domestic and external conditions change, rendering old regulations and institutions obsolete.

Related to the latter point, an open question is how the country avoided being taken off track in 1989 to 1999. By the time the political transition to democracy occurred, the country had already transformed many of its institutions, and the economy was in good health and working fine. Therefore, given the initial conditions, there was little doubt that the "new" economic-development model was the correct one and that there would not be a return to protectionism, fiscal deficits, high inflation, and the like. The policy changes introduced after the transition to democracy have emphasized social programs but for the most part have validated and strengthened the market-oriented reforms introduced since the mid-1970s.

Before closing this section, it is worth noting that the potential benefits to be accrued to the average Latin American country—excluding Chile—from strengthening its institutions and adopting better policies are large. Corbo, Hernández, and Parro (2004) compute the benefits in terms of per capita GDP growth of the average Latin American country adopting institutions of similar quality to Chile's or, even better, Finland's. They find that by having institutions of quality similar to Chile's, the average Latin American country could raise its per capita GDP growth rate by about 1.6 percent per year. Or better still, by having Finland's institutions, the increase would be about 2.3 percent per year.

Conclusions and Overall Policy Lessons

Chile's recent economic history vividly illustrates the importance of institutions in reaching higher and more sustainable economic growth and, equally or even more important, in enhancing an economy's resilience to shocks. In fact, in the past thirty years, the Chilean economy changed swiftly from one suffering from high inflation, large fiscal deficits, multiple exchange rates, financial repression, shortage of goods and services, and a high degree of government intervention to a market-oriented economy with low inflation, a solvent fiscal position, a floating exchange rate, and openness to both trade and financial flows. In the process, many of the country's political, legal, and economic institutions have been overhauled, updated, and strengthened. As a result, the economy experienced a period of rapid economic growth and decreasing inflation between 1985 and 1997, the longest period of fast growth ever. Also, the high growth and targeting of government spending toward the poor has resulted in marked improvements in social indicators as well as in a drastic reduction in poverty levels. But beyond that, during this period no major imbalance arose, and the economy muddled through the Asian and Russian crises relatively unscathed (at least when compared to other emerging market economies).

We strongly believe that Chile's success story is due to the breadth of its reform process, which continues to this date and has been much deeper and broader in scope than the one carried out in other countries. The reform has not only boosted the country's macro fundamentals, attaining macroeconomic stability, but has also upgraded and strengthened its institutions. The high payoff from Chile's reform is due to its scope and continuance through time.

But the institutional build-up process has not been free of trouble. It has had a learning-by-doing component. The debt crisis years of the early 1980s were partly the result of inadequate institutions, in particular those needed to contain moral-hazard and adverse-selection problems in financial markets. And recent problems regarding operational and settlement risks in capital markets—the Corfo-Inverlink affair—show that a lot remains to be done, especially at the micro level.

Drawing from the Chilean experience, Latin American countries should put additional effort into their own reform processes, in many cases completing the so-called first-generation reforms—fiscal stability, trade liberalization, and inflation reduction. But there is also the need to advance second-generation reforms—upgrading the supervisory and regulatory framework of banks, enhancing market competition and market discipline, upgrading the regulatory framework for utilities (including a clear rate-setting mechanism), putting in place a framework for private-sector participation in infrastructure development, and reorganizing pension systems. All these reforms must be implemented irrespective of their difficulty because progress in all areas is needed as reforms are complementary to one another, and stagnation in one area may jeopardize the success of the reforms in others. Beyond that, there are no easy policy recommendations as reforms cannot be easily replicated from one country to the next. Each country has to design and implement its own policies, taking into account its own characteristics: the way China has proceeded in the past two decades is certainly not a replica of measures taken elsewhere.

Nevertheless, the difficulty of the process and the time it takes for reforms to be implemented cannot be an excuse not to do it. The sooner the process gets started, the better for the economy as a whole. In fact, since financial integration and the advances in communications and IT are here to stay, countries can hardly avoid getting their economies in order, both at the macro level (by putting in place mutually consistent fiscal, monetary, and exchange-rate policies) and at the institutional level (by reforming their laws and institutions to provide the right incentives and promote stable rules). Furthermore, the reform process must be permanent as countries should be constantly searching for institutional bottlenecks threatening to slow down growth.

Notes

This paper was prepared for presentation at the National Bank of Poland Conference on Successes and Failures in Real Convergence, Warsaw, October 23–24, 2003. We thank Fernando Parro for his very efficient research assistance.

1. Over the past 190 years, the difference in per-capita income between rich and poor countries has widened notoriously. In fact, in 1830 the ratio of per-capita income between the poorest and richest countries was about one to three; today the same ratio is about one to five hundred (Maddison 2001). Thus, through all these decades some countries—Australia, South Korea, and the United States, among others—have experienced much higher rates of factor accumulation, productivity gains, or both, than others.

2. See Acemoglu, Johnson, and Robinson (2001), Easterly and Levine (2003), Easterly (2002), and Rodrik, Subramanian, and Trebbi (2002).

3. The real exchange-rate appreciation was partly caused by the widespread use of backward indexation mechanisms, especially in wage setting. The latter had been institutionalized in a new labor code introduced in 1979. But it was also partly the result of the large capital inflows—which, in turn, were motivated by the incentives in place in the financial system—that financed a growing current-account deficit.

4. The fiscal cost of the financial crisis is estimated at close to 40 percent of GDP. For more details on the Chilean banking crisis of the 1980s, see Barandiarán and Hernández (1999).

5. Pursuant to the law, the Central Bank is run by a board composed of five members, each one appointed for a term of ten years: every two years a new member is appointed. Board members are nominated by the government but need approval of the Senate. The governor is then chosen among the five board members by the country's president for a period of five years or the time remaining in the member's term, whatever is shorter. The deputy governor is chosen by vote among the other members of the Central Bank Board.

6. Thus, an inflation that started to develop in 1860 was finally controlled by the late 1990s.

7. Capital Markets Reform I.

8. This is a requirement for all publicly issued securities seeking the interest of the pension funds and other institutional investors.

9. The main factors affecting total factor productivity are trade openness, financial development, quality of governance, degree of corruption, quality of the labor force (education), government size, and degree of bureaucracy.

10. Although some authors they do not provide an explanation for the transmission mechanisms, they attribute part of the rise in total factor productivity during the 1990s to the return to democracy (Jadresic and Zahler 2000).

11. This is measured by averaging six categories that include voice and accountability, political instability and violence, government effectiveness, regulatory burden, rule of law, and grant or control of corruption (Kaufmann, Kraay, and Mastruzzi 2003).

References

Acemoglu, D., S. Johnson, and J. Robinson. (2001). "The Colonial Origins of Comparative Development: An Empirical Investigation." *American Economic Review, 91*: 1369–1401.

Barandiarán, E., and L. Hernández. (1999). "Origins and Resolution of a Banking Crisis: Chile 1982–86." Central Bank of Chile, Working Paper No. 59.

Corbo, V., and S. Fischer. (1994). "Lessons from Chilean Stabilization and Recovery." In B. Bosworth, R. Dornbusch, and R. Labán (Eds.), *The Chilean Economy, Policy Lessons and Challenges*. Washington, DC: Brookings Institution.

Corbo, V., L. Hernández, and F. Parro. (2005). "Institutions, Economic Policies, Growth: Lessons from the Chilean Experience." Working Paper 17. Santiago, Chile: Central Bank of Chile.

Corbo, V., and K. Schmidt-Hebbel. (2003). "Efectos Macroeconómicos de la Reforma de Pensiones en Chile." In CIEDESS (Ed.), *Resultados y Desafíos de las Reformas a las Pensiones*. Santiago, Chile: Federación Internacional de Administradoras de Fondos de Pensiones.

Easterly, W. (2002). *The Elusive Quest for Growth*. Cambridge, MA: MIT Press.

Easterly, W., and R. Levine. (2003). "Tropics, Germs and Crops: How Endowments Influence Economic Development." *Journal of Monetary Economics, 50*: 3–39.

Gallego, F., and N. Loayza. (2002). "The Golden Period for Growth in Chile." In N. Loayza and R. Soto (Eds.), *Economic Growth: Sources, Trends and Cycles*. Santiago: Central Bank of Chile.

Held, G. (1989). "Regulación y Supervisión de la Banca en la Experiencia de Liberalización Financiera en Chile (1974–88)." Mimeo, Economic Commission for Latin America and the Caribbean (ECLAC), Santiago.

Hernández, L., and E. Walker. (1993). "Estructura de Financiamiento Corporativo en Chile (1978–1990): Evidencia a Partir de Datos Contables." *Estudios Públicos, 51*: 87–156.

Jadresic, E., and R. Zahler. (2000). "Chile's Rapid Growth in the 1990s: Good Policies, Good Luck, or Political Change?" Working Paper No. 153, Washington, DC, International Monetary Fund.

Kaufmann, D., A. Kraay, and M. Mastruzzi. (2003). "Governance Matters III: Governance Indicators for 1996–2002." Washington, D.C.: World Bank.

Maddison, A. (2001). *The World Economy: A Millennial Perspective*. Paris: OECD.

Modigliani, F., and M. Miller. (1963). "Corporate Income Taxes and the Cost of Capital: A Correction." *American Economic Review, 53*: 433–492.

Rodrik, D., A. Subramanian, and F. Trebbi. (2002). "Institutions Rule: The Primacy of Institutions over Geography and Integration in Economic Development." Working Paper No. 9305, NBER.

6

Economic Resurgence in the Commonwealth of Independent States

Anders Åslund

During the first decade of postcommunist economic transformation, the pattern of economic reform was clear and evident. After 1989, central Europe[1] undertook early, radical, and successful economic reforms, while the twelve members of Commonwealth of Independent States (CIS)[2] pursued slow, gradual, and unsuccessful reforms.

As a result, the aggregate decline in GDP after 1989 was 19 percent in central Europe, 29 percent in Romania and Bulgaria, 44 percent in the Baltics, and 53 percent in the CIS. Moreover, central Europe hit its bottom relatively early in 1992, while the CIS reached it only in 1998. These output declines were highly exaggerated by multiple statistical biases, but a reasonable assessment is that the real decline was about half of the official plunge (Åslund 2002, chap. 4).[3]

The conventional wisdom became that central Europe did everything right and that the CIS countries did everything wrong both economically and politically. By and large, this held true until 1998, the year of the Russian financial crash. The CIS countries lagged behind east-central Europe not only in official economic growth but also in democracy, economic deregulation, financial stabilization, and privatization, and there were strong positive correlations between all these factors (Berg, Borensztein, Sahay, and Zettelmeyer 1999; EBRD 1999; Åslund 2002). Skeptics argued that the distance from Brussels—that is, the European Union—determined the success of transformation.

Since 1999, however, the picture has changed completely. The central European countries had an average annual growth rate of 3 percent from 1998 to 2003, while the nine CIS countries (CIS9) with market economies (Moldova, Ukraine, Russia, Armenia, Azerbaijan, Georgia,

Kazakhstan, Kyrgyzstan, and Tajikistan) have reached an average annual growth rate of 8 percent since 2001. All of a sudden, most CIS countries have had a rate of economic growth more than twice as high as the central European countries. Admittedly, these nine countries are a varied group in terms of economic structure and development, but their postcommunist experiences have been similar, as are their current economic development trends. The purpose of this chapter is to contrast the economic development of these nine CIS countries with the central European countries (CE4) (Poland, the Czech Republic, Slovakia, and Hungary) and to investigate whether the CIS reform countries might be on their way to catching up with central Europe. Three post-Soviet countries (Belarus, Turkmenistan, and Uzbekistan) have stopped short of the transition to capitalism and are not discussed in this chapter. The Baltic countries and southeast Europe cover a middle ground in various ways, so the focus here is on a comparison between the nine CIS reformers and the central European four to achieve the clearest contrast.

Five years is too short a period to say anything definite about long-term economic tendencies, especially in the face of a sharp reversal of prior trends. Economic growth depends on many different factors. Our tentative conclusions must therefore stay hypotheses. Still, considering the large number of countries involved—nine versus four—such a study should be able to say something about plausible long-term developments. Because of the limited period and the peculiarities of the starting point (just after a major output decline and financial crash), we abstain from a full-fledged regression analysis. Moreover, regression analysis reveals correlation but not necessarily causality, and the goal here is to investigate causality. As is shown, several correlations run counter not only to conventional wisdom but also to standard theory and broader multi-country regressions. The aim is exploratory—to establish these strange correlations rather than to submerge them by controlling for various factors. Throughout the chapter, all averages are unweighted because we are interested in qualitative features, rendering each country equally interesting. Weighted averages immediately lead to a dominance of Russia and Poland in the respective country group.

It is important to remember developments in the prior transition. Sheer recovery growth utilizing free capacity is easier to accomplish than growth based on the expansion of capacity. After their large output fall, many postcommunist countries possessed ample excess capacity, and it was much larger in the post-Soviet countries than in central Europe. Several countries achieved high growth in the early stages of their recovery, while their performances diverged later on. Therefore, the relevance of averages is not obvious, and the last year measured is always subject to vagaries. Yet the divergencies in economic growth between the CIS countries and central Europe have been amplified, suggesting that the apparent new trends may last for some time.

Differing Growth Records beyond the Transition

From 1998 to 2003, the nine reformist CIS countries had an average annual GDP growth rate of 6.8 percent, compared with an average GDP growth of 3.0 percent for the four central European countries. This is a big difference. For the last three years, it has risen to an average annual growth of 8.0 percent for the CIS9 versus 3.0 percent for the central European four (figure 6.1). A discrepancy of five percentage units for a

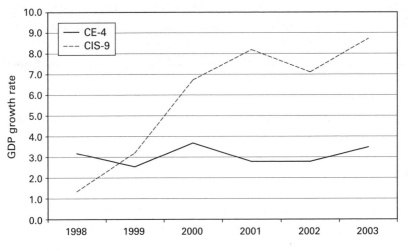

Figure 6.1
GDP growth rates in four central European and nine reformist CIS countries, 1998 to 2003
Source: Table 6.1.

period of three years between two groups of multiple countries suggests that a significant economic diversity has emerged.

To clarify the situation, it is useful to have a look at a table with the annual growth rates for all the countries involved from 1999 to 2003. As can be seen from table 6.1, there is a broad trend that almost all the CIS countries have grown faster every year than almost all the central European countries. After 1999, there are hardly any outliers or relevant statistical caveats, so this is a real general trend. Statistics are shaky, but growth rates are usually perceived as much more reliable statistics than data on the size of GDP, assuming that the size of the underground economy changes only slowly.

The world appears to have turned upside down. What was true of postcommunist economic performance before 1999 appears to have been false since then. In the early transition, the CIS countries were lagging far behind the central Europeans in all market reforms. They are still behind, but all these countries have developed reasonably normal market economies. Figure 6.2 shows a composite transition index, based on measurements of systemic transformation provided by the European Bank for Reconstruction and Development (EBRD).

Since 1998, minimal changes have occurred in the EBRD index, which cast doubt on the relevance of this index after 1998. It looks as if the measurers have gone to sleep because in real life a great deal has happened. Major structural reforms, such as the elimination of barter and radical tax reforms, have had no apparent impact on the transition index, leaving us wondering what this index actually measures.

In the early transition, the key to economic growth was to control inflation. Admittedly, little effect was seen after inflation had been brought down under 40 percent a year (Bruno and Easterly 1998). In 2003, all market economies in the region had inflation under control. In central Europe, average inflation stopped at 3.5 percent a year, while it was 7.2 percent in the nine CIS reformers (EBRD 2003, p. 58). Inflation can hardly explain the difference in performance, and it weighs against the CIS countries.

The degree of deregulation, especially of prices and foreign trade, has appeared to have had the greatest impact on growth in the first decade of transition (Berg, Borensztein, Sahay, and Zettelmeyer 1999). By 2003,

Table 6.1
Annual GDP growth rates (percentage) in four central European and nine reformist CIS countries, 1998 to 2003

	1998	1999	2000	2001	2002	2003	Average (2001–2003)	Average (1999–2003)
Czech Republic	−1.0%	0.5%	3.3%	3.1%	2.0%	2.9%	2.7%	2.4%
Hungary	4.9	4.2	5.2	3.7	3.3	2.9	3.3	3.9
Poland	4.8	4.1	4.0	1.0	1.4	3.7	2.0	2.8
Slovakia	4.0	1.3	2.2	3.3	4.4	4.4	4.0	3.1
CE4	3.2	2.5	3.7	2.8	2.8	3.5	3.0	3.0
Armenia	7.3	3.3	6.0	9.6	12.9	13.9	12.1	9.1
Azerbaijan	10.0	9.5	11.1	9.9	10.6	11.2	10.6	10.5
Georgia	2.9	3.0	1.9	4.7	5.6	8.6	6.3	4.8
Kazakhstan	−1.9	2.7	9.8	13.5	9.5	9.2	10.7	8.9
Kyrgyzstan	2.1	3.7	5.4	5.3	−0.5	5.5	3.4	3.9
Moldova	−6.5	−3.4	2.1	6.1	7.2	6.3	6.5	3.7
Russia	−5.3	6.4	10.0	5.0	4.7	7.3	5.7	6.7
Tajikistan	5.3	3.7	8.3	10.3	9.1	7.1	8.8	7.7
Ukraine	−1.9	−0.2	5.9	9.2	4.8	9.3	7.8	5.8
CIS9	1.3	3.2	6.7	8.2	7.1	8.7	8.0	6.8

Source: EBRD (2003). Assembled official statistics for 2003.

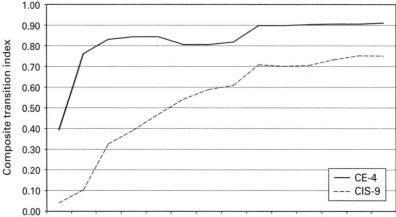

Figure 6.2
Composite transition index for four central European and nine reformist CIS
countries, 1990 to 2003
Source: De Melo et al. (1997); Havrylyshyn and Wolf (1999, p. 34); Åslund
(2002); EBRD (2001, pp. 12, 14); EBRD (2002, p. 20); EBRD (2003, p. 16).

these two EBRD indicators have become all but meaningless for all these
postcommunist economies because virtually all of them had reached the
highest EBRD indicator (EBRD 2003, p. 16). Nor does deregulation appear to be a likely explanation of variations in economic performance.

With regard to privatization, all these postcommunist economies are
similar. By the rather rough EBRD estimate, the private sector generates
from 60 to 80 percent of GDP in these countries (EBRD 2003, p. 16),
with the exception of the slow reformers Moldova and Tajikistan, where
it is only 50 percent of GDP. The average for central Europe is 79 percent, compared with 62 percent in the nine CIS reformist countries. As
privatization has been a positive factor in prior regressions, it does not
appear likely that it has turned negative, especially as it is overwhelm-
ingly privatized industries that have provided the economic expansion
in the CIS countries.

Without pursuing this analysis further, it appears obvious that the differences in economic performance between these thirteen postcommunist
countries can no longer be explained by the transition indicators that
mattered the most in the first decade of transition.

Public discussions tend to focus on the growth performance of Russia and discard it as an effect of high oil prices and sharp devaluation after 1998. However, after five years of high economic growth and substantial real revaluation, the Russian growth rate appears to be accelerating rather than fading. Moreover, Russia's growth rate is actually slightly below the average for the reformist CIS countries, most of which are energy importers. Oil prices and devaluation cannot be the prime explanation, although they kick-started the Russian economy.

Implications of Standard Growth Theory

During the first decade of transition, differences in economic performance among postcommunist countries could be explained with elementary deregulation, financial stabilization, and privatization. As discussed above, all of these countries have now reached quite far in all these regards, and the remaining minor differences are rather negatively correlated with growth. In our investigation, it is therefore natural to turn to modern growth theory, which focuses more on long-term potential and its utilization (Barro and Sala-i-Martin 2004; Sala-i-Martin 1997).

In general, growth is largely explained by prior economic level, economic resources (labor, capital, or investment, including human capital and technology), and the ability to utilize these resources—that is, institutions. However, neither investment nor technology appear relevant explanations of growth in postcommunist transition in the CIS countries. President Vladimir Putin's economic adviser, Andrei Illarionov, usually shows a scatter graph correlating investment as a share of GDP with economic growth. Contrary to ordinary growth theory, Russia actually shows a strongly negative correlation between investment and economic growth over the period 1993 to 2002 (figure 6.3).

This can be explained by several factors. Both physical and human capital was ample and underemployed throughout the region. Investment stayed high, reflecting a soft budget constraint and related waste rather than real investment. Moreover, public investment has steadily fallen as share of total investment, and public investment was never very efficient. Presumably, private investment would be positively correlated to growth, but that indicator is not readily available for most of

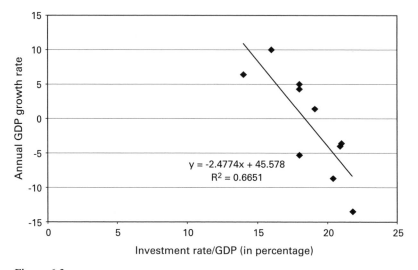

Figure 6.3
Investment rate as proportion of GDP versus GDP growth rate in Russia, 1993 to 2002
Source: EBRD (2001, 2002, 2003).

these countries. If we instead examine the increase in investment in fixed assets and GDP growth in the same year for several transition countries, we find the usual, strong positive correlation between investment and economic growth (figure 6.4). Presumably, an increase in investment reflects rational private investment, while the investment ratio as a whole harbors a lot of unproductive public investment.

Similarly, at this time of restructuring with ample free resources, innovation was not essential for economic growth, while the utilization of available technology was, which is not easily measured. Thus, we dare disregard investment in fixed assets and human capital as well as technology.

Instead, institutional factors appear crucial to growth, while institutions are such a broad and vague concept that everybody tends to have his or her own favorite institutions. Without making any strong theoretical claim, we focus on big apparent contrasts between central Europe and the CIS reformers that are related to economic institutions and have emerged in the last few years and might explain the impressive rise in the latters' economic growth.

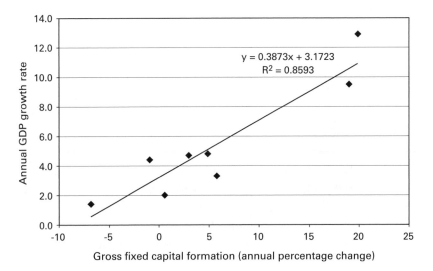

Figure 6.4
Gross fixed capital formation versus GDP growth rate in four central European and four reformist central European countries, 2002
Source: EBRD (2003); table 6.1.
Note: Data not available for Azerbaijan, Georgia, Kyrgyzstan, Moldova, or Tajikistan.

The most striking divide is in public finances—namely, the share of public redistribution in GDP, tax systems, and budget discipline. Another disparity involves labor-market policy. A third one concerns environmental regulation. A fourth great difference lies in the rule of law, as reflected in corruption. Besides, we need to control for the laggard effect—that is, everything else being equal, poorer economies can catch up by imitating richer economies. This chapter disregards external factors, such as market access and foreign investment, as they benefit the central European four (Åslund and Warner 2003). In fact, all the postcommunist market economies are very open economies.

Public Redistribution and Tax System: Keys to Postcommunist Growth?

One of the outstanding features of Western Europe is high public redistribution in the range of 45 to 50 percent of GDP. The socialist economies had about as great a degree of public redistribution. Therefore, this share of public redistribution was widely accepted as natural for post-communist countries, not only by their governments and the EU but even by the IMF and the World Bank.

The Central Europeans swiftly defeated high inflation, and they have continued to collect as large state revenues as before. The CIS countries, by contrast, were unable to do so, facing large and chronic budget deficits until the Russian financial crash of 1998. At that moment, all these governments realized that their only salvation was to adjust their public expenditures to their revenues, and they cut public expenditures dramatically. Today, the difference in public expenditures as a share of GDP is striking—46 percent in the four Central European countries compared with 26 percent in the nine reformist CIS countries in 2002 (figure 6.5).

One reason that the CIS countries were capable of such drastic cuts was their huge enterprise subsidies. According to a World Bank assessment, implicit and explicit enterprise subsidies in Russia amounted to no less than 16 percent of GDP in 1998 (Pinto, Drebentsov, and Morozov 1999). Market economies usually disburse a few percentage of GDP

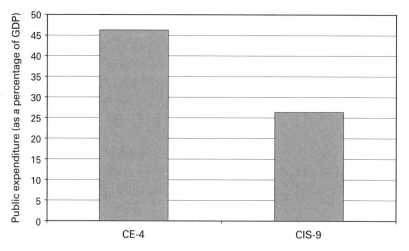

Figure 6.5
Public expenditures in four central European and nine reformist CIS countries, 2002
Sources: Revenue elargissement, Jan. 12, 2004; IMF Country Reports, 2002–2003.

in direct enterprise subsidies, while their social transfers often are huge. Because so much of public expenditures consisted of enterprise subsidies in Russia and other CIS countries, public expenditures could be cut without any perceivable social suffering. On the contrary, their reduction facilitated growth because of the related elimination of barter and the subsequent leveling of the playing field. Therefore, most CIS countries cut their public expenditures by about one-tenth of GDP around Russia's financial crisis of 1998, and much of this sharp reduction fell on enterprise subsidies (Owen and Robinson 2003, p. 101). This is probably a major cause of the rebound of economic growth in the CIS countries. In central Europe, however, public expenditures are predominantly directed to social transfers, which renders it much more difficult to reduce public expenditures there, although social transfers are also likely to reduce growth by weakening the incentives to work.

As economists believing that the market allocates resources more efficiently than the state, we would expect that lower public expenditures would result in higher economic growth (Tanzi and Schuknecht 2000). Figure 6.6 indicates quite a strong positive correlation between low public expenditures and high economic growth. Our hypothesis is that this is the main cause of economic growth being so much higher in the CIS countries than in central Europe.

Strangely, multicountry economic-growth regressions have by and large not shown the very plausible correlation between lower public redistribution and economic welfare. Instead, the broader conclusion is that the quality of government is more important (La Porta, Lopez-de-Silanes, Shleifer, and Vishny 1999; Sala-i-Martin 2002). However, these regressions do not say anything about causality. The Scandinavian countries can get away with big government because of its high quality. For postcommunist countries, the interesting question is how to attain economic growth in the presence of corrupt government. To cure corruption swiftly is not a plausible option, and growth itself is a major cure of corruption. Public expenditures, however, can be cut swiftly, and the first post-Soviet countries that took off (Armenia, Georgia, and Kyrgyzstan) first cut their public expenditures sharply (Åslund 2002, pp. 152–155). Similarly, Russia and Ukraine achieved economic growth only after substantial public expenditure cuts following the financial crisis of 1998.

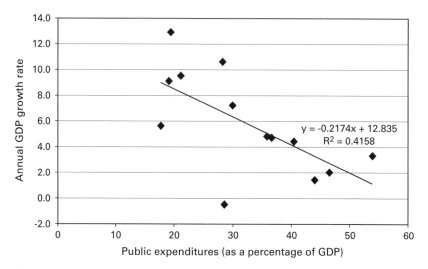

Figure 6.6
Public expenditures as a share of GDP versus GDP growth rate in four central
European and nine reformist CIS countries, 2002
Sources: Revenue elargissement, Jan. 12, 2004; IMF Country Reports, 2002–
2003; table 6.1.

The attitudes to fiscal discipline have undergone a reversal in the
course of the transition. In the early transition, the central European
countries brought their budget deficits under control relatively fast, but
today they maintain steady, large deficits of about 7 percent of GDP
from 2000 to 2003. The CIS reformers, by contrast, had huge deficits
until 1998, but it cost them dearly, and now they have learned their
lesson. The maintain almost balanced budgets with an average deficit of
about 1 percent of GDP in the same period (figure 6.7).

In the early transition, all postcommunist countries adopted amazingly
high tax rates. On the one hand, they thought they needed to maintain
their high public expenditures, and, on the other, they anticipated poor
tax collection. Furthermore, the IMF and the World Bank encouraged
this boosting of tax rates. Gradually, one country after the other reduced
its tax rates. The Baltic countries pioneered radical tax reform around
1994, reducing the number of taxes and introducing low, flat tax rates.
Estonia was the first country to adopt a flat income tax—of as much as
26 percent. Latvia followed with a flat income tax of 25 percent. These

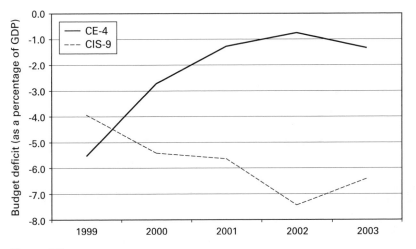

Figure 6.7
Budget deficit as a share of GDP in four central European and nine reformist CIS
countries, 1999 to 2003
Source: EBRD (2003).

Baltic countries did so because of a belief that radical liberal economic
reform would lower public revenues and expenditures. Gradually, the
CIS countries that realized that they had failed to collect their many
high taxes. Georgia opted for a 20 percent flat income tax as early as
1994. Finally, Russia took the prize with a flat income tax of only 13
percent from 2000, and Ukraine followed in 2004. Most reformist CIS
countries have reduced their number of taxes and tax rates radically.
They have also slashed payroll taxes, made them regressive, and cut
profit taxes and value-added taxes. Estonia has abolished the corporate
profit tax altogether, while Kyrgyzstan has minimized it at 10 percent.
Poland, Slovakia, Lithuania, and Latvia have all adopted profit tax rates
of 19 percent.

The rest of central Europe has done little, with the exception of Slovakia, which bravely introduced both a flat personal income tax and a
profit tax of 19 percent before entering the EU (Miklos 2003). Russia
and Ukraine's flat income tax of 13 percent compares with a progressive
income tax peaking at 40 percent in Poland, and the Czech Republic
and Hungary retain similar taxes (Åslund 2002, pp. 228–234). Although
social payroll taxes are still too high in the CIS countries, they have come

down. Kazakhstan leads the pack with a payroll tax of 20 percent, but taxes stay high in central Europe—for instance, 48 percent in Poland.

As early as 1992, Janos Kornai (1992) called the central European countries "premature welfare states." In a seminal paper from 1996, Jeffrey Sachs and Andrew Warner (1996) calculated that the central European countries would not achieve a high growth rate or catch up economically with the European Union if they did not reduce their taxes and social transfers. Unfortunately, their predictions have come true. Postcommunist central Europe never experienced any period of double-digit growth. The peak was 1995 to 1997, when Poland and Slovakia grew by slightly over 6 percent a year. The EU may have many sympathetic features, but economic dynamism is not one of them.

Some argue that these CIS reforms "represented a surrender in the face of widespread bribery and tax evasion, not the victory of a liberal agenda" (Stefes 2003), but liberal thinking develops and wins in such situations. The great liberal revolutions of the 1840s were reactions to the corrupt feudal system. The classical liberal philosophers took the evilness of the state for granted (see Mill 1975), as CIS reformers wisely do. Therefore, economic liberalism won ground in the mid-nineteenth century, as it is now doing in the CIS. In Moscow, extreme liberal thinking is in evidence. Notably, the influential economic thinker Vitaly Naishul (1994) has advocated a true nightwatch state with only 2 percent of GDP in public expenditures. Social democracy requires a belief that the state good, and social democratic parties have grown strong in central Europe, while they are virtually absent throughout the CIS, where few can believe that the postcommunist state may be good, which is the social democratic and West European creed.

Labor-Market Regulation and Payroll Taxes

Another outstanding feature of both the old European social democratic model and socialist economies was heavily regulated labor markets, which were stifled in three ways: direct labor-market regulation, payroll taxes, and social transfers.

Only a few postcommunist countries have formally deregulated their labor markets—notably, Estonia, Latvia, and Kazakhstan, which have all adopted labor codes inspired by the New Zealand labor code, which stands out as a model for liberal Anglo-American labor-market policies. Basic tenets are individual labor contracts and their easy severance. Central Europe, as well as most CIS countries, have maintained heavy regulation of their labor markets, but there is one important difference. In the CIS countries, state regulation is circumvented or even disregarded, rendering labor markets quite free, while labor-market regulations are taken seriously in central Europe.

The greatest apparent difference lies in the social payroll taxes. Most socialist countries had payroll taxes of about 38 percent. After communism, they were boosted to cater for greater social and unemployment protection. The payroll tax peaked at 60 percent in Hungary. Today, payroll taxes have been reduced in many countries, and the picture is as varied as it is fluid. Yet by and large, they have fallen more in the CIS countries than in central Europe. In the CIS, Kazakhstan has taken the lead by cutting its payroll taxes to merely 20 percent and making them regressive like the U.S. social security tax, while the payroll taxes remain high at 48 percent in Poland.

To this can be added the high personal income taxes and social transfers in central Europe discussed above. As expected, the combination of high taxes, high social transfers, and substantial social regulation has led to high unemployment in central Europe, notably 20 percent in Poland and similar heights in Slovakia and Bulgaria, while Russia, which has the best unemployment surveys among the CIS countries, has barely half that unemployment, 8 percent, notwithstanding restructuring and inevitable great regional disparities.

The EU directives on social and employment policies, the European trade unions, and the examples of nonreforming Germany, France, and Italy will not help Poland to liberalize its labor market. East Germany, in particular, appears stuck in a social-welfare trap. It was the first postcommunist country to become a member of the EU, swiftly adopting the whole of *acquis communautaire*. Arguably, its mistake was to price itself out of the market by submitting to West German interest groups that insisted on nearly Western wage levels and the same social benefits (Pickel and Wiesenthal 1997), but the *acquis communautaire* both set the standards and closed the social welfare trap. It also reached the highest official unemployment rate of any postcommunist country at 35 percent (Siebert 1992). Plainly, Russia and Kazakhstan offer better incentives for employers to hire people and for people to work.

Environmental Regulation: Impediment to Growth

The Soviet Union had probably the most ambitious environmental legislation in the world. Unfortunately, most of it has survived. The saving grace is that it is not taken seriously, even if environmental inspectors exploit it for their extraction of bribes. The European Union has environmental legislation that is almost as ambitious, but it is taken seriously.

Alan Mayhew (2000) has estimated the cost to Poland of introducing the 320 EU environment directives and arrived at the staggering sum of 4 to 8 percent of current GDP for the next twenty years. Mayhew and Orlowski (1998) have also calculated that the cost for Poland of complying with EU directives on standards and safety rules in transportation would be somewhat less. Other estimates are lower, but nobody seems to think that the cost to Poland of EU entry will be less than 3 to 4 percent of GDP a year. Most argue that the central European countries need to raise their standards, but the question is how fast. It appears doubtful whether it is advantageous to accept these high costs at this stage of economic development.[4]

The EU regulatory system may put the new EU accession countries in a poverty trap. Again, it is worth remembering hapless East Germany, which adopted the whole of *acquis communautaire* instantly. In spite of huge West German spending on infrastructure and social benefits in East Germany, East German growth remains disappointing (World Bank 2002). Although CIS legislation might be about as rigorous as EU legislation, it does not impede economic growth to the same extent since it is widely ignored.

Positive Correlation between Corruption and Growth

In the general growth literature, corruption has an unequivocally negative impact on growth (Mauro 1995). The persistent accusation against the CIS countries is their far-reaching corruption. There are several mea-

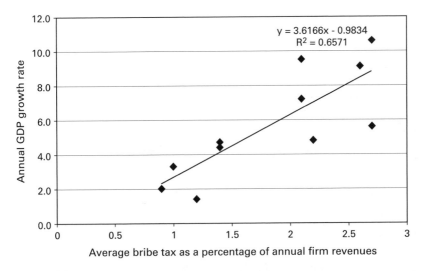

Figure 6.8
Bribe tax versus GDP growth rate in four central Eastern and nine reformist CIS countries, 2002
Source: EBRD (2002, p. 28).
Note: The outliers Armenia and Kyrgyzstan have been removed.

sures of corruption, and they do suggest that the CIS countries have been persistently far more corrupt than the central European countries, which should have a negative impact on their growth.

However, if a scatter graph for 2002 is drawn with the bribe tax of the World Bank and EBRD survey and actual growth rates this year, there is a relatively strong *positive* correlation between corruption and growth (figure 6.8).[5]

If we instead repeat the same exercise with the other major corruption index, the corruption-perceptions index of Transparency International, we also get a clear positive correlation between corruption and growth (figure 6.9). Because it is not plausible that corruption would have a positive impact on economic growth, there are two possible ways of explaining this apparent paradox. One is the development of corruption. Unfortunately, no good statistical time series over corruption exists. It is difficult to establish this change in other indicators of corruption. The corruption-perceptions index of Transparency International (2004) is somewhat useful for this purpose, but it does not evidence any clear

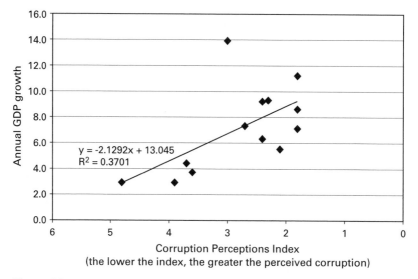

Figure 6.9
Corruption-perceptions index versus GDP growth rate in four central European and nine reformist CIS countries, 2003
Sources: Transparency International (2004); table 6.1.

tendencies. The World Bank and the EBRD, however, carried out large business surveys in most postcommunist countries in 1999 and 2002. They measured the bribe tax as a share of sales. In 1999, it was much smaller in east-central Europe at 1.2 percent, but it stayed the same in 2002. In the nine reformist CIS countries, the bribe tax was on average 3.0 percent in 1999, but it fell substantially to 2.3 percent in 2002 (EBRD 2003, p. 28). If this measurement is correct, it is possibly one of the fastest declines in corruption the world has ever seen.

An alternative explanation is the usual problem of multicausality. Public revenues collapsed in countries with very high inflation, which also aggravated already severe corruption. Thus, high corruption and a sharp reduction of public expenditures went together. There are strong reasons to believe that corruption would fall with less public redistribution and lower taxes, but corruption does tend to be sticky (Treisman 2000). The reformist CIS countries achieved high economic growth only after they had managed to reduce their public expenditures and adjusted them to limited revenues, but corruption stayed high (Åslund 2002, chap. 4).

Thus, high corruption and low public redistribution are causally inter-linked, but it is the reduction of public redistribution that drives growth, while corruption rather impedes it. However, the negative impact of corruption is less than the positive impact from low public redistribution. Moreover, corruption tends to fall with economic growth (Treisman 2000).

Curious Effects of Democracy

In general, democracy and market economies develop together, but historically this relationship is tenuous and not necessarily close (Lindblom 1977). Market economies are more prevalent than democracies. Since 1989, no fewer than twenty-eight countries, from Albania in Europe and to Mongolia in Asia, have abandoned communism. Out of these twenty-eight countries, no less than twenty-five have became market economies, while only thirteen are accepted as full democracies by Freedom House (2004).

During the first decade of transition, the correlation between democracy (political rights and civil liberties as assessed by Freedom House) and economic growth appeared remarkably strong, though Freedom House did not extend its survey to most of the CIS until the end of the 1990s. With the increased growth in the not very democratic CIS countries from 1999, the correlation between democracy and growth turned topsy-turvy from strongly positive to clearly negative in 2003 (figure 6.10).

Now the story is becoming more complicated. The easiest explanation is the multiple effects of EU accession. All the prospective members of the EU are full-fledged democracies because this is one of the fundamental requirements of this very attractive club.

Unfortunately, the EU's impact on economic growth might be less beneficial. New institutional economics teaches us the importance of economic systems and their incentives (e.g., North 1981). The Common Agricultural Policy and EU fishery policy are obviously harmful. Other important institutions are the public redistribution of GDP, the tax system, labor-market regulation, environmental regulations, technical regulations, and corruption. In almost all these regards, the EU is having negative impact.

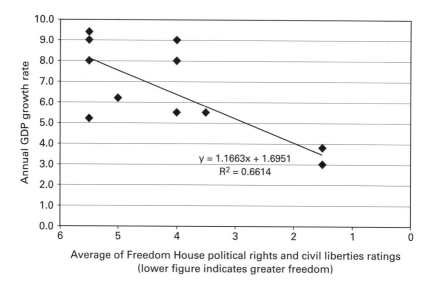

Figure 6.10
Democracy rating versus GDP growth in four central Eastern and nine reformist
CIS countries, 2003
Sources: Freedom House (2004); table 6.1.

The EU is economically a double-edged sword. After all, in the last
decade Europe's strongest economy, Germany, has barely grown by 1.5
percent a year, which amounts to virtual stagnation in per capita terms.
Although the German economic model might appear an extreme version
of the EU model, most EU countries are sufficiently similar so that we
can speak of an EU model. Slovakia's minister of finance, Ivan Miklos
(2003), puts it bluntly: "Europe is hindered by labor market inflexibility,
heavy tax burdens, bloated public sectors, and other competitive constraints, and the gap between the United States and Europe continues to
widen rather than shrink."

Naturally, these facts are being noticed in the CIS. The liberal Russian
economists Vladimir Mau and V. Novikov have analyzed what the *acquis
communautaire* would mean for Russia, classifying its thirty chapters as
desirable, disadvantageous, useful but not essential, or irrelevant. Their
list of advantages is short—the four freedoms (of goods trade, movement
of people, service trade, and movement of capital), the Customs Union,
and company legislation. They consider equally many chapters of the

acquis communautaire as disadvantageous: the Common Agricultural Policy, the fishery policy, taxation, social and employment policy, environmental regulation, and consumer protection. They classify eleven chapters as irrelevant and six as beneficial but nonessential. Competition policy and state aids are considered partly harmful and partly desirable.

The apparent new negative effect of democracy on economic growth may be perceived as the combination of two effects of the adjustment to the EU. One is that the EU demands democracy, which has a positive effect on growth. The other and dominant effect, however, is that the EU encourages economic policies that do not drive economic growth.

Laggard Effect

A widespread observation from economic-growth studies is that laggards tend to grow faster when they have got their economic systems and policies in order. That is *ceteris paribus*, poor countries grow faster than rich countries. This should be of significance because in 2001 GDP per capita of the CIS countries was only 30 percent of the Central European countries (figure 6.11).

The correlation between gross national income in purchasing power parities and GDP growth rate can be seen in figure 6.12. As would be expected, poorer countries are growing significantly faster than the wealthier countries, but the correlation is not very strong. Yet the laggard effect needs to be controlled for, and it could explain slightly more than one percentage unit of the difference in growth rates between the CIS and central European countries (Åslund and Warner 2003).

Conclusion: The West European Model versus the East Asian Model

A remarkable change has occurred in the postcommunist world after 1998. The laggards in the CIS have become the tigers, while the leaders in central Europe have become the laggards. In the early postcommunist transition, Poland and Estonia were the leading radical reformers, but Poland is the star that faded.

Today, Kazakhstan is one of the brightest lights. It has a good liberal tax code with the lowest payroll tax in the region. Public expenditures

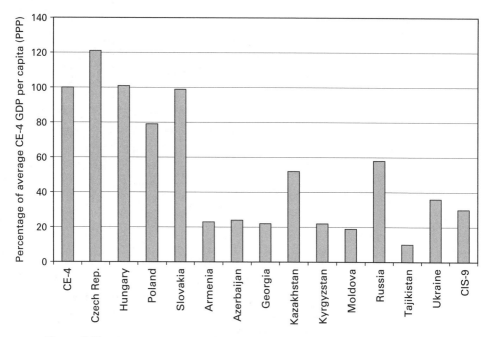

Figure 6.11
Gross national income per capita (PPP) in four central European and nine reformist CIS countries, as a percentage of the central European average, 2001
Source: World Bank Development Indicators, 2003.

have been reduced to 22 percent of GDP. Like Estonia, it has undertaken a radical civil-service reform. Alone in the region, it has carried out a radical Chilean-style pension reform based on private savings. Like Estonia and Latvia, it has deregulated its labor market, promulgating a labor code inspired by that of New Zealand. The privatization of large enterprises has proceeded further than in Poland. Kazakhstan's banking system is the best in the CIS, and it is the only CIS country with investment rating. For the last four years, it has enjoyed an average growth of 10 percent a year, and it is likely to stay close to that level for the foreseeable future, considering its planned oil-production increases and its liberal economic system. This growth is neither accidental nor temporary, while it is also true that Kazakhstan is subject to corrupt and authoritarian rule.

The economic model that is rising in Kazakhstan and other reformist CIS countries appears reminiscent of the East Asian model, which has

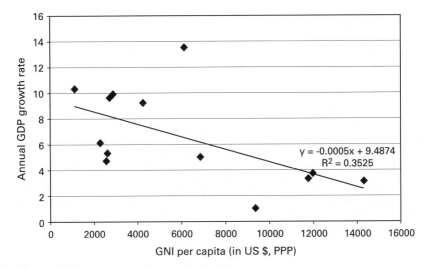

Figure 6.12
GNI per capita (PPP) versus GDP growth rate in four central European and nine reformist CIS countries, 2001
Source: World Bank Development Indicators, 2003; table 6.1.

slowly proliferated with tremendous success. Japan was the first to take off. Four East Asian tigers (Taiwan, Hong Kong, Singapore, and South Korea) followed. China, Thailand, Malaysia, and Indonesia were next. In the last decade, India has taken off, and in the last five years the nine CIS reformers. The Eurasian continent is dominating by similar economic policies and high economic growth, which come to a sudden halt on the border of the enlarged EU. Rather than seeing the last half decade of CIS growth as an exceptional period of recovery or high oil prices, we should note the pattern of proliferation of growth-oriented economic policies.

In this chapter, the salient feature of this model is limited public redistribution, which comes together with low taxes and limited social transfers. A second feature is reasonably free labor markets, and a third characteristic is limited environmental regulation. Our contention is that these three features have generated the high growth in the nine CIS reform countries.

However, these positive features also come with two negative characteristics—substantial corruption and mild authoritarian rule, which paradoxically are also positively correlated to economic growth for the last few years. These two factors might come as part and parcel of the new model. In broader multicountry regressions, it has been shown that corruption is negatively correlated with economic growth (Mauro 1995; Tanzi and Davoodi 1997). With regard to corruption, however, the query needs to be raised when corruption is better than strict regulation. Moreover, democratic central Europe pursues a consistently populist fiscal policy, while the authoritarian CIS government maintain rigorous fiscal discipline. This discrepancy can be explained in many ways, for instance, because of the shock of the 1998 financial crash in the CIS and the demoralizing effect of the EU in central Europe. Nevertheless, regardless of the specific cause, this poor performance is rather embarrassing for new democracies.

Three important hypotheses follow from this chapter:

• First, the major cause of the new high economic growth in the reformist CIS countries is their sharp cuts in public expenditures, accompanied by low taxes and limited social transfers. In general, one of the most important means to achieve economic growth in a corrupt country appears to be to reduce public redistribution.

• Second, the high economic growth in the reformist CIS countries is likely to continue as the current economic policies appear to be deeply imbedded, and these countries watch each other and learn from one another. Meanwhile, there is no obvious reason why economic growth would rise in central Europe until its economic policies are overhauled. So far, only Slovakia has undertaken such an effort.

• Third, over time the CIS countries are likely to encounter increasing tensions between their progressive market-economic models and their regressive authoritarian political regimes. However, this might occur only in the very long term—after one or two decades—if countries such as Singapore, Chile, or South Korea are seen as the most relevant economic models.

The recent strong growth in the CIS countries, however, might still be temporary. An alternative development would be that the combination of corruption and authoritarian rule come to dominate over the nascent liberal economic model in the CIS countries. Argentina under President

Carlos Menem depicts such a seemingly sustainable but in the end temporary growth trajectory. After all, successful economic development under authoritarian rule remains exceptional, and the size of role of the state in the CIS countries remains far greater than in those few successful countries, such as Singapore and Chile under General Augusto Pinochet.

Notes

I want to thank Rashed Chowdhury, who provided me with research assistance and the graphs.

1. "Central Europe" connotes Poland, the Czech Republic, Slovakia, and Hungary in this chapter.

2. The Commonwealth of Independent States consists of twelve countries—from west to east, Moldova, Ukraine, Belarus, Russia, Armenia, Azerbaijan, Georgia, Kazakhstan, Kyrgyzstan, Tajikistan, Turkmenistan, and Uzbekistan.

3. If not otherwise mentioned, all statistics are from European Bank for Reconstruction and Development (2003).

4. Presumably the negative effect on growth will be less because the new member countries do not appear to apply the EU rules rigidly.

5. Admittedly, two extreme outliers have been removed from this graph. One is Kyrgyzstan, which suffered a catastrophe in its dominant gold mine that year, reducing GDP by several percent, and the other is Armenia, which is implausibly assessed as not at all corrupt in this survey.

References

Åslund, Anders. (2002). *Building Capitalism: The Transformation of the Former Soviet Bloc.* New York: Cambridge Unviersity Press.

Åslund, Anders, and Andrew Warner. (2003). "The Enlargement of the European Union: Consequences for the CIS countries." Working Paper No. 36, Carnegie Endowment for International Peace, Washington, DC, April.

Barro, Robert J., and Xavier Sala-i-Martin. (2004). *Economic Growth.* Cambridge, MA: MIT Press.

Berg, Andrew, Eduardo Borensztein, Ratna Sahay, and Jeronim Zettelmeyer. (1999). "The Evolution of Output in Transition Economies: Explaining the Differences." International Monetary Fund Working Paper No. 73.

Bruno, Michael, and William Easterly. (1998). "Inflation Crises and Long-Run Growth." *Journal of Monetary Economics, 41:* 3–26.

De Melo, Martha, Cevdet Denizer, and Alan Gelb. (1997). "From Plan to Market: Patterns of Transition." In Mario I. Blejer and Marko Skreb (Eds.),

Macroeconomic Stabilization in Transition Economies. New York: Cambridge University Press, pp. 17–72.

European Bank for Reconstruction and Development (EBRD). (1999). *Transition Report 1999*. London: EBRD.

European Bank for Reconstruction and Development (EBRD). (2001). *Transition Report 2001*. London: EBRD.

European Bank for Reconstruction and Development (EBRD). (2002). *Transition Report 2002*. London: EBRD.

European Bank for Reconstruction and Development (EBRD). (2003). *Transition Report 2003*. London: EBRD.

Freedom House. (2004). "Freedom in the World 2004." ⟨http://www.freedomhouse.org/research/freeworld/2004/essay2004.pdf⟩.

Havrylyshn, Oleh, and Thomas Wolf. (1999). "Growth in Transition Countries, 1991–1998: The Main Lessons." In *World Development Indicators* (CD-Rom). Washington, DC: World Bank.

Kornai, Janos. (1992). "The Postsocialist Transition and the State: Reflections in Light of Hungarian Fiscal Problems." *American Economic Review, 82*(2): 1–21.

La Porta, Rafael, Florencio Lopez-de-Silanes, Andrei Shleifer, and Robert Vishny. (1999). "The Quality of Government." *Journal of Law, Economics and Organization, 15*(1): 222–279.

Lindblom, Charles E. (1977). *Politics and Markets*. New York: Basic Books.

Mau, Vladimir, and V. Novikov. (2002). "Otnoshenia Rossii i ES: prostranstvo vybora ili vybor prostranstva?" (The Relationship between Russia and the EU: Space of Choice or Choice of Space?). *Voprosy ekonomiki, 6:* 133–143.

Mauro, Paulo. (1995). "Corruption and Growth." *Quarterly Journal of Economics, 110:* 681–712.

Mayhew, Alan. (2000). "Financial and Budgetary Implications of the Accession of Central and East European Countries to the European Union." Working Paper 33. Brighton: Sussex European Institute. In Messerlin (2001).

Mayhew, Alan, and W. Orlowski. (1998). "The Impact of EU Accession on Enterprise Adaptation and Institutional Development in the EU-Associated Countries in Central and Eastern Europe." London: European Bank for Reconstruction and Development. In Messerlin (2001).

Messerlin, Patrick A. (2001). *Measuring the Costs of Protection in Europe*. Washington, DC: Institute for International Economics.

Miklos, Ivan. (2003). "A European Flat Tax." *Wall Street Journal*, May 8.

Mill, John Stuart. (1975). *On Liberty*. New York: Norton. (Original work published in 1859).

Naishul, Vitaly A. (1994). "Economic Reforms: A Liberal Perspective." In Anders Åslund (Ed.), *Economic Transformation in Russia* (pp. 174–181). New York: St. Martin's Press.

North, Douglass C. (1981). *Structure and Change in Economic History*. New York: Norton.

Owen, David, and David O. Robinson (Eds.). (2003). *Russia Rebounds*. Washington, DC: International Monetary Fund.

Pickel, Anders, and Helmut Wiesenthal. (1997). *The Grand Experiment*. Boulder, CO: Westview Press.

Pinto, Brian, Vladimir Drebentsov, and Alexander Morozov. (1999). "Dismantling Russia's Nonpayments System: Creating Conditions for Growth." Moscow: World Bank.

Sachs, Jeffrey D., and Andrew Warner. (1996). "Achieving Rapid Growth in the Transition Economies of Central Europe." Development Discussion Paper No. 544, Harvard Institute for International Development, Cambridge, MA.

Sala-i-Martin, Xavier. (1997). "I Just Ran Two Million Regressions." *American Economic Review*, 87(2): 178–183.

Sala-i-Martin, Xavier. (2002). "Fifteen Years of New Growth Economics: What Have We Learnt?" Economics and Business Working Paper No. 620, Univesitat Pompeu Fabra, June.

Siebert, Horst. (1992). *Das Wagnis der Einheit (The Daring of Unity)*. Stuttgart: Deutsche Verlags-Anstalt.

Stefes, Christoph H. (2003). "Stability vs. Volatility: Why the CIS Is Not a Shining Example for Central Europe." *Demokratizatsiya*, 11(2): 320–323.

Tanzi, Vito, and Hamid Davoodi. (1997). "Corruption, Public Investment, and Growth." International Monetary Fund Working Paper No. 139.

Tanzi, Vito, and Ludgeer Schuknecht. (2000). *Public Spending in the Twentieth Century*. New York: Cambridge University Press.

Transparency International. (2004). *Global Corruption Report 2004*. London: Pluto Press.

Treisman, Daniel S. (2000). "The Causes of Corruption: A Cross-National Study." *Journal of Public Economics*, 76: 399–457.

World Bank. (2002). *Transition: The First Ten Years*. Washington, DC: World Bank.

III

Consequences of Accession to the European Union: Case Studies

7

Spain in the EU: The Key Issues

José Maria Viñals

This chapter assesses the performance of the Spanish economy within the European Union (EU), beginning with what entry into the EU meant for the Spanish economy in terms of structural changes. Developments that occurred in the period 1986 to 1993 were marked by a pattern of growth that proved unsustainable as it was based predominantly on the expansion of aggregate demand in a context in which no solution was found for the main underlying problems that the Spanish economy has traditionally exhibited. Economic developments in the period 1994 to 1998 were marked by Spain's nominal and real convergence toward the Economic and Monetary Union (EMU). Finally, the nature of the challenges posed to the country by EMU membership is explored, and a number of policy suggestions for ensuring that Spain is in a position to best realize the potential gains arising from euro area membership are put forth.

Spain in Europe: Structural Changes

At the political level, Spanish accession to the EU was a resounding endorsement of the fledgling Spanish democracy. In economic terms, it meant the deepening of the opening-up process that began in 1959 with the liberalizing measures accompanying the implementation of the stabilisation plan (Requeijo 2000).

The main structural economic transformation brought about by Spanish entry into the EU has been the *formidable increase in the degree of external openness*. This has been a result, first, of the elimination of barriers to free trade in goods, services, and capital with the rest of the world (Viñals 1992) and, more recently, of Spain's entry into the EMU, which has lifted any remaining obstacles to trade and financial integration within the euro area arising from exchange-rate uncertainties.

Under the provisions of the Treaty of Accession to the European Communities, from 1986 to 1992 the Spanish authorities set about gradually reducing trade tariffs, until achieving the full liberalization of trade with the other EU member states following the creation of the single European market in 1993. Moreover, although it was not compulsory under the Treaty of Accession to follow a precise timetable for the liberalization of international capital flows, the Spanish authorities decided in February 1992 to allow for unrestricted capital flows between Spain and the rest of the world, ahead of the creation of the single European market. Finally, the creation of the EMU and the adoption of the single monetary policy in 1999 have led, on the one hand, to the full integration of national money markets and to the very close approximation of the conditions prevailing on debt markets within the euro area and, on the other, to deeper intra-European trade relations.

These liberalization measures have notably increased the Spanish economy's degree of integration into the rest of the world and have significantly heightened the influence that international and, especially, European factors exert on economic developments in Spain. In respect of trade, the elimination of the tariff and nontariff barriers previously in place has been reflected in an increase in the weight of foreign trade (approximated by the sum of exports and imports, in real terms, as a proportion of gross domestic product, GDP) from 27 percent in 1985 to 63 percent at present. In the financial domain, establishing the free circulation of capital has led to an extraordinary increase in cross-border capital flows (approximated by the sum of proceeds and payments linked to cross-border financial transactions as a proportion of GDP) from 15 percent in 1985 to 1,300 percent at present. This has caused total financial assets and liabilities compared to the rest of the world to rise, respectively, from 23 and 31 percent of GDP in 1985 to 107 and 130 percent of GDP at present. The ongoing economic opening-up process in place since EU entry can thus be asserted to have been the most far-reaching structural change to affect the Spanish economy for many years.

As indicated, Spain did liberalize its foreign trade and capital flows significantly in the period under consideration. However, *the pace of liberalization in each of these two domains was rather different*. In particular, whereas foreign-trade liberalization came about gradually in the period 1986 to 1992 following the timetable set in the Treaty of Accession, the pace of liberalization of international capital flows was much more erratic (at least as far as short-term flows were concerned). This is because the Spanish authorities were obliged to tighten exchange controls in the period 1987 to 1991 to mitigate the inflationary impact associated with the strong capital inflows into Spain. Hence, while it is true that after Spanish EU entry capital flows initially were triggered by favorable economic outlook arising from Spanish EU membership, over time capital inflows tended to depend increasingly on relatively high interest rates, such rates being the undesirable but inevitable outcome of unbalanced macroeconomic policies.

In fact, one of the facts of the Spanish economy within the EU up to the mid-1990s was the tension between a generally expansionary budgetary policy and a relatively tight monetary policy that sought to make headway in combating inflation in a clearly adverse setting. This tension was at the root of the persistent budgetary and current-account imbalances recorded for much of that period.

Another key structural feature associated with the changes in the Spanish economy within the EU is that the *winds of liberalization swept across the different markets with differing degrees of force*. In particular, the external opening-up process had a most significant influence on goods markets and on financial markets as a result of the complying with the liberalization commitments previously entered into under international agreements. However, in other markets, such as those for services and labor, where liberalization required the national authorities to introduce on their own domestic measures, progress was much slower and limited. This explains why for most of the period of EU membership the duality of Spain's economic structure became more accentuated, with industry increasingly exposed to international competition alongside highly regulated and intervened sectors. As explained later on, this lack of synchrony between the liberalization measures implemented in the various markets had a powerful and unfavorable effect on the course of the Spanish economy over quite a number of years.

In sum, weighing up the main structural changes in the Spanish economy after EU accession shows that although wide-ranging liberalization took place as a result of the opening-up process set in train in 1986, this process was not fully extensive to the economic system as a whole with the desirable speed. It was affected by certain underlying problems— unbalanced macroeconomic policies and rigid markets—that did not begin to be resolved until the mid-1990s when economic policies geared to stability and convergence were implemented along the road toward the EMU. Hence, although on balance Spanish EU membership has undoubtedly been favorable overall, it is regrettable that economic policy should not have been geared more promptly and resolutely to stability and that the adaptation of private agents' behavior to the requirements of an increasingly open and internationally integrated economy should have been excessively slow.

Having examined the main changes to the Spanish economic structure arising from EU entry, there follows a brief description of overall macroeconomic developments in the country during the opening-up process and of how these structural changes have influenced such developments.

For a proper assessment of the trajectory of the Spanish economy following EU entry, several periods may be distinguished. The first (1986 to 1993), which covers the phase of economic expansion following Spanish EU accession (1986 to 1991) and the subsequent crisis (1992 to 1993), was characterized by the Spanish economy's inability to grow without simultaneously widening internal and external imbalances. The second period (1994 to 1998) covers the years of recovery and economic expansion in which Spain pursued with increasing determination policies aimed at macroeconomic stability. This allowed it to break free from traditional vicious circles and to achieve high levels of nominal convergence relative to other EU partners, paving the way for Spain's access to the EMU in January 1999. The third period (1999 to 2003) covers Spain's experience within the euro area. This was marked by the maintenance of higher growth rates than those of the area as a whole, by further declines in unemployment, and by the attainment of a balanced budget.

Yet it also saw a resurgence of inflation, which, were it to become entrenched, could significantly harm external competitiveness and jeopardize Spain's economic growth in an enlarged Europe.

From Expansion to Crisis, 1986 to 1993

Macroeconomic Developments

When it joined the European Union, the Spanish economy was in the initial phase of a recovery, following the crisis of the preceding years. In these circumstances, the favorable expectations unleashed by EU membership and the external liberalization measures this entailed helped the economy and contributed to achieving higher growth, investment, and employment (table 7.1).

However, experience shows that a growth process such as that in Spain during these years, based on an expansion of aggregate demand at a quicker pace than that of potential output, leads ultimately to domestic and external imbalances that make its continuity inviable. Thus, during the second half of the 1980s, the lack of resolute budgetary policy measures to counter excessive demand expansion coupled with the absence of structural reforms geared to raising the economy's potential output led to serious problems. This was reflected in the emergence of strong inflationary pressures, higher real interest rates, the erosion of external competitiveness, and the widening of the external deficit. All this has occurred in a context where the brunt of the fight against inflation was borne entirely by monetary policy.

Faced with the evidence of a progressive widening of the macroeconomic imbalances in a difficult social and political context, which gave rise to a general strike in December 1988, the authorities decided to shore up economic policy discipline by entering the exchange-rate mechanism (ERM) of the European Monetary System in mid-1989. Neither the authorities nor economic and social agents appeared to fully realize at that point that the benefits in terms of stability stemming from such a strong exchange-rate commitment could be effective only if accompanied by more austere budgetary policies, wage developments consistent with the exchange rate chosen, and more flexible and competitive markets.

Table 7.1

Macroeconomic development, percentage change (unless otherwise indicated)

	1985	1986	1987	1988	1989	1990	1991	1992	1993	1994	1995
GDP	2.3	3.3	5.5	5.1	4.8	3.8	2.5	0.9	−1.0	2.4	2.8
Fixed investment	6.1	9.9	14.0	13.9	13.6	6.6	1.7	−4.1	−8.9	1.9	7.7
Employment	−1.0	1.9	4.8	3.9	3.6	2.5	0.8	−1.8	−4.1	−0.7	2.5
Unemployment (percentage)	21.5	21.0	20.2	19.2	17.2	16.2	16.3	18.4	22.6	24.1	22.9
Inflation (average)	8.8	8.8	5.2	4.8	6.8	6.7	5.9	5.9	4.6	4.7	4.7
Budget deficit (+) or surplus (−) (percent of GDP)	5.8	6.3	3.8	3.4	3.7	4.3	4.5	4.1	7.0	6.4	6.6
Current account (percent of GDP)	1.6	1.7	0.0	−1.1	−2.9	−3.7	−3.8	−3.7	−1.2	−1.4	1.0

Source: INE (Nacional Statistics Office), Ministerio de Hacienda (Spanish Finance Ministry), and Banco de España.
*Data for 2003: Current-account balance, average 2003q1 to 2003q3.

Consequently, it was no surprise that, with none of the foregoing conditions holding, domestic and external imbalances should have tended to deepen and perpetuate themselves following the peseta's entry into the ERM.

The persistence of increasingly marked macroeconomic imbalances contributed to the progressive erosion of Spanish economic growth against an increasingly adverse international environment. From mid-1992, this opened the way for a deep recession, which was exacerbated by the exchange-rate crises unleashed in the ERM as from the summer that year. The period 1992 to 1993 witnessed one of the heaviest declines in output of recent decades, a marked fall in investment, and in-

	1996	1997	1998	1999	2000	2001	2002	2003	Average 1986–1991	1992–1993	1994–1998	1999–2003
	2.4	4.0	4.3	4.2	4.2	2.8	2.0	2.4	4.2	−0.1	3.2	3.1
	2.1	5.0	10.0	8.7	5.7	3.3	1.0	3.0	10.0	−6.5	5.3	4.3
	2.6	3.3	4.1	5.5	5.5	3.8	2.0	2.7	2.9	−3.0	2.4	3.9
	22.2	20.8	18.7	15.7	13.9	10.5	11.4	11.3	18.4	20.5	21.7	12.6
	3.6	2.0	1.8	2.3	3.4	3.6	3.1	3.0	6.4	5.2	3.4	3.1
	4.9	3.2	3.0	1.2	0.8	0.3	−0.1	−0.3	4.3	5.6	4.8	0.4
	1.2	1.6	0.5	−1.1	−2.5	−2.0	−1.3	−1.7*	−1.6	−2.4	0.6	−1.7

tense job destruction, which moreover contributed to significantly raising the budget deficit.

The economic crisis besetting Spain in 1992 and 1993 reflected the contradictions and problems derived from the low policy discipline in the late 1980s. In particular, far from taking advantage of the economic boom accompanying Spanish EU entry to eradicate fundamental imbalances through the implementation of stability-oriented macroeconomic policies and appropriate structural reforms, budgetary rigor and wage restraint were progressively watered down after 1989. This brought about a situation whereby Spanish growth was increasingly consumption- as opposed to investment-led, in a setting in which wages were growing at higher rates and in which public expenditure and the budget deficit were on a rising trend. A crisis was thus unavoidable.

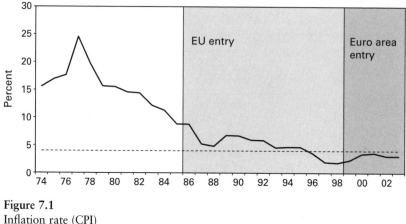

Figure 7.1
Inflation rate (CPI)
Source: INE.

The Main Imbalances

A variable that sums up succinctly the course of *nominal stability and convergence* is inflation. Figure 7.1 shows that inflation was on a declining course from the late 1970s. However, it is worth noting that the Spanish inflationary process appears to have had, until 1994, a floor of 4 percent (in annual average terms), revealing the existence of a resilient inflationary core. The presence until very recently of this inflationary floor is responsible for the fact that despite notable disinflationary progress over the period as a whole, the inflation differential with the EU did not narrow sufficiently (figure 7.2).

Spain's problems in moving forward more effectively and swiftly in respect of nominal stability and convergence were also reflected in the behavior of other nominal economic variables, such as the exchange rate and interest rates. The maintenance of an unfavorable inflation differential leads both to higher long-term interest rates and, eventually, to a depreciation of the currency in foreign exchange markets. Figure 7.3 tracks the effective nominal exchange rate of the peseta and the peseta's long-term interest spread over other European currencies in the period under study, highlighting the difficulties encountered by Spain in achieving nominal convergence.

As regards *stability and convergence in real terms,* for the sake of simplicity the analysis here focuses on the course followed by per-capita in-

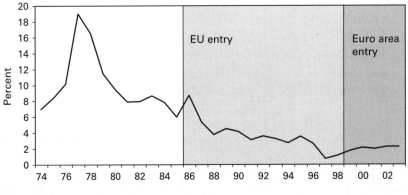

Figure 7.2
Spain's inflation differential compared with the EU's three lowest-inflation countries
Source: Banco de España.

come and unemployment. Spanish per-capita income has tended to grow overall in recent decades. In 1993, for instance, per-capita income in real terms was 44 percent higher than that in 1974 and 33 percent higher than in 1985. Nonetheless, the course of per-capita income relative to the EU differs. Figure 7.4 plots the level of per-capita GDP in Spain relative to the EU. As can be seen, over the period 1974 to 1993 Spain did not converge to the EU. While it is true that significant convergence was achieved in the second half of the 1980s against the backdrop of the strong economic growth accompanying Spanish EU entry, such headway was basically offsetting the heavy backsliding between 1974 and 1985 as a result of the serious and deep-seated economic crisis of those years. Lastly, it should be mentioned that the process of real convergence fell back in the wake of the heavy recession hitting the Spanish economy in 1992 and 1993. Only subsequently was real convergence restarted.

Accordingly, in the light of the above analysis, it can be concluded that the process of real convergence until 1993 depended excessively on cyclical conditions and seemed to encounter a ceiling of 80 percent of the EU per-capita GDP.

A second indicator of the degree of real convergence is the unemployment rate. As figure 7.5 shows, unemployment increased from 2.5 percent in 1974 to almost 23 percent in 1993, although the increases

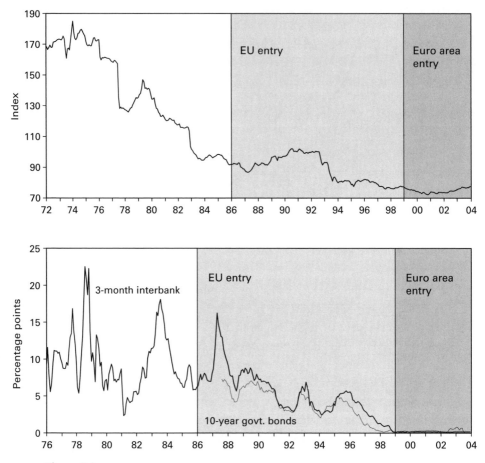

Figure 7.3
A: Nominal effective exchange rate of the peseta; B: Spain-Germany interest
spread
Source: Banco de España.
Note: A drop denotes a depreciation of the peseta.

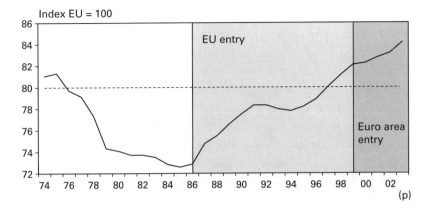

Figure 7.4
Real per capita GDP, Spain and the EU
Source: AMECO.
Note: In all charts, EU refers to EU15.

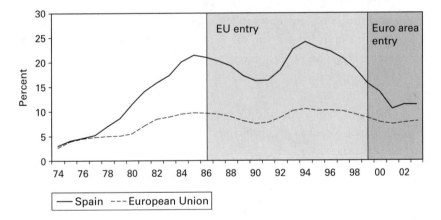

Figure 7.5
Unemployment rate in Spain and the EU
Source: INE and AMECO.
Note: In all charts, EU refers to EU15.

tended to be relatively smaller following Spain's entry into the EU. The behavior of unemployment in the period 1986 to 1993 was clearly more unfavorable than that in the EU as a whole, where it rose from 2.5 percent in 1974 to 10 percent in 1993. Finally, it is notable that the Spanish unemployment rate did not dip below 16 percent even at the height of the economic expansion in the second half of the 1980s.

The proximate cause of the unfavorable behavior of unemployment in Spain throughout these years was the manifest incapacity of the Spanish economy to generate jobs at the pace required by the increase in the labor force. While the latter increased by around 2.5 million people, employment scarcely grew. And more serious still, this relative flatness of total employment was accompanied in the private sector by the destruction of almost two and a half million jobs in the period 1974 to 1993.

In sum, the data clearly reveal that during the initial years of Spanish EU membership (1986 to 1993) the economy failed to progress in certain domains of real convergence and fell back in others. In particular, while there was an improvement in absolute and relative per capita GDP, it was unable to go above 80 percent of the EU level, and unemployment increased even by more than in the EU.

The Obstacles to Stability and Convergence

As postulated by economic principles and extensively confirmed by international experience, it is possible to progress simultaneously and in a durable fashion in nominal and real convergence only if noninflationary demand-side policies are implemented; if a balanced monetary/fiscal policy mix is established; and if structural supply-side policies aimed at ensuring an efficient allocation of resources and the expansion of potential output are pursued.

To what extent were these conditions met in Spain in the period under study? As mentioned, until the mid-1990s the economy followed unbalanced macroeconomic policies that discouraged investment and perpetuated inflationary inertia, while goods and factor markets were dogged by numerous rigidities and inflexibilities. All these contributed to slowing the pace of economic growth and prevented further progress in disinflation.

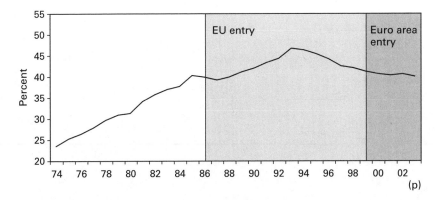

Figure 7.6
General government spending (% GDP)
Source: INE.

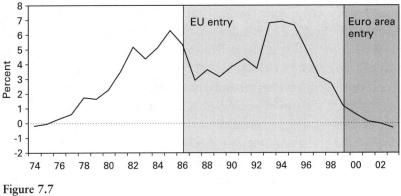

Figure 7.7
General government deficit (+) (% GDP)
Source: INE.

The first underlying problem of the Spanish economy within the European Union was the maintenance for many years of unbalanced macroeconomic policies at whose root there was a structurally very expansionary *fiscal policy*. As figures 7.6, 7.7, and 7.8 show, this was reflected in the increase of public spending from somewhat less than 25 percent of GDP in 1973 to somewhat over 40 percent in 1986 and to almost 46 percent in 1993; in the persistence of a budget deficit which, on average, stood at around 4.5 percent of GDP; and in the strong increase in the level of government debt from 12 percent of GDP in 1974

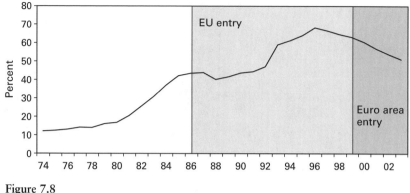

Figure 7.8
General government debt (% GDP)
Source: INE.

to 40 percent in 1986 and to over 60 percent in 1993. The structurally expansionary stance of fiscal policy was largely due to the progressive extension of the welfare state following the introduction of democracy and to the decentralization of the state to enhance the power of regional governments (see Fuentes Quintana 1991). As the maintenance of high budget deficits contributes both to inflationary pressures and to the crowding out of private investment via high real interest rates, this posed a significant obstacle to the achievement of stability and of nominal and real convergence in Spain during this period.

The inadequate workings of goods, services, and labor markets was reflected in the downward stickiness of price and wage growth in the face of adverse economic situations and in the speed at which their growth accelerated in upturns, which gave an inflationary bias to the economy. This asymmetrical behavior of prices and wages was, in turn, the main reason that job creation was limited in periods of expansion and that job destruction was particularly severe during recessions, bearing unfavorably on unemployment.

As to the reasons behind the problems in the *labor market*, several studies (see, for instance, Andrés and García 1992, Bentolila and Dolado 1994, and Marimón 1996) highlight the so-called tax wedge, the lack of competition in the labor market, and the specific nature of collective bargaining arrangements (figure 7.9; see also figure 7.5).

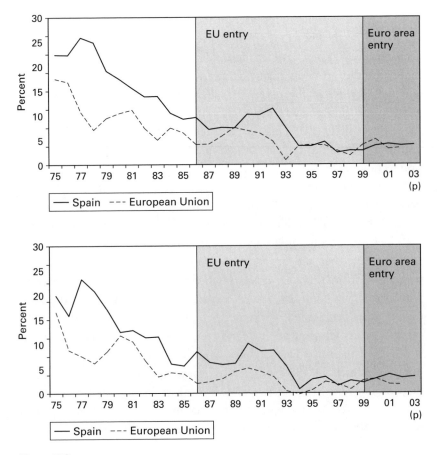

Figure 7.9
A: Compensation per employee (% change); B: Unit labor costs in Spain and the EU
Source: INE, AMECO, and Banco de España.
Note: In all charts, EU refers to EU15.

The tax wedge reflects the rise in total labor costs borne by firms as a result both of the contributions paid by employers and employees to the social security system and of the influence of direct and indirect taxes. In Spain, the growing financing needs of the social security system and the increase in the tax burden during the 1970s and 1980s gave rise to a most significant increase in the tax wedge, placing it among the highest of the EU. This, in turn, led to a reduction in the demand for labor by firms, as they attempted to incorporate labor-saving production techniques.

The ultimate causes of rigidities in the Spanish labor market have been, on the one hand, a legislation strongly protective of employment which restricted labor mobility and reinforced wage pressure and, on the other, the unconditional nature of the unemployment benefit system, which meant that the unemployed scarcely contributed to tempering wage growth at times of crisis. High firing costs prompts employees with permanent contracts to seek higher wage rises than would be the case if firms could shed workers at a low cost and replace them with other workers whose wage demands were more in line with the actual situation of the firm. This explains why the authorities introduced temporary contracts in 1984 with a view to adding flexibility to the labor market. However, this also resulted in duality in the labor market between employees on permanent contracts and those on temporary contracts, which contributed to biasing job creation against permanent-contract jobs.

Other reason for the poor labor-market performance over this period was the nature of unemployment benefits. In Spain, the amount of unemployment benefits increased significantly over time to the point of becoming among the most generous in the EU. Their relatively high level coupled with permissive entitlement terms had the undesirable effect of reducing unemployed workers' incentive to compete for available jobs, thereby limiting their contribution to wage moderation.

A final factor responsible for the unsatisfactory performance of the Spanish labor market in the period considered was the collective bargaining system, through which the wages of most workers were set. As such, bargaining was by industry and province, and as the minimum levels agreed by the firms in each industry and province were binding, a wage remuneration threshold was determined that subsequently would be exceeded in the agreements concluded at the different firms. This wage bargaining system also led an insufficient degree of differentiation in the wage structure by industry, which meant that real wages across the different industries scarcely moved in step with productivity in such industries.

Along with the above-mentioned labor-market problems, there were also serious problems in *goods and services markets*. In particular, certain areas of goods markets and, especially, of services markets remained sheltered from competition, whether due to the internationally nontradable nature of many of these goods and services or as a result of the persistence of competition-stifling regulations in these markets. The lack of sufficient competition meant that firms in these markets could enjoy considerable market power in setting prices and therefore tended to pass through any increase in wage or nonwage costs via prices to safeguard their profit margins (Raymond Bará 1992 and Alberola and Tyrväinen 1999). In turn, this meant these firms were more inclined to yield to workers' wage demands—even in adverse economic conditions—thereby contributing to reinforcing inflationary inertia.

The analysis conducted in this section has highlighted that the source of the difficulties encountered by Spain in attaining greater levels of macroeconomic stability and convergence in the period 1986 to 1993 lay in the implementation of unbalanced macroeconomic policies and in the presence of notable market rigidities at a time when the economy was increasingly exposed to foreign competition. Because it did not promptly resolve these underlying problems, Spain delayed taking full advantage of the potential benefits arising from entry into the EU.

Progress in Stability and Convergence in the Run-Up to EMU Membership, 1994 to 1998

Economic Performance
The most salient feature of the Spanish economic performance in the period 1994 to 1998 was the break with what had been the prevalent pattern in decades—namely, that periods of economic expansion had led to the widening of internal and external imbalances that ultimately choked growth through increases in inflation and the external deficit.

The main cause behind this better economic performance was the growing firmness and resolve with which the policies geared to macro-economic stability and convergence were implemented once the author-ities gave top priority to Spain joining EMU.

With the entry into force of the Maastricht Treaty in late 1993, it was stipulated that countries aspiring to join EMU would have to meet cer-tain criteria ensuring a sustainable degree of nominal convergence. These related to inflation, public finances, nominal long-term interest rates, and the exchange rate. Given the Spanish economy's traditional difficulties in lowering inflation, controlling its budget deficit, and avoiding the contin-uous depreciation of the peseta against the currencies of the core EU countries, few at that time believed Spain could attain the degree of convergence required to be in at the start of EMU. In fact, at the end of 1993 inflation was close to 5 percent, the budget deficit was 7 percent, long-term interest rates stood at over 11 percent, and the peseta had undergone four devaluations since the summer of 1992 against the back-ground of a deep-seated economic crisis.

However, as can be seen in figures 7.10 and 7.11, after 1994 sub-stantial advances in convergence were made, allowing Spain to be among the founding members of EMU in January 1999. Indeed, when the time came for the European Council to assess the convergence conditions, Spain comfortably met the entry requirements established under the Treaty: inflation was only 0.6 percent above that of the three most stable EU countries; long-term interest rates were 0.5 percent above those of the three most stable countries; the budget deficit was comfortably below the reference threshold set at 3 percent of GDP; and the peseta held firm from April 1995 within the ERM of the European Monetary System.

The most relevant feature of Spanish economic performance in the period 1994 to 1998 was that sustained economic growth and employ-ment creation (figure 7.12) were accompanied by lower inflation and bud-get deficits, while the external accounts remained in balance. As earlier mentioned, this shows that nominal and real convergence are fully com-patible processes if the appropriate economic policies are implemented. Figures 7.1, 7.4 to 7.8, 7.12, and 7.13 and table 7.1 reveal how the Spanish economy sustained an average growth rate of 3.2 percent be-tween 1994 and 1998, slightly up from the figure of 3.1 percent for the

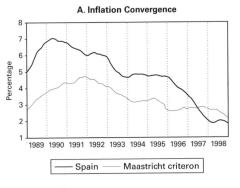

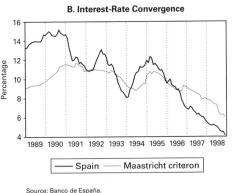

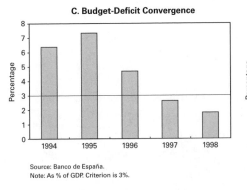

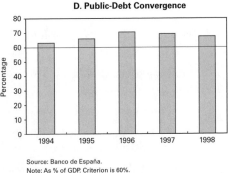

Figure 7.10
Spain's convergence with the European Union countries in accordance with the Maastricht Treaty criteria

period 1986 to 1993. Employment creation was 2.4 percent annually, in contrast to 1.4 percent in the preceding period, which was key in bringing about a decline in unemployment from 23 percent in 1993 to 18.8 percent in 1998. Inflation dipped, on average, from 4.6 percent in 1993 to 1.8 percent in 1998. The budget deficit as a proportion of GDP declined from 7 percent in 1993 to 2.7 percent in 1998. Finally, the balance of payments on current account ran, on average, a surplus of 0.6 percent of GDP in the period 1994 to 1998, compared with an average deficit of 1.8 percent in the period 1986 to 1993.

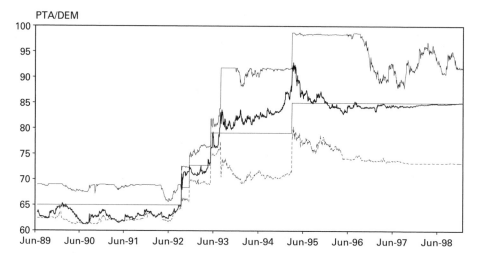

Figure 7.11
The peseta in the ERM (from June 19, 1989 to December 31, 1998)

Stability-Oriented Policies

Undoubtedly, the favorable international environment prevailing during the period contributed to the achievement of greater degrees of stability and convergence. It was one of moderate economic growth without inflationary pressures in a climate of calm in European foreign-exchange markets, which was only sporadically upset. Yet it is primarily in the domestic front where the reasons for the improvement in the Spanish economic situation must be sought. In this respect, and as mentioned earlier, it proved crucial that the authorities should have given priority to achieving macroeconomic stability and convergence, convinced that this was not only necessary to ensure the country's access to EMU but also to lay the foundations for sustained economic growth once Spain was in. This led to *a change in the economic policy regime*, comprising both monetary and fiscal policies and structural reforms.

As regards *monetary policy*, the entry into force of the Law of Autonomy of the Banco de España in July 1994 considerably strengthened the central bank's anti-inflationary stance. The law unequivocally established price stability as the primary goal of monetary policy and provided the central bank with a high degree of independence to achieve

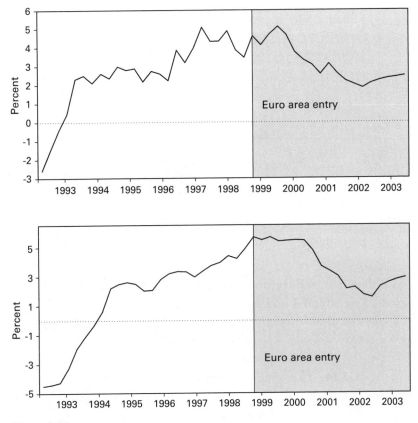

Figure 7.12
A: GDP (% change); B: Employment (% change)
Source: Banco de España.

it. In turn, the adoption by the Banco de España in 1995 of a monetary policy strategy based on the setting of explicit inflation targets contributed favorably to reducing inflation by making the commitment to price stability more visible and effective (see figure 7.13).

Along with reinforcing the stability-oriented stance of monetary policy, the authorities adopted a notably more disciplined *fiscal policy*. This was reflected in greater austerity in the budgetary elaboration process and closer expenditure control to avoid significant deviations from the initially budgeted amounts. As a result of this stricter attitude the budget

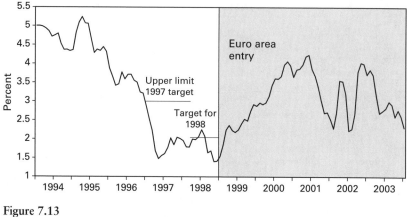

Figure 7.13
Inflation
Source: Banco de España.

deficit decreased and the previous upward trend in public spending was reverted (see table 7.1 and figures 7.6 to 7.8).

Tighter fiscal policy did not only greatly help to achieve stability but also made it possible for the monetary policy stance to be gradually eased, thereby contributing to a more balanced macroeconomic policy mix (figure 7.14). This, in turn, allowed a reduction in the pace of expansion of aggregate demand to rates consistent with the attainment of balanced, noninflationary economic growth.

However, the moderation in the rate of expansion of nominal aggregate demand would not have proved compatible with the slowdown in inflation in a setting of continuously buoyant economic activity without the favorable evolution of *supply-side conditions*, evidenced by wage restraint and more moderate profit margins. In this respect, it may be said that the labor-market reform measures taken in 1994 and 1997 (which were aimed at improving the efficiency of the market by reducing firing costs to lessen the reluctance of firms to offer long-term contracts) contributed favorably to wage behavior and job creation and that the policies of deregulation and privatization pursued during these years introduced greater competition in a number of goods and, especially, services sectors, which had traditionally been sheltered from competitive forces (see Banco de España 1999).

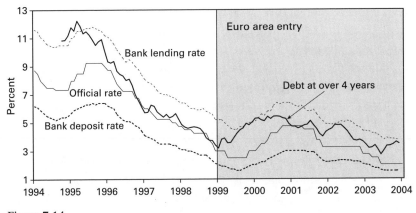

Figure 7.14
Representative interest rates
Source: Banco de España.

The Spanish Economy in the EMU, 1999 to 2003

Participation by Spain in the EMU involves a far-reaching change in the economic and financial environment (Alberola 1998). This environment has become more demanding for several reasons. On the one hand, the move to the single currency eliminates the last barrier (exchange-rate uncertainty) to free trade within the area, paving the way for the full integration of national markets. As a result, Spanish firms are exposed to greater external competition. On the other hand, the single monetary policy entails the disappearance of any scope for monetary or exchange-rate flexibility to alleviate problems of competitiveness arising from higher domestic costs and prices or from asymmetric shocks.

However, the great challenge that the Spanish economy has faced in adapting to the EMU is also a great opportunity to further real convergence. Admittedly, although Spanish growth has overall declined since the start of EMU (4.2 percent in 1999 and 2000, 2.8 percent in 2001, 2 percent in 2002, and 2.4 percent in 2003), the economy has nevertheless grown significantly faster than the euro area. This has been accompanied by a rise in inflation (from 1.8 percent in 1999 to 3.5 percent in 2002 and 3.0 percent in 2003) and a worsening of the current-account balance from a slight surplus to a deficit of close to 1.5 percent of GDP. These developments, though considerably influenced by temporary factors such as the notable rise in energy prices, may—if unchecked—seriously impair competitiveness.

Undoubtedly, the fact that the Spanish economy's growth rate is considerably higher at present than that of other euro area countries reflects the benefits reaped from the efforts in recent years to implement stability-oriented economic policies and structural reforms. But it should not be forgotten that it has also been boosted by the relatively easy monetary and financial conditions that Spain had inside the euro area. It is therefore vital to maintain sufficient countercyclical room for maneuvre regarding fiscal policy and to pursue structural reforms so as to enhance growth potential under conditions of price stability, in step with the requirements implied by euro area membership.

As far as fiscal policy is concerned, it must remain firmly geared to complying with the budgetary rules laid down in the Stability and Growth Pact. In this respect, it is most notable that in recent years Spanish fiscal policy should have moved so swiftly toward a balanced budget, which has contributed to moderating the rate of expansion of aggregate demand. There has thus been a shift from a budget deficit of 2.7 percent of GDP in 1998 to a balanced-budget situation in 2002 and to a slight surplus in 2003.

Moreover, it is also vital to further the implementation of supply-side policies so as to improve the workings of the markets for goods and services and of the labor market. While unemployment has substantially fallen to 11 percent in 2003, fresh steps must be taken in the future to extend the economy's capacity to grow and create jobs. In the labor market, further reforms are needed to enhance its flexibility and efficiency so that more and better jobs can be created. As regards the services sector, important areas are still far from having an appropriate degree of competition, despite recent steps toward deregulation and privatization of certain markets. Hence, the relevance of firmly pursuing liberalization and deregulation policies to improve the level of competition. Finally, to take advantage of the opportunities offered by the new technologies infrastructures must be improved and particular attention should be paid to enhancing education and research.

Conclusions

This chapter has examined what consequences has Spain's integration into the EU in 1996 entailed for the Spanish economy and has also analyzed the main challenges and opportunities resulting from Spain's participation in EMU since 1999. The following main conclusions may be drawn:

• The key structural change arising from Spain's accession to the EU was the formidable increase in external openness resulting from the lifting of the barriers to free trade in goods, services, and capital. In the case of trade, this was reflected in an increase in the weight of foreign trade from 27 percent of GDP in 1985 to 63 percent at present. In the financial domain, proceeds and payments linked to international financial transactions surged from 16 to 1,300 percent of GDP over the same period. Finally, resident-sector assets and liabilities compared with the rest of the world climbed from 23 and 31 percent of GDP, respectively, in 1985 to 107 and 130 percent of GDP at present.

• Whereas Spain significantly liberalized its foreign trade and capital flows by virtue of the commitments entered into under international agreements, in those other markets—for services and labor—where liberalization required the will of the national authorities to apply the relevant domestic measures, progress was much slower and limited. This explains why Spain has had a dual economic structure during all these years where sectors and markets increasingly exposed to competition existed alongside others that were strongly regulated and intervened.

• Spain's accession to the EU unequivocally reveals a favorable balance overall, as testified by the fact that real per-capita income is today around 64 percent higher than in 1985. Yet it is regrettable that economic policy as a whole should not have been oriented sooner toward stability and that the adaptation of private agents' behavior to the requirements of an increasingly open and internationally integrated economy should have been excessively slow. All this has prevented Spain from more fully profiting at an earlier stage from the significant advantages derived from EU membership.

• The difficulties encountered by Spain within the EU to progress more rapidly in nominal and real convergence can be explained by the persistence of certain underlying problems mainly concerning fiscal policy and inefficient market structures. These problems have begun to be resolved only in recent years.

• When the needed change in the economic policy regime was resolutely implemented, the economy reacted very favorably, with significant progress toward stability and both nominal and real convergence being achieved. Consequently, the Spanish experience since 1994 shows that, provided economic policy is well managed, sustained economic growth can be accompanied by low inflation and sound public finances.

• Although the Spanish economy's current situation in the euro area is relatively favorable as far as growth is concerned, it is not so as regards costs and prices, which poses a threat to its competitiveness and, by extension, to future growth. This calls for the continued implementation of structural reforms aimed at enhancing the flexibility of the economy and raising growth potential while maintaining macroeconomic stability. The continued pursuit of stability-cum-growth oriented policies and the complete adaptation of private agent's behavior to the requirements of a dynamic, open, and internationally integrated economy are indispensable for fully realizing the very significant potential benefits associated with euro-area membership.

Note

The opinions contained in this article are exclusively those of the author. A longer Spanish version of this article is being published in *Economía y Economistas Españoles*, volume 8, by Galaxia-Gutemberg and Círculo de Lectores, 2004.

References

Alberola, E. (1998). *España en la Unión Monetaria. Una aproximación a sus costes y beneficios* (Spain Within the EMU: An Approximation of Its Costs and Benefits). Estudios Económicos, Banco de España, núm. 62.

Alberola, E., and T. Tyrväinen. (1999). "¿Hay margen para los diferenciales de inflación en la Unión Económica y Monetaria?" ("Is There Room for Inflation Differentials in EMU?"). *Moneda y Crédito, 208*: 65–120.

Andrés, J., and J. García. (1992). "Principales rasgos del mercado de trabajo ante 1992" ("Stylized Features of the Labor Market in 1992"). In J. Viñals (Ed.), *La economía española ante el Mercado Único Europeo*. Madrid: Alianza Economía.

Banco de España. (Various years). *Annual Report.*

Bentolila, S., and J. J. Dolado. (1994). "Labour Flexibility and Wages: Lessons from Spain." *Economic Policy, 18:* 54–99.

Fuentes Quintana, E. (1991). "La hacienda pública de la democracia española frente al proceso de integración europea" ("Public Finances in Spanish: Democracy Concerning the European Integration Process"). *Papeles de Economía Española, 48:* 2–34.

Instituto de Análisis Económico. (1994). *Crecimiento y convergencia en España y Europa* (Growth and Convergence in Spain and Europe). Vols. 1–2. Barcelona: CSIC.

Marimón, R. (1996). *Economía Española: una visión diferente* (Spain's Economy: A Different View). Barcelona: Antoni Bosch editor.

Martín, C. (1997). *España en la nueva Europa* (Spain in the New Europe). Madrid: Alianza Economía.

Martín, C., J. A. Herce, S. Sosvilla, and F. Velázquez. (2002). *La ampliación de la UE. Efectos sobre la economía española* (EU Enlargement and Its Effects on the Spanish Economy). Barcelona: La Caixa, Estudios Económicos, 27.

Ministerio de Economía y Hacienda. (2001). *Actualización del Programa de Estabilidad del Reino de España 2000–2004* (The Stability Program of the Kingdom of Spain 2000–2004). Madrid: Ministerio de Economia y Hacienda.

Raymond Bará, J. L. (1992). "La inflación dual en España: comportamiento de los precios en los sectores industriales y servicios" ("Dual Inflation in Spain: Price Behavior in Industry and Services"). *Papeles de Economía Española, 52/53:* 46–62.

Requeijo, J. (2000). "El sector exterior español: de los cambios múltiples a la moneda única" ("The Spanish External Sector: From Multiple Exchange Rates to the Single Currency"). In J. Velarde (Ed.), *1900–2000 Historia de un esfuerzo colectivo*. Vol. 1. Madrid: Fundación BSCH-Planeta.

Viñals, J. (Ed.). (1992). *La economía española ante el Mercado Único europeo: las claves del proceso de integración* (The Spanish Economy before the Single Internal Market: The Keys to the Integration Process). Madrid: Alianza Editorial.

Viñals, J. (1996). "La economía española ante el cambio de siglo" ("The Spanish Economy at the Turn of the Century"). In J. Tusell, E. Lamo de Espinosa, and R. Prado (Eds.), *Entre dos siglos. Reflexiones sobre la democracia española*. Madrid: Alianza Editorial.

8

The Spanish Experience in the European Union

Manuel Balmaseda and Miguel Sebastián

The European Union (EU) has been the driving force of economic policy in Spain over the last four decades and the key factor behind the modernization and globalization of the Spanish economy. Its accession to the European Economic Community (EEC) in 1986 was a crucial step in the process of economic and political integration. The process, however, began much earlier, with the implementation of measures (increased competition, privatization of public enterprises, industrial restructuring, deregulation) aimed at modernizing and improving the efficiency of the Spanish economy. These changes, which made it possible for Spain to join the EU and to become a founding member of the European Monetary Union (EMU), were not without cost. Spain's real convergence with Europe ceased for a decade while the reforms were implemented, only to pick up with a greater impetus with the added economic flexibility.

Since 1986, gross domestic product (GDP) per capita has grown at an average annual rate of 2.8 percent. This has made it possible to close the gap that separates Spanish GDP per capita from that of the European Union, converging from 73 percent of the European average in 1986 to 84 percent in 2003. In the same period, the unemployment rate practically halved, falling to 11.3 percent, still the highest among European economies, from the 21 percent rate of 1986. In sum, Spain has achieved greater economic stability and is now an integral part of Europe, economically and politically. It is difficult to disentangle, however, the progress derived from greater economic liberalization from that derived from European integration and greater exchange-rate stability (the entry of the peseta into the European Monetary System and the launch of the single currency).[1]

In spite of this, the process is far from over. Spain's income per capita still stands at 87 percent of the European average. The slow pace of reform, particularly in the labor market, high labor costs leading to persistent unemployment, and an inappropriate policy mix in the late 1980s prevented Spain from reaping the full benefits of integration. Looking forward, the reform process must be reinforced to improve economic competitiveness in an increasing globalized economy. In this light, the imminent enlargement of the European Union will represent a challenge that must be met. In this sense, the integration process is still work in progress.

From Autarky to the Euro

To analyze the recent experience of the Spanish economy, it is important to consider the state of the economy prior to the democratic transition so that the magnitude of changes that have taken place can be understood. The economy under Franco was characterized by the low weight of the public sector (public spending amounted to around 20 percent of GDP) and low fiscal pressure. This contrasted with the predominance of large and inefficient state-owned enterprises (telecommunications, utilities, transportation, shipyards, banking, automotive, mass media, and so on). The economy was highly regulated, and there was no freedom of enterprise. The labor market was marked by its paternalistic nature, with low wages and no freedom of syndication but lifelong employment contracts. With regard to its relations with other economies, Spain lived practically in autarky until the Plan de Estabilización (Stabilization plan) of 1959. The economy was practically closed to foreign trade and investment, with high protectionist measures and exchange-rate and capital-flow restrictions.

The transition to democracy led to changes not only in the political sphere but also in economic terms. The process of European integration has conditioned the progress made by the Spanish economy over the last twenty-five years. Two phases can be distinguished in this period: an initial phase in which the economic structure was transformed (between 1975 and 1986) and a later period marked by European convergence (post-1986). During the first period, Spain had to implement an important program of reforms that transformed both the economic and social structures of Spain. Spain evolved from a highly centralized and intervened economy ruled by an authoritarian regime to a democratic system and a market economy. Spanish markets went through an important process of liberalization and foreign exposure, beginning with the privatization of state enterprises, the deregulation of the overly regulated Spanish economy, and the introduction of a modern tax system. The processes of industrial restructuring and land reform were carried out. Subsidies were lowered, and the labor market was reformed, allowing for the emergence of labor unions and the wage-bargaining process. In this period, the state was decentralized in favor of regional and local governments, and the welfare state (increased health and social security spending) was set in place. The construction of the welfare state and the process of decentralization led to a large increase in public spending, which made the public accounts move from the balanced budget of 1975 to a 5 percent of GDP deficit in 1986. In the labor market, there was a wage boom as a result of the combination of the liberalization of the bargaining process and the maintenance of firing restrictions. In this context, the oil shocks of the late 1970s and early 1980s implied the destruction of a large number of enterprises and unemployment climbed from 4.6 percent in 1975 to 21 percent in 1986. This intense transformation of the productive structure of the Spanish economy was necessary and laid the foundations for the subsequent expansion, but it had a high cost in terms of growth. In those twelve years, the Spanish economy diverged relative to the EU. Its GDP per capita fell by eight percentage points, from 81 percent of the EU average in 1975 to 73 percent in 1986.

During this process, the EU remained the objective of economic policy. It served as a credible excuse for the implementation of policies that, although necessary for long-run growth, induced high short-term costs and hence did not have domestic backing. The European Union remained a goal shared by all economic agents. The integration of the European economies called for fiscal harmonization and consolidation, increased exposure to foreign markets, the liberalization of capital flows, nominal convergence, and the independence of the central banks. In this process, Europe continued to serve as a justification for the implementation of unpopular policies, such as labor reform, privatization, deregulation, foreign direct investment in Spain, and the reduction of subsidies.

European integration was, overall, quite beneficial for the Spanish economy. But the EU is also responsible for not so efficient agricultural and fishing policies and has pervaded Spanish external relations, particularly with Latin America. Additionally, the rigidities in the EU in the labor market (such as high firing costs) and the product markets (such as commerce opening hours or the high cost of starting up an enterprise) and the inherent protectionism of the EU represent a dead weight for the perspectives of Spanish potential growth.

The Economy of European Integration

Nominal Convergence
Nominal convergence has been the paramount objective of Spanish economic policy since 1993. As the achievement of the Maastricht criteria became possible, the financial markets rewarded Spain with a higher probability of accession to the EMU. It also allowed for the reduction of inflation expectations and enhanced the credibility of fiscal policy, giving rise to a virtuous cycle that made it possible for Spain to meet the criteria and become a founding member of the European Monetary Union (figure 8.1).

Inflation   Inflation first began to fall at the end of the 1970s as a result of the new monetary-policy framework adopted by the Bank of Spain (it began to announce a targeted growth rate for the monetary aggregate M3) and the signing of the Pactos de Moncloa. These developments helped rein in inflation from rates in excess of 20 percent at the end of the 1970s to around 5 percent in 1987. After Spain joined the EEC in 1986, the exchange rate became a key variable in the design of monetary policy. Monetary policy was asked to maintain exchange-rate stability with other EEC currencies and bring down inflation. The need to converge toward the inflation rate of the major EEC countries saw interest rates rise to high levels, generating upward pressure on the peseta. Achieving compatibility between the external goal of averting sharp exchange-rate fluctuations and the internal goal of controlling inflation

Figure 8.1
Probability of Spain joining EMU
Source: J. P. Morgan.

was therefore difficult. With the Spanish economy overheating and the consequent worsening of imbalances (external deficit and inflation), inflation rose again to stand at around 6.5 percent in the summer months of 1989. After the peseta entered the EMS1, with fluctuation margins of $+/-6$ percent, pressure on the exchange rate eased. In spite of this, the Bank of Spain held interest rates high, so inflation once again began to trend downward. However, the need for a stable peseta within the EMS placed restrictions on monetary policy, meaning that by itself it could not bring inflation down to the rates prevailing in other countries. Additionally, other key factors hindering the correction of inflation (at a time of economic recession) were the increase in the public deficit (from 3 percent of GDP in 1988 to a peak of 6.7 percent in 1993) and the wage policy of the early 1990s (in which employee compensation rose by 10.4 percent on average in the period 1990 to 1992) (figure 8.2).

The nominal divergence among the member countries of the EMS stood in the way of monetary-policy coordination. Following the drawing up of the Maastricht criteria, economic policies in Spain were aimed at securing compliance with the reference values. Wage moderation and the granting of independence to the Bank of Spain (1994), which

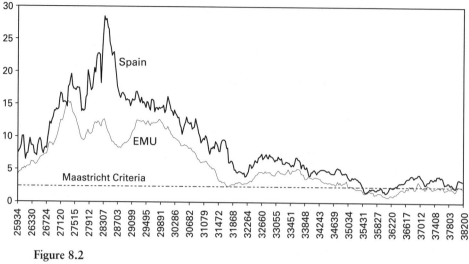

Figure 8.2
Inflation
Source: INE y BBVA.

brought the introduction of annual inflation targets, allowed expectations of inflation to diminish as the likelihood that Spain would form part of EMU increased. After 1996, the Spanish economy experienced a sharp disinflationary process. The growth rate of prices fell from 4.3 percent in December 1995 to 2 percent at the end of 1997, paving the way for Spain to meet the Maastricht requirement. Even though the inflation differential with EMU continued to decline in 1998 (from 0.6 to 0.2 percentage points), the presence of significant rigidities in the Spanish economy prevented further progress. This became apparent in 1999 and 2000 as a result of the reversal of the conditions that had permitted a favorable evolution of the more erratic price components (commodity and food-price developments in 1998) and the application of a policy mix in Spain that was too expansionary.[2] The inflation differential with EMU widened to 1.1 and 1.3 percentage points in 1999 and 2000, respectively. This shows that the recent reduction in inflation was underpinned by the favorable evolution of the more erratic components of the price index, rather than by economic policies aimed at generating greater market efficiency and flexibility (the inflation differential with EMU in the services sector—which in 1997 was one percentage point, as against

0.3 points for inflation overall—widened in 2000 to 1.8 percentage points).

This inflation performance is a cause for concern, since it represents a loss of competitiveness within the EMU, which accounts for around 60 percent of Spanish trade and since the consequences for the formation of inflation expectations and their influence on wage demands were considerable. It must be remembered that wage moderation was the key factor behind the recent cyclical expansion of the Spanish economy. In the Spanish case, the inflation differential is not the result of a faster rate of productivity growth and is not therefore the natural consequence of the convergence process of an economy with a lower per-capita income (the Balassa-Samuelson hypothesis). The risk of the inflation differential becoming permanent arises because of the inflation differential with EMU in both the nontradable and tradable sectors. Furthermore, the impossibility of resorting to competitive devaluations as in the past magnifies the costs associated with the inflation differential due to surplus demand and market inefficiency because it could lead to a permanent and cumulative loss of competitiveness of the Spanish economy.

Public Finances   After the long period of autocratic rule, the decade before Spain entered the EEC (1975 to 1985) was characterized by the gradual adaptation of the country's institutions to the new environment and a sharp increase in the budget deficit resulting from rapid growth in spending outstripping revenue growth. The development of public services and the creation of a welfare state, similar to that of more developed economies, and the increase in public support for crisis-hit sectors are some of the factors behind the rise in public spending (from 20.7 percent of GDP in 1970 to 40.4 percent in 1985). In spite of the increase in revenue from 22 to 34.2 percent of GDP, the result was a sharp deterioration in public-sector finances, from a surplus of 0.6 percent of GDP in 1970 to a deficit of 6.2 percent in 1985. Reflecting this, public debt surged to 45 percent of GDP by 1985, up from 17 percent in 1980. The surge in public spending was partly responsible for the emergence of significant imbalances in inflation and the external sector after Spain joined the EEC. After the peseta entered the EMS, the combination of restrictive monetary policies and the expansionary stance of fiscal policy exacerbated the imbalances that had accumulated during the expansionary phase. Public spending rocketed over these years. The introduction of universal health care, wider unemployment benefit cover, the increase in public employment, and investment policy took public spending up to 47.6 percent of GDP in 1993. Following the economic crisis in the first half of the 1990s and the changes in the EMS, Spain's budget deficit rose once more, confirming that the slight correction seen in the public accounts during the expansion was simply due to the favorable economic context. Thus, in 1993, the budget deficit reached a peak of 6.7 percent of GDP, as against 3 percent in 1988, remaining at similar levels until 1995 (6.6 percent of GDP). The inertia shown by spending led to an increase in the structural component of the deficit, which reached 5.3 percent of GDP in 1993 (3.7 percent in 1988). In this period, structural public spending rose steadily, confirming the expansionary nature of fiscal policy. To strip out the impact of the economic cycle on the public accounts and assess to what extent fiscal policy was restrictive, we have constructed a fiscal indicator, corrected for the cycle, referred to as the *fiscal impulse*, which measures the difference between the structural deficits in two consecutive years. A positive fiscal impulse therefore indicates that fiscal policy was relatively more restrictive and a negative value that it was more expansionary (figure 8.3).

The expansionary nature of fiscal policy at the end of the 1980s and in the early 1990s is apparent in figure 8.4. Thereafter, given the pressing need to lower the deficit to the 3 percent ceiling by 1997, as stipulated by the Maastricht Treaty, Spain's budget deficit dropped over two years by 3.5 percentage points of GDP, to 2.8 percent. As a result, the structural deficit came down by 2.6 percentage points, to stand at 2.5 percent of GDP in 1997. Figure 8.4 confirms the markedly restrictive fiscal policy stance pursued in 1996 and 1997. While an end to the process of expansion in spending, following the overshoot observed in previous years, must be viewed as a positive development, an in-depth analysis of its composition shows that expenditure containment was based primarily on two headings that are unlikely to contribute to the same extent to the reduction of the budget deficit in the future. The first of these, interest payments, fell as a proportion of GDP by 0.5 percentage points, reflecting the positive impact of declining interest rates, while the second, pub-

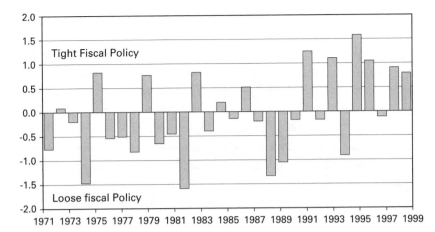

Figure 8.3
Fiscal impulse
Source: Ministerio de Hacienda and BBVA.

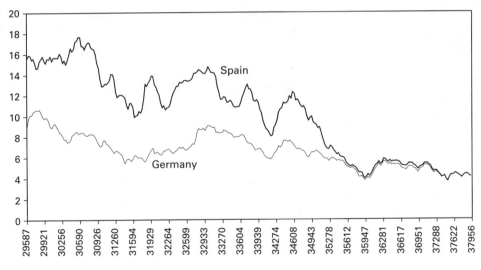

Figure 8.4
Long-term (10 years) nominal interest rates
Source: Bank of Spain.

lic investment declined as a percentage of GDP by 1.2 points. An end to the process of convergence in interest rates with Europe (interest rates on the Spanish Treasury's ten-year bonds fell by 490 basis points over a two-year period) and to the refinancing of debt issued at higher rates suggests that this expenditure heading will make only a modest contribution to the reduction of the budget deficit in the periods ahead. Likewise, if further progress is to be made in real convergence with the more developed countries, the correction of the budget deficit should not be borne by public investment in view of the beneficial impact it has on productivity and competitiveness.

To prevent deficits from rising as in the past and thus hampering the design of a single monetary policy, EU countries signed a Stability and Growth Pact, the aim of which was to establish a deficit ceiling (3 percent of GDP) and set the attainment of a balanced budget as a medium-term goal. During the latter part of the 1990s, Spain's budget deficit continued to fall (to −0.3 percent of GDP in 2000), reaching a balanced budget in 2001. This was partly due to an increased tax-to-GDP ratio, favorable economic conditions, and lower interest payments (−1.4 percentage points). The structural deficit has also continued to shrink to the point of achieving a balanced structural budget at present. This would guarantee a budget deficit of below 3 percent in a recession, as marked by the Stability and Growth Pact.[3]

Interest Rates

The correction of some of the key disequilibria in the Spanish economy (inflation and the budget deficit) has been accompanied by a decline in both nominal interest rates and their volatility. Ten-year rates fell from an average of 16.4 percent in 1983 to a low point of 4.8 percent in 1999. This reduction in rates, which is a reflection of the greater macroeconomic stability and the progress in convergence with the leading European countries, translated into a decline in the long-term interest rate differential between Spain and Germany. The narrowing of spreads speeded up as markets priced-in the growing probability that Spain would be among the first wave of entrants to the Economic and Monetary Union. The probability of this occurring, which in mid-1996 was only around 10 percent, had risen to above 50 percent by early 1997 and to over 75 percent by the summer of that year (see figure 8.1). As a result, the interest-rate differential shrank from 390 basis points in December 1995 to 100 basis points in January 1997 and to 30 basis points in January 1998, only marginally above an average level of 27 basis points since the launch of the EMU. At present, the spread between Spanish and German debt has been eliminated, reflecting the relative favorable behavior of Spanish finances. Lower real interest rates reduce the cost of capital and hence bolster investment and the stock of capital.

The process of nominal convergence has prompted a reduction in real interest rates. At the end of the 1970s, real interest rates began to rise, reaching an average level that was much higher than in the previous decade and much higher than in the EMU (7.7 and 6.7 percent, respectively). From 1999 onward, both the level of interest rates and the differential started to come down (with the exception of 1995) to stand at around 3 percent in both Spain and the EMU at the end of the period. Lower inflation expectations, greater exchange stability, and the correction of the budget deficit lie behind the decline in real interest rates, as these simply reflect the lower risk premium charged on Spanish assets. The decline in Spain's budget deficit has had positive implications for national saving[4] and hence for interest rates. There is an estimated statistically significant negative relationship between fiscal surpluses and real interest rates in Spain (the estimated coefficient is −0.65, similar to the one estimated for the EMU: −0.62). This implies that a 2 percent increase in the budget deficit corresponds to a rise of approximately one percentage point in real interest rates.[5]

Internationalization of the Spanish Economy

Trade Openness

The lowering of trade barriers, the suppression of import tariffs, the adoption of economic policy rules (quality standards, harmonization of indirect taxes), and the increasing mobility of goods and factors of production that comes with greater economic integration, together with the lower cost of transactions and greater exchange-rate stability associated with the single currency, have boosted trade and enhanced the openness of the Spanish economy. In an open economy, a country's external trade

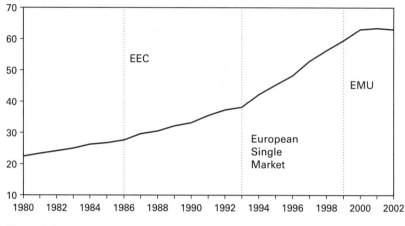

Figure 8.5
Degree of openness of the Spanish economy: $(X + M)/\text{GDP}$
Source: Ministerio de Economía.

is one of the most important and fastest vehicles for the transmission of shocks. This is particularly relevant in today's context in which neither the exchange rate nor monetary policy can be used as mechanisms to correct the impact of asymmetrical shocks on the EMU economies (figure 8.5).

By the time of the launch of the Economic and Monetary Union, the Spanish economy had already transformed, in particular with regard to trade liberalization. Spanish entry into the EEC in 1986 induced a large-scale tariff dismantling, as required by economic integration, and the introduction of the value-added tax (VAT), which had an impact on the performance of Spain's external trade, in general, and of imports, in particular.[6] The launch of the single market, (December 31, 1992) and the successive devaluations of the peseta (1992, 1993, and 1995), with the associated gains in competitiveness, provided an important stimulus to Spanish exports.[7] All in all, by 1999, trade represented 56.4 percent of GDP.

The introduction of the euro in 1999, the consequent reduction (elimination) in exchange-rate volatility, and the lower cost of transactions associated with a single currency encourage trade between the member countries of EMU. Rising trade flows have resulted in a greater cyclical

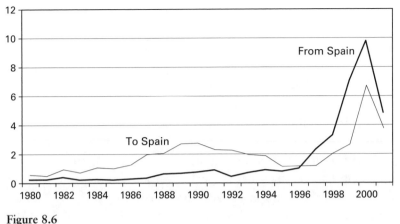

Figure 8.6
Foreign direct investment
Source: Bank of Spain.

alignment of the EMU economies since 1992 and will therefore help dampen Spain's economic cycle and developments in the external sector.

Although the changes in the production structure and hence in the structure of exports[8] will clearly work to stave off the large deterioration witnessed in Spain's external balance in the past, indicators of the degree of competitiveness of the Spanish economy (human capital skills, stock of capital, technological capital) show that significant differences still remain in comparison to the more developed economies. This confirms the need to press ahead with the structural reforms required to enhance economic efficiency.

Foreign Direct Investment
When Spain applied to join the EEC at the end of the 1970s, the perception of foreign investors concerning the economy's growth prospects changed. As a result, foreign direct investment (FDI) in Spain began to rise—slowly at first, in line with the progress being made in the negotiations, and then rapidly, after the EEC entry in 1986. The process of opening to international trade, improved growth potential, falling production costs (lower wages), and lower risk premia in response to the brighter macroeconomic outlook (economic reforms) account for this increase (figure 8.6).

The launching of the euro, as compared to the accession of Spain to the EEC, translated into an increase of FDI into and from Spain but with a predominance of the latter. The increased investment flows were the result, on the one hand, of greater European integration, which called for larger intra-European flows and the internationalization of markets. On the other, the increase in Spanish FDI abroad is a reflection of the maturity of the Spanish economy. The need to seek out new markets with potentially higher returns turned Spain into a net investor of capital (rather than a recipient country as hitherto). In fact, in recent years, Spain has become one of the biggest international investors. It ranked sixth in the world in the year 2000 according to UNO data on foreign investment. According to the Bank of Spain data, in 2000 the flow of Spanish FDI abroad amounted to 9.6 percent of GDP. Specifically, Spain has become one of the main investors in Latin America, not only in relation to its GDP but also in absolute terms. Moreover, the degree of maturity reached by the Spanish market and the potential siphoning-off effect on European capital flows of EU enlargement into central and eastern Europe suggest that FDI in Spain will fall back in the coming years. Spain is therefore likely to continue to be a net capital exporter.

The Role of Structural and Cohesion Funds

The structural funds (reformed in 1988) and cohesion funds (1992)[9] are the instruments designed by the European Commission to develop social and cohesion policy within the European Union (table 8.1 summarizes the importance of EU funds in the four cohesion countries). These funds, which amount to just over one-third of the EU budget, have contributed significantly to reduce regional disparities and foster convergence within the EU. They have played a prominent role in developing the factors that improve the competitiveness and determine the potential growth of the least developed regions.

During the period 1994 to 1999, EU aid accounted for 1.5 percent of Spanish GDP (3.3 percent in Portugal). This is set to fall slightly in the period 2000 to 2006 to 1.3 percent of GDP. The decline reflects, on the one hand, a reduction in structural funds over the new programming horizon (structural funds will represent around 0.3 percent of European

Table 8.1
Structural and cohesion funds

	Greece	Ireland	Spain	Portugal
Percentage of GDP:				
1989–1993	2.6%	2.5%	0.7%	3.0%
1994–1999	3.0	1.9	1.5	3.3
2000–2006	2.8	0.6	1.3	2.9
Percentage spent on gross fixed capital formation:				
1989–1993	11.8	15.0	2.9	12.4
1994–1999	14.6	9.6	6.7	14.2
2000–2006	12.3	2.6	5.5	11.4

Source: European Commission. Estimates based on Eurostat data and forecast for 2000 to 2006.

Union GDP in 2006 compared with 0.45 percent in 1999) and, on the other hand, the impact of enlargement (accession aid).

The magnitude of funding implies that it cannot be omitted from any analysis of the impact of EMU on potential economic growth in the cohesion countries. In fact, the funds have helped minimize the negative short-term impact of compliance with the nominal convergence requirements. EU funding has allowed rates of public investment to remain relatively stable since the mid-1980s, despite the fact that part of the fiscal consolidation process has been achieved at the expense of funding for public infrastructure (figure 8.7).

Figure 8.8 displays the impact on public investment of EU funding in a number of EMU countries. It is interesting to note that the percentage of public investment financed by EU funds has been rising since 1985, to reach average values of 42 percent for Greece, 42 percent for Portugal, 40 percent for Ireland, and 15 percent for Spain from 1993 onward (the year the cohesion funds were ratified). The structural and cohesion funds account for quite a large portion of the public capital accumulated in these countries: 23.5 percent in Portugal in 1997, 17.5 percent in Greece, 13.2 percent in Ireland, and 6 percent in Spain. These effects stand in marked contrast to the modest impact in net contributor countries: the impact in Germany and the Netherlands is estimated at −0.7 and −1.1 percent, respectively, at the end of 1997.

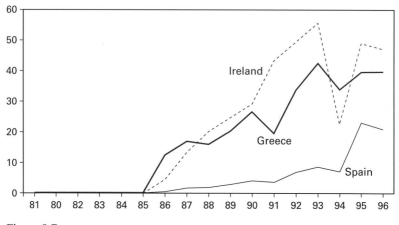

Figure 8.7
Percentage of public investment financed by structural funds
Source: Doménech and Taguas (1999).

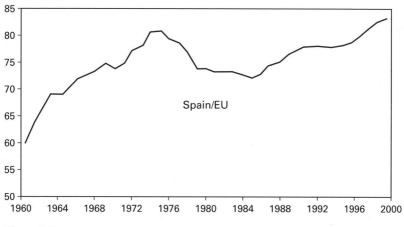

Figure 8.8
Spain's convergence process with EU
Source: European Commission and BBVA.

The Process Is Far from Over: The Challenge of Real Convergence

As already mentioned, the goal of economic and monetary integration in Europe, from an economic standpoint, is, first, to strengthen growth in EU countries as a whole and, second, to nurture the process of convergence between member countries. Spain's participation in the EMU constitutes the culmination of the process of integration of the Spanish economy. Compliance with the accession criteria for the EMU, as laid down by the Maastricht Treaty, enabled the Spanish economy to converge nominally with the countries of the European Union. In the past forty years, per capita income has grown by 2.4 percent annually in the EU, a percentage point slower than in Spain. Productivity, on the other hand, has risen by 2.6 percentage points, also more than one percentage point lower than in the Spanish economy. Nonetheless, despite the great strides made, even if the Spanish economy were to grow at a rate one percentage point faster than the EU, the average differential in the last forty years, in the years ahead, real convergence would still take more than fifteen years to achieve.

Income per Capita and Productivity

In the past forty years, Spain's per-capita income has grown at a rate of 3.4 percent annually. After correcting for purchasing-power parity (PPP), per-capita income has risen by 30 percent more than the average for the European economies. After advancing rapidly up to 1974, the convergence process stalled in the period 1975 to 1984 as a result of the uncertainty associated with the political transition, a wages shock, and the two oil crises. After 1975, Spain's economic and institutional structure had to be modernized and internationalized, shifting from a highly rigid and controlled economy to a more flexible and open one. These years witnessed the industrial restructuring process, including the privatization of state enterprises, clearing the way for considerable gains in efficiency. The process of convergence was not resumed until 1986, partly because of the impetus provided by the membership in the European Union. From 1986 onward, the Spanish economy has been converging continuously with Europe in real terms. Despite the considerable progress made,

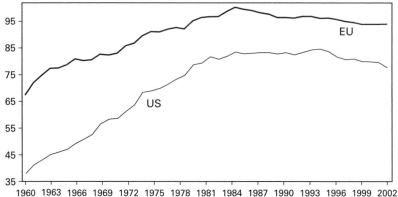

Figure 8.9
Convergence of Spain's labor productivity
Source: European Commission and BBVA.

per-capita income in the Spanish economy is still less than 85 percent of that of the European Union and under 55 percent of that of the United States. The long-term behavior of per-capita income is determined by developments in productivity. In this case, the Spanish experience has been more positive, reaching 80 percent of the apparent labor productivity of the European Union (though the trend in the past five years has been in the opposite direction). The Spanish economy has registered more spectacular gains in productivity than in per-capita income, so that the productivity gap to Europe was almost closed by the mid-1980s. In 1960, the productivity of the Spanish economy was only 65 percent of that of Europe. By 1985, the apparent productivity of labor had practically converged with that of the European Union (97 percent). In the past few years, however, Spanish productivity has grown at very moderate rates, widening the gap to the European Union (figure 8.9).

For a more comprehensive analysis of the behavior of Spanish productivity, we must examine the factors governing its growth. For a global view of the situation, the evolution of other factors of production (capital), the degree of substitution between them, and total factor productivity (TFP), which reflects technical progress in the economy, must all be taken into account. We use a neoclassical growth model to assess the apparent productivity of labor, allowing us to disentangle the contribu-

Table 8.2
Labor productivity (percentage)

	United States	EMU	Spain
1961–1970	2.15%	5.03%	6.71%
1971–1980	1.13	2.83	4.22
1981–1990	1.33	1.71	1.84
1991–2000	1.68	1.46	1.31
1996–2000	2.03	1.16	0.86

Source: European Commission and BBVA.

Table 8.3
Total factor productivity

	United States	EMU	Spain
1961–1970	1.49%	3.06%	5.12%
1971–1980	0.58	1.27	1.75
1981–1990	0.93	0.81	0.59
1991–2000	1.05	0.54	0.00
1996–2000	1.36	0.57	0.13

Source: European Commission and BBVA.

tions of physical capital per worker from the quality of human capital and TFP, measured as the portion of productivity growth that cannot be accounted for by the other factors (tables 8.2 and 8.3).

The evolution of TFP is similar to that of the apparent productivity of labor. In Spain, as in the EMU, TFP has slowed down continuously from 1970 onward. However, its slowdown was much more intense in Spain in the second half of the 1990s. From 1995 to 2000, TFP grew on average at a rate of 0.2 percent, lower than the 0.5 percent rate observed in the EMU. The slower growth rate of TFP in the second half of the 1990s (of the major EMU countries only France recorded a clear recovery in TFP in this period), combined with the advance in TFP in the United States, has widened the existing differential. These differences reflect the technological gap of the Spanish economy overall relative to the EMU and, particularly, to the United States. Spain is far behind other countries in the promotion of R&D. Investment in R&D, as a percentage of

Spain's GDP, has hardly grown in recent years and has remained below 1 percent (compared with 2.6 percent in the United States or 2.2 percent in Germany). It remains at rates similar to Italy's spending on this heading in 1980.

The contribution of the physical capital stock to the apparent productivity of labor in Spain, as a reflection of the process of substitution of labor by capital that took place before 1985 and between 1989 and 1993, has slowed down during the last phase of expansion. This may be a reflection of either the wage containment of the second half of the 1990s or of the moderate increase in investment in relation to other economic expansions (an average of 8.4 percent annually in 1995 to 2000, compared with 13.9 percent in the second half of 1980s).

The stock of physical capital in Spain has increased twelvefold in the last forty years, while in the same period it has increased only eightfold in the EU and threefold in the Organization for Economic Cooperation and Development (OECD). This represents an important impulse to convergence in this factor of production. The most important thrust took place in the second half of the 1980s, owing to the structural change that took place with Spain's entry into the European Community. Another factor (noted earlier) is the impact that the structural funds have had on the accumulation of capital in the Spanish economy. The strong impulse toward convergence in the capital stock that took place in the second part of the 1980s had slowed considerably by the mid-1990s, with the result that convergence was not realized. The Spanish economy's physical capital stock is still around 70 percent of the EU average and is only higher than that of Portugal, Ireland, and Greece. As for public capital, the accumulated stock is a little higher than that of private capital (in EU terms)—that is, 83 percent of the EU average.

All in all, technical progress and the stock of physical capital have contributed only moderately to growth in the productivity of labor in Spain, especially in the last decade. Unlike in the EMU and the United States, in Spain human-capital accounts entirely for the slight increase in labor productivity. This fact is compatible with the increase in the percentage of the working population with higher education (21 percent of the labor force had pursued their studies to a secondary or tertiary level in 1977; in 2000, this figure increased to 71 percent). This permits a certain opti-

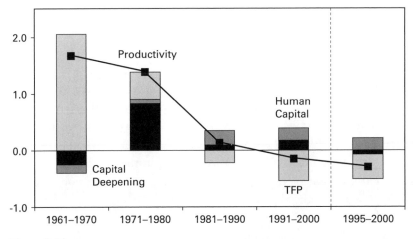

Figure 8.10
Decomposition of the differential in the growth rate of labor productivity between Spain and the EMU
Source: European Commission and BBVA.

mism concerning the future evolution of productivity, as human capital will permit a more efficient use of new technologies. Despite this, Spain's accumulated human capital is still significantly lower than that of neighboring countries (around 75 percent of that of the EMU). The challenge is to continue the process of convergence in human capital while increasing the participation rate to a European level (figure 8.10).

Conclusions

The Spanish experience within the EU has allowed its economy to become integrated internationally and to modernize, thus securing convergence in nominal terms with Europe. This enabled membership in the EMU from the very beginning, which might be considered one of the most important economic achievements of the Spanish economy ever. It allowed for the modernization and internationalization of Spanish firms and gave the economy a strong push into the twenty-first century. However, Spain still finds itself far from achieving its main objective, real convergence. In spite of the progress made, more far-reaching reforms are still necessary to guarantee a sustained future growth. In the decade from 1975 to 1985, the Spanish economy experienced a profound restructuring that coincided with a marked slowdown in the convergence with the EU. The liberalization of the economic structure, however, made room for the subsequent growth acceleration that allowed Spain to enter the European Community and later to join the EMU. In spite of this, as studies from the OECD and the World Economic Forum illustrate, Spain has still one of the highest levels of regulation among OECD countries in both the labor market (collective bargaining, high firing costs, and so on) and in the goods and services market (regulation of trading hours, obstacles to the creation of companies, the slow judicial process).

A flexible economic framework is of special relevance in a monetary union, as monetary autonomy has been surrendered in favor of the union's central bank. The absence of an exchange rate, which could adjust for differing growth rates of prices in the union's member countries, makes price stability a crucial goal of economic policy, as inflation differentials translate into a loss of competitiveness for the high inflation economy. In this context, the sustained inflation differential of the Spanish economy with the EMU worsens the competitive position of Spanish firms.

It has been argued that the inflation differential of the Spanish economy does not pose a threat to future growth, as it is merely the reflection of the Balassa-Samuelson hypothesis. This is not so, as it would imply higher productivity growth in Spain than in the EMU, which is not the case. Additionally, Spanish productivity has been more dynamic in the nontradable than in the tradable-goods sector, which contradicts the assumptions of the Balassa-Samuelson hypothesis. The Spanish inflation differential is due to excess demand (as the EMU's monetary policy stance is too loose for the Spanish economy) and the lack of flexibility in key markets.

In the absence of autonomous monetary policy, fiscal policy gathers special importance because it has to play the dual role of traditional fiscal policy and inflation containment through the expectations channel. In this context, the balancing of the fiscal budget in the medium term, as proclaimed by the Stability and Growth Pact (SGP), is crucial for the maintenance of a stable macroeconomic environment. A balanced budget provides the government with room to maneuver during recessions. The Stability and Growth Pact is necessary because the domestic nature of fiscal policy collides with the EMU character of monetary policy. The SGP, however, should focus on the structural deficit, ignoring fluctuations due to the cyclical behavior of the economy and guaranteeing the soundness of public finances in the medium term. Furthermore, it should not only restrict the deficit allowed to the states but take into consideration the composition of the public finances. The SGP should foment public policies aimed at R&D or the accumulation of human capital, among other, as these increase the growth potential of the economy and yield a positive externality on the rest of the Union members. In this context, the Spanish economy has one of the best track records of its European partners, having balanced the budget and expecting only small deviations from this balance in the future. Now the challenge is on the modification of public expenditures toward more productive uses and toward factors underpinning economic growth. Spain should not fear the free-rider problem of other economies. At the end of the day, the benefits of sound public finances more than outweigh the short-term benefits of free riding.

Notes

1. Integration in an exchange-rate mechanism like the EMS generates a credibility and discipline effect that contributes to a reduction in inflation expectations.

2. The official ECB interest rate in 2000 was on average 4.0 percent, whereas a Taylor-style monetary rule estimated rates of over 6 percent for Spain. The Spanish economy was at a more advanced stage of the cycle than the EMU as a whole, and higher interest rates were needed. Fiscal policy has not been restrictive enough to offset the expansionary monetary policy stance, so that the policy mix was expansionary given the particular cyclical position of the Spanish economy at that time.

3. In the case of the Spanish economy, estimates show that, in the event of a recession, the economic cycle is likely to swell the budget deficit by 1.5 percentage points of GDP, so that the maximum structural deficit compatible with the Stability and Growth Pact is of the order of 1.5 percent of GDP.

4. Note that a four-point increase in the national saving rate raises the rate of GDP growth by 0.3 percentage points (Doménech, Taguas, and Varela, 1997).

5. The result also holds if the structural deficit is used instead. The coefficient for the Spanish economy is estimated to be −0.66.

6. The import of goods and services as a proportion of GDP rose sharply, to 13.6 percent in 1987 from 9.6 percent in 1984, whereas the share of exports shrank slightly, to 15.8 percent of GDP from 16.6 percent in 1984.

7. Exports rose from 17 percent of GDP in 1992 to 27 percent in 1997.

8. In 2000, the technology-intensive sectors represented 22.4 percent of total trade in manufactured goods compared with 19.1 percent in 1999.

9. The creation of the cohesion funds was approved at the Maastricht summit to compensate for the efforts that countries with the lowest per-capita income relative to the EU (Ireland, Greece, Portugal, and Spain) would need to make in the short run to comply with the nominal convergence criteria.

References

Andrés, J., and I. Hernando. (1996). "¿Cómo afecta la inflación al crecimiento económico? Evidencia para los países de la OCDE." Documento de trabajo No. 9602, Banco de España.

Andrés, J., and I. Hernando. (1997). "Does Inflation Harm Economic Growth? Evidence for the OECD." Working Paper No. 9706. Research Department, Bank of Spain.

Andrés, J., I. Hernando, and M. Krüger. (1996). "Growth, Inflation, and the Exchange-Rate Regime." *Economic Letters, 53*: 61–65.

Andrés, J., I. Hernando, and D. López-Salido. (1998). "The Long-Run Effect of Permanent Desinflation." Working Paper No. 9825. Research Department, Bank of Spain.

Bachetta, P., and M. Sebastián. (1998). "Farewell to the Peseta: Macroeconomic Aspects." In *Situacion* (pp. 89–105). Research Department, Banco Bilbao Vizcaya.

Baldwin, R., J. F. Francois, and R. Portes. (1997). "The Costs and Benefits of Eastern Enlargement: The Impact on the EU and Central Europe." *Economic Policy* (April 24): 97–105.

Balmaseda, M., et al. (2000). "The Spanish Economic 'miracle': A Macro Perspective." In *Situacion Spain* (pp. 19–24). Research Department, Banco Bilbao Vizcaya Argentaria.

Bosca, J. E., R. Doménech, and D. Taguas. (1999). "La política fiscal en al Unión Económica y Monetaria." *Moneda y Crédito, 2008*: 267–324.

De la Fuente, A., and R. Doménech. (2000). "Human Capital in Growth Regressions: How Much Difference Does Data Quality Make?" CEPR Discussion Paper No. 2466. Centre for Economic Policy Research.

Dolado, J. J., J. M. Gonzalez-Páramo, and J. Viñals. (1997). "A Cost-Benefit Analysis of Going from Low Inflation to Price Stability in Spain." Working Paper No. 9728. Bank of Spain.

Doménech, R., and D. Taguas. (1999). "El impacto a largo plazo de la Unión Económica y Monetaria sobre la economía española." In *El euro y sus repercusiones sobre la economía española* (pp. 92–138). Fundación BBV.

Doménech, R., D. Taguas, and J. Varela. (1997). "The Effects of Budget Deficits on National Saving in the OECD." Paper presented at the Meeting of the European Economic Association, Toulouse. Mimeo. Ministry of Finance.

European Commission. (1999). "Report on Progress towards Convergence and Recommendation with a View to the Transation to the Third Stage of Economic and Monetary Union. COM (1998) 1999 final, March 25, 1998.

European Commission. (2000). *Public Finances in the EMU*. Reports and Studies No. 3.

European Commission. (2001). "The Economic Impact of Enlargement." *Enlargement papers*. Directorate General for Economic and Financial Affairs.

Hernansanz, C., et al. (2001). "El enigma de la productividad." In *Situacion España* (pp. 25–31). Research Department, Banco Bilbao Vizcaya Argentaria.

Research Department, Banco Bilbao Vizcaya. (1998). "The Competitiviness of the Spanish Economy." In *Situacion* (pp. 47–48).

Research Department, Banco Bilbao Vizcaya. (1999). "Los retos de la economía española." In *Informe anual* (pp. 171–177).

Research Department, Banco Bilbao Vizcaya Argentaria. (1999). "¿Se cumple la hipótesis Balassa-Samuelson para la economía española?" In *Situación* (pp. 51–52). España.

Sebastián, M., and D. Taguas. (1998). "Will EMU Affect Long-Term Growth in Spain's Economy?" Working Paper, Research Department, Banco Bilbao Vizcaya.

Viñals, J., et al. (1990). "Spain and the 'EEC cum 1992' Shock." In *Unity with Diversity in the European Economy* (pp. 145–234). New York: Cambridge University Press.

9

Portugal's Convergence Process: Lessons for Accession Countries

Abel Moreira Mateus

The Portuguese convergence process over the last half century has been a success story. In fact, Portugal is one of the few countries that have changed from a developing to a developed country in the last fifty years.[1] From 1960 to 2003, the gap with the EU15 average decreased from 56.8 to 28 percentage points (28.8 percent), or an annual average of 0.67 percentage points. However, as figure 9.1 shows, the process was not uniform. There were periods of fast convergence, particularly from 1960 to 1974 and again from 1986 to 1997, followed by periods of slow convergence and even divergence.

Among present European Union (EU) member states, Portugal may be the country with the most relevant experience for accession countries, since it experienced an episode of socialism with statization of the economy from 1975 to the mid-1980s. Afterward, there was a process of privatization and liberalization. It is also the country with the most similar position in terms of development in relation to the EU average.

This chapter disentangles the factors behind this performance—the positive factors that induce convergence and the factors that decelerate it. The small growth model presented here encompasses neoclassical and endogenous growth models and tries to identify those factors. Building up human capital has been a determining factor. It is widely known that the buildup of physical capital was quite strong throughout the periods under analysis. However, the residual factors are also essential, and among these, the openness of the economy is crucial and is largely associated with the transfer of technology and intensification of competition. Among institutional factors addressed are macroeconomic stability and developmental orientation. Periods of slow convergence or divergence are

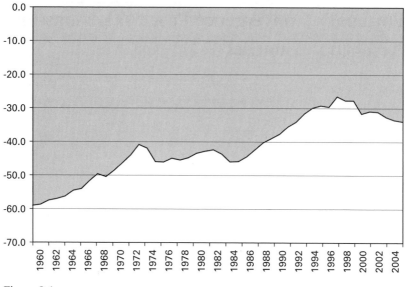

Figure 9.1
Convergence gap, Portugal and the EU15

associated with large macroeconomic disequilibria, institutional instability, and inefficient use of resources, with the state playing a major role.

The good lessons for accession countries are that convergence and even fast convergence is possible, but it is not a mechanical process: it depends on good policies and good institutions. Building up a market and competitive system creates essential infrastructure that is a prerequisite for growth, as is shown by the Portuguese experience in the 1970s and 1980s of socialism followed by privatization and liberalization. The institution building associated with EU accession is nowadays recognized as the most important contribution of EU membership.

The bad lessons are that high transfers of funds may lead to aid dependence and encourage rent seeking, which is detrimental to growth. The emphasis on physical infrastructure, encouraged by EU structural funds, may also lead to a less efficient resource allocation.

The Portuguese Convergence Process, 1960 to 2003

From 1960 to 2003, the gap with the EU15 average decreased from 56.8 to 28 percentage points (28.8 percent) or an annual average of 0.67 per-

Table 9.1
Indices for institutional characteristics

Year	Degree of Openness	Fiscal Pressure	State Intervention	Macro Policy	Foreign Investment	Banking	Prices and Wages	Property Rights	Regulation	Black-Market Premium
1960	3.2	2.0	3.0	1.0	4.0	4.0	4.5	1.4	5.0	2.0
1965	2.9	2.0	2.8	1.5	4.0	3.0	3.5	1.4	5.0	2.0
1970	2.8	2.0	2.8	2.0	3.7	3.0	3.0	1.4	4.0	2.0
1975	3.0	2.7	3.7	3.6	4.0	3.9	3.7	4.7	4.0	3.2
1980	2.5	3.5	3.5	3.0	3.2	3.8	3.2	3.2	3.7	3.3
1985	2.1	3.7	3.3	2.7	3.0	3.7	3.2	3.0	3.6	2.7
1990	1.5	3.6	3.2	2.5	2.3	3.5	2.6	2.7	3.5	2.0
1995	1.3	3.6	3.0	2.3	2.5	3.0	2.0	2.0	3.2	2.0
2000	1.3	3.6	2.5	1.7	2.5	3.0	2.0	2.0	3.2	3.5

Table 9.2
Economic-freedom index

	EF Index	Development Policy	EP Index	TFP Index
1960	199.4	2.0	249.7	126.0
1965	219.4	2.0	259.7	142.1
1970	233.4	1.5	291.7	164.1
1975	135.0	3.0	167.5	183.0
1980	171.0	2.1	230.5	184.1
1985	190.0	2.0	245.0	189.4
1990	226.0	1.6	283.0	200.9
1995	251.0	2.0	275.5	206.5
2000	247.0	2.0	273.5	208.1

centage points. However, as figure 9.1 shows, the process was not uniform. There were periods of fast convergence, particularly from 1960 to 1974 and again from 1986 to 1997, followed by periods of slow convergence and even divergence. The period from 1974 to 1978 was one of fast divergence, followed by an episode of near stagnation up to 1985. Since 1997 and 1998 Portugal has been experiencing an episode of stagnation—a slow divergence that most economists do not expect to end before 2005 or 2006.

The most recent research has brought out the importance of institutions[2] and good policies in explaining total factor productivity (TFP), the most important factor for long-term sustained growth. We closely follow O'Driscoll et al. (2003) and Gwartney (2003) to build indices for each institutional characteristic (table 9.1). We use Driscoll's scale of 0 to 5, on which 0 is the best and 5 the worst grade.

On the basis of the components in table 9.1, we can build the economic-freedom (EF) index presented in table 9.2, as a simple average of the above factors. The economic-policy (EP) index[3] is calculated as a weighted average of the previous index and the development-policy index. This index results from the importance that a developmental policy, reflected in terms of economic policy's development plans and orientation toward growth (a long-term horizon in economic policy), has for economic growth. Table 9.2 also reports a total factor productivity index[4] that is based on an estimate of the Solow residual.

The total factor productivity index shows the highest growth in the fifteen-year period from 1960 to 1974, at an annual rate of 3.8 percent. Similarly to most of the developed countries' experience, the first oil shock caused a sustained deceleration in total productivity growth. There was a further bout of productivity resurgence in the period 1985 to 1990, with an annual growth rate of 2.3 percent.

The EF and EP indices both show a strong increase in the period 1960 to 1975, followed by a precipitate fall in 1975 due to the 1974 revolution that started a socialist experiment in the country, which led to economywide nationalizations overriding property rights and leading to large macroeconomic disequilibria. A fast recovery set in, but it was only in 1985 that the EF index returned to its 1960 level. The indices continued to increase steadily in the 1985 to 1990 period, in association with the reforms that had to be carried out with EC accession. There has been a decrease in the EP index since 1990 largely due to a deterioration in development policy coupled with the decrease in the EF index after 1995 on account of the deterioration in the balance of payments.[5]

Let us study each of the above periods from the perspective of convergence.

The Golden Age of the Convergence Process, 1960 to 1973

At the beginning of the 1960s, Portugal was one of the least developed countries in Europe, with only Greece behind it. But it is precisely at this date that development took off: from an average annual gross domestic product (GDP) per-capita growth rate of 1.6 percent in the previous fifty years, growth accelerated to 6.4 percent in the 1960 to 1973 period. Total factor productivity increased at an average of 3 percent, physical capital 2.6 percent, and human capital 0.6 percent. During the previous two decades, the preconditions for takeoff were being created: electrification, the transport network, universal primary education, the buildup of foreign-exchange reserves during World War II, and the introduction of a more prodevelopmental policy with the First Development Plan of 1953 to 1956. However, one main factor was behind the takeoff: the first wave of European integration with Portugal's membership of EFTA[6] in 1960. In the 1960 to 1972 period, exports grew at an annual rate of 19 percent in volume, within a context of strong European growth and the elimination of tariffs on industrial goods among EFTA trading partners, while Portugal lowered its tariffs in a phased process—five steps of 20 percent until 1977.[7] Manufactured exports boomed: machine tools, paper pulp, textiles, food, and chemicals. This growth took place in an environment of macroeconomic equilibrium and a stable political system, despite the dictatorial Salazar regime and the colonial war. There was a strong developmental policy shift from import substitution in the 1950s and the first half of the 1960s toward export promotion from the mid-1960s to early 1970s. There was also a major institutional change, as the system that created barriers to entry into the field of manufacturing (condicionamento industrial) was abandoned, and more competition was injected in the economy.[8] The investment rate grew from 20 percent in 1950 to a record high of 36 percent in 1973 and there was a large surplus of savings, largely fed by the emigration of more than 10 percent of the workforce to Western Europe.

The Socialist and Statization Period, 1975 to 1985

The golden age suddenly came to a halt with the oil-price shock of 1973, the 1974 revolution that brought democracy to the country,[9] and the populist economic policy associated with the large nationalizations that took place in the 1974 to 1976 period. The external shock due to the oil-price increase, deceleration in the European growth rate, and loss of colonial markets amounted to 8 percent of GDP, with a terms of trade deterioration of 18 percent in the 1974 to 1977 period and a large appreciation of the Portuguese escudo. The internal shock was due to a 35 percent wage increase in 1974 and again in 1975, following the rising expectations due to the revolution. The serious balance-of-payments crisis obliged the government to undertake the first International Monetary Fund (IMF) adjustment program in 1977 to 1979. All major manufacturing firms and the banks, insurance companies, and large farms were subject to nationalization and joined the state enterprises in the infrastructure sectors. The change in property rights and the major institutional upheavals before democratic institutions were built led to temporary productivity losses. From 1973 to 1985, the economy diverged five percentage points from the EU average, with total productivity growth decelerating to 0.8 percent per annum.

An increased budget deficit reaching 13 percent of GDP in 1982,[10] coupled with the second oil-price rise, led to another balance-of-payments crisis that culminated in the second IMF stand-by program of 1983 to 1985. The program reestablished the competitiveness of the economy, and the sharp reversal in the terms of trade in 1984 and 1985 led to a balance-of-payments surplus.

EC Membership and Nominal Convergence Toward the Euro, 1986 to 1996

After about ten years of negotiations and preparation, Portugal joined the EC on January 1, 1986, at the same time as Spain.[11] The first majority center-right government, led by Cavaco Silva from 1986 to 1995, undertook a major program of institutional reform involving privatization and the introduction of a market-oriented economy (figure 9.2). Reflecting the activity in the United Kingdom, Portugal was one the EU countries that introduced an ambitious privatization program. From 1989 to 1995, there were 130 privatization initiatives—starting with the financial sector and manufacturing and then spreading to the infrastructure

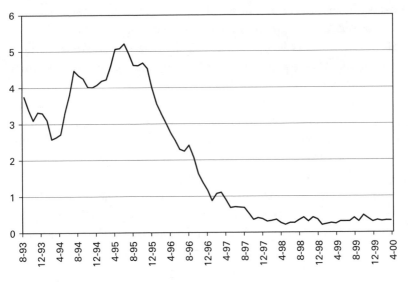

Figure 9.2
Long-term nominal interest rate, differential Portugal and Germany

sector—bringing the enterprise sector under state control down to 10 percent of GDP.

The Portuguese economy expanded 16.6 percent in the ten-year period from 1985 to 1995. Physical capital increased at the rate of 4.4 percent and human capital at 5.5 percent. In the first half of the period, the Solow residual increased at the rate of 3.2 percent; in the second half it declined slightly, due to the recession that set in in 1992 to 1993.

The natural rate of unemployment that had increased from 2 to 6 percent after the 1973 to 1976 shocks, decreased to about 5 percent in 1995.

There are four main impacts of EC membership: trade, investment, transfers, and institution building. These impacts may reinforce one another. The degree of openness increased from 29 to 53 percent of GDP in the period 1985 to 1995, the fastest rise in Portuguese history. The direct impact on exports alone represented 5.6 percent of GDP. After 1988, there was an explosion in the FDI that represented an increase of about 4.2 percent of the productive stock of capital, adding about 0.31 percentage points to GDP growth, per year.[12] The impact of transfers, representing about 2.3 percent of GDP in net terms over the same period, was estimated at about 0.23 percent per year. Combining the three impacts, they represent an impact of 1.1 percent per year or 25 percent of the average annual growth rate: 4.4 percent.

However, we consider the impact on the Solow residual as the most important. Besides the building-up of the market economy, there were major reforms in the fiscal structure (value-added tax and income tax), significant developments in the infrastructure, and a large increase in secondary and university education. There was also a large appreciation of the currency and the persistence of the budget deficit started to threaten the expansion of the economy.

The 1992 to 1998 period marks Portugal's determined effort to reduce inflation and satisfy the Maastricht criteria to be among the founders of the euro. Nominal convergence was achieved by a disinflation policy[13] characterized by the maintenance of a high interest rate[14] and a decline in the budget deficit, although at a slower pace than recommended. In fact, the deficit decreased from 6.5 percent in 1991 to 4.1 percent in 1996. Portugal entered the European Monetary System in 1992, after a heated discussion between the Ministry of Finance (in favor) and the Banco de

Portugal (against), and went through several bouts of exchange-rate speculation. Large foreign-exchange reserves (at a record U.S. $32 billion, or 30 percent of GDP) allowed the country to fight speculation and maintain the escudo within EMS limits.[15] A moderate wage policy and the 1992 to 1993 recession, followed by a slow recovery, also contributed to the moderation of the nominal variables. In 1997, Portugal fulfilled all criteria and was admitted along with nine other countries as a founder of the euro.[16]

The Present Stagnation Period, 1996 to 2004

The success attained in the previous period already contained the seeds of the negative factors that led to the stagnation period of 1996 to 2003, which will perhaps be extended for a few years. There are three major reasons for the stagnation. First, several major reforms required in institutional and economic structures were repeatedly delayed. Second, the lowering of the nominal interest rates, which even led to prolonged periods of negative real interest rates, coupled with overextension of credit by the banking sector, led to the overindebtedness of most economic agents. Third, an accumulation of economic policy errors and loss of competitiveness of the economy led to a slow increase in productivity. Let us look at each factor.

Major reforms that could modernize the economy kept being delayed in order not to incur the short-term political costs of the adjustment, sometimes blocked by interest groups. The weight of the public sector increased steadily, reaching a level of about 8 percent of GDP, above the expected level among EU countries. Labor laws, still anchored in the Constitution, introduced major rigidities in the laying off and mobility of labor. Product markets were still overly regulated, and competition was seriously repressed, mainly in the nontradable and particularly the infrastructure sectors. Education, health, public administration, the pension system, and the legal system were all frequently mentioned as requiring reform and modernization.

With membership of the euro, Portugal lost whatever capability it still had of an independent monetary policy. With the lowering of long-term interest rates to 3 to 4 percent, which were even negative in real terms, banks embarked on heated campaigns[17] to push mortgage credit. As

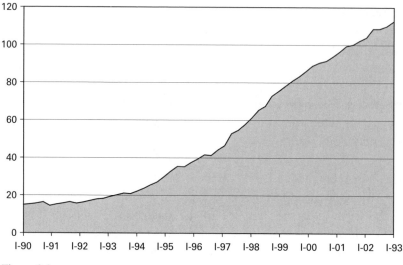

Figure 9.3
Households: ratio of total debt to disposable income

figure 9.3 shows, the ratio of household indebtedness increased from below 40 percent of disposable income in 1996 to above 100 percent in 2002. A similar process took place among private enterprises. In other European countries, central banks acted to break credit expansion by imposing tough prudential criteria or by simple gentlemen's agreements. The Portuguese authorities considered that by doing so they would be interfering with the working of the markets. The high levels of private indebtedness, coupled with the increase in the recourse by the government to securitization, public-private partnerships, and project finance projects, led to a large increase in the external indebtedness of the economy. From a comfortable surplus situation, the stock of debt in the banking system, an actor in the intermediation process, reached about 50 percent of GDP in 2003, and is expected to level off only at a rate of about 70 percent, which is one of the highest in the world among developed countries.

The budget constraint is acting as a lever to slow growth of demand among economic agents, as it can expand only in line with revenue. The present European recession, which has already led to an increase in the unemployment rate in Portugal, from 4 to 6.5 percent, is an important factor in the deepening of the recessionary phase for the country.

Finally, some important economic policies contributed to the present slowdown in the economy. Certain major public investment projects were undertaken in the last decade, amounting to more than 10 percent of GDP, with a very low economic return. Some even had a negative impact.[18] The European Commission has also been responsible, since it does not scrutinize large investment projects carefully, and the pressure to spend builds up as badly designed programs approach deadlines.

Despite the 3 percent ceiling on the budget deficit, spending by the state increased substantially from 1996 to 2002, with the government resorting to several credit vehicles, as in other EU countries. Some of this marginal spending has been of dubious productivity.

Finally, EU transfers, which were instrumental in building badly needed physical infrastructure at the beginning of the membership period, started to ingrain a certain "subsidy dependence" in various sectors of the private economy, which created an obstacle to a rise in productivity. In fact, the single most cited factor of the backwardness of the economy, presently, is the low productivity and loss of competitiveness in large segments of the economy as wages increase, technological upgrading is not undertaken, and Portugal remains the EU country with the lowest level of human capital.[19]

A Growth Model: Factors Explaining the Convergence Process

The previous analysis was mainly based on anecdotal evidence. A growth model can help to disentangle the different factors. We use a generalized growth model of the type proposed by Mankiw, Gregory, Romer, and Weil (1992) and Barro and Sala-i-Martin (1995), which encompasses both exogenous and endogenous growth theories. The following equation puts together a model for the steady-state and a transition equation:

$$\Delta \ln y(t) = a_0 - \phi \ln y(t-1) + a_1 \ln s_k(t) + a_2 \ln h(t) - a_3 n(t) + a_4 t$$

$$+ \sum_j a_{j+4} \ln V_j + b_1 \Delta \ln s_k(t) + b_2 \Delta \ln h(t) + b_3 \Delta \ln n(t)$$

$$+ \sum_j b_{j+4} \Delta \ln V_j + \varepsilon(t),$$

Table 9.3
Total contributions of four factors (percentage)

	GDP Growth	Physical Capital	Human Capital	Openness
Golden age	115%	48%	28%	45%
Statization	45	25	44	8
EC accession	42	12	17	47

where y is GDP per worker, s_K is the gross rate of investment, h is the investment in human capital proxied by the labor force's average years of schooling, n is the growth rate of the labor force, t is time in years, and V is a vector of exogenous variables capturing economic policy. We have included the degree of openness of the economy, the rate of inflation, and the weight of the state in GDP, as well as financial intermediation. The model was estimated for the period 1910 to 2000.[20]

Using the results of the estimation, we computed for each of the previous periods the total contribution of each factor (table 9.3). It is clear from these results that both the golden-age period, with European Free Trade Association (EFTA) membership, and the EC membership period were characterized by the strong impact of the openness of the economy.

We next proceeded to estimate a real convergence equation, explained by investment in physical and human capital, as well as the degree of openness and a macrostability variable, measured by the government deficit. A sample of annual observations was used covering the period 1910 to 2000. The regression equation was corrected for serial correlation, using the maximum likelihood method with an ARCH process and the Marquardt algorithm. All variables have the expected sign and are significant at a 5 percent level, except for the deficit variable. This confirms again a strong influence of both the human capital accumulation[21] and the openness of the economy (table 9.4).

Table 9.5 shows two regressions explaining total factor productivity, TFP (TFP1 for the average years' schooling and TFP2 for a Mincerian definition of human capital). The explanatory variables are the money velocity of M2, which is a proxy for the degree of financial deepening; the degree of openness, measured by the ratio of exports and imports in

Table 9.4
Estimating a real convergence equation

	Coefficient	Standard Error
Degree of openness	25.634	4.352
Human capital	4.476	0.712
Rate of investment	11.315	6.696
Budget deficit	−.069	.079
Constant	21.686	.916

Note: R-squared = .960. Log likelihood = −194.807. F-statistic = 281.810. Akaike criterion = 4.457. Schwarz criterion = 4.678. ARCH coefficient = .835 (s.e. = .343).

Table 9.5
Two regressions explaining total factor productivity

	Degree of Openness	Financial Deepening	Inflation
TFP1	218.093	−4.140	−0.578
	(68.426)	(−16.300)	(1.550)
TFP2	330.545	−4.294	−0.033
	(31.960)	(−9.539)	(−0.437)

Note: The numbers in parentheses below an estimator refer to the *t*-student.

the GDP; and the inflation rate as a proxy for macro stability. The two first variables explain between 89 and 93 percent of total factor productivity. Inflation does not add anything to the explanatory power.

These results show that a 1 percent increase in the degree of openness in the economy adds 0.27 to 0.41 points to the increase in the total factor productivity. An increase of one percentage point in the M2 velocity adds 0.09 points to the productivity of the economy.

Finally, we estimate the impact of the institutional factors studied above on total factor productivity. The impact of the EP index on TFP shows that an increase of one point in the index translates into an increase of 0.49 percentage points in the productivity growth rate. Table 9.6 shows that the improvement in the economic-policy (EP) index is an important factor in explaining the large increase in the TFP of the golden age. The slowdown in the TPF during the statization period was also connected to the deterioration in the EP index, as the recovery in TFP in

Table 9.6
Effect of institutional factors on total factor productivity

	TFP Variation	EP Index	Black Market Premium	Banking	Development Policy
Golden age	59	32	5	25	45
Statization	6	−24	−26	−27	−49
EC accession	17	15	26	19	21

the EC accession period is also related to the improvement in policies and institutions.

An analysis of individual institutional indicators shows the largest impact on TPF of the decrease in the black-market premium, which stands for disequilibria in the balance of payments, the development level of the banking sector, and the position of development policy. As table 9.6 shows, improvement in development policy was the major factor behind the increase in TFP during the golden age. All institutional indicators deteriorated during the statization period. During the accession period, all institutional factors improved consistently.

Lessons for Accession Countries

There is an important difference between Portugal and the largest accession countries. Poland, the Czech Republic, Hungary, and Slovakia were under a socialist regime marked by state intervention and central planning, while Portugal was always a market economy, though with certain connotations of a "corporative state" until 1974. There was always an important entrepreneurial class. In central and eastern European countries, Soviet domination eliminated that class, although older generations had lived under a capitalist system before World War II.

Nevertheless, in terms of its economic and social transformation, among present-day EU member states Portugal may have had the most relevant experience for accession countries, since it experienced an episode of socialism with statization of the economy from 1975 to the mid-1980s.

Good Lessons

The good lessons for accession countries are that convergence and even fast convergence are possible but not through a mechanical process. Convergence depends on good policies and good institutions. Building up a market and competitive system is an essential prerequisite for growth, as is shown by the Portuguese experience in the 1970s and 1980s, where socialism was followed by privatization and liberalization. The institutional building associated with EC accession is nowadays recognized as the most important contribution of EC accession.

The GDP per capita in Portugal is presently about 47 percent above the four largest Central and Eastern European Countries (CEEC). However, as shown in figure 9.4, the stock of human capital is substantially behind those countries. To rebalance their growth path, these economies will have to improve significantly in terms of productive physical investment and, mainly, technological and institutional development. Portugal's experience of economic development over the last four decades is relevant to those countries. Three factors stand out: (1) the openness of the economy and society to technological transfer from the more developed countries, both in technical and institutional terms; (2) the maintenance of micro incentive systems conducive to growth, both in terms of investment and technological and management improvements; and (3) a bias toward developmental policies as well as the maintenance of macroeconomic stability. We conclude that opening up the economy to the external world is equivalent to increasing competition with access to better technology. The two successful phases of growth were clearly linked to European integration: at the center of the process was an increase in competition,[22] which led national enterprises to increase their productivity and caused substantial resource reallocation.[23]

Bad Lessons

Unfortunately, some mistakes were made in the Portuguese experience that should have been avoided. High fund transfers may lead to aid dependence and encourage rent seeking among entrepreneurs, which is detrimental to growth. The emphasis on physical infrastructure, encouraged by EU structural funds, may also lead to a less efficient resource

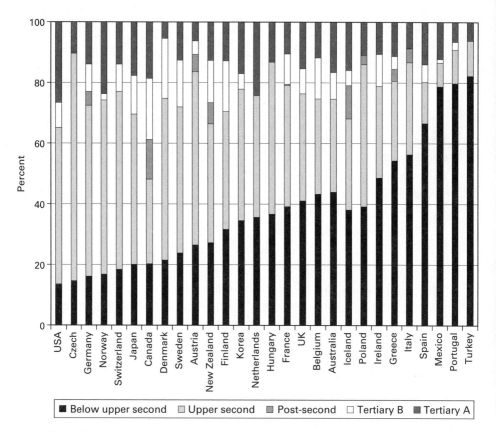

Figure 9.4
Distribution of the population 25 to 64 years of age by the highest completed level of education
Source: OECD, Education at a Glance, 2000.

allocation, and a careful benefit-cost analysis and scrutiny of big projects should be carried out by central governments and parliaments. The momentum of institutional reform needs to be kept up permanently, in view of the major transformations that countries in the transition phase need to confront in the fields of corporate governance, public policies, pension funding, technological and management transfers from developed countries, and so on. Finally, as nominal convergence progresses, the threat of financial crises should be avoided. This is the role of an efficient supervisory system for the financial sector, using mainly a prudential approach. This means that inclusion in the euro zone should not be rushed.

Notes

1. The other countries are the Asian Tigers (Singapore, Hong-Kong, Korea, and Taiwan) and Greece. We use the World Bank's definition of a developed country. Among other criteria, the World Bank uses an income per capita of U.S. $9,656 at 1997 prices.

2. An admirable synthesis and an effort to build a theoretical framework can be found in Acemoglu (2003).

3. The base of all indices is 1910 = 100.

4. The base is 1910 = 100.

5. Reflected in the jump in the black-market premium, signaling disequilibria in the balance of payments.

6. This free-trade area was formed by Norway, Portugal, the United Kingdom, Sweden, and Switzerland.

7. The degree of openness jumps from 15 percent in 1960 to 25 percent in 1974.

8. Foreign competition exerted important pressure. Both phases of European integration were preceded by a heated debate about the impact of foreign competition on the domestic economy. In both cases, entrepreneurial associations and economists argued that the fragility of domestic firms would lead to waves of bankruptcy. This nightmare did not materialize. But two lessons should be learned. First, the country needs to have an equilibrium exchange rate and macro stability so that relative prices lead to a correct resource reallocation. Second, as is argued below, major restructuring in the manufacturing and agricultural sectors will take place, which will be facilitated by flexible product and services markets but, if the labor market does not remain flexible, will lead to a high unemployment rate.

9. Political democratic institutions took some time to be fully operational: most observers place that date in the early 1980s.

10. From 1975 to 1995, the financial costs to the state budget due to state enterprise deficits totaled 21 percent of GDP.

11. Mateus (1999) gives details of the accession process.

12. This is a minimum limit, since it assumes the same marginal productivity as domestic investment.

13. The inflation differential compared with the EU average decreased from six percentage points in 1991 to below 0.5 percentage points in 1996.

14. The three-month real interest rate differential compared with Germany reached six percentage points in 1994 and decreased gradually to about 1.5 percentage points in 1997.

15. The three devaluations were to maintain bilateral parity with the Spanish peseta.

16. The international press, as well as central and northern European governments, did not believe that Portugal would be a founder of the euro. In fact, some observers even propose that the criteria were established to exclude the Club Med. We do not agree with this opinion and consider that the criteria made sense even from a macroeconomic stability perspective.

17. A state bank that had the largest share of the credit markets was one of the leaders in this process.

18. Among them, the 1998 World Exhibition (EXPO 98), overinvestment in road construction, ten new stadiums for the Euro 2004 football championships, a large dam in the Alentejo, and a railway project linking Lisbon and Oporto. The list for future projects goes on: high-speed trains, a new international airport, and so on.

19. One of the main criticisms of the EU structural fund program is that it underinvests in human capital.

20. More elaborate econometric models are estimated in Mateus (2003), including co-integration, but the results remain broadly the same.

21. These results confirm micro studies that show a high rate of return for human capital in the case of Portugal.

22. The OECD has carried out extensive research that proves the importance of regulation and competition in closing the technological gap between the less developed countries and EU levels.

23. All less developed countries in the EU (Spain, Ireland, and, to a lesser extent, Portugal) went through a major restructuring of their productive systems, mainly in manufacturing and agriculture. That restructuring was associated with unemployment rates of up to 20 percent. Restructuring has been more gradual in Portugal, but some economists argue that it has not yet run its full course due to the extensive mechanisms of subsidization. The more flexible wage-rate system, the active informal sector, and the strong construction activity, with higher levels than the above countries, may justify the lower unemployment rates (the peak, so far, was to 8 to 9 percent).

References

Acemoglu, D. (2003). "Lecture Notes for Political Economy of Institutions and Development." Massachusetts Institute of Technology, Cambridge, MA.

Barro, Robert, and X. Sala-I-Martin. (1995). *Economic Growth*. New York: McGraw-Hill.

Gwartney, J., et al. (2003). "Economic Freedom of the World." Annual Report of the Fraser Institute. Vancouver, B.C.

Mateus, A. M. (1999). "Portugal's Accession to the European Union." In G. Biessen, *The Second Decade: Prospects for European Integration after Ten Years of Transition*. The Hague: Ministry of Economic Affairs of the Netherlands.

Mateus, A. M. (2003). "Technological Progress and Growth Factors in the Portuguese Economy." In P. Lains et al., *A New Economic History of Portugal, Nineteenth and Twentieth Centuries*. Lisbon: Imprensade Ciências Sociais.

Mankiw, Gregory, Romer, and Weil. (1992). *A Contribution to the Empirics of Economic Growth. Quarterly Journal of Economics, 107*(2): 407–437.

O'Driscoll, Jr., et al. (2003). *Index of Economic Freedom*. New York City: The Heritage Foundation and Dow Jones and Company.

10

Greece: The Long Process of Economic and Institutional Convergence

Isaac D. Sabethai

The Association Agreement (1961 to 1980) and the Preparation for Accession

Greece signed an association agreement with the European Economic Community (EEC) in 1961 that was virtually suspended during the seven-year military dictatorship (1967 to 1974). Following the reestablishment of democracy in 1974, Greece applied in 1975 for full membership in the European Community. Both the government and a strong majority of the citizens hoped that participation in a larger European family of democratic and economically developed nations would foster political stability in conditions of normalcy and eventually lead to economic prosperity and modernization.

The long and arduous negotiations that followed[1] led to the Treaty of Accession, which was signed in May 1979. The treaty stipulated a period of transition of five years for many issues, seven years for the free movement of workers, and two years for certain items of the *acquis communautaire* related to social policy. An examination of the debate leading to this negotiated outcome—for example, concerning the free movement of labor and social policy (Sabethai 1981)—may be instructive for most of today's acceding countries. Concerning *free movement*, the EEC member countries were not afraid of Greek immigration. Hundreds of thousands of Greek workers had emigrated to West Germany in the 1960s, but a return wave was already under way in the late 1970s because the Greek economy was growing faster than the West German one at the time. The European Commission, however, wanted to set a precedent for Spain and Portugal because it was concerned about possible migratory flows from these two candidate countries that were to become members in 1986. Concerning *social policy*, the Greek government asked for a two-year transitional period to implement two important directives on labor relations[2] because it felt that it was not yet ready to introduce worker-management consultation at the enterprise level, as the directives stipulated.[3]

Accession and Membership: The First Phase, 1981 to 1993

Greece joined the European Community in January 1981. In the first thirteen years of EC membership (1981 to 1993), there was a major effort to maximize the benefits and offset the possible disadvantages of accession. In this period, the slow maturation of Greek society, economy, and institutions, which had started in 1974, was continuing. Greece had lagged behind Western European countries during the interval of the military dictatorship and was now trying to catch up in terms of democratic practices and living standards. Economic agents had to learn to operate responsibly in a free and competitive society—that is, they had to become "social partners" and to stop expecting the state to act both as a provider of first *and* last resort and as a policeman (or mediator). On their part, governments had to accept that a share of power had to be ceded to civil society. Governments also had to learn to avoid the temptation of using fiscal policy (and economic and social policy in general) for short-term electoral gains and to the detriment of future generations. In the 1974 to 1993 period, for example, fiscal and incomes policies were indeed adversely affected by the electoral cycle. Governments were also influenced by the view that expansionary policy could lead to real income gains without increasing inflation; this view proved to be wrong. It is indicative that the general government deficit rose from 2.3 percent of GDP in the 1974 to 1980 period (on average) to 10.9 percent of GDP in the 1981 to 1993 period (on average) (Greek Ministry of National Economy 2001). Also, incomes policies resembled a pendulum: average real wages rose by 4.2 percent in 1982, fell by 2.5 percent in 1983, rose (cumulatively) by 5.5 percent in 1984 to 1985, fell by 13.0 percent in 1986 to 1987, rose by 13.3 percent in 1988 to 1990, and fell again by 8.9 percent in 1991 to 1993 (Bank of Greece 2004, p. 109).

In the same period, the Greek economy had to respond to the challenge of trade liberalization because it was feeling the impact of the lifting of trade barriers. To this end, it was aided by the inflow of Community funds, both for the support of agricultural incomes (under the Common Agricultural Policy, CAP) and for structural intervention (under various schemes, such as the Integrated Mediterranean Programs, the Cohesion Fund, and the first Community Support Framework 1989 to 1993). Still, despite these inflows of funds, the low competitiveness of the Greek economy resulted in a substantial deficit in the balance of current external transactions,[4] which averaged 3.6 percent of GDP in the 1981 to 1993 period (peaking at 8.1 percent of GDP in 1985).

Equally important were, first, the institutional boost provided by the transposition of EEC regulations and directives into Greek law and by their practical implementation, despite problems and delays, and, second, the influence of policy guidelines formulated at the Community level. For example, the years from 1982 up to 1990 witnessed the transposition into Greek law of EEC directives on matters of employment and labor relations.[5]

At this point, it is useful to dwell a little on the meaning and the purpose of the employment and social policy of the European Union (EU). The original Treaty of Rome (article 117) talked about improving the living and the working conditions of the labor force "through their harmonization while improvement is maintained." Additionally, articles 100 and 101 of the Treaty empowered the Council of Ministers to issue directives: first, to harmonize provisions that have a bearing on the establishment and the functioning of the common market, and second, to eliminate differences in national legislation that could cause distortions in the conditions of competition. This has been the legal basis of social policy directives in the EU.

The new European context (because of Greece's accession to the European Community) was one of the factors that led Greek governments, although they were under no formal obligation, to liberalize legislation on labor union rights (1982 and 1988)[6] and on collective bargaining

(1990)[7] and to introduce important elements of labor-market flexibility (part-time and shift work, 1990) (Law 1892 of 1990; see Sabethai 2000).

The result of these various factors was a slow process of Europeanization[8] and modernization. This was marked by ups and downs in GDP (GDP growth averaged only 0.7 percent per annum in the 1981 to 1993 period), in inflation (which fluctuated between 12 to 27 percent in the 1974 to 1993 period and averaged 18.4 percent per annum in the 1981 to 1993 period), and in real wages (as mentioned above). Unemployment rose from 2.1 percent in 1974 to 4.0 percent in 1981 and to 9.7 percent in 1993.[9] It is revealing that most of the restrictive policies or stabilization programs implemented in 1979 to 1981, 1983, 1985 to 1987, and 1991 to 1993 did not yield permanent gains,[10] although they *did* avert a further worsening of the economic situation.

The Second Phase, 1994 to 2000: Preparing for EMU Entry

Things started to change since 1994, when the adoption of the new 1994 to 1999 Convergence Program of the Greek Economy[11] marked a qualitative shift in the economic policy mix. There was now more effective coordination of monetary, fiscal, incomes, and structural policies toward the attainment of low inflation; of low government deficit and debt compared to GDP; and of exchange-rate stability, as the Maastricht Treaty demanded.

In the case of monetary policy, there was a gradual strengthening of its anti-inflationary stance, based on stabilizing the exchange rate of the drachma compared with the European Currency Unit (ECU) (and then the euro) (Voridis, Angelopoulou, and Skotida 2003). This policy was easier to implement without serious losses of actual (as opposed to measured) competitiveness, since part of the real appreciation of the effective exchange rate of the drachma (which would normally indicate a loss in competitiveness) in fact reflected the catching-up process and the Balassa-Samuelson effect. In other words, the rise in the relative price level of Greece compared with its trade partners was partly the result of higher increases in the prices of nontradable goods and services (which did not matter, at least directly, for competitiveness). In the case of tradable goods and services, large productivity gains reduced the inflationary effect of high wage increases and slowed down the erosion of the competitiveness of Greek exports. According to the results of some International Monetary Fund (IMF) studies, as rendered comparable in a recent European Central Bank (ECB) study, the expected inflation differential between Greece and the euro area as a whole, which is attributable to the Balassa-Samuelson effect would be—on the basis of 1995 to 2001 data—of the order of +0.7 to +0.8 of a percentage point (compared to a normalized euro-area harmonized index of consumer prices (HICP) inflation rate of 2 percent). This implies that in 2002 and 2003, when euro-area inflation has been slightly above 2 percent, the Balassa-Samuelson effect would account for approximately half the actual inflation differential between Greece and the euro area (HICP inflation in Greece was 3.9 percent in 2002 and 3.45 percent in 2003) (IMF 1999, chap. 3; IMF 2002, chap. 1; Kieler 2003; ECB 2003; Bank of Greece 2003a, chap. 3).

In the 1994 to 1999 period, the *steady* improvement in the economic situation came to mean that sacrifices were not wasted anymore. Moreover, since the improvement was *visible*, it helped to increase the credibility of the policies followed and made it easier for social partners to adopt a moderate stance with regard to wages and prices: thus unit labor-cost growth slowed down to 2.5 to 3 percent in 1999 from approximately 20 percent in 1990. The most important point is that the 1994 to 1999 Convergence Program relied on a *balanced* set of policy guidelines. Thus, it managed to generate a virtuous circle. Lower inflation (from 20 percent in 1990 down to approximately 2 percent in 1999) led to lower interest rates. In turn, these led to lower government deficits (which fell from 13.6 percent of GDP in 1993 to 1.8 percent in 1999). Lower deficits led to even lower inflation. This also meant that the cyclical fluctuation of certain magnitudes was dampened considerably, thus fostering a climate of stability. Additionally, there has been uninterrupted growth of real incomes since 1994, which has supported the growth of private consumption.

Fiscal policy, however, was not steady enough in the early 1990s, as already mentioned. Also, there were cases when real wage increases exceeded productivity gains in the mid-1990s. Thus, after the hard drachma policy of 1990 to 1997, devaluation and entry into the exchange-rate mechanism (ERM) became necessary in 1998. The inflationary effects of this devaluation were kept small, with help from the social partners and with the use of interest-rate policy, which actually led to some appreciation of the drachma in 1999, and to capital inflows that had to be "sterilized" (Brissimis 2003). Then in 2000, following the decision (taken in agreement with EU organs) for a formal appreciation of the drachma's central rate within the ERM, the drachma started a slide, which led to full convergence of its market rate on its central rate by the end of that year. At the same time, interest-rate convergence was taking place.

Over the same period, inflows from the EU's structural funds (under the second and the third Community Support Frameworks, 1994 to 1999 and 2000 to 2006, respectively) were quite helpful. According to a European Commission report (Commission of the European Communities 2001), inflows of structural funds amounted, on average, to 3.5 percent of GDP annually in the 1989 to 1999 period.[12] It is estimated in the same report that at the end of this period the level of Greek GDP was 9.9 percent higher than it would have been in the absence of these inflows.[13] The inflows of Community funds, together with the fall in interest payments on the public debt, allowed government investment to rise fast without encountering problems of financing. This circumstance also helped to do away (for some time, at least) with the short-run trade-off between inflation and growth. Business investment rose at record rates too, precisely because increased confidence in economic policy led to positive expectations and because firms wanted to prepare for tougher competition once within the Economic and Monetary Union.

By a historical coincidence, during this period, which immediately followed the changes of regime in eastern and central European countries, Greece became a country of net immigration. Foreign, non-EU immigrant workers mainly found employment in services (restaurants, hotels, household services), construction, small-scale manufacturing (especially textiles), and agriculture; their number gradually rose and today they make up approximately 15 percent of the labor force. Their economic activity contributes to GDP growth, strengthens flexibility, averts (or eases) bottlenecks in the labor market, helps to moderate labor-cost growth and inflationary pressures, and augments the revenues of the social security funds. In this sense, the inflow of foreign workers in the 1990s contributed both to the nominal and real convergence of the Greek economy. Government policy is to promote the social integration of legal immigrants.

It is worth noting that during the first wave of legalization, which started in 1998 and ended in 2000, a large number of foreign, non-EU workers (225,000 persons out of 373,000 who registered in the initial phase of the legalization procedure) managed to submit all the necessary documents (including proof of payment of social security contributions). Most of them became "green card" holders. These people are now integrated into the social security system, pay contributions, and receive benefits. There had been common agreement, however, that the total number of non-EU economic immigrants was much higher. Thus, new legislation passed in March 2001 (Law 2910 of 2001) offered illegal workers residing in Greece for at least one year the chance to legitimize their status. This second phase of registration and legalization started in early June and went on until early August 2001. During this two-month period, 351,000 immigrants applied for temporary residence permits. According to more recent data, 505,000 foreign (non-EU) workers are now registered with IKA (the main social security fund); of them, 243,000 come from neighboring Albania; 8,243 workers come from Poland (Greek Ministry of Labor and Social Security 2003, p. 47).[14]

The 1990s were also a period of important structural reforms in the labor and the product markets. In the labor market, the compulsory arbitration of labor disputes (which had been in effect for thirty-five years) was abolished, and a new law concerning free collective bargaining was implemented in 1990. This, together with the abandonment of the automatic wage-indexation system (which, with successive modifications, had constituted the basic mechanism for determining wage increases from 1982 to 1990), clearly had beneficial effects on wage bargaining. The abolition of compulsory arbitration contributed to a healthier structure of the labor-union movement (by objectively favoring the most representative unions); it also contributed to the adoption of a more responsible bargaining stance. The growing realization of some of the Greek economy's structural problems, the lessons drawn from restrictive economic policies (in 1979 to 1981, 1983, and 1986 to 1987), and growing unemployment were additional factors that affected labor-union behavior.

Thus, after 1990 collective labor disputes settled by collective agreements (and not by arbitration, compulsory or voluntary) rose dramatically as a proportion of the total. Since 1991, almost all the national general collective agreements, which determine minimum wages, had a two-year duration. Moreover, strike activity showed a definite downward trend after 1990. Of particular importance, finally, is the fact that free and consensual bargaining, which gradually established itself after 1991, took government policy (such as the official inflation target) into account but in a flexible and nonuniform manner. Thus, the trade-union tactics adopted during 1975 to 1990 were gradually abandoned in the period 1991 to 1996 (if not by all, at least by numerous and important trade unions). These tactics had consisted in demanding very high wage increases at the start of negotiations to create an impression on union members. At the end, however, either comparatively low increases were agreed to, and collective agreements were signed, or even lower wage increases—awarded by the arbitration tribunals—had to be accepted. In the latter case, the trade-union leadership insisted that it did not bear any formal responsibility (Sabethai 1997).

In the 1990 to 2000 period, important labor legislation concerned the implementation of active labor-market policies, the legalization of foreign (non-EU) workers, the annualization of working time, the further promotion of part-time employment, the reduction of social security contributions for low-wage workers, the streamlining of the law on collective redundancies, and so on (OECD 1996, chap. 3; Sabethai 2000). Since 1998, National Action Plans for Employment have been drawn up by Greece (as by other EU countries); this has helped make employment policy more coherent.[15] Most of the above reforms have contributed to labor flexibility. The effect on unemployment was not very visible until 1999; in 2000, however, unemployment started to drop. The limited effect on unemployment reflected mainly the weaknesses of the educational system, the relatively high tax burden on labor, and the remaining product market rigidities. It should be pointed out, however, that the findings of the EU *Ad Hoc Labour Market Surveys*, which were conducted by the European Commission in all EU countries in 1999 among enterprises in industry, retail trade, and services, as well as among employees,[16] support the conclusion that the Greek labor market is characterized by a degree of de facto (rather than formal) flexibility much higher than what is usually believed or admitted (Bank of Greece 2000, p. 58). Of course, some elements of rigidity are also recorded.[17]

In the 1990s, important reforms were also undertaken with the aim of enhancing competition in product markets and reducing the size of the state-controlled sector of the economy. These reforms came under three main headings:

• The privatization program, which involved either full or partial privatization (as the case may be) of state-owned shipyards, oil refineries, banks, and public utilities (in telecommunications, electricity, postal services, water services, port authorities, and so on). For all practical purposes, this program started in 1994 (as part of the 1994 to 1999 Convergence Program), received a boost in 1998 (at the time when the drachma entered the ERM),[18] and has since been expanded. The privatization program, apart from improving market performance, has also helped public finances. In an earlier period (spanning part of the 1980s and part of the 1990s), governments had to face the problem of ailing (overindebted) firms, mainly in the manufacturing sector.

• Market liberalization, which started with the opening up of domestic air travel and of mobile telephony in 1992 to 1993 and went on with the opening up of fixed telephony and of the electricity sector as of 2001. Domestic sea travel followed in 2002.

• The establishment and operation of the Competition Commission and of regulatory authorities in various sectors (telecommunications, postal services, energy and domestic sea travel).

To the above, one should add the liberalization of the banking system (which had started in the 1980s) and the establishment of the independence of the Bank of Greece (Eichengreen and Gibson 2001; OECD 1995, chap. 3; Bank of Greece 2003b, chap. 4, app.).

There have been some clearly positive results in the field of product market reform. The opening up of the telecommunications market has led to lower prices, a wider range and higher quality of services, and an increase in employment. Some positive results have also been recorded in the domestic air transport market, although problems persist. In the electricity market, the opening up is proceeding, but competition will take more time to become effective (heavy investment is required; some institutional wrinkles must be ironed out) (Mylonas and Papaconstantinou 2001; OECD 1998, chap. 4). Greece has obtained derogation until 2006 concerning the opening up of the natural-gas market. The domestic sea transport market was opened up only in November 2002.

All of the above—the new economic policy mix, the more mature attitudes of the social partners, the wide-ranging reforms in labor and product markets, and on a different level the inflows of EU funds and the large influx of foreign workers—had as a result that Greece fulfilled all the *nominal* convergence criteria of the Maastricht Treaty by mid-2000 and became a full member of the euro area in January 2001. The same factors got the process of real convergence of the economy started in 1996.

In retrospect, the twenty-year period between 1981 and 2001 was one of structural change in the economy, attributable partly to EU membership and partly to preexisting tendencies. For example, the structure of production changed significantly. The primary sector's share in GDP fell from 14.5 percent in 1981 to 9.9 percent in 1995 and 7.3 percent in 2000.[19] The share of the secondary sector fell from 29.2 percent in 1981 to 22.4 percent in 1995 and 22.0 percent in 2000. The share of the tertiary sector rose from 56.3 percent in 1981 to 67.7 percent in 1995 and 70.7 percent in 2000. External trade was also affected by EU membership but not dramatically, since Greece had already been linked to the EEC with the association agreement since 1961. Exports of goods and services rose from an average 18.3 percent of GDP in the 1974 to 1980 period to 20.1 percent in the 1981 to 2000 period (and to 22.5 percent in the 1999 to 2003 period); imports of goods and services rose respectively from 23.4 to 27.2 percent of GDP (and to 30.1 percent in the 1999 to 2003 period). In the 1990s, the share of exports to the Balkans, to central European countries, and to the former USSR rose substantially, while the makeup of exports shifted somewhat toward high technology and new products. Finally, between 1983 and 2000 the share of employees (wage and salary earners) in total employment rose from 48.3 to 58.4 percent; their share in nonagricultural employment, however, rose only slightly—from 67.2 to 69.6 percent.

Inside the Euro Area: The First Three Years, Policy Challenges, and EU Enlargement

At the moment of euro-area entry, Greece had been on the path of real convergence for five years already (1996 to 2000); it has remained on this path for the three years that followed (2001 to 2003). During this eight-year period, Greek GDP rose faster than the GDP in the EU or in the euro area. Thus, per-capita GDP was equal to only 65.1 percent of the EU15 average (measured in purchasing-power standards) in 1995 and rose to an estimated 73.5 percent in 2003.[20] This means that the favorable growth differential currently observed is not wide enough to make full real convergence possible *fast enough*. Also, since Greek unemployment is still high (around 9 percent), current growth rates are not sufficient to achieve anything close to full employment within a reasonable period of time.

EMU membership has brought novel challenges. Some key national policy instruments (such as an interest-rate policy and an exchange-rate policy) are no longer available. This means that the importance of fiscal policy, structural policy, as well as of the attitudes and behavior of social partners (especially concerning price and wage increases) has grown—both for dealing with asymmetric shocks and for maintaining and improving competitiveness. Thus, fiscal consolidation and structural reform have to be speeded up.

The 2004 enlargement of the EU adds to these challenges. Greece, Portugal, Spain, and Ireland will lose their current most-favored status with respect to EU structural funds. The new member countries will be net recipients of funds, and both the Common Agricultural Policy (CAP) and the structural policies will be revised, as is already happening. Greece, which is a net recipient of funds today, will probably continue to be one, but net inflows will be reduced.[21] The time profile of the transfers, as well as the size of their reduction, will depend on Greece's differential growth rate,[22] on the changes that will be made to CAP and to the EU's structural policies, and on the transitional arrangements that will be agreed for both old and new members (Bank of Greece 2003a, box IX.2).

In the years to come, the achievement of full real convergence as soon as possible (which is now the major goal of Greek economic policy) *presupposes that nominal convergence—stability of public finances and price stability—will be safeguarded.* Thus, more measures are needed to complete fiscal consolidation (that is, reduce the debt-to-GDP ratio, which stood above 100 percent in 2003,[23] to close to 60 percent), as well as increase productivity and competitiveness. This implies a need for the following:

• Restructuring the general government sector, effectively controlling primary expenditure and completing the tax reform. It will thus become possible to generate new public revenues and also to shift public funds away from interest payments and traditional items of current expenditure, so that they can be used to support employment and entrepreneurship, match or eventually replace EU funds for structural intervention, and help face the financial burden of an aging population (future pension liabilities).

• Increasing labor-market flexibility, putting in place incentives to stimulate labor supply, improving information and matching of supply and demand in the labor market, and overhauling the system of training and education.

• Strengthening competition and opening up sectors, as well as creating a more business-friendly environment by reducing red tape and simplifying regulations on startups, mergers, and acquisitions. This will help attract larger inflows of foreign direct investment (FDI inflows are very low today, no more than 1 percent of GDP), which can contribute to technological modernization and to the introduction of more efficient management strategies.

In conclusion, achieving full real convergence necessitates a concerted and sustained effort—first, mutually supporting policies that inspire confidence both to domestic economic agents and to foreign participants in the markets and, second, social consensus. This is the main lesson for the future from Greece's recently concluded, successful effort for nominal convergence and from its achievement of steadily high real growth, higher than the EU average, which has placed the country on the path of real convergence for the last eight years.

Notes

The opinions expressed in this chapter are the author's and do not necessarily reflect those of the Bank of Greece.

1. From the point of view of the European Commission, two important documents concerning these negotiations are Commission of the European Communities (1976 and 1978).

2. These concerned collective redundancies (Directive 75/129/EEC at the time, today Directive 98/59/EC) and the safeguarding of employees' rights in the event of transfers of undertakings, businesses, or parts of businesses (Directive 77/187/EEC at the time, today Directive 2001/23/EC).

3. At the time, labor relations were still quite tense in Greece. Compulsory arbitration (according to Law 3239 of 1955) was dominant as a method of settling collective labor disputes. Also, various restrictions had been placed on the right to strike and the right to organize (Laws 330 of 1976 and 643 of 1977).

4. On the basis of the balance-of-payments statistics of the Bank of Greece.

5. Directive 75/129/EEC on collective redundancies became Greek law in 1983 (on time). Directive 77/187/EEC on workers' rights in the event of transfers took more time (until 1988). Finally, directive 80/987/EEC on employee protection in the event of employer insolvency became Greek law in 1990.

6. A characteristic example of European political pressure for liberalization was a statement made by the European Commission during the second phase of a long strike by bank employees (the statement was made on January 25, 1980, after the Treaty of Accession had been signed and before it became effective). In an answer to a question by a member of the European Parliament, the Commission said, "By signing the Treaty of Accession, Greece has undertaken to comply not only with the original Treaties and secondary legislation, but also with the general legal principles recognized in the Member States, which, according to the settled interpretation of the Court of Justice, form an integral part of Community law.... The Commission has no immediate plans to adapt the Member States' existing national laws on trade union freedom. This in no way detracts from applicant States' duty to adjust their laws to the *acquis communautaire*, which stipulates *inter alia* respect for the fundamental rights and freedoms enshrined in the legal orders of the present Member States.... Analyzing Greek laws ... is not necessarily a decisive method of establishing beyond doubt whether there is a violation of the principles of freedom of association. However, one may wonder whether the binding nature of arbitration, as laid down in ... Law 3239 of 1955, does not constitute an infringement of the very substance of the right to strike, as enshrined in the fundamental rights and principles recognized in the present Member States." (See Answer to Written Question No 906/79, *Official Journal of the EC*, C 49, February 27, 1980; also see Sabethai, 1982).

7. Law 1264 of 1982 liberalized provisions on the activity of labor unions and the right to strike; law 1767 of 1988 introduced workers' councils at the enterprise level; law 1876 of 1990 repealed the 1955 law on compulsory arbitration and introduced voluntary mediation and arbitration.

8. For the concept of Europeanization, see Featherstone and Radaelli (2003) and Featherstone and Kazamias (2001).

9. Figures from the labor-force survey conducted by the National Statistical Service of Greece.

10. However, some researchers—Hall and Zonzilos (2001)—believe that the drastic cut in real wages during the 1985 to 1987 stabilization program had a long-lasting and substantial downward effect on inflation. Also see Garganas and Tavlas (2001).

11. The Revised Economic Convergence Program 1994 to 1999 (Ministry of National Economy, summer 1994) was accepted by the ECOFIN Council in September 1994.

12. According to a differently based calculation, net inflows from the Community budget (measured after including receipts under the Common Agricultural Policy and subtracting Greek contributions to the Community budget) were equal to 3.2 to 4.5 percent of Greek GDP in the 1990 to 2001 period (see Manassaki, 1998; Bank of Greece, 2003a). It has been estimated that these inflows contributed 0.8 to 1.2 percentage points to the growth rate of Greek GDP (see Bank of Greece, 2002), p. 47, n. 5.

13. Of course, there also exist different views on the subject. *The Economist* (March 27, 2003) quotes an anonymous "senior Greek official in Brussels" as claiming that "the best thing the EU could do for Greece is to cut off the structural funds immediately ...; anybody who works hard at a regular business is regarded as an idiot, since it's much easier to set up a project to draw in European subsidies." There is a grain of truth in this view, since all good things can also be abused. The statement quoted, however, does not describe what usually happens, although it does indicate that there is room for more efficient utilization of EU funds.

14. The full text is available on the Commission's website. Also see OECD, *Trends in International Migration*, annual SOPEMI reports 2001, 2002, 2003.

15. Following the Amsterdam Treaty, the revised text of the treaty establishing the European Community stipulates that member states consider the promotion of employment a matter of common interest and coordinate their action—which is to be supported and complemented by the Community—to this end. This is why annual employment policy guidelines are now issued and national action plans for employment must be drawn up to implement them. The national plans are available at the Commission's Web site (see note 19 above).

16. The detailed findings have been published in *European Economy: Reports and Studies*, No. 4 (2000). The survey among industrial enterprises was also con-

ducted in 1994 and in 1989. For the older surveys, see *European Economy: Reports and Studies*, No. 3 (1995).

17. For a fresh view of rigidities in the Greek labor market (particularly those related to the tax and the social security system), see Burtless (2001).

18. The June 1998 *Update of the Hellenic Convergence Program 1998–2001* contains a detailed exposition of the structural reforms on which the Greek government committed itself when the drachma joined the ERM.

19. National accounts figures used for the 1974 to 1994 period are those estimated by the Ministry of National Economy (2001) to improve comparability with ESA 95 data for the period since 1995.

20. Eurostat, *Structural Indicators*, updated and fully revised in December 2003. Eurostat, however, cautions that measures in purchasing-power standards are "constructed primarily for spatial comparison and not for comparison over time."

21. According to studies by DIW (Deutsches Institut für Wirtschaftsforschung), which include alternative scenarios concerning the allocation and the size of Community funds in 2007 and in 2013, the reduction in per-capita net transfers to Greece in comparison to the 1995 to 1999 average ranges between 3.1 and 17.5 percent for 2007 and between 27.9 and 46.5 percent in 2013, depending on the assumptions concerning Community policies (see Weise, 2001).

22. Conversely, the reduction in net transfers will have an effect on the growth rate of the Greek economy. This effect will depend on (1) the contribution that these transfers have made to the productive capacity of the economy up to now; (2) the effectiveness with which currently incoming transfers are utilized; (3) the extent to which the Greek economy will manage to face up to more intense competition in the enlarged EU market and also take advantage of the greater opportunities that it provides. See Bank of Greece (2002, pp. 47–48).

23. Following a recent reestimation of Greek public-finance statistics by the Greek Statistical Service and by Eurostat, the general government debt has been revised upward from 103 to 110 percent of GDP for the year 2003 (see Eurostat press release, September 23, 2004).

References

Bank of Greece. (2000). *Monetary Policy: Interim Report 2000*. Athens.

Bank of Greece. (2002). *Annual Report 2001*. Athens.

Bank of Greece. (2003a). *Annual Report 2002*. Athens.

Bank of Greece. (2003b). *Monetary Policy: Interim Report 2003*. Athens.

Bank of Greece. (2004). *Monetary Policy 2003–2004*. Athens.

Brissimis, S. N. (2003). "Speaking Notes [on Monetary Policy]." Bank of Greece, May 20.

Burtless, G. (2001). "The Greek Labor Market." In R. C. Bryant, N. C. Garganas, and G. S. Tavlas (Eds.), *Greece's Economic Performance and Prospects.* Athens and Washington, D.C.: Bank of Greece and the Brookings Institution.

Commission of the European Communities. (1976). Avis sur la demande d' adhésion de la Grêce (29 janvier 1976). *Bulletin des Communautés européennes,* Supplément 2/76.

Commission of the European Communities. *Economic and sectoral aspects: Commission analyses complementing its views on enlargement.* COM(78)200 final, Brussels, April 27.

Commission of the European Communities. (2001). *Second Report on Economic and Social Cohesion.* January 31.

Eichengreen, B., and H. D. Gibson. (2001). "Greek Banking at the Dawn of a New Millennium." In R. C. Bryant, N. C. Garganas, G. S. Tavlas (Eds.), *Greece's Economic Performance and Prospects.* Athens and Washington, D.C.: Bank of Greece and the Brookings Institution.

European Central Bank. (2003). *Inflation Differentials in the Euro Area: Potential Causes and Policy Implications.* September. Frankfurt.

European Economy: Reports and Studies. (1995). No. 3.

European Economy: Reports and Studies. (2000). No. 3.

Eurostat. "Second notification of deficit and debt data for 2003." News release 23 September, 2004.

Featherstone, K., and G. Kazamias (Eds.). (2001). *Europeanisation and the Southern Periphery.* London: Frank Cass.

Featherstone, K., and C. Radaelli (Eds.). (2003). *The Politics of Europeanisation.* Oxford: Oxford University Press.

Garganas, N. C., and G. S. Tavlas. (2001). "Monetary Regimes and Inflation Performance: The Case of Greece." In R. C. Bryant, N. C. Garganas, G. S. Tavlas (Eds.), *Greece's Economic Performance and Prospects.* Athens and Washington, D.C.: Bank of Greece and the Brookings Institution.

Greek Ministry of Labor and Social Security. (2003). *National Action Plan for Employment 2003.* The full text is available on the Commission's Web site.

Greek Ministry of National Economy. (1994). *Revised Economic Convergence Program 1994–1999.* Summer.

Greek Ministry of National Economy. (1998). *Update of the Hellenic Convergence Program 1998–2001.* June. Available at the Commission's Web site.

Greek Ministry of National Economy. (2001). *Main National Accounts Aggregates of the Greek Economy 1960–1999 (ESA-95).* January.

Hall, S. G., and N. G. Zonzilos. (2001). "The Determination of Wage and Price Inflation in Greece: An Application of Modern Cointegration Techniques." In R. C. Bryant, N. C. Garganas, G. S. Tavlas (Eds.), *Greece's Economic Perfor-

mance and Prospects. Athens and Washington, D.C.: Bank of Greece and the Brookings Institution.

IMF. (1999). "The Contribution of the Balassa-Samuelson Effect to Inflation: Cross-Country Evidence." In *Greece: Selected Issues* (chap. 3).

IMF. (2002). *Monetary and Exchange-Rate Policies of the Euro Area: Selected Issues.* IMF Country Report No. 02/236, chap. 1.

Kieler, M. (2003). "The ECB's Inflation Objective." IMF Working Paper, May.

Manassaki, A. (1998). "European Union Transfers to Greece: Historical Background and Prospects." Bank of Greece, *Economic Bulletin*, No. 12, December.

Mylonas, P., and G. Papaconstantinou. (2001). "Product Market Reform in Greece: Policy Priorities and Prospects." In R. C. Bryant, N. C. Garganas, G. S. Tavlas (Eds.), *Greece's Economic Performance and Prospects.* Athens and Washington, D.C.: Bank of Greece and the Brookings Institution.

OECD. (1995). *Economic Surveys: Greece* (chap. 3).

OECD. (1996). *Economic Surveys: Greece* (chap. 3).

OECD. (1998). *Economic Surveys: Greece* (chap. 4).

OECD. (2001, 2002, 2003). *Trends in International Migration.* Annual SOPEMI reports.

Sabethai, I. (1981). "Free Movement of Workers and Social Policy." In A. Mitsos et al., *The Accession to the European Communities* [in Greek]. Athens: Synchrona Themata.

Sabethai, I. (1997). "From Contractual Earnings to Labor Costs: Incomes Policy, Collective Bargaining and Inflation (1991–1996)" (in Greek). Bank of Greece, *Economic Bulletin*, No. 9 (March).

Sabethai, I. (1982). "Restrictions on the Right to Strike: Legal Provisions versus Union Action (A Bank Employees' Strike in Greece)." Université de Bordeaux I, *Bulletin de droit comparé du travail et de la securité sociale,* numéro spécial 1982/2 travaux de la conférence internationale de droit du travail organisée par l' Institut de l' Etat et du Droit de l' Académie Polonaise des Sciences, Varsovie, September 21–25.

Sabethai, I. (2000). "The Greek Labor Market: Features, Problems and Policies." Bank of Greece, *Economic Bulletin*, No. 16 (December).

Voridis, H., E. Angelopoulou, and I. Skotida. (2003). "Monetary Policy in Greece 1990–2000 through the Publications of the Bank of Greece." Bank of Greece, *Economic Bulletin* [in English], No. 20 (January).

Weise, C. (2001). "EU Eastern Enlargement Can Be Financed—Increased Need for Reforms—Scenarios for the 2007 and 2013 EU Budgets." DIW (Deutsches Institut für Wirtschaftsforschung), *Economic Bulletin* (October).

11

The Convergence Experience of the Greek Economy in the EU: Lessons for the EU Accession Countries

Athanasios Vamvakidis

The Greek growth experience in the European Union (EU) has had a divergence period (1981 to 1995) and a convergence period (1996 to 2002). Greece became the tenth member of the EU in January 1981 and the twelfth member of the euro area in January 2001. Greece joined the EU with gross domestic product (GDP) per capita at 59 percent of the average in the countries that are in the euro area today. At the end of 2002, Greece's per-capita GDP relative to the euro area had fallen to 56 percent. Has Greece's experience in the EU been one of divergence? The answer is positive for the period up to the mid-1990s (figure 11.1): Greece's relative per-capita output fell by eleven percentage points during this period. Greece started converging in the second half of the 1990s and recovered three-quarters of the lost ground by the end of 2002. In per-capita terms, Greece has grown faster than the euro area every year since 1996, by an annual average of 1.5 percentage points, compared with slower growth by an annual average of 1.4 percentage points in the period 1981 to 1995. What explains these two trends? What caused the break in the mid-1990s? Will Greece continue converging?

The strong growth performance of the Greek economy on the way to the euro and in recent years, compared with a very disappointing performance in the fifteen years following EU entry, is not a puzzle. It can be explained by better macroeconomic policies (fiscal consolidation and price stability) and structural reforms (reducing the role of the state in the economy and liberalizing financial, labor, and product markets)—factors that have been found to lead to faster growth according to the empirical-growth literature. Temporary factors also played a role, primarily the substantial decline in interest rates to euro-area levels in recent

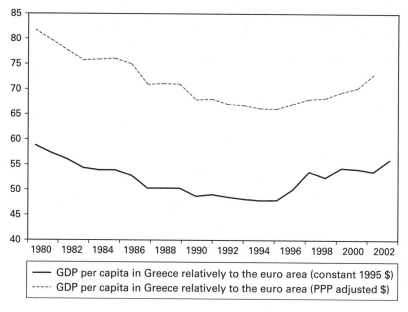

Figure 11.1
Greece, growth performance in per capita terms, 1980 to 2002

years. Some of the reforms may have been difficult for the Greek public to accept, particularly on structural issues that are often decided at the EU level and implemented through EU directives. In fact, the macroeconomic conditions in Greece had deteriorated so much by the mid-1990s that meeting the Maastricht criteria looked almost impossible.

The macroeconomic adjustment and the convergence experience of Greece on the way to the euro suggest a valuable lesson for the EU accession countries: EU participation alone does not lead to convergence; good policies do. Greece experienced divergence up until the mid-1990s because of deterioration in its macroeconomic aggregates and serious structural impediments to growth. Convergence since the mid-1990s went hand in hand with macroeconomic adjustment and progress in structural reforms. Furthermore, Greece's convergence speed is still slower than what estimates from conventional growth models would imply because, despite considerable steps forward in recent years, progress in the above reforms is still insufficient, leaving Greece behind euro-area averages in many areas.

Convergence in Greece after EU Accession

The initial convergence experience of Greece after joining the EU has been disappointing. Keeping everything else constant, Greece should be growing faster than most of the other member states simply because it started with a lower per-capita income. According to empirical evidence, countries do converge after controlling for a number of other growth determinants (see, for example, Barro 1991). Keeping everything else constant and assuming that Greece's steady-state income is determined by the average income of its trading partners, Greece should have grown faster after joining the EU as its steady-state position increased. Assuming a conditional convergence speed—convergence controlling for all other growth determinants—of 3 percent per year (Barro and Sala-I-Martin 1995), Greece should have grown faster than the euro area by 1.4 percentage points after joining the EU and by 1.9 percentage points after 1995, in per-capita terms. Instead, Greece grew less than the euro area by 1.4 percentage points up to the mid-1990s and more by 1.5 percentage points after 1995. Therefore, Greece experienced divergence in the 1980s and in the first half of the 1990s, while the convergence in the second half of the 1990s was not as fast as standard estimates in growth models would imply.

Greece's labor-market performance has also been disappointing since EU participation, although some improvement took place recently. Greece's unemployment rate increased gradually since EU entry from below 6 percent to 12 percent in 1999, before falling to below 10 percent in 2002. Despite strong economic growth since the mid-1990s, no appreciable progress has taken place in increasing employment, and Greece still has one of the lowest participation rates in the euro area. This poor labor-market performance has to do largely with a lack of flexibility in the labor market, where Greece scores poorly despite recent reforms.

Greece's growth experience since joining the EU is not a puzzle. The difference between what convergence should have been in Greece and actual experience is due largely to developments in the main growth determinants found by the empirical growth literature (table 11.1) (Barro and Sala-I-Martin 1995), as well as the considerable decline in interest rates that took place on the way to adopting the euro. Most of the

Table 11.1
Growth determinants in Greece (1980 to 2002) and in the euro area (2002)

	Greece				Euro Area
	1980	1990	1995	2002	2002
Convergence					
GDP per capita relative to the euro area (percentage)	58.7	48.7	47.8	55.9	100.0
Investment					
Gross fixed capital formation (percentage of GDP)	29.2	23.0	18.6	23.1	20.2
Private gross fixed capital formation (percentage of GDP)	14.6	18.7	15.4	19.2	17.3
Public gross fixed capital formation (percentage of GDP)	14.7	4.4	3.2	3.8	2.8
Foreign direct investment inflows (percentage of GDP)	1.4	1.2	0.9	0.0	1.8[1]
Macroeconomic policy					
General government balance (percentage of GDP)	−2.7	−16.1	−10.2	−1.2	−2.3
General government primary balance (percentage of GDP)	−0.3	−5.9	1.0	4.3	0.9
General government total revenue and grants (percentage of GDP)	27.9	32.1	36.5	41.4	46.6
General government total expenditure and net lending (percentage of GDP)	30.5	48.2	46.6	42.7	48.9
Primary expenditure (percentage of GDP)	28.2	38.0	35.5	37.1	45.7
General government debt (percentage of GDP)	25	81	109	105	69
CPI inflation (percentage)	24.9	20.4	8.9	3.9	2.3
Financial sector					
Domestic credit to private sector (percentage of GDP)	43.8	36.3	33.6	63.6[1]	102.8[1]
Lending interest rate (percentage)	21.3	27.6	23.1	7.4	6.1
Interest rate spread (percentage)	6.8	8.1	7.3	4.7	3.3
Human Capital					
Primary school enrollment ratio (percentage)	102.9	97.8	93.9	99.3[2]	104[2]
Secondary enrollment ratio (percentage)	81.2	93.3	95.3	98.4[2]	107[2]
Tertiary school enrollment ratio (percentage)	17.1	36.1	42.3	50.5[3]	52[4]

Table 11.1
(continued)

	Greece				Euro Area
	1980	1990	1995	2002	2002
Labor force with primary education (percentage of total)	.	52.6	49.7	44.8[4]	.
Labor force with secondary education (percentage of total)	.	25.0	28.0	29.2[4]	.
Labor force with tertiary education (percentage of total)	.	11.4	20.9	25.1[4]	.
Public spending on education (percentage of GDP)	2.0	2.4	2.9	3.8[2]	4.8[4]
Structural					
Trade in goods and services (percentage of GDP)	51.4	45.9	42.6	47.4	70.5
Freedom to trade with foreigners (increasing from 1 to 10)	5.6	6.1	6.6	7.6[1]	8.4
Economic freedom index (increasing from 1 to 10)	5.5	5.8	6.3	6.7[1]	7.3[1]
of which:					
Legal system and property rights	5.6	6.8	6.7	5.6	7.8[1]
Business regulation	—	—	4.7	4.8	5.7[1]
of which:					
Starting a new business	—	—	4.2	4.0	5.1[1]
OECD product market regulation index (decreasing from 1 to 3)	—	—	—	2.2[4]	1.7[5]
Labor market regulation index (increasing from 1 to 10)	3.6	3.7	4.0	3.8[1]	4.4[1]
Unemployment rate	5.5	7.0	9.1	9.9	8.4
Employment rate	56.7	57.4	56.4	57.0	63.9
Spending on active labor market policies (percentage of GDP)	—	0.8	0.9	0.8[4]	3.0[5]
Technology					
R&D spending (percentage of GDP)	—	—	0.5	0.7[5]	2.1[2]
Information and communication technology expenditure (percentage of GDP)	—	2.3	3.8	6.1[1]	7.2[1]
Personal computers (per 1,000 people)	—	17	33	81[1]	286[1]

Sources: IFS, WEO, WDI, OECD, Economic Freedom Network.
1. 2001.
2. 2000.
3. 1997.
4. 1998.
5. 1999.

factors that have been found in the literature to explain cross-country and time growth variations deteriorated in Greece during the period of divergence, 1980 to 1995, and improved during the period of convergence, 1996 to 2002. Greece is still not converging as fast as standard convergence estimates would imply because the gap for some of these indicators compared with their levels in the rest of the euro area remains large, especially in the following areas:

• Investment in physical capital followed very closely the growth trend during this period.[1] The share of fixed capital formation fell by ten percentage points in the period 1980 to 1995 and increased by more than four percentage points by 2002 to about three percentage points above the euro-area average. The share of public investment fell considerably after 1980, and it recovered only slightly after the mid-1990s. Most of the investment increase since 1995 was in private investment, which is about two percentage points above the euro-area average.[2]

• Macroeconomic policies also deteriorated considerably after EU accession and up until the macroeconomic adjustment after the mid-1990s.[3] Greece's general government deficit reached double digits as a share of GDP by the end of the 1980s before fiscal consolidation after the mid-1990s brought it down to close to 1 percent of GDP in 2002 (with a primary surplus of more than 4 percent of GDP). Greece joined the EU with a general government debt to GDP ratio of 25 percent and reached 109 percent by the mid-1990s. Public-sector debt remains above 100 percent of GDP despite recent progress in fiscal consolidation. Greece had a high inflation rate when joined the EU. Average annual inflation was 20 percent during the 1980s and the beginning of the 1990s. However, macroeconomic stabilization brought inflation down to single digits by the mid-1990s and to 2.6 percent in 1999. Inflation is currently about 1.5 percentage points above the euro-area average (about one percentage point is explained by Balassa-Samuelson effects) (Swagel 1999). Although fiscal consolidation and policies to bring down inflation can lead to slower growth in the short term, this does not seem to have been the case in Greece. Growth in Greece accelerated after the process of fiscal consolidation started. At the same time, efforts to address fiscal imbalances led to falling inflation rates, despite considerably lower interest rates.

• Greece's human capital is somewhat behind the human capital in the other euro-area countries, according to some indicators.[4] Enrollment ratios for primary, secondary, and tertiary education in Greece are slightly lower than the euro-area averages, but except for primary education, they have increased since EU entry. Public spending on education as a share of GDP also increased, by almost two percentage points since 1980, but remains one percentage point below the euro-area average. However, the stock of human capital, implied by data on the level of education of the labor force, is still relatively low in Greece.

• Greece's growth experience since joining the EU is also due to developments in the financial sector.[5] During the 1980s, the banking sector in Greece was heavily regulated: commercial banks had to invest three-quarters of their deposits to finance preferential activities, 40 percent of which had to be placed in treasury bills; banks were subject to strict branching regulations, restrictions on holdings of assets, and legal barriers to developing new financial products; and large state banks dominated the sector. A far-reaching liberalization of the Greek banking system started during the 1990s: interest rates were liberalized by 1990; rules forcing banks to invest in treasury bills and lend to state enterprises and preferential sectors were abolished in 1993; and capital-account transactions were liberalized by 1994.[6] Furthermore, privatization facilitated consolidation in the sector, while supervision, prudential regulation, and risk-management requirements were strengthened in accordance with the relevant EU directives. As a result, competition increased considerably, reducing interest-rate spreads—from about eight percentage points in the beginning of the 1990s to less than five percentage points in 2002—while bank profitability also increased considerably. The liberalization of the banking sector and the fall of interest rates to euro-area levels resulted in considerable credit expansion, although from very low levels: credit to the private sector fell from 44 percent of GDP in 1980 to 34 percent by 1995 but increased to 64 percent by 2001. However, despite recent consolidation and privatization, state-controlled banks remain an important feature of the Greek banking system, while Greek interest-rate spreads remain above the euro-area average by almost 1.5 percentage points. This suggests, among others, that competition in the Greek banking sector still lags behind that in the euro area.

• Although the Greek economy has been relatively open to foreign competition, its trade share declined during the 1980s and in the first half of the 1990s, and it only partially recovered after the mid-1990s.[7] Greece was an open economy at the time of EU accession, according to the Sachs and Warner (1995) openness measure, which captures many dimensions of protection. However, capital controls during the 1980s resulted in a black-market premium of about 10 percent, significantly distorting trade before the removal of the controls by the mid-1990s.[8] An index of freedom to trade with foreigners, capturing tariff and nontariff barriers and the size of the black-market premium, shows a gradual improvement since 1980. However, Greece has not been as integrated in the world economy as the rest of the euro area. Greece's trade share (the ratio of exports and imports to GDP) of about 47 percent remains well below the euro-area average of 70 percent. And the index of free trade is somewhat lower than the euro-area average.

• The lack of sufficient domestic competition has been another impediment to growth in Greece, but notable progress has been achieved more recently in some sectors.[9] Indices of product-market competition show a gradual improvement since joining the EU. However, many of these indices remain well below euro-area averages (which are well below the levels of these indices in the United Kingdom and the United States). A considerable number of large inefficient state enterprises were privatized during the 1990s. One-stop shops that facilitate the establishment of new businesses and reduce bureaucratic procedures have been established in recent years, but it is still too early to determine their effectiveness. The benefits from domestic competition have been clearly seen in Greece in recent years—in addition to the banking sector discussed above—in the telecommunication sector, where prices have fallen sharply and quality of products and services compares well with EU standards. However, in the electricity sector, efficiency gains have been hampered by continued cross-holdings and high entry barriers. A large number of inefficient state enterprises remain.

• Information technology (IT) and research and development (R&D) spending increased considerably in Greece during the 1990s, although from very low levels.[10] Spending in these areas is still very low in Greece compared with other industrial countries: Greece spends about one-third of what the euro area spends for R&D as a share of GDP and one percentage point less for IT. Internet use indicators and the number of computers per capita also show a relatively large gap in Greece compared with other industrial countries, despite more than doubling since the mid-1990s. Part of this is explained by higher costs in Greece for IT products and internet connection.[11] Low R&D spending has retarded the convergence of Greece, and therefore the increase in spending in this area in recent years, although not enough, is a positive development. However, there is evidence of a shortage of graduates with information technology skills and of limited links between the education system and the labor market, which has resulted in an oversupply of graduates in some sectors and an undersupply in others (especially for the new economy sectors) (Lutz 2001, Vamvakidis 2001b). A recent education reform promises to address this problem, but it is still at the initiation stage.

If Greece had not joined the EU, its growth performance could have been even slower. Greece's participation in the EU implied a change in the set of its trading partners. Recent research has found that the economic conditions in the trading partners of a country have important implications for domestic growth (Arora and Vamvakidis 2005). The growth performance and the relative GDP per capita of the trading partners of a country are positively correlated with domestic growth. This may be driven by spillover effects or specialization in technologically more advanced sectors when exporting to a more advanced country, which may also result in positive spillovers to other sectors in the economy. What do these estimates imply for Greece's growth performance since joining the EU? If Greece had kept the same trading partners as in the 1970s, the estimates suggest that annual growth would had been lower by one percentage point in the 1980s compared with the 1970s and by 0.2 percentage points compared with the actual growth rate in the 1980s. This is explained by two effects: the lower relative per-capita GDP of Greece's hypothetical trading partners in this scenario and their lower growth relative to that of Greece's actual trading partners. However, the acceleration of growth in Greece in the second half of the 1990s is not explained by external factors: Greece's trading partners' growth was almost equal before and after 1995.

The strong acceleration of growth in Greece since the mid-1990s has also been partly driven by temporary factors. Growth has been supported by the decline of interest rates to euro-area levels: the twelve-month lending rate fell from 18.6 percent in 1998 to 7.4 percent in 2002. As noted above, this, as well as the release of blocked excess reserves of banks, contributed importantly to strong credit growth. For example, mortgage lending has been growing in excess of 30 percent in recent years, although from a very low basis. Using estimates based on the Oxford economic-forecasting (OEF) model, growth without interest-rate convergence effects would have been lower by 1.5 percentage points in 2001. Other temporary factors that have supported growth in recent years include the sizable EU transfers, expected to decline considerably in the medium term, and investment for the preparation of the 2004 Olympics.

The Growth Dividend of Reform in Greece

The trend in total factor productivity (TFP) growth in Greece since EU accession is an indication of the growth impact of recent reforms. The previous section argued that the considerably improved growth performance of the Greek economy since the mid-1990s followed macroeconomic and structural reforms that were found in the literature to contribute to faster growth. The stagnation of output in the fifteen-year period following EU accession went together with the deterioration of macroeconomic aggregates and the presence of many structural impediments to growth. Indeed, estimations from a standard production function indicate that TFP growth was negative during the period 1981 to 1995, equal to an annual average of −0.8 percent, while it increased by three percentage points to an annual average of 2.2 percent in the period 1996 to 2002 (figure 11.2).[12]

Estimates from a standard growth model can provide a more concrete indication of the growth dividend of reforms in Greece in recent years. Vamvakidis and Zanforlin (2002) have estimated such a model, which included most of the growth determinants analyzed above. Estimates from this model suggest that the growth dividend from the reforms that took place in Greece in the second half of the 1990s and up to 2002 is

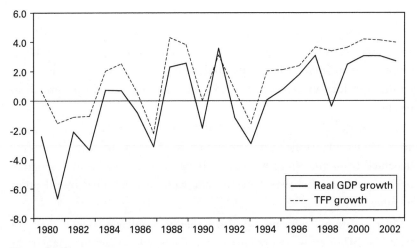

Figure 11.2
Greece, real GDP growth and total factor productivity growth, 1980 to 2002

about 1.5 percentage points annually. Had the values of the growth determinants reached the level in the rest of the euro area, this growth dividend would have been higher by another half percentage point. If these determinants had reached the levels in Ireland, the fastest-growing country in the euro area in recent years, Greece would have grown faster by another half percentage point.

Concluding Remarks: Lessons for the EU Accession Countries and Challenges Ahead

The experience of the Greek economy since joining the EU, both the divergence period of 1980 to 1995 and the convergence period of 1996 to 2002, suggests useful lessons for the EU accession countries:

· The first and perhaps most important lesson is that participating in the EU will not necessarily lead to convergence. Convergence is conditional on good policies—macroeconomic and structural. If such policies are present, countries can benefit from trading within a large market, which includes some of the most developed countries in the world economy.

· The Greek case suggests that macroeconomic and structural reforms do deliver substantial growth benefits. Divergence in the period 1980 to

1995 was clearly connected with steps backward in these areas, while the much improved growth performance in recent years was connected with steps forward. Fiscal consolidation, low inflation, product-market liberalization, labor-market flexibility, and steps in other areas to increase domestic and foreign competition have led to faster growth in Greece in recent years.

• Some of the structural reforms that Greece undertook in recent years are considerably easier to initiate within the EU. Many of these reforms benefited from guidelines from EU directives. They were also acceptable by the public as EU requirements that were also adopted by all other member states.

• Macroeconomic reforms are also easier to implement when they are based on EU or euro-area requirements. The need to meet the Maastricht criteria to be a part of the euro area was one of the main factors, if not the most important factor, that made macroeconomic reforms in Greece possible in the late 1990s. The public supported these reforms because meeting the Maastricht criteria was a priority for Greece. Such reforms are often linked to political costs, but in the case of Greece, exactly the opposite was the case: failing to reform and be a part of the euro area would have implied a large political cost.

Despite the considerable achievements since the mid-1990s in terms of convergence, Greece faces considerable challenges ahead. If anything, the Greek experience since EU accession shows that these challenges cannot be ignored if convergence is to continue and even accelerate. Convergence in Greece is still not as fast as implied by convergence estimates in standard growth models because it still lags behind other industrial countries in many of the factors that support convergence. Furthermore, as noted above, growth in recent years has been in part supported by temporary factors and can continue at its present pace only through further reforms:

• *Fiscal consolidation:* With public debt still one of the highest in the euro area as a share of GDP, bolder fiscal consolidation steps are required, particularly to cut primary spending. Fiscal consolidation since the mid-1990s was based on higher revenues and lower interest payments: primary spending actually increased during this period. Although

Greece spends considerably less than the euro as a share of GDP, Greece also collects considerably less revenue and has a much higher public-sector debt. This leaves cutting primary spending as the main path to fiscal consolidation—in particular given the ongoing tax reform, a positive step, which includes cuts in tax rates. Greece should take advantage of its currently favorable cyclical position for more progress in this area.

• *Pension reform:* Pension expenditures are projected to increase, absent reforms, by more than in any other EU country, almost doubling in relation to GDP (from already relatively high levels) by 2050.[13] Recent reform steps to consolidate the system are positive but have so far failed to address the underlying expenditure pressures. Greece will need to introduce bold reforms in this area to avoid explosive long-term debt dynamics.

• *Reducing inflation:* Despite considerable progress toward price stability in recent years, inflation remains about 1.5 percentage points above the euro-area average. The part of this differential that is not explained by Balassa-Samuelson erodes competitiveness. This deserves serious consideration since monetary union does not provide the option to support competitiveness through devaluations, a solution often used by Greece in the past. Further progress in fiscal consolidation will go a long way to reduce the inflation differential, as will further steps in product-market liberalization.

• *Reducing the role of the state (privatization and product-market liberalization):* Despite recent progress, Greece still scores poorly in indicators of competition and product-market liberalization. Increasing competition in product markets, facilitating new-firm entry, including foreign direct investment, continuing with the ambitious program for privatization, and reducing and rationalizing bureaucratic procedures should be elements of Greece's convergence strategy.

• *Labor-market reform:* The achievement of employment-rich growth requires flexible labor markets (Lutz 2001). An unemployment rate of 8.9 percent (in the second quarter of 2003) for an economy that during the last seven years has been growing by close to 4 percent is a clear indication of a very inflexible labor market. Greece's employment rate—the ratio of the number of employees to working-age population—remained broadly constant since EU entry, and at 57 percent in 2002, it remains well below the euro-area average of close to 64 percent. Greece particularly needs steps to facilitate labor-market entry by women and the young and to increase spending on active labor-market policies. Recent reforms to facilitate the use of atypical labor contracts—part-time employment and fixed-term contracts—are positive steps in this direction and should be pursued further.

Notes

The author would like to thank Thomas Krueger and Mark Lutz for helpful comments. The views in this chapter are entirely the author's and do not necessarily reflect those of the International Monetary Fund.

1. Investment in physical capital is one of the most robust determinants of growth (Levine and Renelt 1992), although the impact can be both ways (Blomstrom, Lipsey, and Zejan 1996).

2. Foreign direct-investment inflows have been very limited in Greece and well below the euro-area average.

3. For the impact of fiscal policy on growth, see Easterly and Rebelo (1993). For the impact of inflation on growth, see Bruno and Easterly (1996).

4. On the impact of human capital on growth, see Benhabib and Spiegel (1994) and Engelbrecht (2003).

5. Indicators of financial-sector development are positively correlated with growth (see Levine, 1997, for a discussion of the literature).

6. For details, see Eichengreen and Gibson (2001) and Vamvakidis (2001a).

7. The literature on the links of openness and growth is vast. For a discussion of the early empirical and theoretical literature, see Bhagwati and Srinivasan (1985). For more recent literature reviews, see Greenaway, Morgan, and Wright (1998), Bhagwati and Srinivasan (2002), Vamvakidis (2002), and Baldwin (2003).

8. The source for Greece's black-market premium is the Barro and Lee data set: ⟨http://www.nuff.ox.ac.uk/economics/growth/barlee.htm⟩.

9. Indices measuring the extent of domestic competition have been found to lead to faster growth (Vamvakidis and Zanforlin 2002). For evidence on the negative growth impact of state-led industrialization, see Sachs (1996).

10. For theoretical foundations of the impact of R&D on growth, see Grossman and Helpman (1991), and for empirical evidence, see Coe and Helpman (1995).

11. For details on information technology and the use of the Internet in Greece, see Vamvakidis (2001b).

12. Some caution would be warranted here, since the improvement in data quality during recent years may explain part of the large break in TFP growth.

13. For details, see IMF Country Report No. 03/156, Lutz (2002), and Börsch-Supan and Tinios (2001).

References

Arora, Vivek, and Athanasios Vamvakidis. (2004). "How Much Do Trading Partners Matter for Growth?" IMF Staff Papers 52 (41), pp. 24–40.

Baldwin, Robert E. (2003). "Openness and Growth: What's the Empirical Relationship?" NBER Working Paper 9578.

Barro, Robert. (1991). "Economic Growth in a Cross Section of Countries." *Quarterly Journal of Economics, 106:* 407–443.

Barro, Robert, and Xavier Sala-I-Martin. (1995). *Economic Growth.* New York: McGraw-Hill.

Benhabib, J., and M. M. Spiegel. (1994). "The Role of Human Capital in Economic Development: Evidence from Aggregate Cross-Country Data." *Journal of Monetary Economics, 34:* 143–173.

Bhagwati, Jagdish N., and T. N. Srinivasan. (1985). "Trade Policy and Development." In Gene Grossman (Ed.), *Dependence and Interdependence.* Cambridge, MA: MIT Press.

Bhagwati, Jagdish N., and T. N. Srinivasan. (2002). "Trade and Poverty in Poor Countries." *American Economic Review, 92:* 180–183.

Blomstrom, M., R. E. Lipsey, and M. Zejan. (1996). "Is Fixed Investment the Key to Economic Growth." *Quarterly Journal of Economics, 111:* 269–276.

Börsch-Supan, Axel, and Platon Tinios. (2001). "The Greek Pension System: Strategic Framework for Reform." In Ralph C. Bryant, Nicholas C. Garganas, and George S. Tavlas (Eds.), *Greece Economic Performance and Prospects.* Athens and Washington, D.C.: Bank of Greece and the Brookings Institution.

Bruno, Michael, and William Easterly. (1996). "Inflation and Growth: In Search of a Stable Relationship." *Federal Reserve Bank of St. Louis Review, 78:* 139–146.

Coe, David T., and Elhanan Helpman. (1995). "International R&D Spillovers." *European Economic Review, 39:* 859–887.

Easterly, William, and Sergio Rebelo. (1993). "Fiscal Policy and Economic Growth." *Journal of Monetary Economics, 32:* 417–458.

Eichengreen, Barry, and Heather D. Gibson. (2001). "Greek Banking at the Dawn of the New Millennium." In Ralph C. Bryant, Nicholas C. Garganas, and George S. Tavlas (Eds.), *Greece Economic Performance and Prospects.* Athens and Washington, D.C.: Bank of Greece and the Brookings Institution.

Engelbrecht, Hans-Jurgen. (2003). "Human Capital and Economic Growth: Cross-Section Evidence for OECD Countries." *Economic Record, 79:* 40–51.

Greenaway, David, Wyn Morgan, and Peter Wright. (1998). "Trade Reform, Adjustment and Growth: What Does the Evidence Tell Us?" *Economic Journal, 108*: 1547–1561.

Grossman, G., and E. Helpman. (1991). *Innovation and Growth in the Global Economy*. Cambridge, MA: MIT Press.

Levine, Ross. (1997). "Financial Development and Economic Growth: Views and Agenda." *Journal of Economic Literature, 35*: 688–726.

Levine, Ross, and David Renelt. (1992). "A Sensitivity Analysis of Cross-Country Growth Regressions." *American Economic Review, 82*: 942–963.

Lutz, Mark. (2001). "Greece Labor Market: Grappling with High Unemployment." IMF Country Report 01/57.

Lutz, Mark. (2002). "Greece: Selected Issue—An Overview of Pension Reform." IMF Country Report 02/58.

Sachs, Jeffrey D. (1996). "Notes on the Life Cycle of State-Led Industrialization." *Japan and the World Economy, 8*: 153–174.

Sachs, Jeffrey D., and Andrew Warner. (1995). "Economic Reform and the Process of Global Integration." Brooking Papers of Economic Activity 1–95.

Swagel, Phillip. (1999). "The Contribution of the Balassa-Samuelson Effects on Inflation: Cross-Country Evidence." IMF Country Report 99/138.

Vamvakidis, Athanasios. (2001a). "The Greek Banking Sector at the Time of EMU Entry: Recent Developments and Challenges Ahead." IMF Country Report 01/57.

Vamvakidis, Athanasios. (2001b). "The New Economy in Greece." IMF Country Report 01/57.

Vamvakidis, Athanasios. (2002). "How Robust Is the Growth-Openness Connection? Historical Evidence." *Journal of Economic Growth, 7*(1): 57–80.

Vamvakidis, Athanasios, and Luisa Zanforlin. (2002). "Selected Euro-Area Countries: The Determinants of Growth—The Experience in the Southern European Economies of Greece and Portugal." IMF Country Report 02/91.

12

Real Convergence within the European Union: The Case of Ireland

Thomas O'Connell and Diarmaid Smyth

For many years, Ireland was something of a European outlier with living standards, as measured by gross domestic product (GDP) per capita, being between just 60 and 70 percent of the European Union (EU) average in the 1960s, 1970s, and 1980s (figure 12.1). It has been only in the last decade or so that Ireland attained real convergence, and this rapid catch-up has attracted a good deal of international attention. Perhaps a more interesting question is why Ireland in large part missed out on the golden period of strong economic growth in Western Europe between the late 1940s and the early 1970s. In their recent review of Ireland's convergence experience, Honohan and Walsh (2002) equally regard the substantial gains of the last decade or so as a deferred and telescoped process compared with the more steady gains of industrialized countries generally over the past half century or so. Ireland's historic failure in the economic field has been its poor employment performance. With this went a traditionally high rate of emigration, most of which could be regarded as involuntary.

The main lesson from the Irish experience is that there are certain key prerequisites necessary to sustain high growth—namely, sound macroeconomic policies, a strong commitment to free trade, a lightly regulated competitive microeconomic environment, and a well-educated and flexible labor force. Furthermore, in Ireland's case as a small open economy, conditions in the international economy have been an important influence on the pace of convergence.

In this chapter, the main factors that contributed to convergence are discussed. I present a view from a central-banking perspective to complement the presentation of my colleague, whose expertise is primarily a

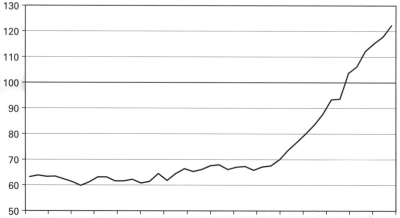

Figure 12.1
GDP per head at current market prices and PPS: EU15 = 100

real-economy one. As a prelude to this, I begin with a brief overview of issues pertinent to recent Irish economic history.

Background

To all intents and purposes, Ireland functioned as an economic region of the United Kingdom through most of the twentieth century. Reflecting the country's history, the major structural and legal institutions of the state have largely mirrored those of the United Kingdom. This provided the essential, if not necessarily sufficient, preconditions for economic development. Since the establishment of the state in 1922, Ireland maintained a no-margins one-for-one link with sterling with complete freedom of capital mobility. This amounted to a currency-board type of regime with monetary conditions set by the hegemonial currency country. There continued to be extremely close trade-, financial-, and factor-market linkages between Ireland and the United Kingdom until recent times. Ireland seemed to meet the optimum currency-area criteria compared with the United Kingdom that should be met in accordance with Mundell's insights (Whitaker, 1973). This monetary regime served Ireland well, until the breakdown of the Bretton Woods arrangements in

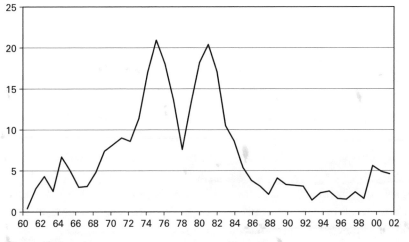

Figure 12.2
Inflation, Consumer Price Index

the early 1970s, which introduced major uncertainties into what the optimal monetary regime should be. The link with sterling began to be questioned in academic and policy circles during the 1970s as Ireland imported a high and volatile inflation rate from the United Kingdom as a consequence of the currency link (figure 12.2). Nonetheless, the monetary and exchange-rate regime continued until the opportunity of joining the European Monetary System arose in 1978 with the prospect of importing lower inflation from the more inflation-averse core EU countries and of developing closer ties with continental Europe. Some commentators at the time noted the apparent paradox that the creation of a zone of monetary stability that the EMS represented coincided with the break up of an existing monetary union.

Ireland adopted predominantly protectionist and inward-looking policies until well beyond the midpoint of the last century. Notwithstanding the small domestic market, the emphasis of development policy was on promoting domestic industry behind high tariff barriers. Not surprisingly, these misconceived policies were not successful in delivering sustained economic growth and higher living standards. Employment failed to increase, and, indeed, emigration for economic reasons rose to very high levels. The legacy of protectionist policies was a small and inefficient indigenous sector, which served the domestic market. The failure of protectionism and overreliance on the agricultural sector were recognized in the late 1950s, and over the course of the next two decades, the economy was progressively opened up to trade and investment.

There were two key strands to the adopted export-led industrial-policy strategy: the elimination of barriers to trade and the adoption of policies to attract inward foreign direct investment. As regards the former, Ireland moved increasingly toward freer trade in the 1960s with tariff reductions in 1963 and 1964. This was followed by the Anglo-Irish Free Trade Area Agreement signed in 1965 and subsequent rounds of the General Agreement on Tariffs and Trade (GATT) from 1967 onward. These developments were followed by perhaps the most significant step of all—namely, Ireland's membership of the European Economic Community (EEC) in 1973. This led to further reductions in trade barriers compared with other EEC countries, with all of these being removed by 1977. These steps intensified pressures on indigenous industry to adapt to the new competitive environment. The importance of the integrated EU market to Ireland and the decoupling that it entailed from the UK economy is elaborated on in chapter 13 by Bradley in this volume.

The second key strand to Ireland's new outward orientation lay in the creation of an industrial promotion agency with the responsibility for promoting an export-oriented manufacturing sector and with a special brief for attracting foreign direct investment. The new outward orientation was underlined by the abolition of corporate taxes on profits from exports. Indeed, since the 1960s to the present day, industrial policy has been geared toward attracting high-productivity export-oriented foreign industries through a combination of a low corporate tax regime and selective grants. At this stage, however, grants are limited, and in fact, Ireland now ranks rather low among EU countries as far as state aids are concerned.

Economic performance from the early 1960s until the problems caused by the first oil shock in the early 1970s was quite good, certainly relative to previous experience. However, despite this growth, no progress was made in closing the gap in living standards between Ireland and its neighbors. At the same time, it has to be recognized that during this period substantial structural changes in the economy had to be effected with the large-scale downsizing of inefficient domestic industry and the modernization of agriculture with attendant large employment reductions in these sectors.

Macroeconomic Activism, 1973 to 1986

Ireland pursued relatively activist macroeconomic policies over the decade and a half or so after the first oil crisis in 1973. In fact, as a consequence, the country has been something of a useful case study in good and bad macro policies. The public has learned the hard way the high cost of pursuing imprudent policies and the truth of the old adage that there is no free lunch. In retrospect, there was a rather naive intention to promote growth through expansionary fiscal policy and a reluctance to accept the negative real income effects of the adverse movement in the terms of trade associated with oil-price increases. During most of this period, fiscal policy was strongly expansionary, with, for example, the current budget deficit increasing from 0.4 percent of GDP in 1973 to 6.8 percent in 1978. From 1976 to 1980, real GDP growth averaged 4.5 percent per annum (see table 12.1).

By the early 1980s, the untenable nature of these policies had become clear. The nadir was reached in 1981, when the government borrowing requirement as a percentage of GDP reached 15 percent (figure 12.3). The mounting fiscal imbalances were coupled with major external imbalances, and between 1978 and 1982, the current account deficit on the balance of payments averaged 10.8 per cent of GDP (figure 12.4). With a small domestic capital market, high government borrowing levels had to be financed overseas with the result of an exploding volume of foreign debt. Consequently, the ratio of debt to GDP increased from approx-

Table 12.1
Main aggregates, annual average percentage change

Variable	1976–1980	1981–1986	1987–1993	1994–2000
GNP	3.7%	1.2%	4.2%	8.5%
GDP	4.5	2.7	4.5	9.3
Inflation (CPI)	14.1	11.0	2.9	2.5
Employment	1.5	−1.1	1.5	5.3

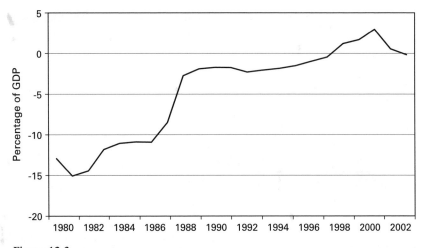

Figure 12.3
Exchequer borrowing requirement

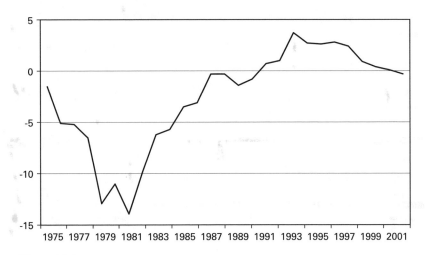

Figure 12.4
Current account balance

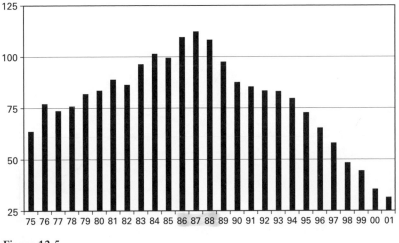

Figure 12.5
National debt

imately 50 percent in the early 1970s to reach 112 percent by 1987 (figure 12.5), with approximately 90 percent of economywide income-tax receipts being used to service the national debt at this time. Indeed, in the early 1980s, total government expenditure averaged 54 percent of GDP (figure 12.6). The critical state of the public finances is summarized in table 12.2 for selected years.

In the monetary sphere, although the Irish pound joined the European Monetary System (EMS) in 1979, there was little monetary discipline because of the large-scale high-powered money financing of the government deficit. Ex ante monetary financing contributed to increases in the money stock of the order of 30 to 40 percent in some years, although the demand for money grew by only a fraction of this. The result predictably was large-scale deficits on the external current and private capital account. With such strong expansionary impulses and the effect of inertial inflation, there was little surprise that the country did not enjoy the low inflation rates of the core EMS countries that some commentators suggested would be realized soon after joining the EMS.

These undisciplined policies were having an equally adverse effect on the real economy. With the exchange rate being supported within the EMS by the proceeds of foreign borrowing, there was a significant

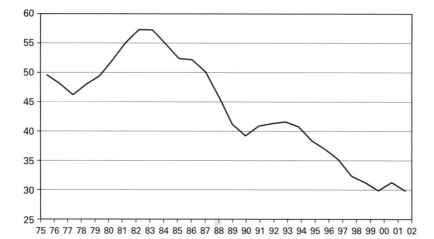

Figure 12.6
Government expenditure

Table 12.2
Government finances, percentage of GDP

Variable	1975	1980	1985	1990	1995	2000
General government balance	−15.8%	−12.9%	−10.8%	−2.2%	−2.2%	4.4%
Primary balance	−10.6	−6.2	−0.3	6.3	4.1	5.5
Total government spending	49.6	52.1	52.4	39.2	38.4	29.9
National debt	63.8	83.7	99.6	87.7	72.9	35.5

Note: Exchequer balance used for general government balance figures prior to 1990.

real appreciation, notwithstanding occasional unilateral DM revaluations within the EMS. In 1983, the economy contracted in real GDP and GNP terms with Ireland's misery index above 24 percent (figure 12.7). Consequently, unemployment and emigration soared in the early 1980s, with the unemployment rate increasing by over ten percentage points to average 17.4 percent between 1979 and 1986. Growth was anemic in contrast to more developed economies, and total employment in the economy fell by 6.4 percent over this period. What little growth there was, was accounted for by the still reasonably strong inflows of

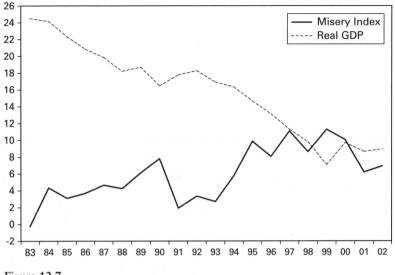

Figure 12.7
Misery index and GDP

foreign direct investment. Since much of this was of a capital-intensive nature, the country experienced what became known as jobless growth.

By the mid-1980s, therefore, the economy had reached a crisis point. Although substantial efforts had been made to arrest the deterioration in the public finances, this seemed like a Sisyphean task for a number of reasons. First, while some progress was made, notably in relation to the primary deficit, a rising stock of public debt and high world interest rates associated with the skewed policy mix in the United States increased debt-servicing costs and made it difficult to make progress. Second, the approach to fiscal consolidation was misconceived. The emphasis was placed on increasing taxes, primarily income taxes. At the same time, unemployment and welfare payments were increased in real terms. At one point, marginal tax rates, including employee social security deductions, on average employee incomes were as high as 77 percent. The effect on work incentives was extremely negative with the emergence of unemployment and poverty traps and, related to this, rising numbers of long-term unemployed.

This approach ran entirely contrary to what experience with successful fiscal consolidation would suggest should have been done (Mackenzie,

Orsmond, and Gerson 1997; Alesina and Perotti 1997). This approach, together with competitive problems associated with a real exchange appreciation, weighed on the real economy and contracted the tax base. The third problem arose from the fact that too much reliance was placed on the EMS exchange-rate arrangement to serve as a nominal anchor when other policies were not consistent with this. Experience shows that it can be a major policy mistake to put too much weight on the nominal anchor role of the exchange rate to stabilize the economy if this gives rise to an overvaluation of the currency. I can recollect Stanley Fischer writing many years ago that persisting with an overvalued currency was the most serious policy mistake of macroeconomic policy generally.

In the early 1980s, no systematic effort was made by the Central Bank to sterilize the large high-powered money creation that flowed from the extensive foreign borrowing of government. These high rates of money creation relative to the demand for money gave rise to substantial exchange-market pressure in the sense of Girton and Roper (1977). At the same time, the exchange-rate obligations of EMS membership called for substantial foreign-exchange intervention by the Central Bank to support the currency. In a nutshell, there was a carousel effect whereby foreign borrowing by government was used to support the exchange rate, which was under continuous pressure as a consequence of money-market imbalances deriving mainly from the monetization of the government deficit. Such a situation could not continue without an unstable explosion of foreign debt. The failed efforts to stabilize the economy were the subject of a study, "Credibility, Debt, and Unemployment: Ireland's Failed Stabilisation," by the late Rudi Dornbusch (1989), although, by the time of publication of his paper, there was a sharp reorientation of fiscal policy, which put the economy back on a sustainable path.

Fiscal Stabilization and Growth

By the mid-1980s, there was a wide public and political acceptance that there had to be a radical reorientation of policy. The era of high public spending financed by large tax increases and substantial borrowing had to end. The major elements of a recovery entailed the following:

• Substantial cuts in nominal public spending;

• A tripartite wage agreement between employers, trade unions, and government whereby low nominal wage increases were traded off against income tax reductions; and

• A devaluation of 8 percent within the EMS.

This reorientation of policy amounted in essence to the adoption of what has come to be known as, in John Williamson's words (1990), the Washington Consensus policy package, in its original form. The main elements of this are macroeconomic stability, economic openness, deregulation, and tax reform.

The external environment in which this adjustment took place became more benign. In particular, world interest rates eased substantially, thereby reducing the large debt-service burden, and economic growth picked up internationally, particularly in the United Kingdom, then and still an important export market for Ireland. Furthermore, the transfer of EU structural funds proved to be particularly useful in the early 1990s, when financial constraints were present, and helped spur a recovery in investment spending after the previous decade. A further channel through which the receipt of EU funds helped to raise the economy's growth potential was through investment in education and training. The structural funds also led to a more rigorous examination of infrastructural needs and improved policy, planning, and evaluation through systematic reviews of investment projects. The importance of the structural funds to the economy and Ireland's role in EU regional policy are discussed in chapter 13 by Bradley in this volume.

In these circumstances, growth resumed with a recovery in both exports and domestic demand. The latter had been very subdued against the background of a deteriorating economy in the first half of the 1980s. In fact, the phenomenon of increased domestic demand in the context of highly restrictive fiscal policy became the subject of a number of studies (Giavazzi and Pagano, 1990). The sharp improvement in the public finances is evident from figure 12.8 (and previous figures 12.3, 12.5, and 12.6), which shows that the primary balance as a percentage of GDP moved into surplus in 1987. From that point on through the 1990s, economic performance was very satisfactory apart from the

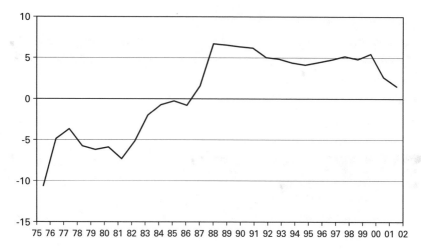

Figure 12.8
Primary balance

temporary difficulties associated with the currency crisis of 1992 and 1993. Indeed, real GDP growth averaged approximately 9 percent from 1994 through 2000 (figure 12.9 and table 12.1). Employment as a lagging variable was somewhat slower to respond; there were, nonetheless, substantial employment increases (figure 12.10 and table 12.1) with over half a million people finding employment over the course of the decade (an increase of 46 percent).

Increasing Real and Monetary Integration in Europe

Ireland's failure to converge prior to the 1990s can be attributed to a number of factors, notably the legacy of protectionism and, related to this, the relative lateness in adopting an outward economic orientation together with major macroeconomic policy errors in the decade between the mid 1970s and 1980s. At the same time, the underlying institutional preconditions were in place to facilitate the attainment of advanced-country living standards.

As the country began to get to grips with the problems of the public finances in the mid-1980s, there were further concerns as the impetus to

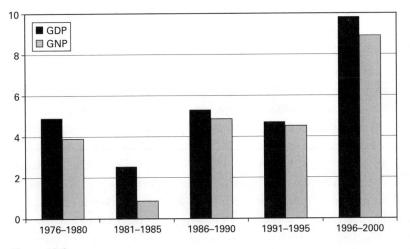

Figure 12.9
Economic growth, annual averages

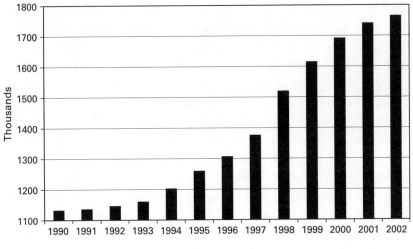

Figure 12.10
Total employment

a more fully integrated EU market and monetary union took hold. To some degree this may have reflected the pessimism of the times. In the first half of the 1980s, over half of the manufacturing jobs that existed five years earlier had been lost, although some of these had been replaced by employment flowing from foreign direct investment. The main concern was that in the single European market and with a monetary union there would be a danger of a substantial divergence in economic performance between core and peripheral regions of the EU (Doyle, 1991). The then governor of the Irish Central Bank at the time stated, in a submission on regional aspects of the EMU to the Delors Report, that Ireland had no intention of being left behind to become the Appalachia of Europe. In the event, the cohesion funds were introduced to prepare the four relatively low-income EU countries for EMU and, in particular, to facilitate further real convergence without putting pressure on the public finances.

The concern was that Ireland was not particularly well placed, both literally and metaphorically, to benefit from the completion of the single European market and the EMU. Unlike the industrial structure of core EU countries—Germany, France, and the Benelux countries—Ireland had only a moderate degree of intraindustry trade with EU countries (Neven, 1990). Ireland was shown to have a revealed comparative advantage in natural resources (food) and high human-capital-type industries. At the same time, other studies (O'Malley, 1990) showed that Ireland was relatively underrepresented in sectors where economies of scale are most important, such as motor vehicles, other transportation, chemicals, and synthetic fibers. These were the sectors that could be expected to gain from scale economies as the EU became more integrated. In a relatively fragmented EU market, however, it was scarcely surprising that, with its small market, such sectors were not very significant in Ireland. According to O'Malley's estimates, only 40 percent of Ireland's industrial employment was in sectors characterized by scale economies compared with 57 percent in the EU generally at the time. Perhaps these concerns were overdone. A Krugman-Venables (1990) analysis would suggest, by contrast, that peripheral low-cost countries could stand to gain from a fully integrated market. In this environment, such countries could benefit as industries sought to establish in low-cost countries from which they could supply the entire market. These factors would be reinforced as trade in more knowledge-intensive lighter products became more important (Krugman, 1997). In such a world, transportation costs became less relevant in industrial location decisions, given the rapid expansion in traded services and higher value-to-weight trade in manufactures. An important related factor was that, in these circumstances, comparative advantage can take on a dynamic character. It need no longer be immutably tied closely to endowments in the old Hecksher-Ohlin sense. Investment in human capital and innovation could alter a country's comparative advantage.

Achieving Real Convergence

The reorientation of macroeconomic policy in 1987 and the favorable international economic environment provided the basis for resumed economic growth after the traumas of the earlier period. Performance improved from 1987 and a period of exceptionally strong growth followed from 1994 until 2000 (see figure 12.9 and table 12.1). Various studies have tried to uncover the reasons for the boom. Perhaps the most authoritative of these are those of the OECD (1999) and Honohan and Walsh (2002). The conclusions of these are that there is no single overriding explanation for this transformation.

A generally recognized essential element was the restoration of stability in the public finances. Having learned from the unhappy experience of earlier fiscal excesses and the great difficulties encountered in trying to redress these, fiscal policy was put on a sound footing. This commitment was underpinned by the need to meet the nominal convergence criteria of the Maastricht Treaty if Ireland were to qualify for EMU. On the monetary front, following the 8 percent devaluation of August 1986, the Irish pound continued to participate in the narrow-band EMS. This served to anchor inflation and inflation expectations supported by the modest nominal pay increases agreed to as part of the social partnership arrangements. As stated earlier, these low pay increases were accepted in the context of a program to reduce the very high rates of personal taxation that had arisen over previous years as the government struggled to reduce the borrowing requirement.

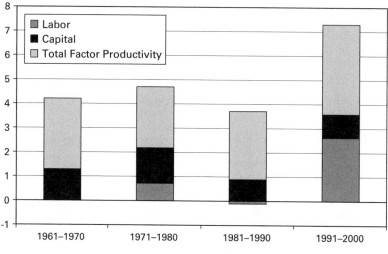

Figure 12.11
Contributions to output growth (GDP)

The second key policy element post-1987 was the pursuit of a process of structural reform and, in particular, tax reform. To some extent, this was driven by the deregulation process in the United Kingdom. As long as Ireland's labor market remained closely tied to that of the United Kingdom, it was clear that policies would have to take account of policy changes being made in the United Kingdom. Furthermore, in the light of significant unemployment traps in the economy and an unsustainably high rate of unemployment in the 1980s, it was recognized that tax reforms were necessary to improve work incentives. Through a series of social partnership agreements, concerted efforts were taken to secure wage restraint in return for tax cuts.

A growth-accounting decomposition of output into its supply-side factors shows that the very substantial increase in labor inputs explains the upturn in performance (figure 12.11 and table 12.3). Just as Krugman showed in relation to the earlier Asian miracle, there was no revolution in productivity performance. Increased labor supply was available from a relatively large inactive proportion of the population, a low female participation rate, and a large pool of unemployed—still 16 percent in 1993. Furthermore, there was a significant amount of underemployment

Table 12.3
Contributions to annual average output growth, percentage of GDP

Variable	1961–1970	1971–1980	1981–1990	1991–2000
Labor	0.0%	0.7%	−0.1%	2.6%
Capital	1.3	1.5	0.9	1.0
Total factor productivity	2.9	2.5	2.8	3.7
GDP	4.2	4.7	3.6	7.3

in agriculture and a relatively strong natural increase in the labor force coupled with a quite elastic supply of labor given the large movements of labor between Ireland and the United Kingdom. In addition, with increased emphasis on education since the late 1960s and active labor-market policies, the average quality of labor was rising substantially. Disincentives in the labor market were improved—substantially on the supply side; less so on the demand side, where taxes and social security contributions were, in any event, quite low by European standards. Since then, Ireland has generally opted for a light degree of regulation of labor and product markets with the object of promoting well-functioning, flexible markets. This has stood the country in good stead over the past decade or more in coping with various vicissitudes.

During the boom period, the country's employment rate increased from a little over 50 percent to over 67 percent, above the EU average; employment itself increased by over 50 percent. A notable feature was that over three-quarters of this increase was accounted by the services sector (figure 12.12). The construction sector also accounted for a significant part of the increase. There was a modest increase in industrial employment and a fall in the number employed in agriculture. The market-services sector in Ireland had long been poorly developed, a point often made by EU Commission commentaries on the Irish economy. A number of factors contributed to this expansion of the services sector. On the supply side, a more strongly probusiness environment was promoted; regulatory reform was progressed, and corporate profits tax on services was progressively reduced from a level of 50 percent to that of industrial companies—$12\frac{1}{2}$ percent. The physiocratic philosophy that previously favored industry had to be altered to ensure a uniform tax

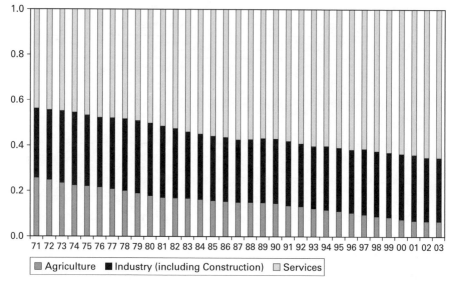

Figure 12.12
Employment by sector, relative shares

treatment of corporate profits for all enterprises on foot of EU legal requirements. On the demand side, higher incomes and a recovery of domestic demand generally from its very depressed levels until the mid-1980s were associated with a rising demand for services. The strong flows of inward direct investment also contributed to this.

Commentators usually attribute an important role to foreign direct investment (FDI) in this catching-up process. The OECD (1999), for example, regards FDI as the most significant factor in explaining the boom. As indicated earlier, the attraction of foreign-owned industry was an important element of Ireland's outward-oriented approach. These foreign-owned firms tended to be larger, more profitable, and more export oriented than indigenous industry. Clusters of high-technology foreign firms developed in predominantly increasing returns to scale sectors of the economy such as chemicals and information technology (see chapter 13 by Bradley in this volume). These firms were attracted to Ireland by low rates of corporation profits tax, ease of access to EU markets, a ready supply of highly skilled labor, and successful targeting by the Industrial

Development Authority. In essence, policies to promote FDI have conformed fairly closely to best practice, as set out by Sachs (1997). Over the years, FDI has undoubtedly brought many benefits. It enabled Ireland to pass relatively seamlessly from a largely agrarian economy to a fairly modern high-technology economy without going through a heavy-industry phase, which most advanced countries had to do. It facilitated the efficient transfer of technology and managerial skills. It also removed what otherwise might have been balance-of-payments constraints, as FDI firms were almost exclusively oriented to supplying export markets. Individually, these firms were generally very large employers by Irish standards, and for this reason, their importance in the economy may have been somewhat overstated. Currently, foreign-owned industrial and service firms employ about 10 percent of the labor force, although they do account for over half of industrial employment.

Coming from a Central Bank, I should say something about the experience with monetary and exchange-rate policy during this catch-up period. While the Irish pound participated in the EMS since the outset and this provided a nominal anchor, the markets and the authorities remained conscious of the importance of sterling, given the still important trade and financial links with the United Kingdom. Whenever sterling depreciated sharply against EMS currencies, pressure was seen on the Irish pound. In fact, the two substantial devaluations of the currency within the EMS—in August 1986 and in January 1993—occurred following substantial depreciations of sterling. Financial-market analysts talked of the Irish pound riding two horses—the EMS and sterling. Indeed, the government-commissioned study of whether Ireland should join the EMU revolved around whether the potential benefits of joining the EMU outweighed the possible costs that might arise from having to deal with possibly wide variations in the sterling-euro exchange rate. The study concluded that the balance of the argument favored participation in the EMU.

A second monetary issue that arose during this catch-up phase related to overheating pressures that emerged in the run-in to the EMU. The Central Bank considered that it would be appropriate to try to maintain relatively high short-term interest rates even though the market was aware that these would be identical to euro-area rates at or even before the inception of the EMU. It is unclear whether these efforts had any material effect on behavior, but it was felt that, at the margin, it was worthwhile taking this restrictive approach.

Current Issues

As a consequence of this strong economic performance over the 1994 to 2000 period, Ireland had closed the gap in employment rates and living standards with the more advanced EU countries that had eluded us for so long. Full employment was reached, and in contrast to earlier decades, there was substantial net inward migration on the part of both Irish people who had emigrated in more straitened times and of those with no previous connection with the country. These major gains have been retained in the more difficult economic conditions of the past few years. As a very open economy, export performance has inevitably weakened, and the relatively large ICT sector, which prior to the international shock to that sector accounted for about a quarter of total manufacturing employment, suffered a significant contraction. Nonetheless, the economy has shown a remarkable resilience. This is so, in particular, for the labor market, with the unemployment rate still at only 4.5 percent. This is attributed, in turn, to the flexibility of the labor market in regard to both remuneration and working-time arrangements in the face of more difficult times.

Toward the end of the catch-up phase, around 2000, significant domestic inflationary pressures began to become evident. This occurred in the context of an economy operating at full capacity and accommodating monetary-policy conditions. Not only were market interest rates negative in real terms (figure 12.13), but the weakness of the euro against both the U.S. dollar and sterling imparted a further boost to Irish exporters. Monetary conditions, therefore, facing Ireland were particularly easy. Various estimates suggested that on the basis of a Taylor rule, for example, interest rates should have been three to four percentage points higher. In addition, with the exchequer overflowing with buoyant tax revenues, fiscal policy tended to be procyclical. While Balassa-Samuelson

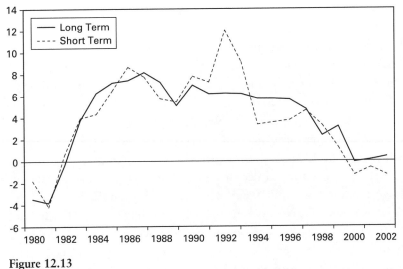

Figure 12.13
Real interest rates

effects were also at work, this can explain only part of the inflation excess over the euro area generally.

An important aspect of these capacity constraints has been the pressure on infrastructure. The rapidity of the convergence process meant that public infrastructure—transport infrastructure, in particular—lagged behind what was required. Other developed countries, for the most part, would have modernized their infrastructure over a much longer timespan against the background of a much more gradual development of their economies. A related issue has been the extremely large rise in property prices. Between 1994 and 2000, house prices rose by 133 percent, an annual compound increase of 15 percent. This has been an ongoing concern to the financial supervisory authorities. While fundamental factors—such as much higher real incomes, basic demographics, employment, and the regime change to a much lower interest-rate environment in EMU—were at work, there remain concerns that prices may have overshot their fundamental values. There is also the possibility that fundamental factors themselves could be vulnerable to extraneous events. Technical studies are inconclusive as to whether there is a bubble in current property prices.

Conclusion

The Irish economy developed rapidly during the 1990s, and the country finally attained the employment rates and living standards of other industrialized countries. Although a small economy, Ireland was relatively late in adopting outward-looking policies that are now seen as an indispensable prerequisite for development; joining the EU in 1973 was the most important milestone in this respect. This led to the single European market in 1992, and ultimately the single currency, the euro, in 1999. These steps toward deeper integration took place in the context of significant inflows of FDI and structural funds from the EU.

The institutional preconditions for real convergence existed in Ireland for many years, but its achievement was delayed by policy errors both macroeconomic and microeconomic (Honohan and Walsh 2002). The pursuit of stability-oriented macroeconomic policies and more liberal microeconomic policies, including tax-benefit reform, laid the groundwork for economic advancement from the mid-1980s on. This reorientation of policy corresponded closely to what later became known as the Washington Consensus in its original form. The takeoff was greatly assisted by benign international conditions. An important slow-burning factor has been the greatly increased resources devoted to education. Although job opportunities were relatively scarce for this more highly educated workforce for some time, they were quickly absorbed into the more knowledge-intensive modern sectors as these expanded as a result of large inflows of foreign direct investment and increased domestic demand. Modest increases in pay, part of a social partnership agreement between employers, unions, and government, were an important factor in facilitating increased employment over much of this period.

The substantial gains made during the catch-up phase have been retained in the present more difficult economic environment. Not surprisingly perhaps, strong growth in this phase has created pressure on the country's infrastructure and greatly pushed up property prices. Foreign direct-investment inflows are unlikely to continue on the scale of recent years; with full employment, these could not easily be absorbed in any event. With Ireland no longer a low-cost economy, there is some concern going forward that there may be some difficulty in retaining a reasonable flow of this investment. More than most small countries, Ireland has an unusually large high-technology industrial structure, the greater part of which is owned by foreign multinational companies. It remains to be seen whether the economy will be sufficiently robust and adaptable to cope in more difficult times. The resilience seen so far in the face of tougher times would lead one to be quietly optimistic in this respect.

References

Alesina, A., and R. Perotti. (1997). "Fiscal Adjustments in OECD Countries: Composition and Macroeconomic Effects." *IMF Staff Papers, 44.*

Dornbusch, Rudiger. (1989). "Credibility, Debt, and Unemployment: Ireland's Failed Stabilization." *Economic Policy, 8:* 173–209.

Doyle, Maurice F. (1991). "Implications of Economic and Monetary Union for Ireland." Central Bank of Ireland Annual Report 1990, Dublin.

Doyle, Maurice F. (1992). "From EMS to EMU: The Case of Ireland." *Central Bank of Ireland Quarterly Bulletin* (Winter): 43–53.

Giavazzi, F., and M. Pagano. (1990). "Can Severe Fiscal Contractions be Expansionary? Tales of Two Small European Countries." *NBER Macroeconomics Annual:* 75–111.

Girton, L., and D. Roper. (1977). "A Monetary Model of Exchange Market Pressure Applied to Postwar Canada." *American Economic Review,* 67(4): 537–548.

Honohan, P., and B. Walsh. (2002). "Catching up with the Leaders: The Irish Hare." *Brookings Papers on Economic Activity, 1:* 1–77.

Krugman, Paul. (1997). "Good News from Ireland: A Geographical Perspective." In Alan Gray (Ed.), *International Perspectives on the Irish Economy.* Dublin: Indecon Economic Consultants.

Krugman, P., and A. Venables. (1990). "Integration and the Competitiveness of Peripheral Industry." In C. Bliss and J. Macedo (Eds.), *Unity with Diversity in the European Economy.* Cambridge: Cambridge University Press.

Mackenzie, G., D. Orsmond, and P. Gerson. (1997). "The Composition of Fiscal Adjustment and Growth: Lessons from Fiscal Reforms in Eight Economies." IMF Occasional Papers 149 (April).

Neven, Damien J. (1990). "EEC Integration towards 1992: Some Distributional Aspects." *Economic Policy,* no. 10: 14–62.

O'Malley, Eoin. (1990). "Ireland." In *Social Europe, a special edition of European Economy on The Impact of the Internal Market by Industrial Sector: The Challenge for the Member States.*

Organization for Economic Cooperation and Development (OECD). (1999). *OECD Economic Surveys: Ireland* (May).

Sachs, Jeffrey. (1997). "Ireland's Growth Strategy: Lessons for Economic Development." In Alan Gray (Ed.), *International Perspectives on the Irish Economy.* Dublin: Indecon Economic Consultants.

Whitaker, T. K. (1973). "Monetary Integration." In *Moorgate and Wall Street: A Review* (Autumn): 4–21.

Williamson, John. (1990). "What Washington Means by Policy Reform." In John Williamson (Ed.), *Latin American Adjustment: How Much Has Happened?* Washington, D.C.: Institute for International Economics.

13

Irish Economic Development in an International Perspective

John Bradley

In a remarkable comment on the state of the Irish economy today, Intel president Craig Barrett recently reflected on why his firm had come to Ireland. Speaking to Thomas Friedman, author of *The Lexus and the Olive Tree*, Barrett said, "We are there because Ireland is very pro-business, they have a very strong educational infrastructure, it is incredibly easy to move things in and out of the country, and it is incredibly easy to work with the government. I would invest in Ireland before Germany or France" (Friedman 1999, p. 188).

It was not always like this. Any Irish person born in the immediate aftermath of World War II has seen their country undergo an extraordinary transformation. Once upon a time we were an inward-looking, inefficient, economic basket case, hemorrhaging our population through emigration. Today, we attract the attention of nations and businesses of the developed and developing world. How did this come about, when as recently as 1988 the *Economist* magazine portrayed us as a beggar nation seeking alms? ("Poorest of the Rich," 1988).

Today Ireland enjoys the many economic advantages that come with membership of the European Union (EU). Among the chief of these is that Irish policy makers—in both the public and private sectors—are able to plan in a more stable environment, with the cooperation as well as with the active financial support of other member states, mediated through the European Commission. However, in today's increasingly internationalized economy, policy-making autonomy has been progressively ceded by small states to supranational organizations. The policy-making autonomy of any small country wishing to be part of this international economy is now heavily circumscribed, and recognizing this fact and exploiting the consequences are wise ways to exercise national sovereignty. Since we belong to the euro zone, monetary policy, as well as the responsibilities for defending the euro against speculative attack, are decided in Frankfurt by the European Central Bank. The Stability and Growth Pact places a welcome constraint on the type of fiscal profligacy that caused the deep recession of the 1980s. Within these policy constraints, our task in Ireland is to embrace with enthusiasm whatever the outcome happens to be, and the outcome so far has been remarkably favorable.

Against this background, I want to examine the Irish economy in an historical and international perspective. In doing so, there is a temptation to focus exclusively on the past decade of rapid growth and convergence and to attribute most of this improvement to EU structural funds. This, indeed, is an interesting story that has attracted considerable international attention. However, in this chapter I wish to place the recent Irish experience in a wider context by comparisons that range across space, across time, and across ideas. For example, the United Kingdom provided the encompassing economic context for Ireland until almost two decades after the end of World War II. Political independence (achieved in 1922) had only a modest impact on Irish economic development, and the then Irish Free State (to become the Republic of Ireland in 1949) continued to function as a regional economy of the British Isles.

During the decade and a half after Ireland joined the then European Economic Community (EEC) in 1973, the small developed core European states became obvious touchstones of comparison, at a time when attempts were being made to diversify the Irish economy away from excessive reliance on the United Kingdom and toward wider European norms and standards. Later, the so-called cohesion states (Greece, Ireland, Portugal, and Spain) became standards of comparison during the 1980s and the 1990s, a period when substantial development aid was forthcoming to these countries from the EU under the enlarged structural fund programs. Today Ireland has many (but not all) of the characteristics of a modern developed economy, and its recent strong growth performance has itself become the object of international interest by the newly liberalized states of central and eastern Europe as they make their transition from Communist autarky and central planning to full integration into an enlarged EU.

The Historical Economic Perspective

The 1960s represented a watershed in economic terms in Ireland. Policy actions taken from the late 1950s and early 1960s onward launched the economy on a development path that differed radically from that pursued before and after independence. The core policy dilemma was not about whether the Irish economy should be open to trade and factor flows with the wider world economy, since Ireland already had a relatively open economy when compared to the other small European states in the late 1950s. Rather, the issue was the nature of this involvement and whether there was to be a break with the heavy dependence on the UK market as the destination for exports of a very restricted variety of mainly agricultural products.

Two key factors served to condition economic performance prior to 1960. The first concerns demographics, emigration, and the openness of the Irish labor market. Ireland was unique in that it experienced a major decline in population between 1840 and 1960. The tradition of migration continued into more recent decades, and Ireland now has the most open labor market in the EU. Today, migration is net inward, and this has served to reduce pressure on wages as the economy grew rapidly from the 1990s. The second concerns the manner in which the economy of the island of Ireland, and later the separate economy of the Republic of Ireland, came to be almost totally dominated by trade and other policy links with Britain; the difficulty in breaking free from this embrace; and the consequences of the British link for Irish policy making. The political incorporation of Ireland into the United Kingdom in 1801 eventually generated forces that led to comprehensive economic and trade integration as well. The full extent of this integration after more than one hundred years of union is illustrated by the UK-Irish trade position from just after independence in 1922 until the early 1960s. For example, the proportion of Irish exports going to the United Kingdom showed only a very small reduction from 98.6 percent in 1924 to 92.7 percent by 1950 and remained above 85 percent until the 1960s.

The failure of Ireland to diversify its economy away from an almost total dependence on the United Kingdom had serious consequences for its economic performance when compared to a range of other small European countries and has been the subject of research and comment.[1] The reluctance of the new Irish public administration to deviate too much from British policy norms has been well documented (Fanning, 1978). The nature of the difficulties faced by Irish policy makers in attempting to break free from the economic embrace of the United Kingdom were reflections of the wider behavior of trade within the EU over the past thirty to forty years. Ireland's relationship with Britain, which had been a very strong dependency prior to 1960, began to weaken only after the shift to foreign direct investment and export-led growth that followed the various French-style programs for economic expansion in the late 1950s and during the 1960s. The forces that brought about this changed pattern of behavior—mainly export-oriented foreign direct investment—are now examined.

Internationalization and Foreign Direct Investment

The 1960s represented a watershed for the Irish economy. Policy changes made from the late 1950s and early 1960s onward launched the economy on a development path that differed radically from that pursued before and after independence. The central policy dilemma was not whether the Irish economy should be open to international trade and investment flows. Rather, the issue was the nature of its international involvement and whether there was to be a break with an almost total dependence on the British market as the destination for exports of a very restricted variety of mainly agricultural products.

To measure the extent to which Ireland lagged behind the other small European states in the late 1950s is a difficult task, since comparisons based on the simple conversion of domestic prices to a common currency are beset by problems. However, from the year 1960 we have standardized data that make this comparison in terms of purchasing-power parity (table 13.1). Ignoring the special case of Luxembourg (which is distorted by its foreign-owned banking sector), the original six member states of the then EEC formed a relatively homogeneous group, with

Table 13.1
GDP per head of population: (PPS), EU15 = 100

Country	1960	1973	1986	1999
Belgium	98.6	104.5	104.2	112.5
Germany	122.1	114.5	116.8	109.1
France	105.3	110.5	109.8	103.7
Italy	87.3	94.0	102.5	101.2
Luxembourg	168.7	153.1	138.8	165.9
The Netherlands	112.1	107.1	102.2	105.3
Denmark (73)	119.9	114.4	117.9	114.6
Ireland (73)	**60.8**	**58.9**	**63.7**	**111.0**
United Kingdom (73)	123.9	104.4	101.9	98.4
Greece (82)	**42.5**	**62.4**	**61.4**	**68.7**
Portugal (86)	**43.2**	**61.1**	**54.0**	**74.1**
Spain (86)	**56.9**	**74.8**	**69.7**	**80.2**
Austria (95)	94.8	98.5	105.4	110.9
Finland (95)	87.8	94.3	100.6	101.8
Sweden (95)	122.7	115.0	112.5	96.5

Source: *European Economy* (1998, pp. 80–81).

Germany leading (at 122 relative to the average of 100) and Italy lagging (at 87). In the case of Italy, its low average concealed the fact that the northern subregions were well above the European average, while the southern (or *Mezzogiorno*) subregion was well below. The other future members of the pre-2004 enlarged EU consisted at that time of five wealthy countries (Denmark, Austria, Finland, Sweden, and the United Kingdom, ranging from the UK's high of 124 to Finland's low of 88) and four much poorer countries (Greece, Spain, Ireland, and Portugal, ranging from Spain's high of 57 to Greece's low of 43).

At the time of the first enlargement in 1973, the Danish and Irish GDP per-capitat figures had changed very little relative to the EU average, but the United Kingdom had declined in relative terms to about the EU average. Since Ireland was a heavily agricultural country even as late as 1973, debate on the wisdom of its entry into the then EEC focused attention on the likely benefits from higher prices of agricultural produce under the CAP rather than on regional policy. In the early years of its membership, the main direct benefits to (rural) Ireland came from the

CAP in terms of greatly increased transfers under the price guarantee section.

An aspect of modern Irish economic development that has attracted considerable attention internationally is the dynamic role played by foreign direct investment (FDI). Ireland is an interesting case study of the effects on a small developing host economy of export-oriented FDI, and this phenomenon has been the subject of much detailed research (O'Malley, 1989; Barry, Bradley, and O'Malley, 1999). The economy emerged in the late 1950s from a heavily protectionist regime, and the switch to openness was more dramatic than in the other European states and was implemented in terms of a vigorous industrial incentive package consisting of a very low corporate tax regime and generous capital and training grants. After a slow start in the 1960s, the foreign sector grew very rapidly during the 1980s and now accounts for about one-half of Irish manufacturing employment and over two-thirds of gross manufacturing output (Barry and Bradley, 1997). Directly as well as indirectly, FDI has affected every corner of the Irish economy.

FDI inflows into Ireland did not go primarily into the more traditional sectors in which the economy had a comparative advantage (such as food processing, clothing, and footwear), mainly because many indigenous manufacturing sectors were largely nontradable (they were directed mainly at serving the small local market), and the substantial high-technology FDI inflows that came to Ireland turned out not to depend on local comparative advantage. Although the outward orientation occurred at a time when the concept of growth poles was universally popular as a spur to development (Buchanan and Partners 1968), the normal processes of clustering and regional concentration in Ireland were impeded both by the branch-plant nature of the investment and by a public policy that encouraged geographical dispersal almost certainly at some expense to strict economic efficiency criteria. However, after more than three decades of exposure to foreign direct investment, Ireland eventually succeeded in attracting sufficient firms in the computer, instrument engineering, pharmaceutical, and chemical sectors to merit a description of sectoral agglomerations or clusters.

The long overdue switch to an outward orientation from the 1960s was an enlightened response to changes in the world economy. The engine of subsequent Irish growth was the manufacturing sector, and the engine of the manufacturing sector was the foreign-owned multinational subsector. Experience led to a better understanding of the benefits to small regions and small states of the increasingly integrated international economy.

On the global economic map, the lines that now mattered were rapidly becoming those defining natural economic zones, where the defining issue is that each such zone possesses, in one or other combination, the key ingredients for successful participation in the international economy. Thus, the rise of the EEC, the development of the Pacific Rim, and the progressive liberalization of world trade under successive GATT and World Trade Organization (WTO) rounds, presented both opportunities and threats to Ireland. But the eventual dominance of the Irish manufacturing sector by foreign multinationals was unexpected and quite unique by Organization for Economic Cooperation and Development (OECD) experience. With falling transportation and telecommunication costs, national economies were destined to become increasingly interdependent, and in the words of President Bill Clinton's former Secretary of Labor, Robert Reich (1993, p. 8): "the real economic challenge ... [of a country or region] ... is to increase the potential value of what its citizens can add to the global economy, by enhancing their skills and capacities and by improving their means of linking those skills and capacities to the world market."

Perhaps the most striking consequence of foreign investment inflows was that it hastened the decoupling of the Irish economy from its almost total dependence on the United Kingdom. Ireland's development dilemma had always been that either it could stick closely to UK economic policy and institutional norms and be constrained by the erratic UK growth performance, with little prospect of rapid convergence to a higher standard of living, or it could implement an economically beneficial and politically acceptable degree of local policy innovation that offered hope of a faster rate of growth than its dominant trading partner. The Irish economic policy-making environment during this period can be characterized as having shifted from one appropriate to a dependent state on the periphery of Europe to that of an region more fully integrated into an encompassing European economy. Starting from the

1960s, FDI renovated and boosted Irish productive capacity. This was a slow process, involving the gradual collapse of many of the previously protected traditional industries and their replacement by more modern highly productive plants in chemicals, computing, and food processing. The evolving EU market (and the single market in particular) provided the primary source of demand for the new export-oriented industries. What was needed was a big push on improvement in physical infrastructure, education, and training, and this arrived in the late 1980s in the form of a dramatic innovation in regional policy at the EU level.

Facilitating Irish Convergence: EU Regional Policy

The importance and emphasis given to regional policy within the EU has greatly increased since the late 1980s, a time when major policy reforms and extensions were introduced in the lead-up to the implementation of the single market and the Economic and Monetary Union (EMU). After the turbulence of the 1970s and the 1980s, economic analysts tended to be more preoccupied with stabilization (very much a national issue) rather than with growth (which usually has spatial and international dimensions). Not until the latter part of the 1980s, when European inflation and unemployment disequilibria were brought more under control (nominal convergence), did a range of longer-term issues (such as real convergence and regional policy) move toward the top of the EU agenda.

The Rise of EU Regional Policy

The progressive enlargement of the EU from its foundation in 1956—when there had been a degree of homogeneity at the national level—brought about an ever increasing degree of socioeconomic heterogeneity with the entry of Ireland, Greece, Portugal, and Spain; the recent entry of low-income states from Central Europe; as well as a growing desire to address regional disparities within nation states as well as between states.

In addition to the simple aspect of enlargement, the internal and external socioeconomic challenges faced by the member states and regions became more complex and forced EU policy makers to address the task of preparing weaker states and regions to handle such initiatives as the single market, the EMU, and the need to prepare for the transition of economies of central and eastern Europe to EU membership.

While nation states have always operated internal regional policies of various types, what is different about the reformed EU regional policy is that significant financial resources were made available by the wealthier member states to fund regional policy initiatives in a limited number of the poorer member states. The available EU budget was initially dominated by the need to support the Common Agricultural Policy (CAP), but there were major expansions in resources to fund the reformed Community Support Frameworks of 1989 to 1993, 1994 to 1999, and 2000 to 2006.

Internal and External Challenges and EU Regional Policy

Progressive trade liberalization within Europe was always likely to entail substantial industrial disruption in the periphery, either defined as the member states on the western and southern edges of the EU or as those subregions of member states that were located far from the centers of population and economic activity. Adjustment problems were therefore likely to be greater in the periphery.

A massive shake-out of jobs in Irish traditional industry occurred as trade liberalization progressed from the mid-1960s and accelerated during the Organization of Petroleum Exporting Countries (OPEC) I and II global recessions of the mid-1970s and early 1980s, even before the formal initiation of the single market in the early 1990s. The low-productivity sectors in Greece, Portugal, and Spain also faced increasingly intense pressures. One of the potential difficulties faced by peripheral economies like Ireland in adjusting to EU membership was the possibility that as trade barriers fell, industries that had a high share of the plants that exhibit increasing returns to scale (that is, plants where productivity increases with size) would be attracted away from the periphery and toward the densely populated core markets. This process led to the decline of many traditional Irish indigenous industries. However, the influx of multinational companies began to partially offset this decline, even in the 1960s. Foreign firms locating in Ireland have tended to be in sectors where there are increasing returns to scale (IRS) at the industry level (computer equipment, pharmaceuticals, instrument engineering) but constant returns to scale (CRS) at the plant level, so the share of Irish employment in IRS sectors has increased substantially. Nevertheless, the underlying trend in manufacturing employment was negative, as labor-intensive firms closed and high-productivity firms set up on "green-field" sites.

The reform of EU regional aid programs into the so-called community-support framework (CSF) in the late 1980s presented EU as well as national policy makers and analysts in countries like Ireland with major challenges. The political rationale behind the CSF came from the fear that not all EU member states were likely to benefit equally from the single market, whose purpose was to dismantle all remaining nontariff barriers within the Union (such as border controls, national-specific product standards, and so on). In particular, the less advanced economies of the southern and western peripheries (mainly Greece, Portugal, Spain, and Ireland) were felt to be particularly vulnerable unless they received development aid (Cecchini, 1988).

What was special about the reformed regional policies was their goal—to design and implement policies with the explicit aim of transforming the underlying structure of the beneficiary economies to prepare them for exposure to the competitive forces about to be unleashed by the single market. Thus, CSF policies moved far beyond a conventional demand-side stabilization role, being directed at the promotion of structural change, faster long-term growth, and real convergence through mainly supply-side processes.

Was Ireland a Case Study of Successful EU Regional Policy?

By the time Ireland joined the European Union in 1973, the program that led to the completion of the single European market had not yet begun. The then European Economic Community was effectively a customs union but was evolving slowly toward deeper integration. The larger wealthier countries feared that in the four poorest member states in the EEC at that time (Greece, Ireland, Portugal, and Spain), where development lagged behind the average, the industrial and service sectors would not be able to withstand the competitive forces that would come from the larger richer core member states.

To help these poorer so-called cohesion countries, generous development aid was made available. We have seen that in 1986, just before the structural funds were expanded, if you set an index of the European average GDP per capita at 100, Greece was at 61, Ireland was at 64, Portugal was at 54, and Spain was at 70. These four countries had many other common characteristics in 1986. They had high actual and hidden unemployment and large agricultural sectors (in the case of Ireland, about 18 percent of the labor force, and in the case of Greece and Portugal, much higher). They had underdeveloped physical infrastructure (in 1986 there were no motorways in Ireland). The unfavorable structure of their manufacturing sectors left them with a preponderance of traditional products (such as food processing, clothing, and textiles) and a lack of modern sectors (such as electronics and pharmaceuticals). In this respect, Ireland was the least vulnerable, since a policy of openness had been pursued since the early 1960s, and considerable industrial restructuring had already occurred. These countries also had a very underdeveloped market-service sector, in particular producer services (that is, services to industry rather than consumer services). From its entry into the European Union in 1973 until the year 1988, Ireland remained at just over 60 percent of the EU average GDP per head. The Irish level of income per capita was about the same as Greece, a bit higher than Portugal, but somewhat lower than Spain.

There is no single simple explanation for the failure of Ireland to converge earlier. Rather, a series of interacting factors were operating. The dreadful state of Irish manufacturing in 1960, after three decades of protection and heavy-handed state interference, could not have been addressed overnight. Unlike the liberalization in Poland, there was to be no big-bang reform, collapse of the old, and growth of the new from a low base. The progress of restructuring, driven by far-sighted industrial incentives such as low corporate taxes and focused aid, proceeded steadily but was rudely and catastrophically interrupted by OPEC I, and a series of disastrous fiscal stimulations from 1977 to 1982 that almost bankrupted the state. The first half of the 1980s were devoted to emergency remedies that slashed public investment programs and drove tax rates up to penal levels. The Irish entry into EMS in 1979, which had held out prospects of importing German nominal stability, failed to deliver since markets had no confidence in the Irish ability to break with the historical UK monetary dominance of the country. Only on the latter half of the 1980s was—so to speak—normal service restored.

With the advent of the single market, the European Union deepened in many different ways. For example, intra-EU trade grew, and trade in intermediate goods (sales to firms by other firms) grew particularly quickly. In the late 1980s, Spain and Ireland had intermediate levels of this type of intraindustry or firm-to-firm trade. Portugal and Greece had very low levels. However, this type of trade is a measure of the differing degree of the integration of these countries into the EU and wider global economy. It is a much better measure than simple trade data.

A gradual restructuring of European industry took place, with the evolution of strategic alliances in manufacturing and services between countries. From being a customs union, Europe evolved toward being a single market. A big shake-out of traditional industry had already taken place in Ireland and Spain prior to the advent of the structural funds in 1989. This shake-out is still underway in Portugal and Greece. In the case of Ireland, it had catastrophic economic effects: the Irish unemployment rate rose to 20 percent in the mid-1980s, and the debt-to-GDP ratio rose to 130 percent. The serious problems of the late 1970s and the first half of the 1980s can be directly attributed to the misguided and ruinous fiscal expansions of 1977 to 1982 (Bradley, Fanning, Prendergast, and Wynne 1985). The collapse of employment and rise in unemployment and outmigration were caused by the accelerated decline of those traditional industries that had managed to survive the slower reforms of earlier decades but that failed in the deep recession of 1981 to 1985. The high tax rates were merely one more nail in the coffin.

It was in this context that the reorganization and massive increase in the EU structural funds took place. About half of the total EU budget— itself about 1 percent of EU GDP—was now to be devoted to structural funds, where previously the agricultural spending under the CAP had dominated the budget. The process started for the five years from 1989 to 1993 (in what was called the Delors I package, after Jacques Delors, then president of the Commission). The next round of structural funds (called Delors II) ran from 1994 to 1999. Each of the four main cohesion countries who were the recipients of most of the aid have had over ten years of sustained high development aid from the EU. In the case of Ireland, under the Delors I package this ran at some 3 to 4 percent per annum of Irish GDP. In the second period, the aid fell slightly as a share of GDP to some 2 to 3 percent, and the third period had still lower rates of transitional aid. Taken together with the domestic cofinancing element, it allowed major investment schemes to go ahead.

The purpose of the structural funds was to generate permanent improvements in economic competitiveness and performance rather than just impart a transitory stimulation that would vanish after the aid was cut off. There were three main channels through which the supply-side effects of the structural fund aid operated.

The first channel was to improve the physical infrastructure, such as roads, rail, ports, and telecoms. A country cannot communicate with the global economy unless these channels operate efficiently and effectively. The second channel was to improve the level of education and training and to enhance the skills of the labor force. You cannot produce world-class goods unless your labor force is well educated and trained. The third channel was to directly assist private-sector firms by subsidizing investment—improving marketing and design skills, R&D, and so on. A fourth channel (intranational regional aid) did not apply to Ireland under Delors I and II since Ireland was such a small and relatively homogeneous country. Portugal, Spain, and Greece have poor regions that suffer relative to others, as does southern Italy (the Mezzogiorno) and the former East Germany.

The goal of the structural funds was to transform the underlying structure of the beneficiary economies and to prepare them to face the competitive forces that were about to be unleashed by the single market. The details and modalities of the implementation have been described elsewhere (Bradley, O'Donnell, Sheridan, and Whelan 1995), and the outcome was very interesting. We noted above the low state of development in the four main recipients of EU aid. By 1999 (at the end of the second structural-fund program), it was at 69. There had been a modest but quite significant increase in living standards. Portugal started at 54 in 1986 and reached 74. Spain started at 70 and reached 80 by the year 1999. But Ireland started at 64 and reached 111. Those figures flatter the Irish performance to some extent, but it represented a massive improvement. Not all of the improvement was due to structural funds. If that had been the case, then we would require explanations of why the other three countries—Greece and Portugal in particular—had not made similar progress, since they all received similar aid in terms of a share of their GDP. We summarize briefly a logical sequence of interconnected effects that brought about that impressive Irish result.

First, the Irish economy in the late 1970s and for the first half of the 1980s was seriously and massively destabilized—with high unemployment, relatively high inflation, and public finances that were almost out of control. But the root causes—the OPEC II global recession and the aftermath of the fiscal profligacy of 1977 to 1982—had now vanished, and the international economy was strengthening.

Second, there were the effects of the structural funds. These had demand and supply effects. As you actually build a road, it injects income and expenditure into your economy. But the long-lasting benefits of building a road come when it is available to connect your cities and to transport goods more efficiently into and out of your economy. So the beneficial effects of structural funds were initially experienced as a construction boom and gradually fed into enhanced supply-side performance as major infrastructural projects were completed.

The third event was the beneficial effect of Ireland joining the European Monetary System (EMS) that was instituted in 1979 and served as a precursor of Economic and Monetary Union (EMU). But the credibility benefits of Ireland's membership in the EMS were delayed by about a decade (see above). The world's financial markets did not believe that the Irish economy could be stabilized successfully and could perform within the constraints of the EMS. So the lower deutsche mark (DM) interest rates did not become available to the Irish economy until the late 1980s, when eventually credibility was established. The convergence of Irish rates to the lower DM ones served to stimulate investment (particularly house building) as well as consumption.

The fourth event was the massive increase in the inflow of mainly U.S. foreign direct investment, most of it in high-technology areas. The characteristics of the global technology boom of the Clinton years are well known, and Ireland was now uniquely positioned to reap the benefits in terms of a massive increase in mainly U.S. FDI. This was in part a spin-off benefit of the structural funds, making use of the improved infrastructure and human capital. It was also due in part to Ireland's access to EU markets for exports produced by multinational companies located and producing in Ireland. Additionally, of course, one of the long-term elements of Irish policy was a low rate of corporate taxation, designed to attract inward investment.

The fifth event concerned the fiscal stabilization of the period 1987 to 1989, where Ireland experienced the nearest equivalent of the type of policy-regime switch that fueled the Polish liberalization. Public consumption was slashed; improved monitoring and evaluation of public investment was instituted (driven by the EU requirements for structural-fund aid). By strongly signaling its firm intention to join the EMU from the start-up—even in the absence of its largest trading partner, the United Kingdom—the benefits of fiscal stabilization were reinforced.

Finally, in Ireland there was an evolving social partnership (involving employers organizations, trades unions, and government) that eased the distribution conflicts and disputes that come with recovery and rapid growth. National wage bargaining for a rolling series of three-year periods were negotiated at rates that preserved the cost competitiveness of the more vulnerable indigenous firms and that eventually were used as a way of lowering the high tax rates that had been inherited from the early 1980s.

After over a decade of structural funds and the single market, how did the cohesion countries perform? In table 13.2, we show the convergence experiences of Greece, Ireland, and Portugal, with Denmark and the United Kingdom (a small rich EU state, as well as Ireland's main trading partner) as comparisons. In all three poor-country cases, convergence has taken place in the decade after the introduction of structural funds. Adaptation to the competitive rigors of the single market and efficient use of structural funds underpin the dramatic convergence of Ireland that coincided with the implementation of the new EU regional policies. The combination of openness and the use of structural funds were the primary forces driving Irish convergence, but the full picture is more complex. Nevertheless, it is the policy of openness and the use of structural funds that served to distinguish Ireland from, say, Greece, which

Table 13.2
Relative GDP per capita purchasing-power parity: EU15 = 100

	1960	1973	1986	2003
Ireland	63.2	60.8	65.8	122.4
Greece	43.8	71.1	62.9	68.4
Portugal	39.6	58.4	54.2	68.8
Denmark	126.2	120.9	117.8	113.8
United Kingdom	123.3	104.2	101.1	104.4

Source: *European Economy*, no. 4 (2003, pp. 120–121).
Note: It should be noted that GDP overstates Ireland's national income (or GNP) by about 15 percent, because of large-scale outflows of corporate profits of foreign-owned multinational firms that operate in Ireland.

had a similar development distance to travel but which has only recently set its wider policy framework in the context of embracing internationalisation. Portugal, on the other hand, is in the process of repeating Irish success. It remains to be seen if these countries can sustain their convergent behavior in times of recession as well as in times of growth.

Conclusions

The opening of the economy and the removal of tariff barriers were necessary policy changes if Ireland was to be kick-started from stagnation. Free trade with the United Kingdom—Ireland's dominant trading partner until the late 1960s—gave the first opportunity of "testing the water" of outward orientation. Free trade with Europe came later when Ireland joined the then EEC in 1973. The strategic orientation of Irish economic policy making over the past three decades has emphasized the need to face the consequences of the extreme openness of the economy, to encourage export orientation toward fast-growing markets and products, and to align the economy with European initiatives. We joined the European Monetary System in 1979, breaking a long link with sterling and escaping from economic and psychological dependency on the United Kingdom. We embraced the single market of 1992 and, most recently, the Economic and Monetary Union from January 1999. The enthusiastic embrace of openness provided the strong and enduring strategic backbone of Irish economic strategy.

But Ireland was not a very attractive investment location in the early 1960s. It was remote and unknown and had little by way of natural resources and no industrial heritage. To offset these handicaps, the main inducement provided to inward investors was initially a zero rate of corporation tax on exports of manufactured goods. Under pressure from the EU, this was later replaced by a low 10 percent tax rate on all manufacturing profits and has recently become a flat rate of 12.5 percent on the whole corporate sector. This tax policy, combined with aggressive and sophisticated marketing initiatives designed by the Irish Industrial Development Agency to attract and aid inward investors, provided the main driving force for the modernization of the economy through export-led growth.

However, the attractive tax rate and the absence of tariffs were only a start and would not in themselves have made Ireland a major destination of high-quality foreign direct investment. Other factors came together to reinforce Ireland's success and interacted to create a virtuous circle of superior performance that replaced the previous vicious circle of decades of underperformance. Educational standards in the Irish workforce had lagged behind the world. Policies were urgently needed to bring about a steady build-up of the quality, quantity, and relevance of education and training, and this had been initiated by far-seeing educational reforms starting in the 1960s. These reforms were extended by the emphasis given to scientific and technical skills through the use of generous EU structural funds from the late 1980s. Although issues of social inequality are still of concern, the general level of educational attainment in Ireland rivals that of other wealthier European countries.

Low taxes, bright people, but bad roads and unreliable phones are incomplete and unsatisfactory recipes for success. As the new EU member states from the central and east European (CEE) economies are now experiencing, improvement in the state of physical infrastructure is demanding in terms of public expenditure. Here, Ireland was remarkably lucky that it was granted so-called Objective 1 status for EU regional policy aid. Because of a generally low standard of living in the late 1980s (less than two-thirds of the EU average), as well as a peripheral location far away from the rich European markets, generous aid was made available to improve infrastructure, train young people, and stimulate the business sector. Few would claim that everything is perfect today, and indeed, growth itself has brought congestion in its wake. But dramatic improvements have taken place in the quality of roads, airports, and telecommunications.

These were the building blocks of the new Irish economy, and they brought success through their interaction and combination. The far-sighted targeting by the Irish Industrial Development Agency of inward investment in clusters of industries in computer equipment, software, and pharmaceuticals was pursued with a degree of diligence and professionalism that became the envy of all aspirant developing countries. Such firms needed highly skilled workers, and these were available in ever increasing numbers from the universities as well as from the assertive and bustling regional technical colleges. Business and knowledge spillovers from the initial clusters encouraged further growth in the high-technology areas and provided the basis for additional benefits, often in the older more traditional areas (such as food processing and clothing) that needed injections of new strategies and technologies. *The Economist*, which had painted so damning a portrait of the Irish economy as recently as 1988, a mere nine years later told a very different story. Ireland was now "Europe's shining light" ("Europe's Shining Light," 1997).

However, there are risks associated with the development path chosen by Ireland. First, the dynamic foreign manufacturing base is concentrated on a narrow range of technologies that can quickly move through maturity and into decline. Second, the policy initiatives that ensured that Ireland enjoyed an advantageous first-mover status in the early 1960s are unlikely to benefit other smaller economies to the same extent.

This is a good time to be Irish, when rapid economic progress has catapulted the country from the role of poor laggard to successful tiger. Not all the explanations are economic. Irish society is at once traditional and modern, and the tension between these forces serves to animate Irish thought and artistic expression. The Irish economy may be small in size, but its policy experiences during the twentieth century provide a rich source of information and guidance for other small countries that seek to develop and prosper.

Note

1. Mjøset (1992) studies Irish economic underperformance and draws carefully from a wide European literature on social and economic development.

References

Barry, F., and J. Bradley. (1997). "FDI and Trade: The Irish Host-Country Experience." *Economic Journal, 107*(445): 1798–1811.

Barry, F., J. Bradley, and E. O'Malley. (1999). "Indigenous and Foreign Industry: Characteristics and Performance." In F. Barry (Ed.), *Understanding Ireland's Economic Growth.* London: Macmillan.

Bradley, J., C. Fanning, C. Prendergast, and M. Wynne. (1985). *Medium-Term Analysis of Fiscal Policy in Ireland: A Macroeconomic Study of the Period 1967–1980.* Research Paper No. 122. Dublin: Economic and Social Research Institute.

Bradley, J., N. O'Donnell, N. Sheridan, and K. Whelan. (1995). *Regional Aid and Convergence: Evaluating the Impact of the Structural Funds on the European Periphery.* Aldershot: Avebury.

Buchanan, C., and Partners. (1968). *Regional Studies in Ireland.* Report Commissioned by the United Nations on behalf of the Irish Government. Dublin: An Foras Forbatha.

Cecchini, P. (1988). *The European Challenge 1992: The Benefits of a Single Market.* London: Wildwood House.

"Europe's Shining Light." (1997). *The Economist,* May 17.

Fanning, R. (1978). *The Irish Department of Finance 1922–58.* Dublin: Institute of Public Administration.

Friedman, T. (1999). *The Lexus and the Olive Tree.* New York: Farrar Straus Giroux.

Mjoset, Lars. (1992). *The Irish Economy in a Comparative Institutional Perspective.* Report No. 93. Dublin: National Economic and Social Council.

O'Malley, E. (1989). *Industry and Economic Development: The Challenge for the Latecomer.* Dublin: Gill and Macmillan.

"Poorest of the Rich: A Survey of the Republic of Ireland." (1988). *The Economist,* January 16.

Reich, Robert. (1993). *The Work of Nations: A Blueprint for the Future.* London: Simon and Schuster.

IV

EMU Entry and Economic Growth

14

When Should the Central Europeans Join the EMU? Reconciling Real and Nominal Convergence

Jacek Rostowski and Nikolai Zoubanov

Prominent European Central Bank (ECB) officials have argued that not just nominal but also real convergence should be required of the central and east European countries (CEECs) that joined the European Union (EU) in May 2004 before they join Economic and Monetary Union (EMU). Thus, Hans Reckers, a Bundesbank Board member, has argued that CEECs should not be allowed to join the EMU before they have achieved gross domestic product (GDP) per-capita levels equivalent to 70 percent of the EU average (Barber, 2000). In fact, the value or stability of a currency has nothing to do with the income of the people who use it. Were this the case, West European currencies would have been much more stable in the 1970s than in the 1870s, whereas just the opposite was true.[1]

One argument that has been made is that according to the Harrod-Balassa-Samuelson (HBS) effect, CEECs are likely to have inflation rates up to 2 percent above the average of the present EMU with each 1 percent increase in productivity differential. On top of this, there may be a demand effect resulting from the demand for nontradables being more income elastic than the demand for tradables. As incomes rise, demand for nontradables rises faster, and unless productivity in the sector rises faster than in the whole economy (which is unlikely), nontradable prices will rise faster than tradable prices. This phenomenon of growth-related relative price changes also happens in current EMU members, but with faster income growth, it would presumably happen faster in CEECs. Adding faster-growing countries with a higher HBS effect and higher demand-effect inflation to the EMU must increase EMU inflation for any given degree of tightness of monetary policy, it is argued. This seems to confront the EMU with an unpleasant dilemma: if the 2 percent ceiling on inflation is to be maintained for the EMU as a whole, interest rates will have to be higher and inflation in slow-growing countries will need to be lower than at present. On the other hand, abandoning the 2 percent ceiling on inflation and allowing CEECs to have inflation rates well above the average of present EMU members (without reducing inflation in the current member states) would, it is claimed, undermine price stability in the whole zone.

However, we have to take a number of other considerations into account. First, both the HBS effect proper and the demand effect are as likely to occur in any rapidly growing economy as in a CEEC. Indeed, these effects have appeared quite strongly in Ireland and to a lesser extent in Spain. They are not particularly the effect of catch-up but simply of faster growth in the country concerned than the EMU on average. To prevent these effects from raising the average inflation rate in the EMU, members should not only refuse to accept CEECs, but *they should also prevent current members from unilaterally undertaking structural reforms that would accelerate their growth*.[2] Indeed, such a moratorium on reform would be particularly important since the CEECs represent only about 6.5 percent of the EMU's GDP. Thus, structural reforms that increased the growth rate by half in France and Italy (which together account for about 40 percent of the EMU's GDP) would be likely to have a much larger effect on EMU inflation than the accession of the CEECs.

Therefore, unless the EMU wishes to remain a low-growth zone, there can be no argument for excluding CEECs on such a basis. Indeed, it may be in recognition of this fact that the Maastricht inflation criterion needs to be fulfilled for only one year. Although low inflation does need to be sustainable to satisfy the Maastricht inflation criterion, it is hard to imagine that expectations of growth-generated relative price changes of the kind we are discussing after the conclusion of the reference period could be held to violate this condition.[3]

Second, the CEECs are so small economically that their accession to the EMU would not in fact require any change in the ECB's inflation target, even if their growth inflation were relatively high. Thus, if CEEC inflation were an improbably high three percentage points above the average of current EMU members, this would mean an increase in the enlarged EMU inflation of 0.2 percent, on the assumption that there were no offsetting effects. If France and Italy increased their long-term growth rate by half, the effect could be twice as large (if we assume that the inflation effect of a growth acceleration would be about half of the acceleration itself).[4] Of course, *even if the EMU-wide inflation target were adjusted upward* to take growth inflation in parts of the zone into account, there would not be any need to adjust the ECB's monetary policy, and therefore *there should not be any effect on the inflation rate in slow-growing countries.*

Third, it is not clear that either the HBS effect or the demand effect on nontradables prices in the faster-growing countries would in fact increase the inflation rate in EMU as a whole, once we take the impact of the higher growth on the nominal exchange rate of the euro into account. While the impact of the two effects on relative prices cannot be avoided, their impact on inflation depends on the monetary stance of the ECB. Therefore, the nominal convergence of inflation, as required by the Maastricht criterion, can in principle be achieved under any rate of productivity growth that underlies the real convergence (of GDP per capita and relative prices). So we question the need for requiring the real convergence of countries before they join the euro zone.

We have developed a simple macroeconomic model of the HBS effect to arrive at the following assertions:

• Euro-zone enlargement to include CEECs can be beneficial for both sides of the process, both applicants and incumbents. While the former will enjoy lower inflation than outside the euro zone and a more stable economic environment, both sides will benefit from lower costs of trade. Therefore, the CEECs should join the EMU as soon as they have satisfied the Maastricht requirements.

• Conventional wisdom has it that if one country is poorer than the other, while it catches up (real convergence), it will exhibit higher rates of growth and inflation than the richer country will (there will be nominal divergence). However, the extent of nominal convergence in fact depends on the monetary policy stance: if it is strictly anti-inflationary, then nominal and real convergences can be achieved simultaneously. Therefore, real convergence of CEECs on the euro-zone average should not be a criterion for their joining EMU.

• It is critical for the union's slower-growing members that they have labor markets flexible enough to align the real wage with real labor productivity. We believe that the labor-market rigidities existing in many euro-zone countries along with slow productivity growth are a probable explanation for the reluctance of some euro-zone officials to admit new members. This is because if nominal and real convergences are reconciled through strict anti-inflationary policies, resulting in appreciation of the euro, and if the euro nominal wage is rigid, then the real wage (as measured in some international currency, such as U.S. dollars) will increase. Unless there is adequate labor-productivity growth, the subsequent increase in export prices in foreign currencies will render the slow growers uncompetitive. However, the answer to this problem is for slow-growing euro-zone members to undertake reforms aimed at fostering productivity growth and improving flexibility of the labor market rather than to exclude fast-growing CEECs from the euro zone.

This chapter is organized as follows. After a brief introduction to the problem, the first section summarizes a mathematical model of the HBS effect in one country (not in a monetary union) and discusses possible implications for the exchange rate and inflation in a fast-growing country that is not in a monetary union, under an anti-inflationary monetary policy stance. The next section summarizes the model's predictions for the case of two countries in a monetary union with uneven growth rates —a fast-growing country (FGC) and a slow-growing country (SGC)— and derives the implications of productivity growth in the faster for the slower. An outline of policy implications following from a theoretical discussion is offered in concluding remarks. A detailed derivation of the results shown in this chapter is offered in the chapter's appendix.

The Starting Point: Uneven Productivity Growth and Inflation Differentials

If the exchange rate is fixed or, equivalently for our purpose, if the two countries share a common currency, the FGC will experience higher inflation than will the SGC. We illustrate this with a model taken from De Grauwe (1992). Consider two countries in a monetary union, A and B, each producing tradable and nontradable goods. Tradable goods are easy to export, so their prices tend to be equal in both countries. Non-tradable goods, though, have such high trade costs that they never enter international trade; hence their prices may vary from country to country. It is further assumed that the shares of nontradable goods in total output are equal in the two countries and that the wage level is the same in both sectors of domestic economy (although not necessarily the same in both countries).

The inflation rate (π) in A and B is defined as follows:

$$\pi_A = (1 - \alpha)\pi_{TA} + \alpha\pi_{NA}$$
$$\pi_B = (1 - \alpha)\pi_{TB} + \alpha\pi_{NB},$$

(14.1)

where a is the share of nontradable goods in the total output and subscripts T and N stand for tradables and nontradables, respectively. Because of the existence of a single currency, inflation rates in tradables are equal across countries. At the same time, inflation in each sector should be equal to differences between the growth rates of wages w and of labor productivity q in respective sectors.[5] If we assume that there is equal productivity growth in nontradables in both countries, we obtain the following equation:

$$\pi_A - \pi_B = \alpha(q_{TA} - q_{TB}),$$

where π_i is inflation in each country and q_{Ti} is labor productivity in the tradable sector. This implies that if A's labor productivity in the tradable sector grows faster than B's, then A will experience higher inflation than will B. So uneven productivity growth implies uneven inflation in a monetary union, which is unavoidable, unless the growth is stopped.

If relatively poor countries tend to grow faster than relatively rich ones, then it may be argued that a certain degree of real convergence may be required prior to accession by the new member states of the EU to the euro zone to ensure parity of the inflation rates within the union. This model, however, does not take into account the effects of monetary policy and of labor-market rigidities on uneven inflation and other macroeconomic problems in a monetary union with variable growth rates. By exploring a model of the HBS effect in detail, we show that labor-market flexibility in the SGC and soundness of monetary policy union-wide will limit the impact of inflation in the FGC on the monetary union as a whole and therefore that countries with higher growth-induced inflation should not be excluded from a monetary union with more stable and slower-growing countries.

The Harrod, Balassa, Samuelson Effect and Its Implications for the Case of One Country

In this section, we discuss the implications of the HBS effect for the price level, output, domestic demand, and export potential in the case of one country and also link it with the monetary-policy stance to show its implications for the exchange rate. It will be shown that productivity growth in the tradable sector leads to appreciation of the country's *real* exchange rate but that monetary policy can be used to trade off *nominal* exchange-rate appreciation and inflation. Besides, in no case will a country experiencing productivity growth lose its competitive advantage in real terms. It has a wide choice of exchange-rate and inflation tradeoffs that do not hurt its position on the world market.

Assumptions
Consider a country S with a small open economy that takes the price of imports and exports as given on the world market. There are two sectors in the economy: tradable (goods available for trade worldwide with reasonable costs of shipping and no significant trade barriers) and nontradable goods (goods so costly to trade that they never enter international trade). The relative unit composite price of nontradables in terms of tradables is set equal to p_S, with an initial value of 1. There are two factors used in production: labor and capital. While S is able to freely import capital from abroad at a fixed interest rate r, the domestic supply of labor is limited and equal to $L_s = L_{TS} + L_{NS}$, where subscripts TS and NS stand for the tradable and nontradable sectors in S, respectively. All factor markets in S are perfectly competitive, which implies that wages are the same across the whole economy. Some other assumptions also apply:

• Output in both sectors is determined by a Cobb-Douglas production function with two factors, labor (L) and capital (K), and constant returns to scale:

$$Y_{TS} = A_{TS}K_{TS}^{\alpha_{TS}}L_{TS}^{1-\alpha_{TS}}$$
$$Y_{NS} = p_S A_{NS}K_{NS}^{\alpha_{NS}}L_{NS}^{1-\alpha_{NS}},$$

(14.2)

where $A_{TS,NS}$ are multipliers that represent the impact of labor productivity growth on output.

• Consumption is determined by a constant-elasticity-of-substitution (CES) utility function:

$$u_S(C) = [\gamma_S^{1/\theta_S} \cdot C_{TS}^{(\theta_S-1)/\theta_S} + (1-\gamma_S)^{1/\theta_S} \cdot C_{NS}^{(\theta_S-1)/\theta_S}]^{\theta_S/(\theta_S-1)},$$

(14.3)

subject to the budget constraint

$$Z_s = C_{TS} + p_s C_{NS} = w_s L_s + r Q_s,$$

(14.4)

where w_s is the equilibrium wage level in S, Q_s is domestic capital plus the current account balance C_{TS}, C_{NS} stand for consumption of tradables and nontradables, respectively, $0 < \gamma_S < 1$ is the share of tradables in total consumption,

$$\theta_S = \frac{d \log\left(\dfrac{C_{TS}}{C_{NS}}\right)}{d \log p_s}$$

is the elasticity of substitution between tradables and nontradables, meaning that with a 1 percent increase in p_S, consumption of tradables grows by θ_S percent relative to that of nontradables.

• The nominal exchange rate between S's currency and other currencies in the world is defined by

$$\varepsilon_{S,i} = \frac{P_{Ti}}{P_{TS}},$$

(14.5)

where $P_{TS,Ti}$ are the nominal prices of tradables in countries S and i. Note that we take into account only the prices of tradables, since for the nominal exchange rate (which is formed as a result of interaction of supply and demand for currencies required to buy goods on international markets) the prices of nontradables should not matter.

• The real exchange rate is, according to the law of one price, initially equal to one for all the countries, which implies that the same bundle of tradable goods costs the same in all countries in terms of a currency convertible worldwide.[6]

• S experiences productivity growth in its tradable sector, $\hat{A}_{TS} = d \log A_{TS} > 0$, and no productivity growth in its nontradable sector. Also, for simplicity, it is assumed that the outer world has zero productivity growth. The assumption of no productivity growth in S's nontradable sector is not crucial to the result yet is helpful for deriving the algebra. Similar calculations can be performed for the general case of nonzero productivity growth but with considerably more technical difficulty.

The Model

We approached a derivation of the HBS effect when we modeled the impact of uneven growth on inflation differentials between two countries. The model we considered there was too simple to catch any other effect than the inflation differentials. We now undertake some more careful modeling to show other implications of productivity growth. We start with the case of one country to show the basic intuition and then proceed to the case of two countries to see the spillover effects of productivity growth from one country within a currency union to another. Throughout this chapter, we use the modeling framework of Obstfeld and Rogoff (1996), with several extensions and minor alterations.

Given the above assumptions and applying basic algebra, we obtain that in the presence of labor productivity growth in the tradable sector of S's economy $\hat{A}_{TS}$, the relative price of nontradables in terms of tradables changes by

$$\hat{p}_S = \frac{\mu_{NS}}{\mu_{TS}} \hat{A}_{TS}, \tag{14.6}$$

where $\mu_{TS,NS} = 1 - \alpha_{TS,NS}$, the shares of labor in the output of tradable and nontradable goods in S, respectively. That is, a small change (say, 1 percent) in labor productivity in tradables causes an μ_{NS}/μ_{TS} percent increase in the relative price of nontradables.

Given the utility function (14.3), we obtain the following expression for the real aggregate price level in S, P_S:

$$P_S = [\gamma_S + (1 - \gamma_S) p_S^{1-\theta_S}]^{1/(1-\theta_S)}. \tag{14.7}$$

Log-differentiating (14.7), we obtain

$$\hat{P}_S = (1 - \gamma_S)\hat{p}_S. \tag{14.8}$$

This result suggests that the real aggregate price level in S increases by $(1 - \gamma_s)$ percent with each 1 percent increase in p_s, or, equivalently, by $(\mu_{NS}/\mu_{TS})(1 - \gamma_s)$ percent with each 1 percent increase in tradable-sector productivity. So we have derived the HBS effect in its initial formulation: wealthier countries tend to have higher price levels. With output growing in S due to increased productivity, its wealth increases, but so does its price level. Now comes the implication for the real exchange rate: assuming that there is no productivity growth in the reference country i, S's real exchange rate in terms of i's currency appreciates because S has become a more expensive country.

Further Implications
Following the derivation summarized above, one can derive many macroeconomic implications. We are particularly interested in seeing what this may mean for other countries that are in a monetary union with S. The impact of higher labor-productivity growth in S comes through two channels: (1) changes in trade flows within the union caused by increased production capacity and income in S and (2) the monetary policy that is uniform for all countries in the monetary union.

We first explore the impact of productivity growth on S's output, consumption, and trade patterns. Initially, growth in labor productivity leads to an increase in per-worker output in the tradable sector from which that growth has originated. The increase in output is rewarded by a higher wage in both sectors, since the labor market in S is perfectly competitive, which will contribute to growth of the total income. The total income growth will lead to an increase in demand, both for tradables and nontradables, hence the increase in imports of other tradables not produced in S, as well as growth in exports of TS (the part of its tradable output that is produced but not consumed in S). However, because the excess output of tradables can be exported while nontradables must be consumed within the country and because changes in demand do not necessarily have to match those in the output, there needs to be a reallocation of labor between the two sectors of the economy. This will define how much of its tradables S will be able to export.

Let us summarize the results so far. The growth in per-worker output in tradables is equal to

$$\hat{y}_{TS} = \frac{\hat{A}_{TS}}{\mu_{TS}}, \tag{14.9}$$

which means that with a 1 percent productivity growth in tradables, per-worker output in this sector grows by $1/\mu_{TS}$ percent. If we redo these calculations for the nontradable good, NS, we get

$$\hat{y}_{NS} = \frac{\hat{p}_s + \hat{A}_{NS}}{\mu_{NS}} = \frac{\hat{p}_s}{\mu_{NS}}, \tag{14.10}$$

which is equal to the growth of output per worker in the tradable sector if we apply equation (14.6). This result is paradoxical but only at first sight: since the wage and interest rate are the same in all sectors of the economy, labor and capital are employed up to the point where their marginal products are equal for all sectors. Actually, this is one of the implications of the HBS effect: the relative price of nontradables makes up for the gap in real productivities between tradables and nontradables.

If the wage is paid according to the marginal product of labor, its growth will match the growth of output per-worker,

$$\hat{y}_{TS} = \hat{w}_S.$$

This implies that the nominal price of tradables (if we were to introduce one at this point) stays the same as before the labor productivity shock $\hat{A}_{TS}$. This result goes to show that any other country trading with S will not experience inflationary pressure from importing TS because its price does not change due to the productivity increase.

Recalling the budget constraint, we see that with a 1 percent increase in w_s, the total income, Z_s grows by φ/μ_{TS} percent with 1 percent increase in productivity, or by φ/μ_{NS} percent with a 1 percent increase in p_s.[7] With income increasing, demand for tradables increases by

$$\frac{\varphi}{\mu_{NS}} - (1 - \gamma_S)(1 - \theta_S)\%$$

with each 1 percent increase in p_s or by

$$\left[\frac{\varphi}{\mu_{TS}} - (1 - \gamma_S)(1 - \theta_S) \right] \cdot \frac{\mu_{NS}}{\mu_{TS}} \%$$

with each 1 percent increase in A_{TS}, both in physical and value terms (since tradables are used as a numeraire).

The demand for nontradables, however, increases at different rates in physical and value terms, since their relative price p_s also changes. In value terms, the demand for nontradables grows at $\varphi/\mu_{NS} + (1 - \theta_s)\gamma_s$ percent with every 1 percent increase in p_s or

$$\left[\frac{\varphi}{\mu_{NS}} + (1 - \theta_S)\gamma_s\right] \cdot \frac{\mu_{NS}}{\mu_{TS}}$$

with every 1 percent increase in A_{TS}, which is faster than the growth in demand for tradables and faster than the growth of income. This implies that the share of expenditure on nontradable goods grows with improvements in productivity (and the economic growth that results from it), which is supported by rich evidence of changes in the composition of GDP as countries get richer (for example, growth of the share of services).[8]

While overproduced tradables may be exported, nontradables must be consumed within the country. Equating the changes in demand for nontradables and their output, we obtain that the nontradable sector employment should go up by

$$\hat{L}_{NS} = [\varphi - \mu_{NS} \cdot (\theta_S + (1 - \gamma_S)(1 - \theta_S)) - (1 - \mu_{NS})] \cdot \frac{1}{\mu_{TS}} \qquad (14.11)$$

with each 1 percent increase in labor productivity in the tradable sector. From (14.11) we can see that the higher θ_S, the lower is the growth of employment in the nontradable sector.[9] Indeed, if nontradables are well substituted for by tradables (θ_S approaching 1 from below), there is no need to produce more nontradables because the actual demand for them will not grow even though income will (if $\theta_S = 1$ and $\varphi < 1$, employment in the nontradable sector should actually fall). On the other hand, if nontradables are not easily substituted for by tradables, there will be a higher growth of employment in that sector to meet the growing demand.

Theoretically, there need not be an increase in unemployment because of labor reallocation: production of nontradables will exactly meet the demand for them, and every extra unit of tradables produced will be sold on the world market. However, because of structural rigidities and imperfect competition on the world market, a country experiencing productivity improvement may find it difficult to sell all its extra output of tradables abroad, and then unemployment may rise. Analysis of this situation is beyond the scope of this chapter, but some empirical evidence of this can be found in Gordon (1998).

Bringing together the changes in income, demand, and sectoral employment, we obtain that the country's tradable output grows by $1/\mu_{NS} + v$ percent with each 1 percent increase in p_s, where

$$v = -\frac{\Delta \cdot \hat{L}_{NS}/100}{L_S - \Delta} \cdot 100.$$

The growth of total output is a weighted average of the growth rates of tradable and nontradable outputs.

Finally, the net increase in S's export potential is

$$\frac{1 - \varphi}{\mu_{NS}} + (1 - \gamma_S)(1 - \theta_S) + v\%$$

with each 1 percent increase in p_s. This is very likely to be positive, suggesting that a country experiencing productivity growth tends to have its current-account balance improved through exports. The extent to which it can do so depends on the economy's structural parameters and consumer preferences. A high share of labor employed in the stagnant nontradable sector dampens the effect on the economy as a whole of productivity growth in tradables. A high share of labor income in GDP creates higher internal demand for tradables. Low substitutability between tradables and nontradables reduces the effective internal demand for tradables, thus increasing export potential. On the other hand, if nontradables are easily substituted by tradables, there is little room for a substantial increase in export potential because much of the increase in output would be eaten up by domestic consumers.

A Monetary Policy Link

Notice that none of the derivations above depend on nominal prices (in other words, they are correct for any numeraire), since they were calculated for relative prices. But now we can link the HBS effect with monetary policy and the nominal exchange rate. Although the HBS effect is modeled using relative prices, we can introduce money in this model if we assume a certain monetary policy stance. Consider two possible different cases of a neutral monetary policy: when the money stock grows proportionally to the GDP (that is when $M/Y = const$) and when the money stock is constant irrespective of output changes.

The Case When $M/Y = const$ Recalling Friedman's formula, $MV = PY$, $M/Y = const$ implies that the aggregate *nominal* price level, P_n, stays constant unless there are changes in the velocity of circulation. Since the relative price of nontradables rises to guarantee that the average price level P_n remains constant, its base (that is, the nominal price of tradables) should fall. But in that case, because of competitive forces, the country's nominal exchange rate must appreciate, thus bringing the price of its tradables back to the international level.

Formally, the nominal price level is equal to the real price level multiplied by some numeraire η, for which it is convenient to use the price of tradables:

$$P_n = \eta \cdot P_S = \eta \cdot [\gamma_S + (1 - \gamma_S)p_S^{1-\theta_S}]^{1/(1-\theta_S)}. \tag{14.12}$$

Log-differentiating (14.12), we get

$$\hat{P}_n = \hat{\eta} + \hat{P}_S = \hat{\eta} + (1 - \gamma_S)\hat{p}_s. \tag{14.13}$$

Then, to keep the above constant, we need $\hat{\eta} = -(1 - \gamma_S)\hat{p}_s$—that is, the numeraire should fall by $(1 - \gamma_s)$ percent with each 1 percent increase in p_s or, equivalently, by $(\mu_{NS}/\mu_{TS})(1 - \gamma_s)$ percent with each 1 percent increase in tradable-sector productivity.

Recalling the formula for the nominal exchange rate between countries S and i (eq. (14.5)) and log-differentiating it, we obtain

$$\hat{\varepsilon}_{S,i} = \hat{P}_{Ti} - \hat{P}_{TS} = \hat{P}_{Ti} - \hat{\eta}.$$

Since we have assumed that there is no productivity growth in the rest of the world, P_{Ti} should not change, so that we have the nominal exchange rate appreciating by $(1 - \gamma_s)$ percent with each 1 percent increase in p_s. It should now be clear that S does not lose competitiveness because its exchange-rate appreciation is exactly matched by the fall in its domestic price of tradables.[10]

The Case When $M = const$ A constant money supply implies a reduction in the aggregate price level and a fall in the price of tradables even greater than that in the previous case. The exchange-rate appreciation is greater, but as before, such exchange-rate appreciation does not mean any loss of competitiveness because it proceeds just to the point where the domestic price of tradables equals their international price.

$M = const$ means $\hat{P}_n + \hat{Y} = 0$, so that the nominal price level should fall by as much as the total output would grow as a result of the productivity increase (or by as much as the relative price of nontradables increases, which is equivalent). The total output growth associated with a 1 percent increase in p_S is

$$(1 - \gamma_S) \cdot \left(\frac{\varphi}{\mu_{NS}} - [\theta_S + (1 - \gamma_S)(1 - \theta_S)] \right) + \gamma_S \cdot \left(\frac{1}{\mu_{NS}} + v \right) = \psi \text{ percent.}$$

Then P_n should fall by ψ percent, which means that the price of tradables drops by $(1 - \gamma_s + \psi)$ percent, which is more than in the previous case. Again, the nominal exchange rate should appreciate by the same percentage.

There is also a wide range of exchange-rate and inflation tradeoffs in which the money stock grows faster than output, which leads to less exchange-rate appreciation but more inflation. Suppose M/Y is not constant but rather is $\hat{P}_n = k > 0$. Then $\hat{\eta} = k - (1 - \gamma_S)\hat{p}_s$. Since it still holds that $\hat{\varepsilon}_{S,i} = \hat{P}_{Ti} - \hat{P}_{TS} = \hat{P}_{Ti} - \hat{\eta}$ and we continue to assume that there is no price changes in country i, then $\varepsilon_{S,i}$ appreciates by exactly $k - (1 - \gamma_S)\hat{p}_s$. This implies that whatever growth the money stock may have, the exchange rate is a mirror image of the movements in the numeraire, and therefore there is no loss of competitive advantage for the countries experiencing the HBS effect but no gain either.

We have thus seen that productivity growth in S has an impact on income, production, consumption, the price level, and the exchange rate in country S. Now we aim to explore what spill-over effects these changes have on S's monetary union partners.

Two Countries in a Monetary Union: What Influence Does the HBS Effect in One Country Have on the Other?

Preliminary Observations
Now that we have studied the implications of the HBS effect for one country, we are ready to examine its impact on other countries tied

to the faster-growing country by a monetary union and therefore by a common monetary policy. All the implications for one country derived in real terms are still valid. However, there are some differences in the effects of monetary policy and some feedback from the FGC on its slower-growing monetary union partner:

• The fall in the numeraire required to keep the aggregate price level unchanged is smaller now because the slower-growing country does not experience an increase in its price level.

• The SGC may have its exports (and employment) increase through the increase in demand in its faster-growing partner, but taking full advantage of this requires flexible labor markets—namely, the ability to index the wage to the numeraire (the exchange rate) to stay competitive.

• If labor markets in the SGC are rigid, it will be difficult for the SGC to export more, and employment may fall—unless there is adequate growth in labor productivity.

• However, if there is no productivity growth in the SGC and it is unable to make its labor-market flexible enough, the union's Central Bank might consider tolerating higher inflation for the union as a whole, thus keeping the inflation rate and hence real wages in the SGC at their previous levels.

To illustrate this formally, consider an SGC named G forming a monetary union with S where productivity grows faster than in G. Let S produce one tradable good AS that it can export worldwide and sell at the world's prevailing price. G produces two tradable goods: AG (identical to AS) and BG, which S cannot produce. Goods AS, AG, and BG are also produced and traded worldwide. Both G and S are small countries relative to the size of the world market, so the price elasticity of demand for their exports is assumed to be infinite.

All the assumptions made earlier for S are valid for G, except that G does not experience productivity growth. Again, this is not a crucial assumption, but it does greatly simplify calculations. All the conclusions are valid even if there is some productivity growth in G (lower than in S), although they become less pronounced.

In addition to the assumptions made in the previous section, we now introduce utility measures for the whole $G + S$ union and for both tradable goods (*A* and *B*). We continue to use CES utility functions. The advantages of the CES utility function are that it allows easy aggregation of the goods entering it and that the price index implied by it can contain aggregated prices of the component goods indexed in the same way at different relative prices between the components. Furthermore, since we calculate the effects in percentage points, we are free to choose suitable initial values of relative prices, which greatly simplifies calculations and serves for clarity of results.

Thus, introducing a CES utility function for the $G + S$ union including aggregate goods **S** and **G**,

$$u(C_{G+S}) = [\delta^{1/\theta} \cdot C_G^{(\theta-1)/\theta} + (1 - \delta)^{1/\theta} \cdot C_S^{(\theta-1)/\theta}]^{\theta/(\theta-1)},$$

where δ = share of *G*'s economy in the union and θ is the elasticity of substitution in consumption between goods **S** and **G** (in fact, the propensity to migrate), we derive the **G** + **S** aggregate price index in the usual way as

$$P_{G+S} = [\delta + (1 - \delta)\rho^{1-\theta}]^{1/(1-\theta)},$$

where ρ is the relative price of good **S** in terms of good **G**. From here we can immediately see that if a 1 percent increase in p_S causes a $(1 - \gamma_s)$ percent increase in P_S, then it also causes a $(1 - \delta)(1 - \gamma_s)$ percent increase in P_{G+S}, by analogy with eq. (14.8). Thus the presence of a slower-growing country in the union will attenuate the exchange-rate realignment required to keep the nominal price level constant.

Another lesson is that the HBS effect in *S* does not have any bearing on inflation in *G*. As was shown previously, $\hat{y}_{TS} = \hat{w}_S$, so that the nominal price of tradables stays unchanged. Thus, there will be no HBS-effect-caused price growth in *G* because of trade with *S*, no matter how much the price index in *S* appreciates due to the HBS effect (as long as there is no autonomous HBS effect in *G* itself).

In this section, implications of growth in the FGC for the SGC will be derived only for the $M/Y = const$ case. However, one can use intuition and insights from the previous section to see that in the case of fixed money stock, the implications to be derived will be qualitatively the same, except that the magnitudes of deflation and exchange-rate appreciation will be bigger.

The Impact of Growth in S on Output and Employment in G: The Flexible Labor-Market Case

Recall from previous derivations that a 1 percent increase in p_s results in a $\varphi/\mu_{NS} - (1 - \gamma_S)(1 - \theta_S)$ percent increase in demand for tradables, including good BG. How does G benefit from the increase in demand for BG in S? If G is a net exporter of good BG and faces constant long-term marginal costs MC (because of constant returns to scale in the production function), transportation costs for delivery outside the $G + S$ union T, the world's price level WP, and the aggregate downward-sloping intraunion demand curve D_{S+G}, then the picture looks as shown in figure 14.1.

G sells BG worldwide at WP (and covers transportation costs) and within the union at MC. The volume of exports to the world is unaffected by the increase in demand within the union, so the union consumes the output of BG that is left. Because of transportation costs, every increase in demand for BG in the union is met by increased production of BG in G, not in the world. Then for every 1 percent increase in p_s, G gains

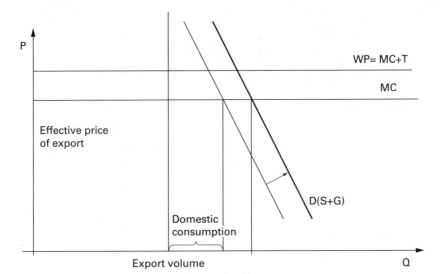

Figure 14.1
The effect of the HBS effect in S on the intraunion exports from G

$$\frac{\varphi}{\mu_{NS}} - (1 - \gamma_S)(1 - \theta_S)\%$$

in employment[11] in the sector meeting S's demand for BG and a corresponding increase in income. And G's ability to satisfy S's increased demand depends on having extra labor available, which may come through a decrease in structural and frictional unemployment or simply from workers choosing to work longer hours. Alternatively, in the absence of the HBS effect in G one can relax the assumption of a limited workforce, admitting some immigration into G.

The Impact of Growth in S on Nominal Price Levels

As has been shown, each 1 percent increase in p_S causes a $(1 - \delta)(1 - \gamma_s)$ percent increase in P_{G+S}. Therefore, to keep the overall nominal $G + S$ price index constant, the numeraire in $G + S$ (that is, the price of its tradable goods) has to go down by the same percentage, which implies a corresponding nominal exchange-rate appreciation but no loss of competitiveness for either S or G, just as in the case of one country. However, because of differences in growth rates, we now have S's price level increasing and G's decreasing: P_S rises by $(1 - \gamma_s) - (1 - \delta)(1 - \gamma_s) = \delta(1 - \gamma_s)$ percent (because it is cushioned by its slower-growing neighbor), but P_G goes down by $(1 - \delta)(1 - \gamma_s)$ percent.

The Impact of Growth in S on Output and Employment in G: The Rigid Nominal-Wages Case

Nominal-wage rigidity can be a real threat to a slow-growing country in a monetary union with a faster-growing country, especially when the union's monetary authorities adopt a strong anti-inflationary stance. A rigid labor market means that P_G goes down while the wage does not, leading to real wage increases in G unmatched by productivity growth. Therefore, the demand for labor will decline. Because of subsequent nominal exchange-rate appreciation in the union's currency, there will also be a drop in G's exports to the rest of the world (as MC in the production of BG in the world's currency, such as U.S. dollars, shifts upward) and an increase in its imports as marginal cost in the production of AG increases and marginal cost in the production of AS remains constant.

All this will increase G's unemployment and worsen its current account. True, these negative effects will be mitigated by real earnings growth, but the per-capita earnings growth for those in employment must, in its turn, be set against the drop in employment. For G to avoid job cuts and a decline in income from exports, the central bank of the $G + S$ monetary union would have to issue more money than would be enough to satisfy $M/Y = const.$ A good choice would be to set $\hat{M} - \hat{Y} = (1 - \delta)(1 - \gamma_S)$ for each 1 percent increase in p_S, in which case the price level in G would stay unchanged, although at the price of somewhat higher inflation in the union as a whole.

We next examine the impact of wage rigidity for employment and output in both the short run and long run.

Short-Run Impact We use two definitions of the short run: as the period in which capital-to-labor ratio is fixed at its historical level and as the period in which the stock of capital is fixed. Both definitions lead to fundamentally the same results. Namely, in the short run, without an adequate growth in labor productivity, the increase in the real wage renders G's exports uncompetitive on the world market, no matter how labor intensive they may be. In this situation, G faces the choice of either withdrawing from the world market or subsidizing the exports of the industries that have costs higher than revenues. However, because of the transportation-cost barrier, domestic production will not stop completely.

In the case of a fixed K/L ratio, real marginal costs grow at $(1 - \alpha)$ percent with each 1 percent increase in the real wage—that is, at $(1 - \delta)(1 - \gamma_s)$ percent with each 1 percent increase in the relative price of nontradables in S. This implies that, under given technology, the only way to prevent average costs from growing (that is, for exports to break even) is to avoid wage increases in the absence of adequate labor productivity growth. If the wage grows unmatched by productivity, exports become uncompetitive and the workers lose their jobs.

If there were some productivity growth, the growth of marginal costs MC would be

$$d \log(MC) = \hat{w}(1 - \alpha) - \hat{A}.$$

So it would be possible to offset the increase in costs due to real wage increases by sufficient increases in labor productivity. Notice here that for a given productivity growth in S's tradable sector it takes much lower (but nonzero) productivity growth in G's tradable sector to restore G's competitiveness. With a 1 percent increase in A_{TS}, p_S goes up by $\mu_{TS}/\mu_{NS} < 1$ percent (eq. (14.6)), then the wage in G increases by $(\mu_{TS}/\mu_{NS})(1 - \delta)(1 - \gamma_s)$ percent, which requires a $(\mu_{TS}/\mu_{NS})(1 - \delta) \cdot (1 - \gamma_s)(1 - \alpha)$ percent increase in A in the production function, which is much less than the 1 percent improvement in productivity in TS. Therefore, G can cope with the impact of productivity growth in S if it ensures that its workers continue to receive their marginal product.

When capital stock is fixed, we come to fundamentally the same results, with the difference that it is now possible to trim *marginal* costs down to the $WP - C$ level by decreasing the output of BG and substituting labor by relatively cheaper capital. However, with the real wage increase unmatched by productivity growth, it is impossible to restore *average* costs, so that the export industry will see the capital invested in it wearing down without replacement. As a result, production of BG will decline until it is revived by adequate labor-productivity growth.

For intraunion exports of AG, the situation is similar: since S is now the most efficient producer of A, the intraunion exports of AG will decline until they ultimately become negligible. However, with intraunion sales of BG the situation is different: because of the protection offered to G's producers by transportation costs of B from the rest of the world, it is cheaper for S to buy BG than its analogue on the world market. This implies that there exists a finite price elasticity of exports on the intraunion market, $-\sigma$ percent per each 1 percent increase in price. Thus the producers of BG meeting the demand from S do not have to shut down or ask for subsidies. Nevertheless, they will also experience a decrease in output and employment.

With a 1 percent increase in p_S, marginal costs of good BG increase by $(1 - \gamma_S)(1 - \delta)(1 - \alpha')$ percent, where $(1 - \alpha')$ is the share of labor in the production of BG. The increase in the price of good BG relative to the price of AS (not of AG because there is no point in buying A at a dearer price from G than it can be obtained domestically in S) is also $(1 - \gamma_S)(1 - \delta)(1 - \alpha')$ percent. Assuming a CES demand function for goods A and B in both countries, the demand for B from S falls by $[\omega + (1 - \beta)(1 - \omega)](1 - \gamma_S)(1 - \delta)(1 - \alpha')$ percent, where ω is the elasticity of substitution in consumption between A and BG and β is the share of BG in total consumption of tradables by S. However, with income in S rising, the net increase in demand for BG is

$$\lambda = \frac{\varphi}{\mu_{LNS}} - (1 - \gamma_S)(1 - \theta_S)$$

$$- [\omega + (1 - \beta)(1 - \omega)](1 - \gamma_S)(1 - \delta)(1 - \alpha') \text{ percent} \qquad (14.14)$$

per 1 percent increase in p_s, the sign of which is ambiguous. One insight of the expression above is that if good BG is capital intensive, then nominal wage rigidity in G does not have too great an impact on demand for BG in S, but otherwise G is likely to lose sales even in friendly S.

Depending on the sign of (14.14), there may be a growth in employment in the part of sector BG that serves demand from S (although now considerably reduced), while in sector AG there is clearly a fall in employment. So the only hope for G's exports to S to recover is for higher exports of BG, which is not produced in S and which it is cheaper for S's consumers to buy from G than to import from the world market (up to the point at which the increase in the price of GB corresponds to the transportation cost of bringing B from the world market).

With employment and output in export sectors decreasing in G, the trend in domestic sales will also be downward. Increases in wage costs will lead to higher unemployment, which will further reduce consumption. True, the increase in per-capita labor income may stimulate demand and thus reduce the layoffs, but it will not completely offset the divestment of labor because of the substitution effect between labor and capital. Therefore, although the situation with the total output is unclear, in the end we observe a decrease in employment in the sum of the tradable and nontradable sectors, except as regards BG, where the situation with employment is uncertain.

Long-Run Impact   As falling output in the tradable sector of G develops in the long run, capital use can be adjusted to its most efficient level. With wages remaining rigid and in the absence of labor-productivity growth, G will lose its competitiveness on the world market because there will be no way to adjust its marginal costs back to the world price. Changing the technology parameter, alpha, will not reduce costs either. Since it is hardly possible that the government will subsidize G's industry in the long run, inability to adjust marginal costs down will result in withdrawal of G's goods from the world market.[12] On the intraunion market, the situation will be the same as described for the short run. Again, as in the short-run case, if there were adequate labor-productivity growth, the marginal costs would not increase so that G would remain competitive in the world market.

Other Implications   The wage rigidity in G has further repercussions for its economy, especially for income and employment. The fall in domestic output will worsen G's current account. Domestic demand in G will be damaged by unemployment: although there will be an increase in real wages, some labor will be divested, thus lowering aggregate demand. Some second-order effects (such as demand switching from AG to cheaper AS, labor migration from G to S, and market segmentation) could also be modeled.

It does not take an advanced modeling exercise to make the important point here: in slow-growing parts of a monetary union, wage rigidities seriously damage the economy by reducing employment and income and depriving citizens of a great deal of the potential benefits that their faster-growing partner countries could bring. Therefore, governments in SGCs should focus not on trying to delay the accession of new, faster-growing members or on hindering growth-accelerating reforms in their current partners but rather on institutional reforms to enhance the flexibility of their own markets.

Another solution for the dilemma of the SGC with inflexible labor markets is for the currency union's Central Bank to allow slightly higher inflation in the union by running more expansionary monetary policy to keep that in G from turning negative. However, this would be not for the sake of faster-growing S (it is doing equally well at whatever unionwide inflation rate) but to help G's workers keep their jobs, in spite of their nominal wage rigidity and the ensuing mismatch between real wages and productivity in G. Such an increase in the union's inflation, however, would not have to be met by increases in the interest rate, as long as price increases in nontradables in S are caused by productivity (and therefore production) growth in S's tradables sector.

Concluding Remarks

Being in a monetary union with a faster-growing country can be beneficial for a slower-growing one because of the opportunity to increase intraunion exports by taking advantage of lower trade costs. Yet if the slower-growing country has a rigid labor market, it may face problems with its exports within and outside the union because in that case the nominal wage rigidity will result in a higher dollar price of its exports.

There are three possible strategies to cure the slower-growing country's problem of wage and productivity mismatch in the presence of a rigid domestic labor market:

• *Allowing slightly more inflation unionwide* while keeping inflation in the slow-growing country unchanged. But once again we would like to stress that the higher inflation rate will be allowed not because of the FGCs but because of inability of the governments of SGCs to bridge the gap between nominal wages and labor productivity in their economies.

• *Improving labor productivity in the slow-growing country.* Increased labor productivity will offset the real wage growth resulting from appreciation of the union's currency so that the slow-growing country can maintain its competitiveness. This need not exactly match the labor-productivity growth of the workers in S: calculations suggest that the labor-productivity increase in G need only be a fraction of that in S to restore G's competitiveness. This is because the effect of inflation in S on unionwide inflation is attenuated by the share of its economy in the union. So labor-productivity growth in the monetary union can still be uneven (faster in S) without having G lose its competitiveness (its ability to sell tradables).

• *Implement labor-market reforms* to improve flexibility. This is the best alternative to improving labor productivity. It might require reducing the minimum wage; decreasing social security provisions, severance pay, and vacations; or increasing the working week. Although efficient economically, however, this might be unacceptable politically, since it is hard to persuade the general public to make sacrifices, especially when it is argued (quite opportunistically) that the need for these sacrifices comes from accession of the new countries in the union.

Finally, because slower-growing countries can benefit from being in a monetary union with faster-growing ones, they should seek to increase trade and economic relations with fast growers. However, in a monetary union consisting of unevenly growing countries, the choices are either easy but not welcome (allowing for more inflation in fast-growing countries even after their accession to the monetary union) or good but hard to implement (improving labor productivity and labor-market flexibility in the slower growers).

Appendix: The HBS Effect Model in Detail

Here we derive the results shown in the main text of this chapter in more detail to enable readers to obtain the same algebraic results themselves. Calculations that were made in the main text of the chapter are therefore not repeated here.

Define the output per employed unit of labour as $y = Y/L$. Then take a constant-returns-to-scale Cobb-Douglas production function (eq. (14.2)),

$$y_{NS,TS} = (p_S)A_{NS,TS} \cdot k_{NS,TS}^{\alpha_{NS,TS}},$$

where $k = K/L$. By assumption of perfectly competitive factor markets and CRS,

$$y_{TS} = A_{TS} \cdot k_{TS}^{\alpha_{TS}} = rk_{TS} + w_S \quad \text{and} \quad y_{NS} = p_S A_{NS} \cdot k_{NS}^{\alpha_{NS}} = rk_{NS} + w_S. \tag{14.15}$$

Log-differentiate equations (14.15) to get

$$\hat{y}_{TS,NS} = \frac{rk_{TS,NS}}{rk_{TS,NS} + w_S}\hat{k}_{TS,NS} + \frac{w_S}{rk_{TS,NS} + w_S}\hat{w}_S, \tag{14.15a}$$

which is equivalent to

$$\hat{A}_{TS} + \alpha_{TS}\hat{k}_{TS} = \alpha_{TS}\hat{k}_{TS} + (1 - \alpha_{TS})w_S \quad \text{and}$$

$$\hat{p}_S + \hat{A}_{NS} + \alpha_{NS}\hat{k}_{NS} = \alpha_{NS}\hat{k}_{NS} + (1 - \alpha_{NS})w_S,$$

where we have made use of the fact that the shares of capital and labor in the total output are equal to α and $(1 - \alpha)$, respectively. Define $1 - \alpha = \mu$. Then

$$\hat{A}_{TS} = \mu_{TS}\hat{w}_S \quad \text{and} \quad \hat{p}_S + \hat{A}_{NS} = \mu_{NS}\hat{w}_S,$$

which gives us

$$\hat{p}_S = \frac{\mu_{NS}}{\mu_{TS}}\hat{A}_{TS} - \hat{A}_{NS}. \tag{14.16}$$

But remembering that we assume no growth in S's nontradable sector, equation (14.16) simplifies to

$$\hat{p}_S = \frac{\mu_{NS}}{\mu_{TS}}\hat{A}_{TS},$$

which is the result reported in the main text of the chapter.

By maximizing the utility function (14.3) subject to the budget constraint (14.4), we get the following demand schedules:

$$C_{TS} = \frac{\gamma_S Z_S}{\gamma_S + (1 - \gamma_S)p_S^{1-\theta_S}}, \quad C_{NS} = \frac{p_S^{-\theta_S}(1 - \gamma_S)Z_S}{\gamma_S + (1 - \gamma_S)p_S^{1-\theta_S}}. \tag{14.17}$$

By substituting equations (14.17) back into the utility function (14.3), we get the overall price level defined as minimum expenditure required to buy one unit of consumption:

$$P_S = [\gamma_S + (1 - \gamma_S)p_S^{1-\theta_S}]^{1/(1-\theta_S)}. \tag{14.18}$$

Log-differentiate eq. (14.18) to obtain

$$\hat{P}_S = \frac{1}{1 - \theta_S}\frac{(1 - \theta_S)(1 - \gamma_S)\hat{p}_S}{[\gamma_S + (1 - \gamma_S)p_S^{1-\theta_S}]}. \tag{14.19}$$

Remembering that we have set $p_s = 1$ initially, eq. (14.19) simplifies to

$$\hat{P}_S = (1 - \gamma_S)\hat{p}_S,$$

as reported in the chapter. We now derive further implications of the HBS effect in S.

Changes in Output per Worker

Recall that $y_{TS} = A_{TS}k_{TS}^{\alpha_{TS}} = rk_{TS} + w_S$ (eq. (14.15)). Differentiate with respect to k_{TS} to get

$$\alpha_{TS} A_{TS} k_{TS}^{\alpha_{TS}-1} = r. \tag{14.20}$$

Then log-differentiate (14.20) to get

$$\hat{a}_{TS} + \hat{A}_{TS} + (\alpha_{TS} - 1)\hat{k}_{TS} = \hat{r}.$$

Because r and α are constant, the above reduces to

$$\hat{k}_{TS} = \frac{\hat{A}_{TS}}{\mu_{TS}}. \tag{14.21}$$

Combining eqs. (14.15a) and (14.21), we obtain the results reported in the main text:

$$\hat{y}_{TS} = \hat{k}_{TS}. \tag{14.22}$$

Redoing these calculations for the nontradable good *NS*, we get

$$\hat{y}_{NS} = \hat{k}_{NS} = \frac{\hat{p}_s + \hat{A}_{NS}}{\mu_{NS}} = \frac{\hat{p}_s}{\mu_{NS}}. \tag{14.23}$$

Changes in Wages and Total Income

Recall from previous derivations that

$$\hat{A}_{TS} = \mu_{TS} \cdot \hat{w}_S, \quad \text{or} \quad \hat{w}_S = \frac{\hat{A}_{TS}}{\mu_{TS}}.$$

We then obtain that $\hat{y}_{TS} = \hat{w}_S$, which proves that there will be no inflationary pressure on S's trade partners because of the HBS effect in S.

Recall the budget constraint (eq. (14.4)). Clearly, with a 1 percent increase in w_s, Z_s grows by

$$\varphi = \frac{w_S L_S}{w_S L_S + r Q_S} \text{ percent.}$$

Since

$$\hat{w}_S = \frac{\hat{A}_{TS}}{\mu_{TS}} = \frac{\hat{p}_S}{\mu_{NS}},$$

Z_s grows by φ/μ_{TS} percent with a 1 percent increase in productivity, or by φ/μ_{NS} percent with a 1 percent increase in p_s. With income increasing, demand should also increase, but its increase need not necessarily match the output increase, so that we may have a change in S's export potential, which we will not be able to calculate before we explore how domestic demand reacts to the increase in productivity.

Changes in Domestic Demand

Log-differentiate the optimal demand schedules (14.17) to get

$$\hat{C}_{TS} = \hat{Z}_S - (1 - \gamma_S)(1 - \theta_S)\hat{p}_S \quad \text{and}$$

$$\hat{C}_{NS} = \hat{Z}_S - [\theta_S + (1 - \gamma_S)(1 - \theta_S)]\hat{p}_S. \tag{14.24}$$

Because $\hat{Z}_S = (\varphi/\mu_{NS})\hat{p}_S$, the net increase in domestic demand for tradables is

$$\frac{\varphi}{\mu_{NS}} - (1 - \gamma_S)(1 - \theta_S)\%$$

per each 1 percent increase in p_s, or

$$\left[\frac{\varphi}{\mu_{TS}} - (1 - \gamma_S)(1 - \theta_S)\right] \cdot \frac{\mu_{NS}}{\mu_{TS}} \%$$

per each 1 percent increase in A_{TS}. Analogously, the net increase in demand for nontradables is

$$\frac{\varphi}{\mu_{NS}} - [\theta_S + (1 - \gamma_S)(1 - \theta_S)] \text{ percent}$$

and

$$\left[\frac{\varphi}{\mu_{TS}} - [\theta_S + (1 - \gamma_S)(1 - \theta_S)]\right] \cdot \frac{\mu_{NS}}{\mu_{TS}} \text{ percent}$$

per each 1 percent increase in p_s and A_{TS}, respectively.

In value terms, though, the demand for nontradables grows as follows:

$$\hat{p}_s + \hat{C}_{NS} = \hat{Z}_s + (1 - \theta_s)\gamma_s\hat{p}_s = \left[\frac{\varphi}{\mu_{NS}} + (1 - \theta_S)\gamma_s\right]\hat{p}_s,$$

which is $\varphi/\mu_{NS} + (1 - \theta_s)\gamma_s$ percent with every 1 percent increase in p_s, or

$$\left[\frac{\varphi}{\mu_{NS}} + (1 - \theta_S)\gamma_s\right] \cdot \frac{\mu_{NS}}{\mu_{TS}}$$

with every 1 percent increase in A_{TS}.

Reallocation of Labor

Recall that the physical output of nontradables is equal to $Y_{NS} = A_{NS} \cdot k_{NS}^{\alpha_{NS}} \cdot L_{NS}$. Log-differentiate this, remembering that $\hat{A}_{NS} = 0$, to get

$$\hat{L}_{NS} = \hat{Y}_{NS} - \alpha_{NS}\hat{k}_{NS} = \hat{C}_{NS} - \alpha_{NS}\hat{k}_{NS},$$

since nontradables do not enter international trade. We already know what $\hat{C}_{NS}$ and $\hat{k}_{NS}$ are eqs. (14.23) and (14.24), so just by bringing them together we get

$$\hat{L}_{NS} = [\varphi - \mu_{NS} \cdot (\theta_S + (1 - \gamma_S)(1 - \theta_S)) - (1 - \mu_{NS})] \cdot \frac{\hat{A}_{TS}}{\mu_{TS}},$$

or

$$\hat{L}_{NS} = [\varphi - \mu_{NS} \cdot (\theta_S + (1 - \gamma_S)(1 - \theta_S)) - (1 - \mu_{NS})] \cdot \frac{\hat{p}_S}{\mu_{NS}}.$$

Changes in Total Output

We continue to assume that labor reallocation does not cause unemployment. Before the productivity shock, the amount of labor employed in the nontradable sector was

$$\frac{\gamma_S(w_S L_S + r Q_S)\mu_{NS}}{w_S} = \Delta,$$

and therefore $L_S - \Delta$ units of labor were employed in tradables. If with a 1 percent increase in p_s there is an $\hat{L}_{NS}$ percent increase in the labor employed in nontradables, then the tradable sector is going to have $L_S - \Delta \cdot (100 + \hat{L}_{NS})/100$ units employed, thus growing by $-(\Delta \cdot \hat{L}_{NS}/100)/(L_S - \Delta) \cdot 100 = v$ percent.[13] Then tradable output grows at

$$\hat{Y}_{TS} = \hat{y}_{TS} + \hat{L}_{TS} = \frac{\hat{p}_S}{\mu_{NS}} + v\hat{p}_S, \tag{14.25}$$

which is $1/\mu_{NS} + v$ percent per each 1 percent increase in p_s. The growth of total output is a weighted average of the growth rates of tradable and nontradable outputs.

Changes in Export Potential

Given that consumption of tradables grows by $\varphi/\mu_{NS} - (1 - \gamma_S)(1 - \theta_S)$ percent and that tradable output grows by $1/\mu_{NS} + v$ percent (eq. (14.25)), the net increase in S's export potential is $(1 - \varphi)/\mu_{NS} + (1 - \gamma_S)(1 - \theta_S) + v$ percent per 1 percent increase in p_s.

We next examine the case of the two countries, S and G, in a monetary union. While the situation with flexible labor markets in G is relatively simple and was presented in the main text of the chapter in sufficient detail, the rigid-labor-market case needs more explanation. We therefore explore the impact of wage rigidity for employment and output in G in detail both in the short run and long run.

Short-Run Impact

In the case of a fixed K/L ratio, the CRS Cobb-Douglas production function can be transformed as follows:

$$Y = AK^\alpha L^{1-\alpha} = Ak^\alpha L,$$

where $k = K/L$, which is fixed. The total cost function in this case is trivial:

$$C(w, r, Y) = L(rk + w) = \frac{rk + w}{Ak^\alpha} Y, \tag{14.26}$$

from which we derive the marginal (and average) cost function:

$$MC = \frac{rk + w}{Ak^\alpha}. \tag{14.27}$$

Log-differentiate (14.27) to get

$$d \log(MC) = (1 - \alpha)\hat{w}, \tag{14.28}$$

which implies that, under given technology, the only way to prevent average costs from growing (to break even with exports) in the absence of adequate labor-productivity growth is to avoid real wage increases. If the real wage grows unmatched by productivity, exports become uncompetitive, and the workers lose their jobs.

If there were some productivity growth, eq. (14.28) would look different:

$$d \log(MC) = \hat{w}(1 - \alpha) - \hat{A}.$$

So it would be possible to offset the increase in costs due to real wage increases by sufficient increases in labor productivity. Notice here that for a given rate of productivity growth in S's tradable sector, it takes much lower (but nonzero) productivity growth in G's tradable sector to restore G's competitiveness.

When capital stock is fixed, we come to fundamentally the same results, with the difference that it is now possible to trim *marginal* costs down to the $WP - C$ level by decreasing the output of BG and substituting labor by relatively cheaper capital. However, with the real wage increase unmatched with productivity growth, it is impossible to restore *average* costs, so that the export industry will be making negative profits.

Consider the output per unit of capital,

$$y = Y/K = A(L/K)^{1-\alpha} = Al^{1-\alpha} \tag{14.29}$$

where $l = L/K$.

Derive l from the above equation, and substitute the result back to the total cost function per unit of capital:

$$c = C/K = wl + r = r + w(y/A)^{1/(1-\alpha)}.$$

Derive the marginal cost function and log-differentiate it (holding A and r are fixed):

$$MC = \frac{1}{1-\alpha} \cdot \frac{w}{A^{1/(1-\alpha)}} y^{\alpha/(1-\alpha)}$$

$$\hat{MC} = \hat{w} + \frac{\alpha}{1-\alpha} \hat{y}.$$

We see that it is now possible to manipulate output to keep marginal costs unchanged. To keep $\hat{MC} = 0$ in the absence of productivity growth, the following must hold:

$$\hat{w} = \frac{\alpha}{1-\alpha} \hat{y}$$

—that is, with every 1 percent increase in wage, output must contract by $(1 - \alpha)/\alpha$ percent, which, given our production function, is equivalent to a $1/\alpha$ percent drop in employment.[14] Log-differentiating the average cost function,

$$AC = \frac{r}{y} + \frac{w}{A^{1/(1-\alpha)}} y^{\alpha/(1-\alpha)},$$

we get

$$\hat{AC} = \frac{r}{y} + \frac{w}{A^{1/(1-\alpha)}} y^{\alpha/(1-\alpha)} = (1-\alpha)\hat{w} + \hat{y} - \hat{y} = (1-\alpha)\hat{w}. \tag{14.30}$$

So it is not possible to adjust the average costs to their previous level, unless there is an adequate growth in labor productivity. If there is none, then the exporting industries will make losses and, if not subsidized, will have to withdraw from the market. However, if we assume that capital, once allocated to production in a particular sector, cannot be reallocated to another (so that it effectively becomes a bygone cost), then exports of *BG* will not collapse immediately. What will collapse is returns to the owners of capital used in the production of *BG*, who will effectively suffer a capital loss. Such a situation will lead to a slow decline in *BG* production, as capital used in the sector declines through depreciation and is not replaced.

Long-Run Impact

In the long run, capital use can be adjusted to its most efficient level. With wages remaining rigid and in the absence of labor productivity growth, *G* will lose its competitiveness on the world market because there will be no way to adjust its marginal costs back to the world price.

To see why marginal costs cannot be adjusted downward with real wage increases and zero productivity growth, consider the cost-minimization problem with a Cobb-Douglas production function with CRS:

$$\min wL + rK, \quad s.t. \quad AK^{\alpha}L^{1-\alpha} = Y.$$

After some algebraic manipulation, we get the demand functions for capital and labor:

$$K = \frac{Y}{A} \cdot \left[\frac{\alpha}{1-\alpha} \cdot \frac{w}{r} \right]^{1-\alpha}, \quad L = \frac{Y}{A} \left[\frac{1-\alpha}{\alpha} \cdot \frac{r}{w} \right]^{\alpha}$$

and then the total cost function:

$$C = \frac{Y}{A} \left[\frac{r}{\alpha} \right]^{\alpha} \cdot \left[\frac{w}{1-\alpha} \right]^{1-\alpha}$$

and marginal costs:

$$c = \frac{1}{A} \left[\frac{r}{\alpha} \right]^{\alpha} \cdot \left[\frac{w}{1-\alpha} \right]^{1-\alpha}, \tag{14.31}$$

which in this case are equal to average costs. We see that marginal costs are now constant regardless of the volume of output, so that we cannot simply reduce them by reducing output. Changing alpha does not solve the problem, either. To see this, log-differentiate (14.31), holding A and r fixed to get

$$\hat{c} = -\alpha\hat{\alpha} + (1 - \alpha) \cdot \left[\hat{w} + \frac{\alpha}{1 - \alpha}\hat{\alpha}\right] = (1 - \alpha) \cdot \hat{w}.$$

Again, as in the short-run case, if there were adequate labor-productivity growth, the marginal costs would not increase, so that G would remain competitive in the world's market. This can be seen immediately from eq. (14.31).

Notes

1. It may be the case that a certain minimum level of income is required for a society to be able to support various sophisticated institutions, such as advanced forms of banking supervision, which may be helpful in protecting the political system from demands for inflationary finance. However, the more advanced CEECs already have such institutions in place.

2. This would be necessary for countries to avoid the demand effect. Structural reforms in the tradable-goods sector would be additionally dangerous.

3. The reference period is that for which the conformity of a country with the criteria is assessed. What could be targeted by the sustainability requirement would be various tricks such as delaying administered price or negotiated wage increases into postexamination years or fulfiling the criterion thanks to an unsustainable nominal appreciation.

4. The same assumption applied to an excess of CEEC inflation of three percentage points above the EMU average inflation during 2000 to 2002 of 2.5 percent would imply improbably high CEEC-wide growth rates of 7 to 8 percent per annum.

5. That is,

$$\pi_{TA} = \hat{w}_A - \hat{q}_{TA}$$
$$\pi_{NA} = \hat{w}_A - \hat{q}_{NA}$$
$$\pi_{TB} = \hat{w}_B - \hat{q}_{TB}$$
$$\pi_{NB} = \hat{w}_B - \hat{q}_{NB},$$

where $\hat{x} = d \log x$ is the rate of change in relative terms. We can now derive nontradable inflation as a function of tradable inflation and productivity in both sectors:

$$\pi_{NA} = \pi_{TA} + \hat{q}_{TA} - \hat{q}_{NA}$$
$$\pi_{NB} = \pi_{TB} + \hat{q}_{TB} - \hat{q}_{NB}.$$

By substituting these back to equation (14.1), we get

$$\pi_A = (1 - \alpha)\pi_{TA} + \alpha(\pi_{TA} + q_{TA} - q_{NA})$$
$$\pi_B = (1 - \alpha)\pi_{TB} + \alpha(\pi_{TB} + q_{TB} - q_{NB}),$$

which implies

$$\pi_A - \pi_B = \alpha(q_{TA} - q_{TB}) - \alpha(q_{NA} - q_{NB}).$$

6. This, however, does not mean that identical bundles of consumption goods, both tradable and nontradable, should cost the same in all countries, since prices of nontradables may vary from country to country. Moreover, the model of the HBS effect that we present offers one possible explanation to why total costs of the same unit of consumption goods may actually differ across countries.

7. This is because Z_s grows by $\varphi = w_S L_S / (w_S L_S + rQ_S)$ percent, and

$$\hat{w}_S = \hat{y}_{TS} = \hat{y}_{NS} = \frac{\hat{A}_{TS}}{\mu_{TS}} = \frac{\hat{p}_S}{\mu_{NS}}.$$

8. The net increase in demand for nontradables in real terms is

$$\frac{\varphi}{\mu_{NS}} - [\theta_S + (1 - \gamma_S)(1 - \theta_S)] \text{ percent} \quad \text{and}$$

$$\left[\frac{\varphi}{\mu_{TS}} - [\theta_S + (1 - \gamma_S)(1 - \theta_S)] \right] \cdot \frac{\mu_{NS}}{\mu_{TS}} \text{ percent}$$

with each 1 percent increase in p_s and A_{TS}, respectively.

9. Unless S has negative financial wealth so that its share of labor in output is above 1.

10. In a more complex setup, though, when we have to deal with nontradable inputs into tradable goods, there may be some loss of competitiveness, but the question then is whether such goods should be classified as fully tradable.

11. If there is a CRS technology in place.

12. Of course, this is true for the case of infinite price elasticity of exports. In another framework, where countries are assumed to have some pricing power on the world market, higher costs would mean a reduction of exports and not their complete cessation (Dixit and Stiglitz 1977).

13. The same sort of calculation can be performed for each 1 percent increase in A_{TS} using eq. (14.6).

14. Consider that $\hat{l} = \hat{L} - \hat{K} = \hat{L}$.

References

Barber, Tony. "EU hopefuls likely to suffer if Danes vote 'no.'" *Financial Times* (London edition). 26 September 2000, pp. 10.

De Grauwe, P. (1992). "Inflation Convergence during the Transition to EMU." Centre for Economic Policy Research (CEPR) Discussion Paper Series No. 658.

Dixit, A., and J. Stiglitz. (1977). "Monopolistic Competition and Optimum Product Diversity." *American Economic Review*, 67: 297–308.

Gordon, R. J. (1998). "Is There a Tradeoff between Unemployment and Productivity Growth?" NBER Working Paper No. 5081.

Hämäläinen, S. (2003). "EU Accession: Challenges for Retail Banking." Keynote address made at the Conference on Retail Financial Services in the New Europe, European Financial Management and Marketing Association, Warsaw, April 28–29. Available at ⟨http://www.ecb.int/⟩ (key speeches).

Obstfeld, M., and K. Rogoff. (1996). *Foundations of International Macroeconomics*. Cambridge, MA: MIT Press.

15

Is Full Participation in the EMU Likely to Favor or Slow Real Convergence?

Iain Begg

Along with the single market and monetary union, one of the fundamental aims (article 2, Treaty on European Union (TEU)) of the European Union (EU) is to promote economic and social cohesion, an expression which is interpreted in title XVII (article 158, Treaty establishing the European Community (TEC)) to mean "reducing disparities between the levels of development of the various regions and the backwardness of the least favored regions or islands, including rural areas." Clearly, this wording signals that a key element of cohesion is the promotion of convergence in the sense of reducing disparities in GDP per head: in other words, real convergence. Entry into stage 3 of the EMU—that is, full membership of the euro area—requires countries to pass the entirely different test of fulfilling the nominal convergence criteria set out in the Maastricht Treaty. Real convergence means that poorer countries and regions should, by having relatively higher growth, catch up with the richer, whereas nominal convergence has the more limited ambition of ensuring that a country's fiscal and monetary position is compatible with the obligations of monetary union, irrespective of its growth rate. At the time of writing, most of the member states that joined the EU in 2004 are within striking distance of the nominal-convergence criteria, having achieved a substantial degree of disinflation. However, as their economies adjust to EU membership, it may prove difficult to maintain these gains.

Deciding whether to participate fully in monetary union, particularly for the new member states, will necessarily require a balancing of different considerations. On the one hand, as Leszek Balcerowicz explained in 2001,[1] early "entry of the candidate countries into EMU would allow them to start reaping the related advantages (more price transparency, reduced transformation costs, stronger macroeconomic framework)" as quickly as possible and would help to consolidate the momentum toward structural reforms. He also argues that setting a firm deadline is advantageous and that his reasoning is applicable to most of the new members. The Centre for European Policy Studies (CEPS) (2002) also supports early EMU entry for most of the new members on the grounds that a stable macroeconomic framework is an essential precondition for real convergence.

Opponents of early participation in the EMU, on the other hand, are concerned that the EMU will impose too rigid a macroeconomic policy framework on countries that are bound to face turbulent times as they continue to restructure. The new members will have to cope with the demands of transition not only to a market economy but also to the EU single market (for a summary, see Landesmann and Richter 2003). The core of this latter position is that a greater degree of flexibility will be required and that the capacity to adapt monetary conditions and alter the nominal exchange rate will be essential tools. There are also many factors to consider, as the evidence from the last forty years for the current members reviewed by Barry (2003) shows. The principal obstacles to convergence according to Barry have been labor-market rigidities (especially Ireland prior to 1973 and Spain during the 1980s), ill-judged macroeconomic policies (all the cohesion countries from the mid-1970s to the late 1980s), and weaknesses in public administration, especially in many backward regions. Rostowski (2003) also highlights the risk of macroeconomic instability, a possible "capital inflow stop" and thus a risk of currency depreciation, but he draws the opposite conclusion that the answer is to move rapidly to adopt the euro. He argues that the effect may be to damage the prospects for real convergence and that this is the worst possible outcome, especially if pressures for easy monetary policy crate unsustainable short-term booms.

In assessing the balance between these effects, it is important to distinguish between the phase of transition from the current position to full participation in EMU and the medium- to long-term effects of being part of the euro area. The transition (stage 2 of the EMU) implies adjustment costs associated with nominal convergence, and these, depending on the changes that have to be engineered, may have a limited, adverse impact on real convergence. Full membership of the euro area, by contrast, means making a different form of adjustment—namely, to the EMU policy framework—and ensuring that the impact on the real economy is positive so that real convergence occurs. Some critics argue that the structures of the economies of the new EU members are so different from the core euro-area countries that the former will not find it easy to live with the euro and that real convergence will suffer. But as Rostowski (2003, p. 1008) argues, "the balance of the argument appears to lie definitely on the side of EMU accession," and evidence in chapter 14 in this volume by Rostowski and Zoubanov reinforces the message.

For both the EU15 and the new members, several real convergence challenges have to be confronted. Four very different (though possibly overlapping) types of convergence problem can be identified:

• *Lack of development* has meant that many parts of the enlarged EU are deficient in the dynamic sectors of activity that have supported economic advances. Such regions typically have large, often low-productivity agricultural sectors and did not experience large-scale industrialization. In much of southern Europe, until quite recently, agriculture remained a dominant industry, and there was relatively little industrialization. High natural rates of labor-force growth (that is, where the entry of youths into the labor market is substantially higher than the retirement of older workers) have traditionally characterized much of southern Europe, as well as Ireland, and have led to a steady emigration of working-age individuals.[2] Advances in agricultural productivity have meant that fewer workers can be supported by farming, with the result that in such regions there has been a drift of population toward urban centers. This pattern of a shakeout in agriculture is likely to be repeated in many of the new members from central and eastern Europe and could result in severe problems of adjustment in those regions where agriculture currently accounts for a high share of employment.

• *Peripherality, remoteness, or inaccessibility* are purely geographical disadvantages that amount to a permanent competitive disadvantage that is unlikely to be easily countered. Most of the currently designated less favored regions are on the periphery of the EU, suggesting that this, in itself, is a significant reason for support. The notion of peripherality as a geographical one of distance from an economic core implies that transport costs are the main obstacle, but it may be more accurate to analyze peripherality in terms of marginalization in a wider sense. It is also important to note that there are many relatively prosperous regions (the Prague region, Grampian in the United Kingdom, Uusimaa in Finland) in ostensibly remote locations, whereas some of the less favored regions, such as Hainaut in Belgium or the Saarland, could scarcely be more centrally located relative to the EU center of gravity.

• *Loss of competitiveness* can arise for a variety of reasons and can be especially hard to reverse if cumulative processes reinforce the initial loss. In some of the rustbelt regions of northern Europe (such as South Yorkshire in England and parts of Wallonia in Belgium or the Ruhr in Germany), where the decline of agricultural employment occurred at an earlier stage, regional problems are associated mainly with the decline of staple industries, especially coal mining, steel making, textiles, and shipbuilding. By contrast, the sunrise industries, such as computer software or biotechnology, are drawn to different sorts of locations, often environmentally more attractive and without a strong industrial tradition, examples being the Toulouse area in France or parts of Bavaria. For most of the regions affected by industrial decline, adjustment has proved to be slow and painful, instead of happening quickly as might be predicted by the more sanguine economic theories. Here, too, the reliance on old industry and the poor environmental conditions in many regions of the new member states is inauspicious.

• *The consequences of economic integration* can be pronounced where the dismantling of barriers and reconfiguring of policy or regulatory frameworks may in themselves precipitate regional problems. The impact of integration can arise in a variety of ways, analyzed notably in new-economic-geography (NEG) approaches (Krugman and Venables 1996; Puga 1999). If integration tips the balance of industrial organization in favor of economies of scale and scope, the effects may systematically affect a whole region, although the NEG analyses tend to have conflicting views on what the outcomes will be, depending on the assumptions made about labor mobility and wage flexibility. At a macroeconomic level, other mechanisms come into play. In particular, a changed macroeconomic policy mix may have an uneven regional incidence.

All four categories of regional problem are in evidence in the EU15 at present. Eastern enlargement of the union will, moreover, bring new demands on policy. EU policies to promote cohesion (through the structural funds and the Cohesion Fund) focus principally on enhancing the long-run competitiveness of weaker regions. Current eligibility rules distinguish between two classes of recipients: the lagging regions (those with a GDP per head relative to the EU of 75 percent or below (objective 1 of the structural funds) and other regions facing socioeconomic restructuring (objective 2). Nearly all the regions in the former group have been slow to develop and tend to have above-average proportions of primary industry. Objective 2 regions, by contrast, have generally seen an erosion of competitiveness.

These questions about convergence point to a number of awkward tradeoffs that need to be explored in considering the merits of quick accession to the full EMU. The aim of this chapter is to assess the issues raised by looking at the conceptual arguments and at the emerging evidence from the early years of the euro. Both are surprisingly inconclusive, and the chapter therefore also tries to explore the circumstances in which full monetary union is likely to be more advantageous. The next section sets out the broad lines of the debate on the balance of effects of joining the EMU rapidly. After a brief discussion of the record after five years of the euro, the chapter concludes with a review of policy issues.

The Impact of the EMU

That the EMU changes the economic environment, perhaps radically, is generally accepted, and there is broad agreement on several of its expected effects. Equally, there are possible outcomes where neither theory nor evidence provides a solid basis for judgment and where there is no easy way of reconciling the conflicting views. Three different categories of effects, all of which bear on real economy performance, can be delineated (table 15.1):

• *Macroeconomic changes*:   The new policy regime might alter the manner in which policy is conducted and require the country to acclimatize and then to develop new accommodations between policy actors and objectives. Thus, a general fall in interest rates (expected from the single

Table 15.1
The impact of EMU on cohesion

Mechanism	Effect	Incidence and Impact on Cohesion
Macroeconomic shifts	Change to the new policy regime recasts established policy signals and rules	Affects all members of the EMU, but spatial impact uncertain; depends on willingness and capacity to adapt
Acclimatization in the short term to new policy settings	Low nominal interest rate; impact on asset prices; disparities in real rates	Previously inflation-prone countries face overheating; thus far, positive for less prosperous areas but increases prospect of macroeconomic imbalances
Adoption of stability-oriented macro policy approach	Alters government and financial-market behavior	Most pronounced for those who have to change most, with need for policy learning; risks from Balassa-Samuelson effect for countries with least developed service sectors
Labor market and transformations of it	More of the burden of adjustment falls on labor market	Creates problems for least flexible regions; could aggravate unemployment in weaker regions
Systems for wage setting	Influence on wage flexibility and scope for short-term adjustment	Potentially damaging for areas with rigid systems and engenders problems of social cohesion (insiders and outsiders)
Geographical, sectoral, and occupational mobility	Affects medium-term scope for labor-market adaptability to deal with competitiveness problems	Induced pressures from migration; could lead to brain drain (gain); possibility of aggravated imbalances within countries

Table 15.1
(continued)

Mechanism	Effect	Incidence and Impact on Cohesion
Regulatory setting and institutions underpinning labor market	Shapes long-term potential for adjustment through the supply-side	Adverse for less developed economies that lack training provision, especially where de facto regulation is pronounced
Induced effects on economic structure	Market opening accelerates pace of restructuring	Potential threat to least competitive; likely to widen existing disparities; may also create new problem areas
Regional industrial specialization	Mix of centripetal and centrifugal NEG consequences	Initially favors core regions; creates opportunities for low-cost areas; ambivalent overall
Concentration of financial services	Lowers intermediation margins; enhances pool of liquidity and supply of risk capital	Regions with weak financial sectors lose activity; ambivalent overall but gains for capital regions

Note: Reproduced from Begg (2003).

currency) will favor relatively indebted countries. Curbs in public expenditure to meet the EU's fiscal rules, by contrast, may result in lower discretionary public spending, with a disproportionate effect on regions most dependent on net fiscal transfers and possibly an adverse effect—at least in a transitional phase—on public investment. Longer term, the promise of the EMU is to deliver a stable macroeconomic environment conducive to a higher sustainable growth rate.

• *Labor-market transformations*: An important consideration in this context is the ease with which countries are likely to be able to render their labor markets more flexible. The difficulties in Germany in pushing forward labor-market reforms may be in the limelight at the moment, but there is also evidence that there is a lack of adaptability on the part of lagging countries (Algoe and Alphametrics 2002). Equally, the EMU may be the trigger for reform that has lasting benefits so that again there may be a disjunction between short-term transition costs and longer-term benefits.

• *Induced effects on economic structure*:   The longer-term competitive position of the economy might be shaped when the competitive position of different areas and supply-side developments are altered.

In looking specifically at the challenges surrounding the EMU that are faced by the new members of the EU, three general questions arise. First, are stabilization and growth at odds with each other for any country contemplating whether to participate fully in the EMU? Balcerowicz states that "we should not oppose nominal and real convergence. One should not assume there is an unavoidable conflict between the two." Equally, any such conflict may, above all, be a matter of timing: the medium- to longer-term benefits of stabilization may be uncontested, but if rapid transition is very costly, does it make sense?

Second, if the EMU delivers its promise of higher growth in the medium- to long-term, will it benefit the richer parts of the union at the expense of the poorer? In similar vein, will the advantages *within* countries be evenly spread or unbalanced? Third, is the particular institutional form of the EMU—especially the fiscal rules that govern both the transition to stage 3 of the EMU (the convergence criteria) and full participation (the Stability and Growth Pact)—likely to be an obstacle to successful economic development by the new members?

Stabilization Effects

There is little dissent from the view that there are long-run benefits to be realized from the enhanced stability that will be achieved by full participation in the EMU. Instead, the issues surrounding stabilization are more about the short- to medium-term effects. The expected gains in stabilization come about because full participation in EMU immediately confers on the country that joins commitment and credibility benefits that it would otherwise find it very difficult to achieve. It is generally accepted that these gains will have to be paid for in the transition to the EMU and possibly beyond. The argument about transition costs is straightforward, if empirically contentious. Countries with inflation rates or fiscal ratios above the Maastricht thresholds will have to rein back the economy to attain the required macroeconomic balance and, in so doing, must expect to lose output growth. Whether doing so is costly will depend partly on whether the initial macroeconomic position was a sustainable one: Greece (latterly) and Ireland (in the late 1980s) can be portrayed as examples of a shift to sound macroeconomics that paid very rapid dividends and possibly even constituted an expansionary fiscal contraction. The extent of any output loss will depend on a range of influences, such as the magnitude of the adjustment that has to be made, the sequencing of different stages, whether it takes place in a generally buoyant or stagnating economic environment (both internally and among key trading partners), and the potential conflict that might be engendered in making the adjustment.

Certainly, countries that have to travel a long way to achieve nominal convergence might be expected to have to forgo more growth to attain a stabilized economy than those that have to make only minor adjustments. There is also a significant risk of instability from early membership of ERM II (Pelkmans and Hobza 2002), a system that requires a fair degree of nominal convergence to be generally beneficial for its participants but could prove to be damaging if exchange rates tend to diverge. As Landesmann and Richter (2003, p. 28) note, several of the CEECs have suffered "major exchange-rate crises which entailed exchange-rate realignments (Czech Republic 1997, Slovak Republic 1999; see also the realignment in Poland 2002, etc.)." They therefore contend that joining the EMU swiftly could necessitate the overriding of other macroeconomic policies while at the same time slowing structural reforms. Both could result in heavy costs in terms of output forgone, although the fact that the countries have already achieved much in nominal convergence should limit this effect. They also point to the fact that one potential adjustment mechanism—migration—will be even weaker than it is at present in the EU15 because of the agreement on a seven-year transitional period. A further important element in the macroeconomic assessment of early EMU entry is whether capital flows are likely to have a destabilizing impact. In this regard, the free capital movement that characterizes all current and new EU members means that there is limited scope for dealing with destabilizing capital flows. Here again the implication is that full EMU participation would be beneficial compared with ERM II and that the transition is the risky and potentially costly phase.

But it can be argued, just as persuasively, that if the pursuit of EMU constitutes a shift from bad to good policy, then the process may well be unambiguously beneficial. A question to pose, therefore, is whether the pre-EMU policy regime was one that favored growth or instead had a debilitating effect. For example, the Greek economy appeared to pick up from the mid-1990s onward as the macroeconomic excesses of the previous decade were replaced by more sensible policies. Ireland, too, rapidly saw benefits as the large deficits and high debt of the decade before were brought under control from the late 1980s onward. Indeed, the transformation of Irish macroeconomic policy in the late 1980s is regarded as one of the foundations of that country's subsequent spectacular growth (Barry 1999). By contrast, both the French and Italian economies seemed to lose dynamism during the 1980s and 1990s, first through targeting the exchange rate to stay in the exchange-rate mechanism of the EMS and then in making the further adjustment to the EMU. It is, perhaps, salient that the small open economies have, on the whole, found it easier to adjust than their larger peers. EMU can also act as an external benchmark cum incentive for policy improvement, and there is evidence that it contributed to the recasting of policy in Greece (with results that can be regarded as positive for growth) and Italy (though with, thus far, less encouraging outcomes). Whether Italy would have been any better off if its macroeconomic policy had been looser is an open question: GDP growth might have been more robust but only at the cost of prolonging the adjustment period.

Once in the EMU, a country has to adapt to a policy regime that is radically different. In particular, it has to recognize that the European Central Bank will deliver price stability and that resorting to inflation as an adjustment mechanism or to calling on the central bank to print money to finance expenditures are no longer options. Adjustment to shocks, symmetric or asymmetric, will require the creation of room for maneuver in fiscal policy, while also obliging the supply side to assume a greater share of any burden. Consequently, the fiscal authorities will have to adapt, and labor-market actors will have to recognize that monetary policy can no longer accommodate inflationary pay deals.

Interterritorial Disparities

Even if the EMU does fullfil the expectation of its supporters that it will facilitate stable growth in the EU as a whole, there is no guarantee that the resulting growth will be balanced, whether among member states or regions. Yet there is by no means a consensus in the literature on how the furthering of economic integration by monetary union will affect disparities. In the Delors report (CEC 1989, para. 29), which paved the way for the euro, the fear was expressed that "historical experience suggests, however, that in the absence of countervailing policies, the overall impact on peripheral regions could be negative." This statement echoed concerns expressed in the Padoa-Schioppa report (1987) and led directly to the acceptance that there should be some sort of compensatory policy to ensure cohesion. The thrust of much of the new economic geography analysis as applied to European integration is that integration does indeed favor core areas at the expense of the periphery. But the outcome will be the result of a balancing of different effects (succinctly summarized in Krugman 1998) that can sensibly be assessed only empirically.

An alternative view is that EMU will provide a stimulus to the less competitive countries and regions that will enable them to make a leap forward, the implication being that separate currencies have acted as a barrier to economic development. Possible explanations for such an advance include the overcoming of inhibitions on factor movements that have prevented optimal allocation of resources, especially investment flows, and the negative effects of markets fragmented in a way that has slowed innovation and the exploitation of economies of scale. The Sapir report notes that "growth may have a negative effect on cohesion if market forces lead to a widening of the income gaps between regions or between individuals. In the case of economic convergence between regions there is little evidence of such effects and, on the contrary, lagging regions have provided a boost to overall EU growth" (CEC 2003a, p. 2). The same report also states that although redistributive policies have helped to ensure social cohesion, they may have done so "at the expense of lower incentives for growth" (CEC 2003a, p. 3). The inference to draw is, perhaps, that EMU provides a new setting within which what matters are the detailed policy choices made by the acceding country rather than more theoretical analyses of the optimality and overall impact of monetary union. State-aid policies that shore up inefficient industries or welfare arrangements that provide few incentives for increasing employability, for example, might be adopted to ease adjustment problems but have the effect of inhibiting growth.

Institutional Factors

The recent controversies surrounding the Stability and Growth Pact (SGP) have prompted searching questions about whether the current policy framework is appropriate. The EMU policy regime combines a specific philosophy of economic policy, a novel distribution of responsibility between the national and supranational levels of economic governance, and a reconfiguration of policy instruments and targets. It is easy to forget just how profound the change is. In addition, because of political imperatives that have resulted in a delicate balance of power between member states and the supranational level, appropriate means of coordinating a range of national policies have had to be established. A key question in this regard is whether what might be called the Artis-Buti policy framework[3] goes far enough in assigning policy roles. In this conceptualization (to simplify greatly), monetary policy (and hence the ECB) plays the primary role in responding to symmetric shocks to the euro-area economy, while fiscal policy provides the means to deal with national differentiation. A related but separate question is whether national inflation rates matter and thus whether anyone should lose sleep if they diverge, provided the overall euro-area rate is on track.

The successive controversies surrounding the SGP have prompted searching questions about whether the current EMU policy framework is appropriate, and although criticisms center on the SGP, other dimensions of economic policy making also come under scrutiny (Pisani-Ferry 2002). In particular, what has become known as the Lisbon Agenda—shorthand for a range of supply-side (or structural) reforms—has come to be seen as an essential complement to the EMU. For the new members, it can be argued that bringing these supply-side considerations into the equation must be part of the decision on how rapidly to move to full participation in the EMU.

Equally, if the SGP is problematic for growth in EU15 insofar as it tends to be procyclical and deters public investment—problems that have been acknowledged in a communication published by the Commission in 2004 (CEC 2004b)—what about the new members? For Buiter and Grafe (2004, p. 2), the answer is clearcut: "both the Stability and Growth Pact and the Broad Economic Policy Guidelines currently in place are ill-designed to address the economic realities of countries that differ significantly from the current EU average as regards their expected future inflation rates and real GDP growth rates, and their inherited stocks of environmental and public sector capital." The same authors (Buiter and Grafe 2002) nevertheless believe that the new members should accede to the EMU at the earliest possible opportunity, arguing that the benefits of a correct "fiscal financial program" are paramount. But the implication is that the fiscal rules may well water down the potential benefits. The dilemma here is that EMU is a package deal that includes fiscal rectitude, yet the new members (and indeed countries such as the United Kingdom, which have neglected public investment) have obvious needs for enhancement of infrastructure and other forms of public capital. Given that there is a disposition to revise the SGP after the debacle of the "let-off" for France and Germany at the Ecofin meeting of November 25, 2003, one way forward will be for the new members to lobby for revisions that take more account of public investment.

The Timing of EMU Effects

A number of phases can be envisaged for the different effects of monetary union. The first is nominal convergence, which in the EMU model has had to take place prior to joining the currency. Second, there is assimilation to the resulting new regime. Then follow the medium- to longer-term real economy effects described in the second and third segments of table 15.1.

The nominal-convergence phase has proved to be a testing one for many countries because the obligation to consolidate public finances tends to mean a combination of tax increases and public spending cuts that dampen demand. In the EU as a whole, public spending fell by some three percentage points between 1995 and 2003,[4] with most of the change matched by a fall in public deficits. There are circumstances in which the holy grail of an expansionary fiscal contraction can be achieved, especially if fiscal restraint permits a markedly looser monetary policy, but the consensus is that most member states lost potential output during the 1990s as they struggled to meet the Maastricht criteria. The rationale is, plainly, that once the adjustment is complete, the member states can build on the platform of their consolidated public finances to achieve more rapid growth. Indeed, this is the underlying promise (and premise) of the EMU. Another major issue is the price level. In all the new member states, these are well below EU15 levels: according to a recent report by the Organization for Economic Cooperation and Development (OECD) (2003), the price level in the accession countries, measured in 2001, was just 51 percent of the EU15 level. The lowest recorded level was the Slovak Republic at 39 percent; the figure for Hungary was 46 percent, for Poland 56 percent, and for Slovenia 65 percent; while Cyprus topped the list at 85 percent. One potentially disruptive factor is the so-called Balassa-Samuelson effect (see chapter 14 by Rostowski and Zoubanov in this volume for a full explanation of the effect), which arises because productivity in the tradable sector of the economy rises more rapidly than in the rest of the economy, but relative wages do not adjust. If the effect is substantial, measured inflation will be higher, but the competitiveness of the tradables sector will be scarcely affected. By causing a real exchange-rate appreciation, there may be problems in maintaining the combination of stable nominal exchange rates and low inflation required for EMU accession. Again, the rules and economic common sense risk being at odds. However, the evidence from chapter 14 suggests that the effect will not be that great so that there may not be much to fear.

To bring these together, a useful analytic device for looking at the impact of the single currency is the *j*-curve, traditionally employed to assess devaluations (figure 15.1). If the country does not accede to the full EMU, it might be expected to maintain a steady rate of growth but to forgo the boost to growth that arises from greater macroeconomic stability. When the decision is taken to seek full participation in EMU, the process of nominal convergence may cause initial dislocations that result in a loss

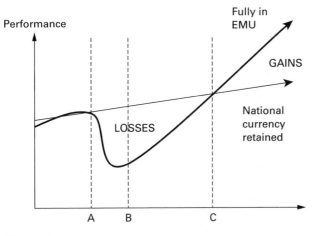

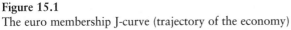

Figure 15.1
The euro membership J-curve (trajectory of the economy)

of performance. This is captured in the figure in the period A-B and in the downward movement along the *j*-curve. It can be argued that this was true for several EU15 countries during the 1990s. Subsequently, however, the benefits of stabilization manifest themselves in a better trajectory for performance: this is the upward slope of the *j*-curve.[5] The length of period B-C will depend on how quickly the country adapts to the new macroeconomic regime. One of the challenges of joining EMU is to optimize the shape of the *j*-curve. An ideal policy will have little or no initial loss of performance, a short wait until improvements kick in, and a steep upturn. Greece in the late 1990s might be seen as an illustration in that it seems to have avoided the dip and moved straight to the upturn, although the recent expansion of its deficit may hint at a day of reckoning to come (partly as a result of heavy public spending related to the 2004 Olympic games). The one to be avoided will have such severe short-term costs that it is politically awkward. Figure 15.2 illustrates these extreme cases.

The Macroeconomic Record of the Euro

With the euro having now been in place for close to six years and a fair degree of consensus on macroeconomic projections covering 2005, there

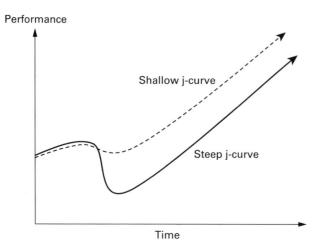

Figure 15.2
The euro membership J-curve (trajectory of the economy)

is now enough information to attempt a provisional assessment of its initial macroeconomic effects. In terms of growth, the outcome is, perhaps, surprising: the core countries, other than Luxembourg, have performed relatively poorly, while the periphery countries (with the exception of Portugal) have prospered, as can be seen from figure 15.3. Moreover, the difficulties confronting Germany, Italy, and France have become more pronounced since the downturn of 2001, and the Netherlands has seen a marked reversal of the dynamism it exhibited in the late 1990s. These trends go a long way to explain the tensions that have arisen in relation to the Stability and Growth Pact.

However, although seven years have to be seen as more than a temporary phenomenon, the apparently favorable impact of the EMU on several peripheral countries may well be the result of factors other than the single currency. Among the reasons for the disparate performances of the euro-area economies since 1999, four deserve particular attention. First, there is the gain in credibility that accrues to countries that had previously faced an interest-rate surcharge because of fears about long-term inflation. This would have benefited, primarily, the southern member states. Second, debt service has become much cheaper as countries have benefited from falling national debt stocks and lower coupon rates. As a

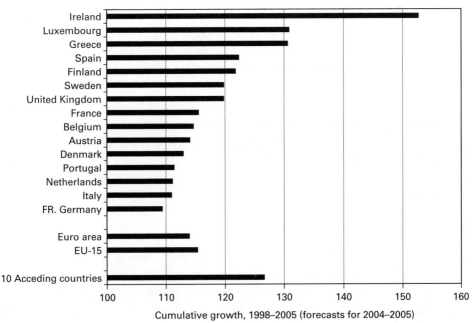

Figure 15.3
Growth of EU economies since the advent of the euro
Source: European Commission spring 2004 macroeconomic forecasts.

result, the shackles on fiscal policy in these countries have been relaxed. Third, by managing to maintain growth above the EU average, the faster-growing countries have avoided the fiscal squeeze that has affected Germany and France, generating a virtuous circle effect. A fourth effect stems from the parities at which countries fixed their currencies to the euro. By common consent, Germany has had a rate that has been relatively uncompetitive, whereas other countries—notably Ireland and Spain—may perhaps have had a competitive advantage. For the core economies, especially Germany and Italy, structural problems are often cited as an explanation for the difficulties besetting them. It is, though, easy to forget that these structural challenges are of long standing and cannot be directly associated with the euro.

In Ireland's case especially (also in Portugal), a further effect has been rapid asset price inflation manifesting itself, above all, in the property market, while elsewhere strains have emerged on the current account of the balance of payments. The EMU, in short, has been accompanied by signs of macroeconomic imbalance, although only in Portugal has this been translated into a fiscal position incompatible with the SGP.[6] Indeed, there is more than a little irony in the growing problems that Germany and France have in conforming to the pact at a time when the majority of the supposedly more vulnerable countries have been doing well. The underlying question, however, is whether the temporary benefits will subsequently be reversed. In practice, the answer will depend on the degree to which the economies themselves adapt.

Policy Implications and Conclusions

The early years of the euro have, in several respects, confounded the fears about divergence and give some support to those who argue that the EMU will foster more rapid real convergence. But the jury remains out, if only because so many of the supply-side indicators remain tilted against the poorer parts of the EU15 (Begg 2003). By inference, the same conclusion would be drawn about the new members.

When the ten new members joined the EU in 2004, cohesion was expected to be high on the agenda in at least two key respects. A first question is how quickly countries acceding to the EU should seek to embrace full monetary union. Three options can be delineated:

• Entering into stage 3 of the EMU as rapidly as possible (a form of big bang),

• Remaining for an extended period in exchange-rate mechanism (ERM) II to assist acclimatization but with the corollary that monetary policy would remain with the member state, and

• Retaining flexibility in the exchange rate to deal with possible shocks or problems associated with transition both to EU membership and more comprehensive market-economy structures.

Devereux (2003) models the second and third options and shows that in most respects, the ERM option is the least attractive for reasons that are well covered in the literature. Being part of ERM only partly captures the benefits of the fixed exchange rate and notably forgoes the credibility gains that would arise from full participation in the EMU, leaving the currency (and the economy) vulnerable. Retaining exchange-rate flexibility would, according to Devereux's simulations, make it easier to ensure efficient adjustment to cyclical and structural shocks. A rapid move to full participation in EMU, keeping the transitional ERM II stage to a minimum, may however be better.

The advent of the new members will prompt a rethinking of both the nature of cohesion policies and the regions that should be eligible for them. How direct European Community assistance to lagging regions is reformed will be a key part of this rethinking, but questions also arise about striking a balance between cohesion and catch-up, the role of domestic policy in fostering change, and the appropriate pace of progress toward full adoption of the European social model. Enlargement is bound to require major changes in the way in which structural operations are conducted, and difficult questions arise about how to deal with the accession of so many regions with low per-capita GDP. As a backdrop to the discussion, the following points are worth noting (CEC 2001, 2003a, 2003b; Begg 2003; Boldrin and Canova 2003; Hallet 2002):

• There seems little disposition to change one of the key features of the structural funds, which is that regions with a GDP per head (measured in purchasing-power standards (PPS), which correct for price-level differences between countries) below 75 percent of the EU average are classified as objective 1 (lagging behind) and are entitled to the highest level of Community support.

• Because the accession of the ten new members due to enter in 2004 implies an increase of almost 20 percent in the population of the EU but barely 4 percent in GDP measured in current euros, the average GDP per capita of the EU will fall by about ten percentage points.

• Nearly all the regions of the ten new member states will be below the revised 75 percent threshold for objective 1 status calibrated on EU25, but the majority of the EU15 regions currently classified as objective 1 will be lifted above it by what has become known as the statistical effect. Yet the absolute prosperity of the latter group will be unchanged.

• At present all the richer member states continue to receive some allocations from the structural funds under objective 2 (which mainly targets regions facing industrial decline and undiversified rural areas) or objective 3 (designed for labor-market interventions, mainly to deal with unemployment, anywhere in the Union).

• Following accession, the number of member states that are net contributors to the Community budget can be expected to increase. Despite the arrival of so many new members who might be expected to support a higher budget, the fact that the budget requires unanimity means that it is highly unlikely that the current ceiling of 1.27 percent of EU GDP will be increased.

• The maximum level of support for any region is to be capped at 4 percent of its GDP, a figure set to ensure that the capacity of an economy to absorb the resources is not exceeded, although it is a blunt limit that takes little account of differences in absorptive capacity.

• Evidence on the effectiveness of the structural funds is patchy and in some respects inconclusive. Some authors (such as Cappelen, Castellaci, Fagerberg, and Verspagen 2003) find that the cumulative effect of cohesion policies has been positive, whereas others (such as Boldrin and Canova 2001) are quite scathing, while Hallet (2002) pleads for a more subtle assessment.

• Doubts have also been raised about the orientation of policy, especially an excessive focus on infrastructure, leading to the criticism that there are insufficient efforts to institute a comprehensive development framework (Barry 2003).

Cohesion policy consequently faces a number of dilemmas. First, it will have to provide for a larger objective 1 population while also satisfying the member states and regions that currently receive support. Second, there are awkward questions about whether all member states or just the lagging countries should be eligible for aid. Third, there are many questions about the focus and administration of structural policies. A key recommendation of the Sapir report is "that EU convergence policy should concentrate on low-income countries rather than low-income regions, and that eligibility for access to EU assistance should be reviewed at the end of each programming period. In addition, convergence funds allocated to low-income countries should focus on two areas—(1) institution building and (2) investment in human and physical capital—leaving beneficiaries free to decide how to allocate resources across different national projects" (CEC 2003a, p. 6). In its third cohesion report, the commission of the European Communities (CEC) signaled how it proposes to develop cohesion policy (CEC 2004a), and the proposals for the structural funds beyond 2006 will give a priority to achieving real convergence. Details, however, remain to be settled and will, no doubt, give rise to tense negotiations.

Although the costs of extending the EU's structural operations to the new members is surprisingly low at present, it could rise to become more contentious for a reason that has received little attention. If (as they would be expected to do, not least because of the Balassa-Samuelson effect) price *levels* in the accession countries start to rise, the cost to the EU budget of a transfer amounting to 4 percent of GDP will also rise. A simple exercise shows what is at stake (table 15.2). In 2000, the aggregate GDP of the ten CEEC countries,[7] measured in euros, was 395 billion, just 4.4 percent the aggregate of the EU15 and the CEEC10's current GDP. In PPS terms, the GDP per head was more than twice as high at 9.6 percent (yielding a per-capita figure of 38 percent) and can be used as a measure of the potential for price convergence. The last line of the table shows the cost of a transfer of 4 percent of GDP based on the current price level and the price level if full convergence occurs (as measured by using the PPS values). The effect would be to increase the cost of structural operations in the CEECs from a very

Table 15.2
Potential cost of transfers to CEECs if price convergence occurs

All Data for 2000	Current Price GDP (billion euros)	GDP Based on PPS per Head (billion euros)
GDP of the 10 CEE countries	394.9	906.5
EU15 GDP	8,523.9	8,523.9
Total EU25 GDP	8,918.8	9,430.4
Cost of 4% transfer (4% of row 1)	16.0	36.3
Transfer as percentage of EU25 GDP (row 4 as percentage of row 3)	0.18	0.38

Source: Author's calculations from Eurostat data.

manageable 0.18 percent of EU GDP to a much more demanding 0.38 percent. Although this is manifestly a simplistic calculation, it should be noted that the two figures differ purely because of a nominal change and thus imply no *real* convergence, yet the impact would be to make a politically awkward hole in the EU budget.

There is another side to the 4 percent ceiling, which also warrants mention. If crudely applied, this ceiling will have a perverse distributive effect. Richer recipients, especially if they have a higher price level, will receive proportionately much more. This can again be illustrated using 2000 data, this time looking at the per-capita cost to the EU budget of a transfer of 4 percent of GDP to each of the CEECs. From this calculation, it can be seen (table 15.3) that the biggest per-capita cost to the EU budget would be for the two most prosperous accession countries (Slovenia and the Czech Republic) and the smallest the two poorest (Bulgaria and Romania). If parts of the richer countries such as the Czech Republic are excluded (notably the booming Prague region), the per-capita transfer would fall accordingly, but to put the estimates for the richer accession countries in perspective, they are of similar orders of

Table 15.3
The likely payments to accession countries

Accession Country	Current GDP (billion euros)	Population (millions)	Cost of 4% Transfer (billion euros)	Per Capita Cost to EU (euros)	GDP per Head (EU15 = 100)
Bulgaria	13.0	8.211	0.52	63	28
Czech Republic	55.0	10.283	2.20	214	59
Estonia	5.5	1.444	0.22	152	38
Hungary	50.3	10.068	2.01	200	51
Lithuania	12.2	3.700	0.45	122	33
Latvia	7.8	2.432	0.31	127	30
Poland	171.0	38.654	6.84	177	40
Romania	40.0	22.458	1.6	71	23
Slovenia	19.5	1.986	0.84	393	69
Slovakia	20.9	5.395	0.78	156	48

Source: Author's calculations from Eurostat data.

magnitude to the current transfers to Greece and Portugal and hence by no means unrealistic. The dilemma here is that the 4 percent limit has been set to reflect what any receiving nation can reasonably absorb and to this degree makes sense, especially if it is recognized that much of the expenditure would fall on the construction sector. Equally, if the money is used to purchase goods and services from abroad at world prices rather than indigenous output at domestic prices, the least well off will be penalized by the mechanical operation of the 4 percent rule. This, plainly, is a thorny issue.

A specific challenge will be how to respond—if at all—to any widening of regional disparities within the new members. There is already evidence from some countries that capital regions have gained most from the postcommunist transition, and the experiences of Portugal, Ireland, and Greece suggest that market forces have favored agglomeration in favored regions at the expense of the most backward regions. According to the Commission's second progress report (CEC 2003b), for example, the Mazowieckie region (which includes Warsaw) converged from 43 percent of EU GDP to 59 percent between 1995 and 2000, whereas the regions on the Polish eastern border remained at just over 26 percent of the EU average.[8] Moreover, it is often the case that the return on investment in, for instance, R&D will be higher in more competitive regions, raising questions about how active policy should be elsewhere (see, for example, Rodríguez-Pose 2001). To the extent that growth is fueled by the performance of leading regions, competitiveness imperatives would caution against countervailing policy. But will there be enough trickle-down to make such internal divergence palatable and politically acceptable?

There is, therefore, much to sort out about real convergence, and it is clear that reaching convincing conclusions is not easy. It may be that asking how rapidly to seek full participation in EMU is not the question that should be posed. Rather, attention needs to focus on whether the overall mix of policies and economic conditions will be conducive to comfortable membership of the euro area, including adequate real convergence. In part, this concerns the nominal variables, but judging by the EU15 experience, it is also important to emphasize different aspects of the *E* in *EMU*—that is the real economy. Key issues include labor-market conditions, administrative capacity, and the approach to public investment. Efficient use also has to be made of support policies such as the structural funds, notably ensuring that they dovetail well with indigenous policies, as in Ireland (FitzGerald 1998).

Concluding Remarks

Real convergence is a dimension of the EMU that has received insufficient attention, yet it is also one for which neither theory nor empirical evidence provide altogether convincing answers. For countries contemplating full participation in the EMU, the underlying challenge is not so much *whether* EMU will result in real convergence as *how* to ensure that it does. Accession to the euro area will probably impose some costs in a transitional phase but is expected to deliver longer-term benefits. There may therefore be a tradeoff. To be eligible for stage 3 of the EMU, the new members must first fulfill the Maastricht nominal convergence. Most of them proved able to deal with the immediate inflationary consequences of the transition to market economies and now have values for the indicators that are close enough to the required thresholds to be attainable. They should, in principle, be able to achieve the criteria fairly easily, but the question that now presents itself is whether the costs associated with maintaining these nominal values are too high for now and might be inimical to real convergence. This chapter has argued that there are risks in this but that they are outweighed by the longer-term benefits.

However, the long-term benefits cannot be taken for granted, and the difficulties now apparent in some EU15 countries testify to the problems of further adjustment beyond the point of entry into the euro. For the new members, the experience of over a decade of rapid structural change will be both an advantage and a potential threat. The advantage is that the imperative of structural change should have become accepted, although the other side of the coin is that a transition fatigue may have set in that prompts voters to says enough is enough. EU assistance via the structural and cohesion funds can be a help in this regard but will not be sufficient on its own. The trick, in short, will be to flatten the dip in the *j*-curve and to ensure that the upswing phase is sustained, such that the transition to the euro is not overly costly.

Notes

1. Speech to the Eleventh European Banking Congress, Frankfurt, November 23, 2001.

2. Ironically, low fertility in recent years in many of these areas will mean that there is an emerging problem of a growing elderly dependent population. In this regard, too, the outlook in many new members is not encouraging.

3. See, for example, the model developed in Artis and Buti (2000) and some of the contributions to Brunila, Buti, and Franco (2001) and Buti, von Hagen, and Martinez-Mongay (2002).

4. If certain transactions related to East German restructuring (dealt with outside the excessive deficit calculation methodology used here) are taken into account, the cut in expenditures is even more pronounced.

5. As applied to devaluation, the j-curve approach analyzes the response of the trade balance. It posits an initial terms of trade loss giving rise to a worsening trade balance but a subsequent improvement as increased price competitiveness boosts exports. The difficulty with devaluation, however, is that it risks higher inflation by raising the price of imports, which leads to a further loss of competitiveness. There is no reason to expect such a third phase from full participation in the EMU unless there are longer-term incompatibilities between the monetary conditions under the EMU and those that the economy needs.

6. In any case, Portugal has shown that it could exercise the political will to rein in the deficit.

7. Including Bulgaria and Romania, which are not expected to join the EU before 2007.

8. These figures are measured in PPS. They have to be treated with some caution because of intracountry disparities in price levels and the incidence of undeclared activity.

References

Algoé Consultants with Alphametrics Limited. (2002). "The Construction of an Index of Labour Market Adaptability for EU Member States." Report for the European Commission. Brussels.

Ardy, B., I. Begg, W. Schelkle, and F. Torres. (2002). *EMU and Cohesion: Theory and Policy.* S. Joao do Estoril–Cascais: Principia.

Artis, M., and M. Buti. (2000). "'Close to Balance or in Surplus': A Policy-Maker's Guide to the Implementation of the Stability and Growth Pact." *Journal of Common Market Studies, 38:* 563–591.

Barry, F. (Ed.). (1999). *Understanding Ireland's Economic Growth.* Basingstoke: Macmillan.

Barry, F. (2000). "Convergence Is Not Automatic: Lessons from Ireland for Central and Eastern Europe." *World Economy, 23:* 1379–1394.

Barry, F. (2003). "Economic Integration and Convergence Processes in the EU Cohesion Countries." *Journal of Common Market Studies, 41*(5): 897–921.

Begg, I. (2003). "Complementing EMU: Rethinking Cohesion Policy." *Oxford Review of Economic Policy, 19*(1): 161–179.

Boldrin, M., and F. Canova. (2001). "Inequality and Convergence in Europe's Regions: Reconsidering European Regional Policies." *Economic Policy, 16:* 207–253.

Boldrin, M., and F. Canova. (2003). "Regional Policies and EU Enlargement." In B. Funck and L. Pizzati (Eds.), *European Integration, Regional Policy and Growth.* Washington, DC: World Bank.

Brunila, A., M. Buti, and D. Franco (Eds.). (2001). *The Stability and Growth Pact: The Architecture of Fiscal Policy in EMU.* Basingstoke: Palgrave.

Buiter, W. H., and C. Grafe. (2002). "Anchor, Float or Abandon Ship: Exchange Rate Regimes for the Accession Countries." *Banca Nationale del Lavoro Quarterly Review, 221:* 1–32.

Buiter, W. H., and C. Grafe. (2003). "Patching up the Pact: Some Suggestions for Enhancing Fiscal Sustainability and Macroeconomic Stability in an Enlarged European Union." *Economics of Transition* 12, pp. 67–102.

Buti, M., J. von Hagen, and C. Martinez-Mongay (Eds.). (2002). *The Behaviour of Fiscal Authorities.* Basingstoke: Palgrave.

Cappelen, A., F. Castellaci, J. Fagerberg, and B. Verspagen. (2003). "The Impact of Regional Support on Growth and Convergence in the European Union." *Journal of Common Market Studies, 41:* 621–644.

Centre for European Policy Studies (CEPS) Macroeconomic Policy Group. (2002). *The Euro at Twenty-five: Special Report on Enlargement.* Brussels: CEPS.

Commission of the European Communities (CEC). (1989). *Report of the Study Group on Economic and Monetary Union* (the Delors Report). Brussels: CEC.

Commission of the European Communities (CEC). (2001). *Unity, Solidarity, Diversity for Europe Its People and Its Territory: Second Report on Economic and Social Cohesion.* Luxembourg: OOPEC.

Commission of the European Communities (CEC). (2002). *Second European Scoreboard on Innovation.* Brussels: CEC.

Commission of the European Communities (CEC). (2003a). *An Agenda for a Growing Europe: Making the EU Economic System Deliver.* Report of an Independent High-Level Study Group Established on the Initiative of the President of the European Commission (the Sapir Report). Brussels: European Commission.

Commission of the European Communities (CEC). (2003b). *Second Progress Report on Economic and Social Cohesion.* Luxembourg: OOPEC.

Commission of the European Communities (CEC). (2004a). *A New Partnership for Cohesion: Convergence, Competitiveness Cooperation*. Luxembourg: OOPEC.

Commission of the European Communities (CEC). (2004b). "Strengthening Economic Governance and Clarifying the Implementation of the Stability and Growth Pact." COM(2004) 581, Brussels, September 6.

Devereux, M. (2003). "A Macroeconomic Analysis of EU Accession under Alternative Monetary Policies." *Journal of Common Market Studies, 41*(5): 941–964.

FitzGerald, J. (1998). "An Irish Perspective on the Structural Funds." *European Planning Studies, 6*(6): 677–694.

Hallet, M. (2002). "Income Convergence and Regional Policies in Europe: Results and Future Challenges." Paper presented at the Congress of the European Regional Science Association (ERSA) in Dortmund/Germany, August 28–29. Available at ⟨http://www.ersa2002.org⟩.

Krugman, P. R. (1998). "What's New about the New Economic Geography?" *Oxford Review of Economic Policy, 14*: 7–17.

Krugman, P. R., and A. J. Venables. (1996). "Integration, Specialisation, Adjustment." *European Economic Review, 40*: 959–968.

Landesmann, M., and S. Richter. (2003). "Consequences of EU Accession: Economic Effects on CEECs." WIIW Research Report No. 299, Vienna.

Organization for Economic Cooperation and Development (OECD). (2003). *France*. Paris: OECD.

Padoa-Schioppa, T., M. Emerson, M. King, J. C. Milleron, J. H. P. Paelinck, L. D. Papademos, A. Pastor, and F. W. Scharpf. (1987). *Efficiency, Stability and Equity: A Strategy for the Evolution of the Economic System of the European Community*. Oxford: Oxford University Press.

Pelkmans, J., and A. Hobza. (2002). "A Sound Enlargement of Euroland." CEPS Briefing note. Brussels: CEPS.

Pisani-Ferry, J. (2002). "Fiscal Discipline and Policy Coordination in the Eurozone: Assessment and Proposals." Paper prepared for the European Commission President's Group of Economic Analysis. Brussels.

Puga, D. (1999). "The Rise and Fall of Regional Inequalities." *European Economic Review, 43*: 303–334.

Rodríguez-Pose, A. (2001). "Is R&D Investment in Lagging Areas of Europe Worthwhile? Theory and Empirical Evidence." *Papers in Regional Science, 80*: 275–295

Rostowski, J. (2003). "When Should the Central Europeans Join EMU?" *International Affairs, 79*: 993–1008.

V

Conclusion

16

Concluding Comments

Leszek Balcerowicz

In this chapter, I briefly present some basic facts about economic convergence and divergence over the last 200 years and then discuss how the problem of long-run growth has been treated in the economics literature. Institutions are the key explanatory variable in the deeper analysis of the relative pace of development. In the heart of the chapter, I formulate three broad propositions regarding convergence. These place the chapters of this book in a broader framework.

Economic Convergence and Divergence

• It is believed that prior to 1800 living standards differed little across countries and time (Parente and Prescott 2000, p. 23). Modern economic growth started around 1800 in Western Europe (and its ethnic offshoots) bringing about an unprecedented acceleration in the growth of living standards in Western countries: their per-capita GDP from 1820 to 1989 grew about eight times as fast as in the precapitalist epoch (Maddison 1991, p. 48). Such acceleration did not take place in other countries until about 1950. Thus, "the big story over the last 200–300 years is one of the massive divergence in the levels of income per capita between the rich and the poor" (Easterly and Levine 2000, p. 18).

• As is well known from the work of Kuznets, Solow and others, productivity increase plays the most important role in countries at the technology frontier. Factor accumulation can also play an important role in countries that are converging toward the technology frontier, as can the reallocation of labor from agriculture to the modern sector.

• While the Western countries as a group surged ahead, there was a substantial convergence of income levels in the West itself. The most widespread and intense convergence occurred from 1950 to 1973, when all the Western economies grew considerably faster than the United States (which grew at 2.2 percent). The fastest growth per capita was achieved by Japan (8 percent), Italy (5 percent), Germany, Austria (4.9 percent), and France (4 percent) (Maddison 1991). Spain surged ahead from 1961 to 1975 with a growth rate of 6.9 percent. A true growth miracle happened during the 1990s in Ireland, a case discussed in this volume.

• The post–World War II period brought about an accelerated convergence among Western countries and an impressive catching-up of some other economies—particularly in Japan and among the East Asian tigers. China entered the race in the late 1970s and increased its per-capita income from 6.7 percent of the Western European average in 1976 to 17.9 percent in 2001. A slower but still impressive catching up has been achieved more recently by India. Outside Asia, Chile (also discussed in this volume) has been a growth leader over the past fifteen years.

• However, there were also important examples of divergence during this period, most notably in Africa and to a lesser extent in Latin America, as well as among the former Communist economies. From 1970 to 1998, per-capita income fell in thirty-two countries, while only seven developing countries showed rapid convergence. However, China and India are among the seven fast-growing countries. As a result, 70 percent of the population of the developing countries lives in countries where per-capita income growth has exceeded that in the developed economies, while less than 10 percent lives in countries where average income declined (*World Economic Outlook* 2000, pp. 15–16).

The reader may want to check the robustness of the conclusions of this volume by asking whether the prescriptions for convergence advanced in earlier chapters also explain the many cases of divergence in the world— that is, whether divergence is explained by the absence of the conditions stated in the volume as being necessary for convergence.

The Problem of Convergence and Divergence in the Economic Literature

The emphasis on growth in the economics literature has varied over time. It was the main topic for Adam Smith and his followers and successors, including Karl Marx. The marginalist revolution in the late nineteenth century shifted economists' attention to the issues of market exchange and allocation under given resources—technology and the consumers' tastes. This static tradition was taken up and developed in general-equilibrium theory. Nor did monetary and macroeconomic analysis focus on long-run growth until after World War II.

Within the analytic literature, early models by Harrod and Domar were the precursors of two generations of growth models, those originating from Solow (1956) and the ever-growing endogenous-growth theory approach starting from Lucas (1988) and Romer (1986). Within this literature, Barro pioneered cross-country econometric research on the determinants of longer-term growth.

Schumpeter (1983), one of the few to break away from the dominant static analysis of his time, can retrospectively be identified as a pioneer in the modern analysis of both growth and development. He focused on major technological breakthroughs and on the related role of the entrepreneur defined as a person implementing inventions in business practice. However, his views on what institutional framework is conducive to technical change were rather ambivalent.

Issues of risk taking and technical change also surfaced in the debate over whether socialism can be as economically efficient as capitalism. Lange (1936) argued that the first-order conditions for a static optimum could as well be implemented by a planner as in a market system. Critics, notably Mises (1951) and Hayek (1935, 1949), emphasized issues of uncertainty and change and the need for incentives. Subsequent experience awards the victory in the debate to the latter group.

Starting after World War II, the economic profession and multinational organizations had to address the problem of underdevelopment in the poorer countries, now named the less developed countries (LDCs). Among the pioneers in this literature were Albert Hirschman (1960),

Arthur Lewis (1960), Paul Rosenstein-Rodan (1961), and Walt Rostow (1971).

Two basic approaches to the study of longer-term growth can be distinguished. The *quantitative approach* limits its attention to quantitative variables (inputs), particularly land, labor, capital, and productivity. The institutional framework of the economy is typically taken as given or is only briefly discussed. The *qualitative approach* omits or goes beyond the quantitative factors and includes variables of a qualitative nature, most often institutional. Note that the distinction refers to the nature of the explanatory variables rather than the mode of analysis, which can be quantitative in both cases.

So long as growth theory and empirical work remains within the traditional quantitative framework, it is guaranteed to omit variables that are clearly crucial for growth (for example, whether an economy is socialist or capitalist, as in the cases of North and South Korea or East and West Germany). It is possible to include measures of institutional variables (such as the extent of democracy and the monetary and fiscal frameworks) in empirical work, which has thus begun to bridge between the quantitative and qualitative approaches.

Within the qualitative approach, one can distinguish two main and conflicting economic directions, free market and statist. The *free-market approach* is rightly associated with Adam Smith and classical economics. Smith stressed the positive role of market competition, a product of economic freedom, and was very critical of monopoly. He emphasized the "unproductive" nature of the public sector and was skeptical of public regulation of the economy.[1] Smith's basic insights were maintained by his classical followers and successors, including J. S. Mill (1909), according to whom the state's despotism, including predatory or arbitrary taxation, is much more dangerous to a nation's progress than almost any degree of lawlessness and disturbance in the "system of freedom."

The *statist direction* regards the free market and the related limited state as fundamental obstacles to economic development and consequently recommends the state's expansion as the key to growth. This tradition included the mercantilists, so much criticized by Adam Smith, but found its most vocal and somewhat paradoxical exponent in Karl Marx.

While praising the technological dynamism of capitalism, he predicted its demise, pointing out (among other things) the allegedly destructive role of the "anarchy of production"—that is, of market competition.

Marx's central message was implemented in the form of the planned or command economy. North (1998, pp. 100–101) notes that "it is an extraordinary irony that Karl Marx, who first pointed out the necessity for restructuring societies to realize the potential of new technology, should have been responsible for creating economies that have foundered on these precise issues."

Schumpeter's writings display a similar, if not so visible, tension. In (1934) he claims that some of the motives of entrepreneurs may be present in noncapitalist systems and that capitalist profit motive can be replaced. In (1962) he goes much further and stresses that industrial managers under socialism would be instructed to produce as economically as possible and as a result "in the socialist order every improvement would theoretically spread by decree and substandard practice could be promptly eliminated" (p. 196).

Reflecting the view that Soviet growth in the prewar period and the Great Depression showed the superiority of extensive state intervention, the early post–World War II development economists postulated that a free market in the LDCs cannot be relied on to produce growth and that the state can successfully generate a takeoff by concentrated investments, protectionism, and forced industrialization at the cost of agriculture.[2]

The failure of state-led development, including the crisis and breakdown of Soviet socialism, has demonstrated the bankruptcy of the statist approach and contributed to the revival of a free-market orientation in development economics. This shift was helped by the increased focus on institutions and institutional variables, among them freedom of international trade, property rights (Alchian 1977, Pejovich 1974), public-choice theory (Buchanan 1989, Tullock 1998, Niskanen 1971), constitutional economics (Hayek 1960, Buchanan 1989), interest-group theory (Olson 1965, Becker 1984), and economic history (North 1998). Empirical research linked economic growth to the development of the market-oriented financial sector (Beck, Levine, and Loayza 1999; Rajan and Zingales 2001) and to economic imbalances and inflation, products of unconstrained governments (Fischer 1991). Various indexes of economic freedom were developed since the 1980, and a strong link between the extent of that freedom and economic growth was shown (Scully 1992; Hanke and Walters 1997).

Summing up this section: developments in economics during the last twenty to thirty years have increased the importance of the problem of economic growth, have rehabilitated the role of institutional variables, and have shifted attention to the classical issues of economic freedom, the market, and the limits of government. This transformation is far from finished. Few, however, would today object to North's (1998, p. 98) assertion that "the central issue of economic history and of economic development is to account for the evolution of political and economic institutions that create an economic environment that induces increasing productivity."

Institutions, Policies, and Systems

According to North (1998, p. 95): "Institutions are the rules of the game in society; more formally, they are the humanly devised constraints that shape human interaction. Thus, they structure incentives in exchange, whether political, social or economic."

I use this definition as a point of departure to make some distinctions that are useful in further analyzing the convergence problem. To avoid confusion, one should determine the relationship between institutions and policies. Policies can be divided between those that change the institutional framework (reforms or structural reforms) and those that act through macroeconomic variables without changing the institutional framework (macroeconomic policy). However, macroeconomic policy is influenced by the institutional framework (such as the position of the central bank, the fiscal framework, or social policy regulations), and more fundamental changes in the macroeconomic situation may require reforms of these institutional variables.

The institutional framework is most frequently analyzed by categorizing the institutional systems of different countries, as countries vary the most in institutions. These systems are classified under various criteria. I find the traditional criterion of individual economic freedom, inversely related to the role of the state, a useful one in this respect. However, it requires a little elaboration.

Economic freedom can be expressed through the concept of property rights, which have several dimensions. Three types of *property-rights regimes* can be identified: open or liberal, which allows the choice of both private and cooperative types of enterprises; closed, which ensures the monopoly of just one type of nonprivate firm: mostly state-owned or labor managed; and mixed, which preserves the monopoly of state-owned enterprises (SOEs) in some sectors (such as oil in Mexico or copper in Chile).

The open system gives rise to a private-enterprise economy, the closed system produces an economy dominated by socialist firms, and the mixed regime creates a mixed-ownership structure (for more, see Balcerowicz 1995). The most basic difference in the extent of economic freedom can be captured by this simple classification. Privatization of SOEs increases the extent of economic freedom in the economy and is a natural supplement of moving from a closed to open property-rights regime.

However, there are some other dimensions. One is the *extent of freedom* enjoyed by the official holders of rights. Soviet socialism not only prohibited private entrepreneurship but also strongly limited the autonomy of SOEs so that market mechanisms were replaced by central planning (nonmarket coordination). Other systems did not go so far. Here one speaks of the attenuation of privately held property rights through regulation or taxation, both of which reduce the extent of economic freedom.

Some regulations (for example, price controls, barriers to entry, and import protectionism) strongly limit competition. They should be singled out as *anticompetitive regulations*, which lead to distorted market economies and—in the extreme—to a market economy without competition.

Countries differ sharply in the extent of governmental regulations of various sectors and markets. The most pronounced differences among contemporary economies are present in the labor market and in the service sectors, especially in retail trade, the financial sector, and construction. These differences have a profound impact on the pace of technological change and on productivity growth as market- or sector-specific regulations limit the flexibility of supply and the pace of restructuring (see, for example, Scarpetta, Hemmings, Tressel, and Woo 2002). Large differences in the extent of regulations of the same sectors among countries with a similar per-capita income produce significant cross-country differences in their productivity. And large differences in the extent of regulations of various sectors in the same country are responsible for their equally striking productivity differences (Lewis 2004). This shows the power of institutional variables and suggests that a country institutional system may include various institutional subsystems that sharply differ in the extent of economic freedom.

Taxes directly reduce the benefits of effort. Some of them, like anticompetitive regulations, distort the way that effort is used. Thus, what matters for convergence is not only the level of taxes but their structure as well (see, e.g., Leibfritz, Thorton, and Bibee 1997). Countries differ in both of these dimensions considerably.

Another dimension is the level of the state's protection (enforcement) of property rights, which is also referred to as the extent of the *rule of law* (with respect to economic freedom). Here we come to the basic issue of the nature of the state—whether it is a *protective state* (Brunner 1998) or a *predatory state* (Olson 1982). Differences and changes in the extent of the protection of private property rights have an important impact on economic growth.[3] And if the protection of property rights is positively linked to economic growth, then its unequal distribution across society matters both for growth and for equity. This point was powerfully argued by De Soto (2000) with reference to the enormous size of the informal sector in Latin American economies.

Relying on the classic criterion of economic freedom, we can now define more concretely the *direction* of institutional change. The following institutional changes move in the free-market (liberal) direction:

- A shift from the closed- (or mixed-) to an open-property-rights regime,
- Privatization of stated-owned enterprises,
- Elimination of or reduction in anticompetitive regulations and in other restrictive regulations (liberalization or deregulation),
- An increase in the state's protection of private property rights, and
- Reduced taxation.

The change in the statist direction includes a shift to closed- or mixed-property-rights regimes, nationalization, increased taxation, increased restrictive regulations, and reduced protection of private property rights. Radically reduced levels of this protection are a defining feature of failed states where ostensibly state-run agencies are in fact instruments of a private plunder. This situation of anarchy may be distinguished from the statist systems.

Finally, let us make one more distinction. Growth trajectories differ enormously in the extent of their variability (OECD 2000; Easterly and Levine 2000). Some countries grow steadily, while some others are plagued by frequent development breakdowns. These differences are due partly to differences in the external shocks that hit economies. However, some negative shocks are produced at home, and countries may differ in their ability to cope with external shocks.

It is accordingly useful to distinguish two types of institutions *propelling institutions*, which determine the systematic forces of growth, and *stabilizing institutions*, which determine the frequency and severity of domestic shocks and the capacity of the economy to deal with external shocks. Propelling institutions include various dimensions of property rights and the level of rights protection, as well as the extent of anti-competitive regulations. Stabilizing institutions include institutional constraints (if any) on monetary and fiscal policy, some institutional features of the financial sector and its environment (the extent of market discipline, the relationship between the state and the banks, prudential regulations, supervisory institutions), and institutional characteristics of the labor market. There is some overlap between the two types of institutions—for example, the institutional structure of the labor market belongs to both of them.

Since Keynes, the economic profession has focused on analyzing the self-equilibrating properties of the macroeconomy, taking the market structure of the economy as given. While there is much to be discussed in this regard, there is little doubt that the worst breakdowns in economic growth in the contemporary world have occurred under extended and not laissez-faire states and because of the actions of the governments of former states.

A country's growth trajectory depends on the strengths of its propelling and stabilizing institutions. When both are strong, growth is fast and relatively smooth. When both are weak, growth is slow and interrupted by serious breakdowns (as has occurred in some countries of Africa and Latin America). In the intermediate case, propelling institutions are strong, but stabilizing institutions are weak (such as South Korea, Thailand, and Indonesia before the 1998 crisis), or the propelling institutions are weak and the stabilizing institutions strong (such as Portugal under Salazar until the economic liberalization in the 1960s).

Some Propositions about Convergence

We draw on the case studies in the book and a broader literature in formulating several propositions on convergence:

Proposition 1: No poor country has lastingly converged under any variation of a statist institutional system. By implication, an institutional change that results in such a system also precludes lasting convergence.

The main varieties of statist systems are as follows:

1. Systems with a closed-property-rights regime (that is, with a ban on the creation of private firms). The main example is Soviet socialism in which, in addition, central planning replaced coordination by the market.

2. Systems with nominally liberal- or mixed-property-rights regimes but having at least one of the features:

2.1. A dominant state sector;

2.2. Very limited competition due to strong anticompetitive regulations on entry and on imports of goods, capital, and technology;

2.3. Other very restrictive regulations impacting the adoption of new technologies, especially restrictive labor practices or a high level of job protection.

Characteristics 2.2 and 2.3 imply a strong attenuation of private property rights.

2.4. The protection of property rights is limited to a privileged minority, while a large part of the population operates in the informal sector;

2.5. A low general level of protection;

2.6. A profound weakness of stabilizing institutions, leading to chronic or frequent and profound macroeconomics imbalances.

A failed state system is defined by a very low level of protection of property rights and, in the extreme, by a negative protection (predatory state).

The main and sufficient reason for the failure of statist systems to produce convergence is the weakness of the propelling institutions. This precludes efficiency-enhancing technical change. In addition, incentives under Soviet socialism pushed managers in the direction of efficiency-reducing change (for more on this, see Balcerowicz 1995). Characteristic 2.6 blocks convergence because of chronic and profound macroeconomic imbalances, which hurt growth through several channels. Argentina's recent breakdown shows once again that fundamental weaknesses of stabilizing institutions may overpower the results of genuine market-oriented reforms and lead to catastrophic consequences.

Several of the case studies demonstrate how statist elements blocked convergence or even produced divergence in the countries in question. After the golden age of convergence during 1960 to 1973, Portugal's economy diverged relative to the EU average during 1975 to 1985 as a result of large-scale nationalization and the relaxation of macroeconomic discipline (Mateus, chapter 11). Greece diverged with respect to the EU in the period 1981 to 1993, mostly due to expansionary fiscal policy (Sabethai, chapter 16; Vamvakidis, chapter 19). Ireland barely converged under the protectionist and inward-looking policies that continued until the 1950s and under the macroeconomic activism of 1973 to 1986 (O'Connell, chapter 12; Smyth, chapter 18; Bradley, chapter 5). Chile, under interventionist government and rampant fiscal deficit, was diverging after World War II until the 1970s (Corbo, chapter 6; Hernandez, chapter 8).

After their periods of divergence, all these countries responded to institutional change with accelerated growth.

Proposition 2: All successful cases of sustained convergence have happened under more or less free-market systems (nonstatist regimes) or during and after the transition to such systems (due to institutional change in the free-market direction).

Note in particular the second category in the above proposition. This means that the acceleration of growth does not have to wait till the completion of the reforms—that is, until achieving "good" institutions. Rather, *growth may accelerate during the reforms*: improvements in the direction of a market system can increase growth. These can be called *transition effects*, whose existence I stress because some economists seem to overlook them. The transition effects increase growth because they increase productivity in the previously repressed sectors (such as agriculture in China or retail trade in the Soviet system) or because the previous incentive structure encouraged massive waste (command socialism). Such transition effects tend to expire after a certain time period.

There is still much debate about what types of institutional change are of key importance for starting and sustaining economic convergence. The IMF (2000, pp. 114–115) notes that "the bulk of development research reveals neither a unique set of preconditions that are always present during economic takeoff nor an easily identified set of impediments that have prevented poor countries from sustained growth." But the article lists "macroeconomic stability, sound institutional arrangements, and openness to trade" as the key factors promoting growth.

Parente and Prescott (chapters 13 and 14 in this book) assert that "a country will catch up to the leading industrial countries only if it eliminates constraints relating to the use of technology" and recommend joining a free-trade club as a way to do so. The concepts of obstacles to technology adoption and of the role of free-trade clubs are certainly important in explaining successes and failures in convergence. However, it appears that the authors implicitly assume the presence of additional conditions, such as an open-property-rights regime, the predominance of private firms, sufficient protection of property rights, and sufficient strength of stabilizing institutions. These conditions may be empirically related to the convergence or presence of a free-trade club, but that needs to be demonstrated.

In chapter 9, Philip Keefer presents an empirical analysis that suggests that constraints on government decision-making contribute to economic growth but the mere fact of holding elections does not. This finding confirms the insights of classical economists that a limited government, the obverse side of proper and secure property rights, is a key to development.

We could also remember J. S. Mill's warnings that a democratic government is not immune to the temptation of infringing on individual liberty.

All the case studies presented in this book (Finland, Spain, Portugal, Greece, and Chile) show that convergence was due to some combination of market-oriented reforms and, if necessary, macroeconomic stabilization.

Some exceptionally rapidly growing countries have been referred to as the *growth miracles*. Some have argued that a growth miracle can occur only in countries that start with a large development gap and especially a large technology gap relative to the leader. This is Gerschenkron's advantage of backwardness (Gerschenkron 1962; see also Maddison 1991), a view that is shared by Parente and Prescott (2000).[4]

However, as the case of Ireland examined in this volume (chapters 12 and 13) shows, it is not necessary to begin far behind to become a growth miracle. In seeking to explain the Irish miracle, O'Connell and Smyth (chapter 12) stress the role of the radical shift in policies in the second half of the 1980s. The budget deficit was decisively reduced, and tax rates were reduced in exchange for increased wage flexibility. This policy change took place in a reasonably free and very open economy with an effective legal framework and in a nation with strong ties to the United States and Europe. The macroeconomic shift under such conditions released two forces of accelerated growth: increased labor-force participation and increased inflows of foreign direct investment (FDI), coming to a large extent from the U.S. multinationals. Foreign direct investment was further encouraged by the low rates of corporate taxation. In his chapter on Ireland (chapter 13), Bradley discusses the important role of trade liberalization in the 1950s and 1960s and of fiscal consolidation in the late 1980s. However, he focuses on the inflows of FDI and on the positive impact of the EU structural funds. He refers to the latter's role as only "facilitating" convergence.

Explanations for growth miracles can be grouped into three main categories: miracles that are ascribed to some special state interventions (such as directed credits or state-led industrialization), miracles that are ascribed to a combination of special state interventions and an improved general framework for private economic activity, and miracles ascribed solely to an improved general framework for private economic activity.

A closer look at the experience of exceptionally fast-growing countries in Asia and elsewhere suggests that the third explanation is most plausible. The argument is that while the miracle economies differed in the extent of special state interventions (for example, none in Hong Kong but present in most other countries), they had one thing in common: a large dose of market reforms, which, combined with their initial conditions, ensured a larger extent of economic freedom than in other developing countries. In addition, an analysis of special interventions in the miracle countries suggests that they tended to obstruct rather than promote long-term growth—as, for example, the state-led heavy industrialization drive in South Korea in the 1970s (see, e.g., Quibria 2002).

Wing Thye Woo's chapter (chapter 4) on Chinese exceptional growth since the late 1970s is especially instructive. The author contrasts the experimental and the convergence explanations of Chinese growth. He analyzes the dual-track pricing system (DTPS), SOE reform, and township and village enterprises (TVEs). The experimental school praises these half-way or third-way reforms for their supposed role in defusing social tensions during the reform and in preventing transformational recession and fostering growth.

The convergence school to which Woo belongs stresses that the faster the convergence to the institutional framework of a market economy, the better the results. Woo shows that the DTPS, TVEs, and shape and pace of Chinese reforms more generally were the result of factional political struggles and compromises within the ruling group. He describes how DTPS and TVEs generated massive corruption and consequently deep social discontent and as a result have been replaced (DTPS) or are in the process of being replaced by more free-market solutions.[5] He further points out how reforms of a dual-track variety contributed to the disintegration of the Soviet economy from 1989 onward and how the big-bang stabilization and liberalization in Vietnam and Laos in late 1986 have led to accelerated growth and not to transformational recession.

In his view, the key to the Chinese growth miracle lies in the interaction of the initial economic structure (a huge and repressed agricultural sector with a lot of surplus labor) and market-oriented reforms. Given this economic structure, very different from the one of Russia, reforms in China released huge transitional effects. Woo emphasizes that in

China faster market reforms were associated with better economic results. Along this line, we can add that the substantial external opening (trade, FDI), by far exceeding that in India, has also been a critical factor in China's growth miracle.

Proposition 3: While all the successful cases of sustained convergence have taken place under more or less free-market systems or during and after the transition to such systems, not all market-oriented reforms have led to lasting convergence.

It is all too easy to find examples of market-oriented reforms that failed to produce lasting convergence. There are at least three categories of reasons for such failures. First, reforms are frequently announced but not implemented or are implemented to a lesser extent than planned. Second, reforms may be implemented initially but then reversed or seriously attenuated. In both these cases, critics may blame the announced reforms, rather than the failure to implement them, for the failure to converge.

Third, some authors acknowledge that it was the reversal of reforms and not the reforms themselves that caused a lack of convergence but blame the reforms and the reformers for their rejection, linking them to social or political protests. Such critics tend to take it for granted that there existed some milder reforms, which, if implemented, would have avoided the protests while producing the desired economic results.

There are nonetheless genuine reasons why market reforms may fail to generate lasting convergence. Let me note three, which should be regarded as hypotheses meriting future research:

• Market-oriented reforms may fail to produce convergence if they are incomplete in a critical way, in particular by violating crucial complementarities.

One example would be introducing a fixed-exchange regime without adequately strengthening the fiscal framework (Argentina). Another is external opening with very rigid markets and barriers to job creation that hamper the reallocation of labor from sectors exposed to competition. Yet another is the opening of the capital account in the presence of an insufficiently strong macro framework and financial system.

An important research and policy question is to discover which partial reform packages can be introduced successfully and which are likely to fail. Quite likely, a package that does not leave any part of the economy in critically bad shape is more likely to generate convergence than a package—even a very ambitious one—that leaves a major weakness in a significant part of the economy. However, under certain initial conditions a rather large minimum scope (threshold) of reforms may be required if they are to be sustained and to produce convergence. This was, for example, the case of centrally planned economies (Balcerowicz 1995).

• Market-oriented reforms may fail to generate convergence if some of their crucial details are badly structured and induce operational failures. Examples include a serious misspecification of the initial level of a fixed exchange-rate peg or a wrong incentive structure in the bankruptcy law.

• Some regions may be of such an inhospitable nature or so distant—in terms of transportation costs—from large markets that no profitable economic activity can develop there (Gallup, Sachs, and Mellinger 1998). In such situations, market-oriented reforms cannot produce lasting convergence. However, such a geographical predicament at the country level, while present in parts of Africa and on other continents, is still relatively rare, as there are few countries with a sizable population that consist only of inhospitable and distant regions.

These remarks focused on the link between the nature of a country institutional system and convergence. On a deeper level, one can ask what accounts for changes or differences in this system. Such a question, however, would require another book.

Notes

1. "No regulation of commerce can increase the quantity of industry in any society beyond what its capital can maintain. It can only divert a part of it into direction into which it is by no means certain that this artificial direction is likely to be more advantageous to the society than that into which it would have gone on its own accord" (Smith 1999).

2. For more of the analysis of the old development economics, see Bauer (1998), Brunner (1998) and other authors in Dorn, Hanke, and Walters (1998).

3. However, this importance depends on the nature of rights that are protected. The protection of state's rights under a closed property-rights regime includes a fight with the informal market, and this is not unequivocally positive for economic growth. So the positive impact of the increased protection of property rights for growth is unquestionably true for private property rights.

4. Gomułka (1999), by contrast, maintains that growth miracles are more likely to happen in middle-income than in very backward countries because the former have in place more preconditions for an accelerated technology transfer than the latter.

5. Woo's criticism would apply among other authors to Dani Rodrik's claim (2003) that very different and unorthodox arrangements work as long as they are in agreement with first principles such as protection of property rights, market-based competition, appropriate incentives, and so on. He then claims that both private and public property rights constitute a "plausible diversity" within the "first principles." Evidently Rodrik's first principles are very elastic and accommodate both capitalism and socialism.

References

Alchian, A. (1977). *Economic Forces at Work*. Indianapolis, Liberty Press.

Balcerowicz, L. (1995). *Socialism, Capitalism, Transformation*. Budapest: Central European University Press.

Bauer, P. (1998). "The Disregard of Reality." In J. A. Dorn, S. H. Hanke, and A. W. Walters (Eds.), *The Revolution in Development Economics*. Washington, DC: Cato Institute.

Beck, T., R. Levine, and N. Loayza. (1999). "Finance and the Sources of Growth." World Bank Working Paper No. 2057, Washington, DC.

Becker, G. S. (1985). "Public Policies, Pressure Groups, and Dead Weight Costs." *Journal of Public Economics*, 28(3), pp. 329–347.

Brunner, K. (1998). "The Poverty of Nations." In J. A. Dorn, S. H. Hanke, and A. W. Walters (Eds.), *The Revolution in Development Economics*. Washington, DC: Cato Institute.

Buchanan, J. (1989). *Explorations into Constitutional Economics*. College Station, Texas: Texas A&M University Press.

De Soto, H. (2000). *The Mystery of Capital: Why Capitalism Triumphs in the West and Fails Everywhere Else*. New York: Basic Books.

Dorn, J. A., S. H. Hanke, and A. W. Walters. (1998). *The Revolution in Development Economics*. Washington, DC: Cato Institute.

Easterly, W., and R. Levine. (2000). "It's Not Factor Accumulation: Stylized Facts and Growth Models." Mimeo, Washington, DC.

Fischer, S. (1991). "Growth, Macroeconomics, and Development." NBER Working Paper No. W3702, Cambridge, MA.

Furubotn, E., and S. Pejovich (Eds.). (1974). *The Economics of Property Rights.* Cambridge: Ballinger Publishing Company.

Gallup, J. L., J. D. Sachs, and A. D. Mellinger. (1998). "Geography and Economic Development." NBER Working Paper No. W6849, Cambridge, MA.

Gerschenkron, A. C. (1962). *Economic Backwardness in Historical Perspective.* Cambridge, MA: Harvard University Press.

Gomulka, S. (1999). "Growth Convergence: A Comment on Sachs and Warner." In L. Orlowski (Ed.), *Transition and Growth in Post-Communist Countries.* Northampton: Edward Elgar Publishing.

Hanke, S., and S. J. K. Walters. (1997). "Economic Freedom, Prosperity and Equality: A Survey." *Cato Journal, 2:* 117–146.

Hayek, F. A. (1935). "The Present State of the Debate." In F. A. Hayek (Ed.), *Collectivist Economic Planning.* London: Routledge.

———. (1949). "Socialist Calculation III: The Competitive 'Solution'." In *Individualism and Economic Order.* London: Routledge.

———. (1960). *The Constitution of Liberty.* Chicago: University of Chicago Press.

Hirschman, A. O. (1960). *The Strategy of Economic Development.* New Haven: Yale University Press.

Lange, O. (1936). "On the Economic Theory of the Socialist Economy." *Review of Economic Studies, 4:* 53–71.

Leibfritz, W., J. Thornton, and A. Bibbee. (1997). *Taxation and Economic Performance.* Paris: OECD.

Lewis, W. A. (1960). *The Theory of Economic Growth.* London: George Allen and Unwin.

Lewis, W. (2004). "The Power of Productivity: Wealth, Poverty, and the Threat to Global Stability." Chicago: University of Chicago Press.

Lucas, R. E. (1988). "On the Mechanics of Economic Development." *Journal of Monetary Economics, 22(2):* 3–42.

Maddison, A. (1991). *Dynamic Forces in Capitalist Development: A Long-Run Comparative View.* Oxford: Oxford University Press.

Mills, J. S. (1909). *Principles of Political Economy with Some of Their Application to Social Philosophy.* London: Ashley.

Niskanen, W. (1971). *Bureaucracy and Representative Government.* Chicago: Aldine/Atherton.

North, D. C. (1998). "Institutions, Ideology, and Economic Performance." In J. A. Dorn, S. H. Hanke, and A. W. Walters (Eds.), *The Revolution in Development Economics* (pp. 95–108). Washington, DC: Cato Institute.

Organisation for Economic Co-operation and Development (OECD). (2000). *Economic Outlook 67.*

Olson, M. (1965). *The Logic of Collective Action: Public Goods and the Theory of Groups.* Cambridge: Harvard University Press.

Olson, M. (1982). *The Rise and Decline of Nations: Economic Growth, Stagflation, and Social Rigidities.* New Haven, CT: Yale University Press.

Parente, S., and E. C. Prescott. (2000). *Barriers to Riches.* Cambridge, MA: MIT Press.

Quibria, M. G. (2002). "Growth and Poverty: Lessons from the East Asian Miracle Revisited." ADBI Research Paper No. 33, Tokyo.

Rajan, R. G., and L. Zingales. (2001). "Financial Systems, Industrial Structure, and Growth." *Oxford Review of Economic Policy, 17*(4): 467–482.

Rodrik, D. (2003). "Growth Strategies." NBER Working Paper No. 10005, Cambridge, MA.

Romer, P. (1986). "Increasing Returns and Long-Run Growth." *Journal of Political Economy, 94*(5): 1002–1037.

Rosenstein-Rodna, P. N. (1961). "International Aid for Underdeveloped Countries." *Review of Economics and Statistics,* 43(2), pp. 107–138.

Rostow, W. W. (1971). *The Stages of Economics Development, Second Edition.* Cambridge: Cambridge University Press.

Sachs, J. D., and A. M. Warner. (1995). "Economic Reform and the Process of Global Integration." *Brookings Papers on Economic Activity, 1:* 1–118.

Scarpetta, S., P. Hemmings, T. Tressel, and J. Woo. (2002). "The Role of Policy and Institutions for Productivity and Firm Dynamics: Evidence from Micro and Industry Data." OECD Economics Department Working Paper No. 329, Paris.

Schumpeter, J. A. (1983). *The Theory of Economic Development.* Oxford: Oxford University Press. (Original work published in 1934.)

Schumpeter, J. A. (1962). *Capitalism, Socialism and Democracy.* New York: Harper Torchbooks. (Original work published in 1942.)

Scully, G. W. (1992). *Constitutional Environments and Economic Growth.* Princeton, NJ: Princeton University Press.

Smith, A. (1999). *The Wealth of Nations.* London: Penguin Books. (Original work published in 1776).

Solow, R. (1956). "A Contribution to the Theory of Economic Growth." *Quarterly Journal of Economics and Statistics, 70*(1): 65–94.

Von Mises, L. (1951). *Socialism: An Economic and Sociological Analysis.* New Haven: Yale University Press.

World Economic Outlook. (2000). Washington, DC: IMF.

Index